Eyewitness

THE ESSENCE

SIMON & SCHUSTER PAPERBACKS
New York   London   Toronto   Sydney

to Power

OF LEADERSHIP
NIXON TO CLINTON

David Gergen

To Anne,

Christopher, and Katherine

for their love

Simon & Schuster Paperbacks
Rockefeller Center
1230 Avenue of the Americas
New York, NY 10020

Copyright © 2000 by David Gergen
All rights reserved,
including the right of reproduction
in whole or in part in any form.
First Simon & Schuster Paperbacks edition 2005
SIMON & SCHUSTER PAPERBACKS and colophon are
registered trademarks of Simon & Schuster, Inc.
For information about special discounts for bulk purchases,
please contact Simon & Schuster Special Sales:
1-800-456-6798 or business@simonandschuster.com.
Designed by Edith Fowler
Manufactured in the United States of America

20 19 18 17 16 15 14 13 12 11

The Library of Congress has cataloged
the hardcover edition as follows:
Gergen, David R. (David Richmond), [date]
   Eyewitness to power : the essence of leadership :
Nixon to Clinton / David Gergen.
      p.   cm.
   Includes bibliographical references and index.
   1. Presidents—United States—Case studies.
2. Executive power—United States—Case
studies.   I. Title.
JK516 .G493 2000
973.92—dc21   00-57386
ISBN-13: 978-0-684-82663-9
ISBN-10:   0-684-82663-1
ISBN-13: 978-0-7432-0322-7 (Pbk)
ISBN-10:   0-7432-0322-4 (Pbk)

Contents _____

Eyewitness
to Power

Preface

IT IS JUST POSSIBLE that we are living at the dawn of a new golden age.

America's two core ideas, freedom and capitalism, are catching fire around the world. Just as sweeping are revolutions in information technology and the life sciences that are still in their infancies. And the United States itself has the potential to achieve enormous good, having gained a preeminence in economic, political, military, scientific, and cultural influence that has not been matched since the days of ancient Rome. Taken together, these forces could lift future generations to the distant, sunny upland envisioned by Woodrow Wilson, where people celebrate "with a great shout of joy and triumph."

But progress will be neither sure nor inevitable. Much of it will rest upon the quality of our leaders, starting with America's president.

It is worth remembering that the twentieth century began in an air of triumphalism, too. Experts looked ahead and saw an unparalleled opportunity for human advancement. But over the next fifty years, a new dark age descended, as men plunged into the bloodiest wars in history and Depression struck. Just after World War I, there were twenty-nine democracies; by the middle of World War II, only twelve. Trade among nations withered and not until the 1970s reached the same levels of intensity as at the beginning of the century.

What went wrong? Bad leadership was a large part of the answer. British historian John Keegan writes that the political history of the twentieth century can be found in the biographies of six men:

Lenin, Stalin, Hitler, Mao Tse-tung, Roosevelt, and Churchill. Four were tyrants. Had Roosevelt and Churchill not rallied the Western democracies, civilization might have perished. As it was, we survived by the skin of our teeth.

Everyone who has worked in government, a corporation, a professional group, or a nonprofit knows that leadership matters. Arthur Schlesinger, Jr., points out that in 1931, Winston Churchill was almost killed when he crossed Park Avenue one night in New York City, looked the wrong way, and was knocked down by a car. Fourteen months later, Franklin Roosevelt was almost killed when an assassin in Miami opened fire upon an open car in which he was riding; the man sitting next to him, the mayor of Chicago, was mortally wounded. Would history have been any different if Churchill and Roosevelt had died then? Terribly. As Schlesinger snorts, one can hardly imagine Neville Chamberlain or Lord Halifax giving voice to the British lion or John Nance Garner guiding the allied powers to victory. At a moment of crisis, the quality of a nation's leader can be decisive.

Some argue that with the end of the Cold War and the advent of the information age, the American presidency has shriveled in importance. It is true that some of the powers of the office have devolved to others, and, for the most part, that is healthy.

But the presidency remains the center of our democracy. The man who occupies that office—and, one day soon, the woman—will always be the single person who can engage the dreams and mobilize the energies of the country behind large, sustained drives. Generally, we are a people who like to get on with our lives without paying much attention to Washington. But there are times when we have to act together. Dwight Eisenhower liked to think of us as a people who are at our best joining up with a wagon train heading west and working together to get over the mountains. Once in California, people go their own ways. The American president is always the one who will organize the wagon train.

If we are to realize a new golden age, it will be vital that our next presidents exercise a wisdom and will that help us to move steadily forward. They must work to keep the world on a stable, upward course, even as they fight off bouts of isolationism at home and rising resentment of American power overseas. They must manage a dynamic economy with a light hand, even as they seek to ensure that people left behind have more equal opportunities in life. They must be good stewards not only of the United States, but also of earth itself. Increasingly, they must make difficult decisions about technology and science that will transform the way we live.

All of this will require of our presidents that they know how to lead—that they bring to bear the qualities of personal character, idealism, political skill, and organizational strength that give power to their office. Leaders, some believe, are born, not made. It certainly appears that many of the best of the past century—Churchill, the Roosevelts, Gandhi, Mandela, Golda Meir, Martin Luther King, Jr.— had leadership in their bones. But each of them gained enormously by studying and drawing upon the experiences of others. Training and understanding of the past have been indispensable to the preparation of most leaders.

This book is an attempt to help. It is a privilege for any American citizen to serve in the White House. I have been unusually blessed by serving there under four presidents. Three of them were Republicans: Richard Nixon, Gerald Ford, and Ronald Reagan. The fourth was a Democrat: Bill Clinton. Along the way, I have also had an opportunity to work for George Bush when he was first seeking the presidency and to work with Jimmy Carter after he left the post.

Rather than inflict a personal memoir upon readers, I try here to bring together what I have learned about presidential leadership. The bulk of the book will trace out the lessons I carried away from the presidents I served in the White House. In the final chapter, I will step back and bring together the main themes, setting forth seven lessons that seem fundamental. While the discussion will focus primarily upon the presidency, I believe the conclusions drawn apply as well to other fields.

Woven through these reflections will be bits and pieces of my own story, so the reader will know the context in which I am writing. I started out in the Nixon White House looking through a keyhole. If there was someone more junior on staff, I never met him. But I was lucky enough to begin working directly with that president and was closer still to his successors. While there were many ups and downs, I was fortunate to have served with the presidents I did and to have observed them struggling with the exercise of power.

SOME CAVEATS ARE IN ORDER.

I do not promise that these thoughts will be strikingly original. To a considerable extent, what I know comes from experiences shared with others or was passed down to me from mentors who were generous with counsel and friendship. Over time, many of us acquired a common folk wisdom that is reflected here. Nor I am seeking to make news. Rather, I hope that by looking at four presidents over thirty years, we can all gain perspective on how people in that office—and in others—can exercise responsible leadership.

A reader looking for tidbits of gossip or personal slams may also wish to go elsewhere. This book is not of the kiss-and-tell genre, revealing intimate conversations from within, nor is it an attempt to settle scores. If anything, in a search for fairness I have tried to tip in the other direction.

Readers will notice that the president is always described as a "he" and references to gender are usually in the masculine. That is because the presidency so far has remained in male hands. But I hope that one day soon we will elect our first woman president. We are long overdue. A successful woman in that office could do more to cleanse and lift the quality of our public life than almost anything imaginable.

I should also warn that the conversations I have described here are not verbatim recordings. I did not keep a White House diary. What I have attempted is to reconstruct conversations as best I can, relying upon memory, files, and published documents. If I have misquoted anyone to ill effect, I apologize. Where I was hazy, I have left out quotation marks.

Finally, I have tried to write in a spirit of goodwill toward the presidents I have known. Since this book is an attempt to help others, there are occasions when I feel compelled to say what went wrong in an administration or to describe the personal shortcomings that damaged a president's leadership, but I have tried to do so with respect. And I have tried to be evenhanded by describing the very real strengths that each man brought to the job.

Our culture is too quick to tear down our presidents once they are in office. All of the six men I have known in the office—from Nixon to Clinton—have been patriots who cared deeply about the fate of the country. Several of them made terrible blunders, but they all struggled and fought to create a better world. We would not be at peace today, enjoying a chance for a golden future, had they not been men of accomplishment as well.

Those of us who have been privileged to serve on a White House staff have a special obligation to remember the best of the presidents we served. Leaving the Nixon staff in 1970, Daniel Patrick Moynihan offered a farewell thought that should guide all who labor in that house:

"I am one of those who believe that America is the hope of the world, and that for the time given him the President is the hope of America. Serve him well. Pray for his success. Understand how much depends on you. Try to understand what he has given of himself. This is something those of us who have worked in this building with him know in a way that perhaps only experience can teach."

Richard Nixon

1

The Stuff of Shakespeare

I<small>T MAY SEEM PERVERSE</small> to begin a book about leadership with Richard Nixon. No modern president has been more reviled by his enemies while in office, and none has been more rebuked by historians after leaving. When Arthur Schlesinger, Jr., asked three dozen historians in 1996 to rank the overall performance of America's presidents, they placed Nixon in the bottom tier, along with two notorious failures, Ulysses S. Grant and Warren G. Harding. Nixon will never be forgotten—and perhaps never fully forgiven—for the sins of Watergate and the long period of national turmoil that ended in his resignation on August 9, 1974, the only man to endure such a disgrace.

In the 1980s, Senator Bob Dole was strolling into the Gridiron dinner in Washington when he spied three former presidents sitting at the dais: Ford, Carter, and Nixon. "Look," he deadpanned, "See No Evil . . . Hear No Evil . . . and *Evil!*" Dole was actually a longtime Nixon loyalist and delivered a moving eulogy at his funeral, but he never passes up a chance to deliver a zinging one-liner, and he knew he was capturing what many Americans have come to think of our thirty-seventh president. Years of attacks, dismissals, and editorial cartoons—not to mention his own misdeeds—have left an indelible brand.

More recently, the National Archives has released 445 hours of tape recordings of Nixon's private conversations in 1971, when he was angry about the leakage of the Pentagon Papers. By any standard, his comments to his staff are vile and repulsive. He calls Senator Edward M. Kennedy a "goddamn lily-livered mealy-mouth." Tip O'Neill, then Democratic whip of the House, is "an all-out dove and a vicious bastard." The Supreme Court is "a disaster." Nixon rants: "You've got a senile old bastard in Black. You've got an old fool and black fool in that Thurgood Marshall. Then you've got Brennan, I mean, a jackass Catholic." Justice Potter Stewart, an Eisenhower appointee, is "a little dumb" and "a weak bastard" who has been "overwhelmed by the Washington Georgetown social set."

Even worse is his anti-Semitism. "The Jews are all over the government," he complains to Bob Haldeman, his chief of staff. "Most Jews are disloyal." Later he instructs Haldeman: "I want you to look at any sensitive areas where Jews are involved." There are exceptions, he said, "but, Bob, generally speaking, you can't trust the bastards. They turn on you. Am I wrong or right?" Talking about Daniel Ellsberg, suspected of leaking the Pentagon Papers, Nixon reveals one of the roots of his feelings: "Incidentally, I hope to God he's not Jewish, is he? . . . The only two non-Jews in the Communist conspiracy were Chambers and Hiss. Many felt that Hiss was. He could have been a half, but he was not by religion. The only two non-Jews. Every other one was a Jew. And it raised hell with us."

What could such a man possibly tell us about leadership? Plenty, as it turns out. Many of his lessons are actually uplifting, just as many are cautionary tales of how a leader can pull himself down. There is a rich vein here if one takes a little time to tap into it.

In fact, Richard Nixon was the most fascinating man I have met in thirty years of public life. Those of us who worked for him in the White House found him almost impossible to fathom. Ray Price, his principal speechwriter, later wrote a book about the experience and, trying to describe Nixon, turned to Churchill's famous comment about Russia. "It is a riddle wrapped in a mystery inside an enigma," said Churchill. Scattered through the memoirs of former Nixon aides are descriptions of him as "weird," "mysterious," "the strangest man I ever knew." Yet, to a person, those who have written accounts of working with him, hearing him speak privately, and watching him make decisions have come to the same conclusion: there were also times when he was a towering president. I agree.

There was a side to Nixon, not reflected by Watergate or by the tapes, that to this day has inspired a legion of fine public servants. When his comments about Jews have been released in recent years, it is striking that the first to spring to his defense have been his former Jewish advisers. The late Herbert Stein said that he felt only the utmost respect and friendship from Nixon. Leonard Garment, a former Wall Street lawyer who joined up with Nixon in the 1968 campaign and stayed by his side through his presidency, pointed out that Nixon had appointed numerous Jews to his administration, including Alan Greenspan and Bill Safire. Sure, wrote Charles Krauthammer, Nixon was a "seething cauldron of inchoate hatreds." But he was also "the man who cut through the paranoia and fear and opened the door to China, fashioned détente and ushered in the era of arms control—something less psychically roiled presidents had not been able to do."

Americans could see that Nixon was tightly coiled, but they too decided to judge him mostly by his works—just as they have judged Bill Clinton. Throughout his life on the political stage, spanning more than a quarter century, large numbers looked upon Nixon as a forceful leader. After his first four years in the White House, Nixon amassed over 60 percent of the popular vote in 1972, the second-largest landslide ever recorded. His margin of victory in that reelection—18 million votes—remains the biggest in history. With the exception of Franklin Roosevelt—the Babe Ruth of twentieth-century politics—only Nixon has been nominated by his party for high office in five different national elections. Three times, he was the Republican nominee for president, twice for vice president.

Anyone who can rally so many Americans behind him election after election exercises a hold upon the popular imagination that is worth understanding. *Time* magazine put him on its cover no less than fifty-six times. There will never be a monument to Richard Nixon in Washington. But when he died in 1994—two decades after he resigned—there was an outpouring of public sympathy that suggested he went to his grave commanding the respect of millions. Visitors from around the world still stream to his museum and birthplace in Yorba Linda, California. His biographers speak of the third quarter of the twentieth century as the Age of Nixon, and he competes with Ronald Reagan and John F. Kennedy as America's most important political figure in the past half century.

That a leader could rise so high and then fall so low is also a tale worth understanding. Nixon had it all and kicked it away. He complained later that he had simply made a bad mistake and it was really his enemies who destroyed him. "I gave them a sword and they stuck it in," he growled to David Frost, a comment that an embittered Bill Clinton might have made later on. But Nixon, like Clinton, knew better. He had brought himself down.

The Nixon story, then, offers the stuff of Shakespeare. There is much here from which future leaders can learn. I do not pretend to

21

understand the full tale. I was not an intimate who talked with him every day, only a young, junior member of his White House staff. But he certainly taught me a lot about leadership.

An Introduction to Valhalla

When students learn that I began working in the White House in my twenties, they frequently ask, "How did you get there?"

Most VIPs make their first entry into the West Wing through the front door. New members of the staff use a side door. I started in a closet.

While serving in the Navy in the late 1960s, I was reassigned from a ship in the Far East to a desk job in Washington. With the Vietnam War sucking in thousands of young draftees, controversy was swirling around the Selective Service System, and the Nixon White House was moving aggressively to straighten out the agency. A dear friend and former roommate, Jonathan Rose, was a young aide to Nixon and was asked to assemble a group of junior officers who could serve as advisers to the new head of Selective Service, Curtis Tarr. Jon placed a series of calls, one to me, and since I had already put in nearly two years aboard ship, I was ready. The Navy sent me to Selective Service.

Plump! I landed in the middle of a city where I had never worked, sitting two blocks away from the White House as all hell broke loose about the inequities of the draft. Tarr and our small team went to work in a hurry. One morning, Jon called and asked if I could visit with him in his second-floor office in the West Wing. Our meeting had to be hush-hush—absolutely no one was to know, he said, not even Tarr—because he wanted my unvarnished views of Selective Service and how to fix it.

It was my first visit to the White House. Moments after I was surreptitiously ushered into Jon's office that afternoon, his secretary knocked at the door. "Curtis Tarr is here to see you, Jon," she said. Panic. You can't get out the door without Tarr spotting you, Jon said. There's only one solution: "You've got to hide in my closet!"

"Jesus, Jonathan. Your closet?"

"We don't have any choice. And, don't worry, he will only stay five minutes."

In I went.

Some closets in the White House, I discovered, are bigger than you might think. This one had a light and even a phone. But it was also bloody cold, and as fate would have it, Curtis had a lot on his mind. He and Jon talked on for about an hour, while I stood there freezing. Nature began calling, so I quietly picked up the phone and buzzed Jon's secretary, Marie Smith. "Marie, you've got to get me the hell out of here. Please go in and slip Jonathan a note that I'm getting desperate." She ushered Tarr out.

Jon was more amused than I was. But seeing White House life through a keyhole, I discovered, was often the way I would feel in the next few years.

Toward the end of that year, 1970, I was preparing to muster out of the Navy and was interviewing for a job at the Institute of Government at the University of North Carolina in Chapel Hill, not far from my hometown of Durham. My friend Jonathan intervened again. "The President has just named Ray Price to head up the speechwriting team here, and Ray is scouting for an assistant. He's terrific. Why don't you come over and interview with him?" Jon said.

I went to see Ray on a lark. He occupied a spacious office in the southwest corner of the Old Executive Office Building, where one could feel the presence of ghosts even more than in the West Wing. Ray already had some excellent candidates, and I doubted I was a good fit. Growing up in North Carolina, I told Ray, I didn't know any Republicans. While I was in college, Democrat Terry Sanford was our governor and he more than anyone else drew me into public life. One of my most rewarding experiences was working for him on civil rights. And, in 1968, I voted for Humphrey, not Nixon. That, I thought, would finish our conversation, but Ray wanted to keep talking.

I told him that I was a firm believer in Nixon's foreign policy, including Vietnam. Since I was sailing on a ship out of Japan during the late 1960s, I was never radicalized by the turmoil at home, and I thought it important to persevere in Vietnam. But he should know that on domestic issues, I was a moderate on many key questions and a liberal on civil rights. While I was pleasantly surprised by Nixon's domestic record—he was much more progressive than I had been led to believe by the press—I was certainly not as conservative as some of the men around Nixon like Pat Buchanan. Ray responded that Nixon liked a diversity of voices on his staff. Some people in the White House would oppose my joining up, but there were a number of others with my views on board already, some in speechwriting. I would feel more at home than I thought, he believed. No doubt it also helped in his eyes that we had both gone to Yale.

23

I liked Ray instantly and also sensed I could entrust him with my fate. He had run the editorial page of the *New York Herald Tribune* in its halcyon days of the mid-1960s, when Jock Whitney was publisher. In 1964, Ray had penned a famous editorial endorsing Lyndon Johnson over Barry Goldwater, but Ray had remained a conservative with a strong belief in restraint and moderation. He was one of the first principals to join up with the Nixon campaign of 1968 and went on to become a confidant, an alter ego, and an inspired wordsmith for the new president.

The more we talked that day, the more we bonded. By the end of the conversation, he promised he would get back to me soon. If we were to work together, perhaps we ought to do it on a trial basis, which seemed sensible to both of us. If he had known less about my background and more about my slipshod habits in organizing paperwork, I doubt he would have touched me with a barge pole.

But a short while later, Ray called with a one-year job offer, and I arrived at the Nixon White House in January 1971. Little did either of us realize that my one-year stint would turn into more than three and a half years and one of the best growing-up experiences a person can have.

Getting to Know "RN"

Richard Nixon paid me precious little attention the first time we met. That occurred in the mid-sixties when I was a student at the Harvard Law School, looking ahead to military service and weighing whether I would eventually return to North Carolina or perhaps try out Wall Street. Nixon was temporarily out of politics. After his loss in the 1960 presidential campaign and his humiliation in the 1962 California gubernatorial race, he had gone east to nurse his wounds and practice law, preparing his comeback.

When word spread that Nixon was coming to Cambridge to interview law students for prospective jobs at his New York firm, most of us jumped for interviews. After passing an initial screen by junior partners, a few were admitted to a private session with The Man. There he was, the deep basso voice, the jowls, the eyes that penetrated to your core. Or did they? As we talked, his eyes quickly strayed over my shoulder to a television set that was quietly broadcasting the World Series. He let his other partner do the talking while he watched the game.

24

As we said good-bye, I needled him a little. "What's the score?" I asked. He relayed it good-naturedly, then added a piece of advice that proved helpful. "You're signing up for the Navy, huh? Well, don't go into the Judge Advocate General Corps as a lawyer. Become a line officer," he said. "That way you'll get some real leadership training. You'll be a lot better off later on." I took his advice and wound up as a damage control officer on a repair ship, the USS *Ajax* (AR-6). Learning to control damage, it turned out, was the best possible preparation for my coming years in the White House.

Joining the Nixon staff in early 1971, halfway into his first term, I was on the third rung of the staff, kids to be seen and never heard. Republicans like hierarchy and order; they're not like Democrats, as I saw later on, who thrive on chaos and creativity. Ike had taught Nixon that a good organization will never guarantee an effective leader, but a bad organization will kill you every time. So, he established a strong top-down system and brought in Bob Haldeman, John Ehrlichman, and Henry Kissinger to run it for him (Nixon himself was no manager). Haldeman was the first chief of staff in the White House since Eisenhower left,* while Ehrlichman and Kissinger became the czars of domestic and foreign policy. When I got there, they had the place under lock and key.

Nixon was famously aloof and preferred that most of his staff communicate with him on paper rather than face-to-face. Lyndon Johnson had a White House phone that had direct extensions to sixty people; Nixon kept a phone with direct lines to only three—the so-called "Teutonic trio." Those three, along with his faithful administrative assistant, Rose Mary Woods, were also the only ones who seemed to enjoy "walk-in" rights. A few of the young guard, like Dwight Chapin, were favored with frequent visits to his office because they had marched with him in the campaign. Almost everyone else on staff waited to be called.

But speechwriters, I found, have a dispensation from God. The policy-makers and political advisers have usually spent years in their fields before taking a job at the White House. They worked hard to earn a seat at the table. Most of them have trouble, however, translating their ideas into public prose, and they need speechwriters around to help them. If they think the Muse may have touched your brow, you can be a twenty-eight-year-old with no experience and they will invite you to their meetings. It's exhilarating to be a

25

*Kennedy and Johnson preferred to operate without a formal chief of staff.

White House wordsmith when you are young. You may not shape history, but you have a ringside seat watching others make it. Over time, you may even add a finishing touch or two.

Ray Price wasn't ready to have me write or edit anything yet—that would come later—but he did have a special assignment that I loved. Nixon wanted a representative of the writing shop to sit in on his meetings with the cabinet and congressional leaders so we could take notes of what he was saying and pass them around the shop. He frequently used those occasions to try out thoughts and ideas that could form the basis of public speeches. Ray would naturally attend the more sensitive sessions, but when he was busy—and the work always piled up—he asked me to substitute, taking a seat along the wall. I happily agreed, wondering whether this was where it all happened.

It didn't take long to see that cabinet meetings were exactly where it didn't happen. The cabinet members Nixon had so proudly presented to the nation on live television early on were now treated more warily. Nixon's staff regarded a few as continuing loyalists but thought others had "gone native"—they had joined the camp of their entrenched bureaucracies, so despised by the White House. Nixon was always urging his cabinet to sell his programs harder and take more political heat for the administration, but he and his staff were sucking most of the real power back into the White House. Cabinet and congressional sessions could still be wide-ranging, even robust, but the big decisions were made in the White House.

Even so, those sessions in the cabinet room gave me a chance to see Nixon up close. I was immensely impressed. It was true what his lieutenants had been saying: unlike the man we saw on television, sweating and uncomfortable, this Nixon could be dazzling. His conversations were heavily sprinkled with historical references, and he spoke knowingly of leaders like Charles de Gaulle, Winston Churchill, Shigeru Yoshida, and Lee Kuan Yew. If the conversation turned to domestic fare, he spoke with equal facility about local leaders in downstate Illinois or the Panhandle of Florida. Whatever the issue, an insight would roll out. He wasn't showing off; he had just seen more, studied more, and reflected more than anyone else in the room. I would not see his intellectual match until Bill Clinton came to Washington. Moreover, he acted on his knowledge. As he told the staff, he wanted to be the man in the saddle, not the man saddled by events.

26

Later on, Nixon was about to make a live radio broadcast from the Oval Office and wanted to make massive revisions in his speech draft. He and press secretary Ron Ziegler were poring over the text at his desk, while Nell Yates, a pillar of many administrations, was retyping pages at a furious clip just outside. I was helping the President with suggestions and racing back and forth to Nell. To my astonishment, Nixon began cursing up a storm. I hadn't heard anyone that crusty since I left the Navy.

"What in the world is happening?" I asked Ziegler.

"Don't worry," Ron replied. "He can get like that. That's a signal that he trusts you when he starts talking like that in front of you. It's his way of letting off steam."

I didn't hear Nixon like that often, but that moment has replayed in my head several times since transcripts have appeared from the secret tape recorder he kept in the Oval Office. His barnyard epithets were so raw that when he released some transcripts during the Watergate turmoil in order to show his innocence, the release backfired. Even though many words were redacted, the public was horrified that their president spoke like that. The transcripts, as Teddy White wrote, shattered their romantic dream about the presidency.

The tapes that have come out since have further tarnished his reputation, especially among the young, who never saw him at his best. They create an impression that he was not only churlish and anti-Semitic but also small and stupid. They stand in sharp contrast to the transcripts that have been so carefully released from the Kennedy files, which show him resolute and sophisticated during the Cuban missile crisis. Clearly, a number of Nixon's comments are indefensible. No leader should speak that way, even in private to those he trusts. The fact that earlier presidents like Harry Truman were known to use racist language about blacks and Jews is not an excuse. Eisenhower would have served as a good model for Nixon. As Stephen Ambrose has written, Ike confided his darkest thoughts to his pillow.

But in judging Nixon, one should also keep him in perspective. Yes, he was tormented and vented more than he should. However, the tapes that have been released are not the full measure of the man. Certainly, the Nixon most of us saw in the White House spoke, thought, and acted most of the time in ways that were far loftier and more inspiring. The Nixon I heard in the cabinet room and increasingly in his office and elsewhere spoke with intelligence and fluidity about the world. He could be riveting. He could also be mean and ruthless, no doubt, and he could be deceptive and manipulative. He thought all of those qualities necessary in his job. But no one else

27

on the American stage in the past thirty years, including Henry Kissinger, has demonstrated a deeper grasp of foreign affairs. When international crises broke out after he left office, one of the first questions of every president I have known since has been: I wonder what Nixon thinks?

The tapes that have been released so far show Nixon at his ugliest. The taping system was only up and running full-time by 1971, when he was under heavy stress. Perhaps one day we will hear other tapes recording him at his best. For the sake of historical balance, I hope so.

As I saw more of him, I realized that Nixon could switch on his public face in an instant. On a morning that is still memorable, I was standing in a small antechamber outside the Oval Office, waiting to give him a paper before he walked into a cabinet meeting. He came out, sullen, brooding, mean-looking, and took my paper with little more than a grunt. I wouldn't have dared cross his path in a dark alley. Three steps later, he straightened up, threw back his shoulders, summoned a smile—the mask was on just as he stepped into the cabinet room. "Ladies and gentlemen, the President!" All stood and applauded.

On another occasion, I had a speech draft from our shop that we had to deliver to him around nine o'clock at night. We were too late for the pouch that the staff secretariat collected at the end of the day, so I walked it over to the residence, where an usher could take it up to him. No, said the usher, he's bowling and wants you to bring it to him personally. Bowling? Where? The thought conjured up images of a smoke-filled hall and pairs of tacky bowling shoes. I didn't even know there was an alley in the White House.

Over at the Old EOB, deep in the basement, the usher said. Armed with his directions, I set out among the catacombs and piping of the EOB and, sure enough, tucked far away was a small door that opened into a single lane. And there was Richard Nixon, the leader of the free world—dress shoes, a pressed white shirt with cuff links, dark tie—bowling alone. No Secret Service men were in sight. I felt strangely drawn to him that night, so vulnerable and lonely he seemed, the trappings of power temporarily fallen away. The image comes to mind of James Goldman's title for a play about Henry II, *The Lion in Winter.* The Nixon I knew seemed like a wounded lion— he could be magnificent at times, striding the world, but he was always nursing huge inner damage, something that made you wince for him. At one moment he could be splendidly remote, almost regal,

28

and in the next, snarling and angry at any hiss that came from the bushes.

There was also a clumsiness about Nixon, both physically and socially. Sometimes he could barely make his fingers work a dial telephone. In a well-remembered incident in 1971, Ron Ziegler had arranged a photo op commemorating the President's birthday. Reluctantly, Nixon agreed to walk along the beach at San Clemente, a California spot that was home to the "western White House" and a welcome refuge from Washington. Imagine the horror among the staff when photos came back of him walking stiffly on the sand in a windbreaker, dark trousers . . . *and black wing-tipped shoes.*

Occasionally, his words were out of sync with the rest of him. In a speech, he might cup his hands in the form of a globe and say, "It takes a strong man . . ." Then, just the wrong second, he would straighten his hands to show an upright man while he said, ". . . to shape the world." Haldeman recounts that Nixon once ordered him to eliminate soup from state dinners because "men don't really like soup" but that Manolo Sanchez, the President's valet, confided the real reason: Nixon kept spilling soup down his vest. Extremely shy, Nixon also hated small talk and wasn't good at it. In a motorcade in Florida, a cop on a motorcycle fell and Nixon, compassionate, stopped everything so he could console him. But as the man lay on the ground, the only thing he could think to ask him was how he liked his job.

It was obvious to all of us how precious his daughters, Tricia and Julie, were. Julie in particular was one of the few people to whom he seemed to relate naturally, not through his intellect. Yet he would have the staff meet privately with the girls to give them a message he felt awkward in conveying himself. He would even send directives to his wife, Pat, on White House stationery with the heading: "To: Mrs. Nixon, From: The President." Or on a hot summer day, as is well known, he might sit in the coldest air-conditioning with logs blazing in the fireplace. A strange man? Of course. But, over time, as I saw his strengths and vulnerabilities, I was one of many on staff who came to like him—even in his strangeness.

His Dual Personality

One of the first lessons about public life, I discovered, is to choose 29
your mentors wisely. In my case, I was plain lucky. Ray Price was a

wonderful introduction to the Nixon White House and, more than that, to the high standards that leaders should set. He could see I was young and eager—too eager, in fact—to grab the brass ring. He set out to help me grow up.

Each week in those days, citizens were writing about forty thousand letters, cards, and telegrams to the President, and Ray thought it important that Nixon read a sample of two dozen or more of the most interesting, including those that were negative. He would get a better feel for what people were thinking outside Washington, and we might spot some speech nuggets. The correspondence unit, which reported to Ray, would cull the arrivals and send us a large stack. One of my early assignments was to read them and propose the weekly sample. It was more interesting than I expected. Americans pour out their hearts to their president and are not shy about asking for personal help and advice on matters ranging from Social Security to divorce. The American president was truly a father figure, at least back then. Privately, Nixon referred to himself in the same way and relished that role, writing that "each day [is] a chance to do something memorable for someone."

Late on a Friday night each week, Ray and I would sit down together and sift through the letters I was suggesting. Inevitably, a letter would spark conversations about Nixon, life at the White House, and the ways of the world. Our sessions often stretched past midnight, as Ray quietly told me all about the man we worked for, the men he had brought with him, and how important Nixon's success was to the country. It was my tutorial from one of the President's most trusted advisers.

Nixon, he explained, was blessed with a very bright side, but mostly hidden from public view was a dark, thunderous aspect. Inside the White House, a titanic struggle was under way between those who naturally appealed to his better qualities and those who played upon his demons. Our job, he said, was to strengthen his positive instincts. If only that side prevailed, Nixon had the capacity for enormous achievement.

Ray and others like Leonard Garment, Bill Safire, George Shultz, and Arthur Burns believed that Richard Nixon had within him the capacity to be a statesman who could indeed build the "lasting structure of peace" that he dreamed about. These were serious men who had given up satisfying jobs on the outside because they were convinced Nixon stood on the threshold of greatness. To them, Nixon was the real thing, a genuine and inspired leader who was working to achieve peace, not just talking about it.

30

But there was another side to his nature—insecure, secretive, angry, vindictive—that lurked beneath the exterior and was rarely seen except by those closest to him. Nixon knew it was there and thought there were times when he needed to be mean in order to retain power in the face of countless hostile forces. It was easy, Ray said, for an adviser like Chuck Colson and others to exploit that dark side by warning him of the enemies at the gate and urging that swift, brutal action be taken. Nixon would easily succumb and lash out at his foes, real and imagined. If that side ultimately prevailed, Ray warned, the Nixon presidency was doomed. It was an eerie prophecy, one that I recalled years later in trying to sort out Bill Clinton's complex personality.

In his memoirs of the Nixon years, *Before the Fall*, Bill Safire provided a similar, if more expansive, metaphor. "Think of Nixon as a layer cake," he wrote. "The public face or crust is conservative, stern, dignified, proper." The first layer underneath is the "progressive politician" seeking to become another Disraeli; underneath, "an unnecessarily pugnacious man" who is self-made, self-pitying, but not self-centered; the next layer down is the poker player; underneath, "the hater, the impugner of motives"; another layer down, the realist; then "the observer-participant" who sees himself as a third person; beneath, "the man of extraordinary courage"; and finally the loner. People tend to see only the layer they want to see. "But the whole cake is the 'real' Nixon, including some layers I have not mentioned because I do not know. When you take a bite of the cake that is Nixon, you must get a mouthful of all the layers; nibbling along one level is not permitted."

Bill had insights into Nixon that over time made more and more sense to me. But in my first years at the White House, I was struck with great force by Ray's simpler metaphor—the uneasy co-existence of the bright and dark sides of Nixon's soul. Was this who Nixon truly was? In college, I had read Shakespeare's tragic portrayal of King Richard II, who stepped down from his throne, a senseless victim of an inner struggle between brilliance and despair. The famous Greek and Elizabethan tragedies were also cautionary tales of how fatal flaws had undermined Creon, Lear, and Agamemnon, but those were fabled figures whose stories stretched back thousands of years. Did the same drama live on in the man from Whittier, California, who kept an office down the hall from ours in the Old EOB?

31

Psychologists have written about the bright and shadow sides of personalities. Again, however, their books rang more of theory than of the modern presidency, where the sun came up every day on a beehive of people in coat and tie scurrying from one meeting to the next, memos written, decisions made. The Nixon I caught glimpses of in those early days seemed buoyant and in command, at ease with power. But my education was just beginning: the Watergate break-in was more than a year away, and there was much I didn't know. Nearly thirty years later, it is clear that Ray Price had figured out Nixon from the beginning.

2

The Bright Side

Richard Nixon called me in the early fall of 1993, about six months before he died. He was coming to Washington and wondered if we might have breakfast in his suite at One Washington Circle, a modest hotel where he liked to stay. I was working by then at the Clinton White House. Of course, I replied, and wondered if Mack McLarty, the chief of staff, might join us, to which Nixon readily assented.

As we sat down, it was obvious that Nixon had two purposes in mind: to find out what was happening in Washington, feeding an intellectual appetite that remained voracious until the end, and, more to the point, to have me carry messages to his successor. Good for him, I thought, still trying to shape the world.

After telling us that the administration must maintain strong economic ties with Russia—a familiar theme—and suggesting that Clinton was courting political trouble by encouraging his wife to be out front on health care reform ("She's too tough in her appearances"), Nixon turned to the issue uppermost in his thoughts. "The President hasn't been outspoken enough in his support of NAFTA," he said, referring to the controversial trade agreement with Mexico and Canada, then facing a perilous journey through Congress. "He's been in the weeds on this, hanging back too much. Tell him there are things worse than losing. He has to stand up for the principle of free trade."

Then Nixon added his special touch: "If he wants to know why

33

he should be for NAFTA, tell him to study the repeal of the Corn Laws in Britain. That should convince him."

Repeal of the Corn Laws? Only Nixon. In the nineteenth century, the farmers of Great Britain fought fiercely to preserve the Corn Laws, which placed high tariffs on agricultural products coming in from other countries. The battle over their repeal stirred a tumultuous debate about threats to the British way of life, just as NAFTA was doing in the United States. History shows that Parliament's vote to tear down the barriers in 1846 not only marked a turning point toward an era of freer trade, but also paid enormous benefits for Britain, catapulting the nation into a dominant position in the world economy. Nixon's analysis was precisely on point. It was also characteristic of the man. He loved to read about great events and great leaders of the past and draw upon them to assess the present.

That conversation, my last with Nixon, brought back a flow of memories of what it was like to work in his White House and why, for so long, we on staff admired him. More than any other president in the twentieth century, save Woodrow Wilson and Dwight Eisenhower, Nixon was a serious student of power and leadership. Wilson, the only chief executive with a Ph.D., had written memorable treatises about the powers of Congress and the president long before he set foot in Washington. Nixon never had as much formal education, but he applied himself as earnestly in learning about men in power and, as a Quaker, embraced Wilson's idealism. He even asked to sit at Wilson's desk.

Until the 1970s, when roughly half his papers were opened, scholars did not appreciate how diligently Eisenhower had studied the arts of leadership while in uniform, especially working under Douglas MacArthur and George Marshall, or how wily he had been. With the publication of Fred Greenstein's book *The Hidden-Hand Presidency,* Ike's stature has properly grown. Nixon had the advantage of studying under Eisenhower and, when his turn came, tried to blend Ike's tough-mindedness with Wilson's idealism, an approach that continues to recommend itself today. Long after he left office, Nixon, ever the student, mulled over the mysteries of leadership in one of his best books, *Leaders.*

The tragedy of Nixon's life is that he could not live up to his own standards. He had learned what it takes to be strong and effective, and he often climbed to the peaks, but he could not stay there. Something inside pulled him down. Until his final fall, however, he taught those of us who worked for him many lessons about the positive qualities that are needed for the exercise of leadership.

34

For two years, I mostly learned from the back benches. Approaching the 1972 Republican Convention in Miami, Dwight Chapin formed a small planning group and invited me to join. "You're in charge of the convention script," he told me. That was less impressive than it sounded. I was to coordinate all of the speeches in the hall, ensuring that they stayed within tight time constraints and didn't slop over each other. Implicit was the challenge of keeping the speeches crisp and fresh for the large audience that watched conventions in those days.

Stagecraft, I was finding, is an important element of modern politics, and no one practiced it more assiduously than the Nixon team. For fun, someone hooked me up with Bob Hope's comedy writers and I asked them to come to Miami. Two of them holed up in a Miami hotel, maintaining an open telephone line to our convention trailer. As they watched the convention on television, they would think up gag lines. Then I or someone else would trot their jokes over to the next speaker just as he was going up to the podium. A good use of your tax dollars, right? But the convention was a smashing success on television.

When the elections were over and Nixon had won the landslide he was seeking, Ray Price surprised me by deciding that he would like to leave his post as head of the speechwriting and research team. He wanted to stay on at the White House as "house philosopher," and Nixon agreed, so long as Ray would continue to handle big speeches. Ray asked me to serve as his successor.

It was an immensely flattering suggestion. Writers of strong talent would be reporting to me, and as a team we could have a significant impact upon Nixon's next term. Altogether, we had about fifty people in our department—writers, researchers, administrative assistants, and members of the correspondence unit. I had thought of going home to North Carolina after the elections, but this was a chance I could not pass up. I was thirty years old, eager to grow and to climb.

For the rest of Nixon's presidency, I ran that writing and research team, a wonderful bunch. I was also among a cadre of other junior staffers moving into midlevel positions for the second term, running policy shops, scheduling, advance, and related activities. Most of us marched together through the Watergate hell and became friends for life. But that was still far off. For now, my job was drawing me closer to the President himself. I never became a confidant, but he often took me in hand, as he did others, trying to teach me how the game was played at the top.

35

What I saw in those days was mostly his bright side. Before he self-destructed, Nixon was among the best of modern presidents. Now I could see why—how he drew upon his years in the wilderness, his inner steel, his understanding of history, his personal mystique, the men and women he attracted to government, and upon the way he molded his staff. Most of all, I saw how his strategic vision was central to his success.

It may seem that by emphasizing his positive qualities first, I am not wholly objective. I plead "guilty as charged." I remain grateful to Richard Nixon for helping me get started in public life, and as I hope these pages reflect, my respect for his accomplishments continues, even as I believe it important for others to understand what went wrong, too. It is also true that only by understanding just how towering his strengths were can we appreciate the depths. Let's look at his core strengths one by one.

His Years in the Wilderness

In the presidential election of 1960, some 60 million Americans went to the polls. Nixon lost to Kennedy by 119,000 votes—fewer than 1 vote per precinct. Question: Would Nixon have been a better president in 1961 than he was after he was elected in 1968? No one knows for sure. But certainly Nixon thought he was more effective because he *lost* his first national election.

He still had the campaign bug after that defeat and quickly mapped out plans to run for governor of California two years later, a move to keep his career alive while permitting him to sit out the 1964 race against Kennedy. California voters had a different idea. They dealt him a second, humbling defeat, electing Democrat Pat Brown instead, and it appeared that he was through forever.

As it turned out, his banishment from politics was one of the best things that ever happened to him. It prepared him to lead. For most of the next six years, as he wandered in the political wilderness, he finally had a chance to deepen and broaden himself intellectually, something that few politicians on today's fast track ever take the time to do. Clinton, for example, paid a price for not having time away from politics for personal growth, and so did Lyndon Johnson. They were both catapulted into the presidency before they had a clear idea of what they wanted to do with it or, in Clinton's case, had settled down.

Certainly, Nixon had never taken time for reflection before.

From the day he was a thirty-five-year-old freshman Congressman and first met Alger Hiss until he was beaten in his twin election bids in the 1960s, his time on the national stage had been jam-packed. He did not know his family very well, much less himself. The process of self-renewal began in 1961, when he took ten months off between campaigns to write about his life. The book that emerged, *Six Crises*, helped him to begin making sense of who he was, where he had gone wrong, and how to prepare for future office. For his chapter on Khrushchev, he wrote later, he spent six days in a Los Angeles hotel room, working fourteen hours a day and taking all his meals there. It was a rushed job, patterned a little too obviously after Walter Bedell Smith's book on Eisenhower's six major decisions. But his book became a best-seller and began a period of personal enrichment that continued until he went to the White House in 1969.

People who saw him in his "out" years found him not just restless but anxious to learn everything he could about international affairs and about the exercise of power. He visited four continents, investigating conditions, examining the interests and motivations of other nations, and expanding his storehouse of contacts. Highly disciplined most of his life, Nixon took ample amounts of time to read and to write out his thoughts. Gradually, he developed a more sophisticated, tempered, longer-range view of world affairs that became the foundation for his presidency.

Looking back after he left the White House, Nixon concluded that his time out of office had been one of his most productive periods. And he took pride that great statesmen of other nations had followed a similar path. "De Gaulle in his 'wilderness' years, Adenauer in prison and in the monastery, Churchill out of power, de Gasperi in the Vatican library—all had time to reflect, and all used it well. I found that some of my own most valuable years were those between the vice presidency and the presidency, when I was able to step back from the center of events and look in a most measured way at the past and the future," he wrote in 1982. He was particularly impressed that both Churchill and de Gaulle, when rejected and out of power, had used their time to do some of their finest writing. It was no surprise, then, that Nixon turned back to writing after he resigned from office in 1974. It was his path to whatever redemption he might find.

Nixon no doubt liked to dramatize this "wilderness" theme because it gave him one more link to his heroes. He was thrilled when he heard in the 1960s that de Gaulle thought Nixon had the makings of leadership because he, too, had "crossed the desert." It is difficult to say that Nixon gained as much from his time out of power as some

37

others have. Franklin Roosevelt's struggle with polio during the 1920s, for example, provides one of the most inspiring stories in politics. By the account of most historians, his trial transformed him as a man and as a leader. Had Nixon faced a personal struggle as serious as FDR's and achieved his emotional maturity, Watergate might never have happened.

Even so, the Nixon story does underscore an important lesson: years in the wilderness may appear to be a sure path to oblivion, but, if seized upon as an opportunity for personal growth, can actually become a springboard to serious leadership. They represent the "withdrawal and return" that Arnold Toynbee has described, "the hero's journey" in the phrase of Joseph Campbell. Churchill, de Gaulle, Gandhi, Roosevelt—and, yes, Nixon—all discovered that central truth.

An Inner Steel

In the summer of 1974, as his presidency was crumbling, I was among those who accompanied Nixon on a tour of the Middle East. Heading in, we stopped for an overnight rest in Salzburg, and the next day, Nixon was experiencing serious pains in his left leg. The White House physician discovered he had phlebitis, an inflammation that, if intense, can send a fatal blood clot to the brain, as it almost did two months after his resignation. The doctor, the staff was told, advised him to cut his Middle East schedule in half.

When the physician left, Nixon called in our chief advance man, Ron Walker. "Ron, this trip is important. *Double* the schedule."

When some of us heard that tale, we wondered whether Nixon had become suicidal. Before the trip, he had speculated that an assassin might send him home in a pine box and maybe that would be the best way to end things. But, over the years, I have come to see his response to phlebitis as characteristic of the man: when faced with bad news, he didn't flinch but plunged ahead with even more grit. That toughness became his hallmark and proved to be an indispensable element of his success in politics. He was indomitable.

I never knew where that toughness came from. From the adversities of childhood, when two of his brothers died and his family faced hard times? The rough-and tumble of his early campaigns for the House and Senate, when he turned mean and came to be known as Tricky Dick? From the constant pounding he took from the political establishment after he took down one of their bright lights, Alger

38

Hiss? From the crises and defeats that so often smashed into his life? Or was it just sheer orneriness? Even myopic grandiosity? Whatever its origins, he was the toughest man I have ever met in politics—and he was proud of it. "The strongest steel always comes from the hottest fire," he used to tell us during Watergate.

In his biography of Nixon, *One of Us,* Tom Wicker, the former *New York Times* columnist, relates a story from an early personal crisis. Nixon, thirty-nine, had served only four years in the House and two in the Senate when Dwight Eisenhower surprised the country by selecting him as his vice presidential running mate. Ike knew the nomination would help to mollify the Taft wing of the party, which thought its man should be at the top of the ticket. Ike barely knew Nixon at all.

Just as the fall campaign began, the *New York Post* printed a sensational story charging that Nixon had a secret slush fund, drawn from campaign contributions, and that he dipped into it for personal use. Nixon indeed had a fund, but it was on the up-and-up. There was no scandal there. Nonetheless, the smear took hold and produced a frenzy in the press, especially because Ike wavered on his nominee. Nixon had never been hit so severely and pressure built for him to resign from the ticket. He decided to make a nationally televised address pleading his case.

Three days after the story broke, Eisenhower finally called, but instead of offering encouragement, he said it was up to Nixon to decide his fate. Feeling abandoned, Nixon boiled over, giving Eisenhower a lecture. "There comes a time in matters like these when you have to shit or get off the pot! The great trouble here is the indecision."

Nixon went on to Southern California, where he holed up with his longtime adviser, Murray Chotiner, and prepared notes for his live address. An hour before he was to leave for the studio, Tom Dewey—Mr. Republican himself, twice the nominee of his party, and an Eisenhower intimate—called. "There has just been a meeting of all of Eisenhower's top advisers," Dewey said, "and they have asked me to tell you that it is their opinion that at the conclusion of the broadcast tonight you should submit your resignation to Eisenhower."

Dewey and Co. probably thought they had delivered the knockout punch. Here was a powerless junior senator given an order directly by the party establishment and indirectly by the most popular man in America: "Scram!" Nixon would surely be gone by midnight. But they misjudged their man. Angrily, he responded: "Just tell them . . . if they want to find out they'd better listen to the broadcast . . . and tell them I know something about politics too!"

Nixon privately decided to go ahead with a ploy he had been mulling over with Chotiner. Instead of resigning or leaving the decision in Eisenhower's hands, he would ask viewers to send telegrams and letters to the Republican National Committee advising him on his next step. He didn't ask Eisenhower, Dewey, or anyone else for permission. He also made his personal finances public and suggested that all other candidates do so as well, something Eisenhower was loath to do. Eisenhower was surprised and stung by the way Nixon had boxed him in and, by some accounts, never fully forgave him.

As it turned out, Nixon did know something about politics. Watching his "Checkers" speech a half century later, one is struck by how lugubrious and cloying it is. In the context of his times, however, Nixon made a huge impression upon his viewing audience, the largest ever to watch a live political event until then. Telegrams and letters poured into GOP headquarters, urging him to stay on the ticket. Ike quietly embraced him and the scandal evaporated. It was the first time in history that a major political figure had so masterfully used the new medium of television to swing the country—a point Nixon remembered long after. More to the point, the pros knew that Nixon was a man who had twice stood up to the hero of Normandy. He had stood up to the entire Republican establishment. And he had won! That's guts.

There were many instances of Nixon's toughness in the years that followed—his steadiness in 1956 when Ike almost knocked him off the ticket for reelection; his bravery in 1958 during a trip to Latin America with his wife, Pat, when he walked directly into a mob of angry, anti-American students in Lima and was nearly killed by another mob in Caracas; his willingness in 1960 to concede a razor-thin defeat to John F. Kennedy rather than insisting on recounts in Illinois and Texas, where there were well-founded suspicions of voting fraud. All those are thoroughly described elsewhere.

What I saw in the White House was a man who was pummeled unmercifully and still held his head up. The beatings Nixon took were far worse than anything any president has received since, including Clinton. In private, Nixon could be nasty, profane, and, in his most intimate moments, horribly self-pitying. Publicly, he insisted upon hiding his bitter side until the day he resigned, and even then—as we listened to his emotional speech in the East Room and

40

waved good-bye from the lawn—he kept his composure. Ray Price captured the moment perfectly in a memo he wrote that fateful day describing Nixon as "a beaten man doggedly playing it out." Honor lost, he still had his dignity.

Americans have a gritty respect for someone who can dish it out and also take it. They never looked upon Nixon as a hero, nor did he see himself that way. They sensed he was insecure and vindictive. But they saw he had an inner toughness, and many thought a president needs that to lead the country. They were right.

Drawing Upon History

Daniel Patrick Moynihan, then a Harvard professor who had worked for both Kennedy and Johnson, joined Nixon's White House staff in 1969 as Counselor to the President for Domestic Affairs. Nixon reveled in Moynihan's rich intellectualism and buoyant spirit. At the President's request, Moynihan gave him a list of books worth reading. Nixon immediately obtained them, and when he awoke at 2:00 A.M. or so, as he often did, he would pore over Robert Blake's biography of Disraeli, trying to relate the leadership of one of Britain's most illustrious prime ministers to contemporary America. He talked about that biography so often to me and others that it still has a place on my bookshelf, along with several others he recommended.

To Nixon, history was a handmaiden to leadership. He drew upon it in three ways: to gain a broader perspective on his own times; to impress upon listeners his place in the sun; and to find role models for action.

While he spent much of his time reading about foreign leaders, he also took notes repeatedly on his predecessors, analyzing their greatest qualities and evaluating how he measured up. He was looking for insight, guidance, and, of course, reassurance. In his private, small sessions with his top three advisers—Haldeman, Ehrlichman, and Kissinger—he frequently referred to lessons he found in American and European history. Commiserating with Kissinger over the domestic turmoil caused by Vietnam, Nixon told him that their problems might be more substantial than anyone's except Lincoln, whose difficulties overshadowed everyone else's by a wide margin. "He commented," writes Haldeman in his diaries, "that Lincoln had cannons in the streets of New York to shoot draft resisters; that he

41

had a rebellious Cabinet; Stanton wouldn't speak to him; his wife's insanity and her two brothers killed in the Southern side of the war, etc. All of these, added up, make our situation look pretty simple."

He liked to talk about the lessons of other wars, too. He and Kissinger had running discussions about the relative merits of German generals in World War II, a subject dear to Henry. Or he might focus on the failure of Erich Ludendorff's big offensive in World War I or MacArthur's misjudgments at Yalu. When was a war moral? he might ask. He watched the movie *Patton* as many as five times, urging others to reflect upon the general's leadership. Patton, he told Haldeman, "inspired people, charged them up," and a chief of staff has to do this. That was "pointed," Haldeman notes sourly.

Isaiah Berlin has observed that an ability to look backward was Churchill's greatest gift, while an ability to look forward was FDR's special talent. Nixon was no Churchill and no Roosevelt, but because he steeped himself in history, he was very good at looking in both directions. He was convinced that his very capacity to see the road behind enabled him to see where the road was heading. It is a priceless asset for a leader.

A danger facing any new politician in Washington today is to begin living entirely in the present; the same holds true for journalists. The temptation is overwhelming because the city is so attuned to the latest tidbit of news, the hottest piece of gossip. You can dine at the finest tables or win a spot on cable news if you can deliver juicy morsels of inside, up-to-the-minute "news." But those leaders who have successfully guided the fate of nations, while living in the present, have also spent their time on a higher plane that is less cluttered with minutiae. As scholar Ronald A. Heifetz puts it, a leader must be able to "get on the balcony," observing the patterns of action from afar so that he may participate in them more effectively. No one loved detail more than Churchill, but his schooling in history enabled him to rise above and see the arc of events more clearly— where things had come from long ago, where they were portending now.

Nixon was accustomed to measuring time in decades and centuries, so he liked to think about what forces would be at work a decade or century hence. In his book *In the Arena,* he writes that in making policy decisions, he was looking for headlines not tomorrow but the day after tomorrow. That's disingenuous. He cared deeply— too much so—about the next morning's headlines. But he also cared a great deal about headlines far down the path, and that not only distinguished him as president, but also made him a far better strate-

42

gist. His capacity as a visionary exceeds that of other presidents in modern times and was squarely based upon his understanding of history.

As speechwriters, we were expected to look through books of our own, searching for historical nuggets that we could drop into a text, giving his speeches more life and inspiration. Nixon especially welcomed anything from the founders, Lincoln, the Roosevelts, Truman, or Eisenhower. Madison and the first Adams mattered more to him than Washington, while Jefferson and Andrew Jackson never seemed to move him. Churchill was always a gold mine, of course, and he could never get enough of de Gaulle.

Nixon once asked Ray Price to compile a notebook of favorite anecdotes, so that he could keep it in his desk and brush through it just before he appeared in the Rose Garden to welcome the Jaycees from Oklahoma. We applied ourselves diligently, pulling together about a hundred, and Nixon got a kick out of the final product. Later on, one of our best speechwriters, James C. Humes, wrote a book entitled *Instant Eloquence* that contains many of Nixon's chestnuts; I still recommend it to young speechwriters.

It is surprising that few politicians appreciate how much a capacity to speak knowledgeably from history can enhance the stature of a leader. As bright as he is, Clinton rarely cites historical parallels to buttress his initiatives, and neither of the candidates trying to succeed him shows much interest. The point was not lost on Nixon nor on Truman, the Roosevelts, Lincoln, and a host of others.

Typically, as recorded by Haldeman in his diary, Nixon once told a congressional delegation over breakfast how Disraeli had once borrowed part of his rival's agenda, pushing through an extension of the voting franchise. In the next election, an enlarged but ungrateful electorate threw out Disraeli and elected his rival, William Gladstone. To laughter, Nixon explained he wanted to push forward his own agenda of reforms (some of which were borrowed from Democrats) but was expecting a more positive result in the polls. When a president talks to members of Congress in that way, they feel he is talking up to them, not down, and they are complimented.

The very fact that Nixon spoke with authority about the past also gave him an aura of distinction, a sense that he might be above the pack. He knew that if he recited the deeds of great men, his listeners might think that, possibly, he was among their company. People were drawn to him in part because they wanted to touch history themselves; listening to him seemed to magnify him even as it enlarged them. The stories were often self-serving, of course; they

43

could also be maudlin. But for a while—until his own misdeeds overwhelmed him—the stories strengthened him. For a brief moment, Nixon seemed as if he could be destiny's child.

By studying the lives of great men, Nixon sought one other asset: to find role models for action. Disraeli was certainly one model, and a worthy one, too. As a Conservative prime minister in the latter nineteenth century, Disraeli was famous for co-opting the agenda of the Whigs and is now known as the father of Britain's welfare state. Disraeli's leadership also broadened the base of his Conservative Party and shaped Tory traditions for years thereafter. Bringing Democrat Pat Moynihan to the White House as one of his two counselors in 1969, Nixon was patterning himself after Disraeli, and in the years that followed proposed some of the most progressive reforms in years. Some of it did not pass, but much of it did in areas such as the environment, cancer research, workplace safety, and education. In his new study, *The Presidency of Richard Nixon*, historian Melvin Small entitles his chapter on the administration's domestic record "Disraeli Redux." An appropriate choice.

Yet Nixon's search for role models could also be hazardous. No one exercised greater hold over Nixon's imagination than Charles de Gaulle. He admired de Gaulle's role in the Resistance during World War II, but, more than that, de Gaulle had shown keen respect for him during a time when most people counted Nixon out. After his two defeats in the early 1960s, Nixon continued to roam world capitals, a solitary and seemingly broken man. The ministers of most governments found it inconvenient to see him, and he was shunted off to meals with lower-ranking deputies and American Foreign Service officers. De Gaulle was more astute: having come back from oblivion himself, he calculated that Nixon might one day be president and rolled out the red carpet. Invited to the Elysée with wife Pat, Nixon purred while de Gaulle predicted that he would one day enjoy "a top capacity" in the United States. That generosity did more than seal a friendship; it also turned Nixon into a devoted follower for the rest of his life.

De Gaulle did have positive impacts. He had the same quality that Nixon valued in himself: a capacity to look over the heads of his contemporaries toward the far horizon. Nixon especially appreciated that in the 1930s, as a lieutenant colonel in the French army, de Gaulle foresaw the changing nature of warfare. Set-piece battle strategies had been rendered obsolete by the invention of the internal combustion engine, de Gaulle wrote in a book entitled *The Army of the Future*: "The machine controls our destiny." Thereafter,

44

de Gaulle stood virtually alone in arguing the ineffectiveness of the Maginot Line in protecting France from Germany, and, of course, history bore him out within less than a decade. De Gaulle instilled in Nixon a belief that a leader, whether on a battlefield or in the White House, must have the prescience that comes from a combination of intelligence and instinct.

De Gaulle also helped Nixon see that people want more out of life than material gain. They aspire to higher purposes, and a leader who can summon them to something beyond themselves can touch off revolutionary changes. Repeatedly, both in public and private, Nixon quoted de Gaulle's line from the Resistance that "France cannot be France without greatness." Like de Gaulle, Nixon was a fervent nationalist and he tried to rally the United States to high ambitions. His inaugural in 1969 talked of "our summons to greatness," and his reelection campaign in 1972 called for a New American Revolution. Nixon could not inspire people the way de Gaulle could, but in seeking to propel himself and the United States to Olympian heights, he enlarged the vision of what he was trying to achieve as president.

But aping a European leader like de Gaulle had its perils. One was trivial and exposed Nixon only to ridicule. White House guards showed up for work one day looking like palace guards from Ruritania, wearing uniforms Nixon had ordered to make them appear more regal. Reporters guffawed so loudly that he was forced into an instant retreat. Those uniforms never made it to the Smithsonian; they were donated to a college marching band and, who knows, may have wound up in a Gilbert and Sullivan production.

A more serious peril lay in following his hero's style of governance. De Gaulle was notoriously aloof, acting in isolation and often without consultation. "L'état, c'est moi," Louis XIV once said, but de Gaulle might have said it equally well. While he spoke as the voice of the people, he had little interest in mixing with them, nor did he seem to care much for politicians, the press, or anyone else. He was imperious and haughty, and were it not for the traditions of France stretching back over centuries—and refreshed as recently as Napoleon—he would not have gotten away with it. One cannot imagine a political leader like de Gaulle surviving long on British soil—or American. He lacked a democratic temperament.

Unfortunately for Nixon, trying to emulate de Gaulle only reinforced his own worst instincts. Nixon, as we have seen, was by nature a loner, a shy man who preferred to work out grand solutions in his own mind—or with a partner like Henry Kissinger. He didn't enjoy the hurly-burly of politics, nor was he naturally drawn to the arts of democratic leadership. By staying above the fray, Nixon never forced himself to build the personal relationships and observe the traditions of normal democratic politics. He came to believe that the exercise of power is the same thing as the exercise of leadership— and, in a democracy, they can be different. We shall explore that point more fully in the next chapter because it is fundamental to Nixon's ultimate fall.

What is the lesson here? That history is an invaluable resource for a leader, but one that must be used wisely. Nixon certainly gained much from it as president. Instead of choosing de Gaulle as his point of reference, however, he would have been far better off if he had stuck to figures who represented the best of the American democratic tradition—men like Teddy Roosevelt, Wilson, and Eisenhower. He admired all of them but he chose to follow de Gaulle. It was a mixed blessing.

Maintaining a Mystique

Charles de Gaulle wrapped himself in a mystique that was mesmerizing to Nixon. What was his secret? How could a leader turn men in the street into faithful believers? Charismatically challenged himself, Nixon studied him closely. Only after his hero died did he discover some of the answers in a series of lectures that de Gaulle had given at the French War College in 1932, long before he rose to prominence. They are reprinted as a book, *The Edge of the Sword*, a gem that is difficult to find in the United States. Nixon called it "a manual for leadership," and I assign portions of it to students today.

There, de Gaulle argues that a leader "must be able to create a spirit of confidence in those under him. He must be able to assert his authority. . . . Certain men have, one might almost say from birth, the quality of exuding authority, as though it were a liquid, though it is impossible to say precisely of what it consists." Authority, de Gaulle asserted, is more than the formal power that comes from holding office or rank; it is the informal power that comes from the respect and deference of others and thus can be infinitely greater in impact.

To achieve that authority, de Gaulle believed that a leader must have more than character and grandeur; he must also preserve his innermost self from public appropriation. "First and foremost, there can be no prestige without mystery, for familiarity breeds contempt.

46

All religions have their tabernacles, and no man is a hero to his valet." De Gaulle did not try to manufacture or create a false self, as some politicians do. Rather, he intentionally created a distance between his real self and others that helped to elevate his public persona and, because it was done without condescension, increase his popular appeal.

Once again, de Gaulle could be the wrong model if taken too far by an American leader. Nixon told me how he wished he could adopt de Gaulle's approach to press conferences—two a year with about a thousand journalists beneath crystal chandeliers in the Elysée Palace. Resplendent in full military dress, de Gaulle would stand and speak for about twenty minutes on a single subject of his choice and would then answer questions—no more than three and all apparently planted by his press office in advance. After that, he would sweep out of the room. I can think of a half-dozen American presidents who would have loved that model, especially Nixon, Carter, and Bush. As Nixon would add, "But it would be wrong."

No American president can be as reclusive as de Gaulle, withdrawing from the give-and-take of democratic politics. Yet de Gaulle did have a valuable point in arguing that a leader should have a measure of reserve, giving himself space in which to think and keeping parts of himself private. A leader must not try to manufacture or create a false self for public consumption. One who lives by illusions will ultimately fail. A leader must be true to people, even as he remains true to his own inner core.

A solitary man who needed space for thinking, Nixon often disappeared for parts of the day into a quiet study, usually in the Old Executive Office Building or upstairs in the White House residence, away from the bustle and formality of the Oval Office. The announced purpose was to give himself a chance to reflect, write, and decide on issues of the day. It took months for several of us in a subsequent White House to persuade a younger, more exuberant Bill Clinton to set aside more time for reflection. He, too, found that he became more effective.

Admittedly, Nixon could also waste extraordinary amounts of time when tucked away in the Old EOB. Instead of grand thoughts, he might call in Haldeman for rambling bull sessions that could last four hours or more and generate pages of instructions to the staff on matters big and unbelievably odd. (Among my favorites was a memorandum from Haldeman to the military aide at the White House, conveying Nixon's instructions: "The President would like to have the bowling ball man come in and fit Mrs. Nixon and Tricia

47

for balls as soon as possible.") Still, those hours of seclusion also encouraged Nixon to make some of the most far-reaching decisions of his presidency.

I saw with Nixon how much a president can gain from preserving a realm of personal privacy. In today's therapeutic politics, political leaders feel a compulsion to spill out their inner emotions on television, Oprah-style. We come to know too much about them. They become too familiar. The nadir was reached, of course, when Clinton told an MTV audience about his underwear. But many others have told us about the dynamics of their marriages, the problems of their small children, the trauma they experienced when a sibling died. While voters need to see and evaluate the character of the men and women they are electing, politicians who babble on about their inner lives rob themselves of their own dignity. It is far better to protect and hold sacrosanct one's inner self, as FDR, Truman, Eisenhower, Kennedy, and Reagan did.

Nixon appreciated that point, just as he did the importance of not becoming overexposed as president. He ensured that neither his aides nor the press could poke into his personal life or that of his family. His wife, Pat, did not want to become public property and she never did. His daughters, Julie and Tricia, both had splendid weddings after he was elected president, but neither of them became public celebrities. Just as the Clintons succeeded in drawing a protective cloak over their daughter, Chelsea, the Nixons did with their daughters—and everyone gained.

Nixon had recognized the power of prime time television since the night of his Checkers speech, and he made more prime time appearances—thirty-two speeches and press conferences in six years—than any other president. But he insisted, wisely, that he not become overexposed. "No more than four prime time speeches a year," he told me, "and each one has to count." Toward the end of his life, Nixon thought that Clinton was badly overexposed, undercutting his effectiveness. His audiences were tuning out. To Nixon, a leader must create a degree of suspense so that people *want* to know what he has to say on an issue. He can't be entirely predictable, nor should he become just another talking head.

Cultivating an air of mystery was also essential, he believed, in the conduct of diplomacy. Bob Haldeman records in his memoirs that walking together on a beach one day, Nixon related a "madman theory" of international politics—that if other nations thought he was tough, vindictive, even a little mad, they would more likely stay out of America's way. Who knows where he might strike next? In her extensive research, biographer Joan Hoff was unable to find any evidence supporting Haldeman's theory. But on staff we certainly believed that Nixon intentionally kept adversaries off guard by occasional bouts of erratic behavior and menacing signals.

There were times when some of us on the staff thought he went too far. Over the Christmas season of 1972—when peace seemed almost within grasp in Vietnam—Nixon ordered up a relentless bombing campaign against Haiphong Harbor, sending protesters into the streets and the press into hyperventilation. So prolonged was the bombing that we worried it was killing innocent people—and perhaps our chances for peace. Had he finally careened over the edge? As it turned out, I was also one of those who was wrong. His hard nose forced the North Vietnamese back to the bargaining table. Steel does matter—both external and internal—as I came to learn.

The point here is not to recommend that a political leader have a streak of madness. But there is value in having a president like Nixon, known to carry a big stick, and willing to use it if rashly provoked. The ardor for terrorism by Libyan strongman Muammar al-Qaddafi noticeably cooled after Reagan ordered up air strikes that nearly took him out. While he still remains in power, Saddam Hussein has not threatened his neighbors so seriously since Bush responded with massive force. Outbreaks of terrorism seem to have subsided since Clinton ordered up air strikes in Pakistan and Sudan. Those same presidents realized, as did Nixon, that in some flash points around the world, ambiguity about America's intentions can also be useful in preserving peace. For a good many years, China and Taiwan have been reluctant to attack each other across the Straits, not completely sure what the American response would be.

In recent years, some of Nixon's critics like Oliver Stone have seized upon his elusive nature to portray him as a drunken, twisted egomaniac who might have blown up the world. Those portraits are wrong and unfair. The air of mystery about him was a strength, not a weakness. The Nixon I saw used it with considerable thought and in a way that generally strengthened prospects for long-term peace.

A Flow of Talent

On the first Wednesday of November 1972—about 6:00 A.M., as I recall—my beeper went off furiously. I had been asleep only a couple of hours after a night of revelry. That Tuesday night, Nixon had just won reelection, beating McGovern in a landslide.

49

Foggily, I called the White House. There was an urgent message waiting, asking me to come in for a meeting late that morning. "Be there. It's a command performance."

The only thing I recall clearly was my pleasure at the prospect of the meeting. I had never worked in a presidential campaign before and looked forward now to joining the rest of the writing and research team as our superiors thanked us for our labors and painted a glorious picture of the years ahead.

How little I still knew. As we arrived that morning, there were a few thank-yous, all perfunctory. That wasn't the real reason we were called together. President Nixon did want us to know that he appreciated our efforts, but now he wanted our immediate resignations! Every one of us! Across the federal government, some one thousand people were asked to submit letters. It was the biggest purge of political appointees by any administration in history. I was instantly cured of my hangover.

The ax that Nixon swung that day still symbolizes, in my judgment, one of the low points of his presidency. It was one of the worst mistreatments of a staff I have seen in thirty years. "The first act of a leader is to define reality," Max DePree has written. "The last is to say thank you." Nixon should have had the good grace that Wednesday morning to call his various teams together and praise them for their extraordinary efforts on his behalf and to pledge that he would dedicate his second term to living up to the trust so many had placed in him. Instead, he became arrogant—a failing that has tripped up many a president, especially just after reelection.

But buried within the needless brutality was an idea that was right and, had it been executed differently, would have been understood at the time. Nixon's inner purpose, I eventually learned, was to weed out "strap-hangers" within the administration, keep the performers, and pump in some new recruits as quickly as he could. The mass resignations gave higher-ups a chance to review everyone's record and then invite some to stay on for the second term while letting others quietly disappear.

Nixon was acting upon two assumptions, both right. He knew from history that a second-term president has only the briefest time to make his mark before his power seeps away. Power in the presidency is evanescent: it can come in a rush, but it also tends to evaporate overnight. A president must know how to draw upon it quickly, putting it to full use, or he will never achieve great goals. Nixon understood that and was seeking a fresh burst of energy as his second term began.

His other assumption—and the main point of discussion here—is that a president, to be effective, needs a steady stream of talented, fresh lieutenants around him to carry forward the projects of government. George Patton used to say that there are more tired division commanders than tired divisions, and all tired men are pessimists. Nixon admired Patton's ruthlessness in getting rid of underlings who were inadequate so that his army could always perform at top efficiency. Nixon, like Patton, went too far. (Once again, he chose a role model too much like himself.) But one has to say this for both Nixon and Patton: they both managed to recruit some excellent people around them and they both got results.

Looking over Nixon's presidency, it is clear that the people he brought into public life were one of his greatest strengths and became one of his greatest legacies.

The dedication in 1990 of his library in Yorba Linda drew together a wide array of former presidents, cabinet members, and other major figures, almost all of whom had roots in the Nixon era. Among those who came were the Republican Big Four—Nixon, Gerald Ford, Ronald Reagan, and the sitting President, George Bush—who gathered for the first time in nearly a decade. Each of the others knew that had it not been for Nixon, he might never have made it to the White House. Ford was an obvious case.

In 1970, Nixon had encouraged Bush to put his political career at risk by giving up a safe House seat to run for the Senate from Texas. Even though Bush lost to Democrat Lloyd Bentsen, he was still considered a rising star and Nixon was eager for him to stay in public life. Bush, I am told, had his eye on the number-two post at Treasury, where he might one day move up to become secretary; the Nixon White House initially marked him out for a deputy post at Commerce. Fortunately for Bush, Nixon eventually decided the young Bush ought to have some foreign policy experience and dispatched him to the United Nations. Bush turned the post into a training ground in international affairs and rapidly ascended toward the presidency in his own right.

Of the subsequent Republican presidents, Reagan owed the least to Nixon. But even he would not have jumped into politics in 1966, running for governor of California, had not Nixon lost to Pat Brown four years earlier. Despite their ideological differences, Reagan also gave Nixon strong support during his presidential years and Nixon asked Reagan to undertake some foreign missions that burnished his credentials.

Nixon not only opened a door for future presidents, but re-

51

cruited the most talented team of Republicans to the rest of the executive branch of any president since Teddy Roosevelt, more than sixty years earlier. Not even Dwight Eisenhower, whose presidency was much more successful than Nixon's, brought as many men and women to Washington who played principal roles in subsequent administrations.

Nixon's principal environmental adviser, John Whitaker, provided within a recent issue of the *Presidential Studies Quarterly* a roster of men and women who first came into government in the Nixon years and went on to high posts in subsequent administrations. Nixon, of course, did not recruit each of them directly, but he was the magnet. He also gave instructions to his personnel team about the kinds of people he was looking for, and in the case of cabinet members, interviewed them before their appointments. Among those flowing into government were one future president (Bush); five secretaries of state in succeeding administrations (Henry Kissinger, Alexander Haig, George Shultz, James Baker, and Lawrence Eagleburger); five secretaries of defense (James Schlesinger, Donald Rumsfeld, Caspar Weinberger, Frank Carlucci, and Dick Cheney); a chairman of the joint chiefs of staff (Colin Powell); two secretaries of the treasury (William Simon and Jim Baker); and three directors of the Office of Management and Budget (Carlucci, Shultz, and Richard Darman). Paul Volcker first entered public life at the Nixon Treasury Department and his successor at the Federal Reserve Board, Alan Greenspan, had just signed up for a stint in government when Nixon resigned. Greenspan soon became a star in the Ford entourage. Four Nixon recruits later served as White House chiefs of staff (Rumsfeld, Cheney, Baker, and Kenneth Duberstein). Elliot Richardson, Carla Hills, Brent Scowcroft, and Ann McLaughlin are all Nixon alumni, as are senators Daniel Patrick Moynihan (a veteran of the Kennedy and Johnson administrations, too), John Warner, and Robert Bennett. So far, four Nixon alumni have run for president in their own right—Lamar Alexander, Pat Buchanan, Al Haig, and Don Rumsfeld. And the chief justice of the Supreme Court, William Rehnquist, first came to Washington as head of the Office of Legal Counsel in Nixon's Justice Department.

Of course, Nixon also set a modern record for the number of top appointees who went to jail—among them his attorney general, his White House chief of staff, his chief domestic adviser, his general counsel, his top political adviser, and scores of others. He also showed spectacularly poor judgment in the selection of Spiro Agnew as vice president. But the fact that so many others not only

52

survived but were a bulwark of strength in the Ford, Reagan, and Bush administrations gives testimony that, just as in so many other areas, Nixon offered two faces to the world—one dark, the other brighter than remembered.

After the library gathering in Yorba Linda, I wrote in *U.S. News & World Report* that even as the dedication failed to bring absolution, it did show that his impact upon American life stretched far beyond the day he resigned. I also pointed out some of the alumni who came. His daughter Julie sent a note saying nothing gave Nixon greater pride than the people he had recruited and helped train for future leadership.

Molding His Team

Earlier presidents had kept only a few people around to help with speeches, such as Judge Samuel Rosenman in the Roosevelt years. Ted Sorensen was also Kennedy's general counsel. LBJ pulled together the first speechwriting staff at the White House, but he, too, relied heavily upon other advisers for his speeches—men like Harry McPherson. Nixon was the first to assemble a large team of writers and they were the finest any White House has seen since. Peggy Noonan compared them to the "Murderers' Row" of the 1927 Yankees.

In the opening days, Ray Price, Bill Safire, and Pat Buchanan were on the front line, and a former editor of *Time,* Jim Keogh, was the chief. By the time I began running the shop, they had all moved on and so had Ken Khachigian. But we continued to have a crackerjack team. Several of them went on to prominence: John McLaughlin; Ben Stein; Lee Huebner, who became publisher of the *International Herald Tribune;* and Aram Bakshian, Jr., who later headed up Reagan's first speechwriting team. Others are less in today's limelight but were no less valuable then, among them John Andrews, Noel Koch, Vera Hirschberg, John Coyne, Jack McDonald, and Rodney Campbell.

By habit and inclination, speechwriters exercise more personal license than would pass muster in the West Wing. After I became straw boss, two of them would disappear to the National Press Club for long lunches. I never objected because they each turned in polished speeches by the end of the day. Only later did I learn that one came back soused and the other covered for him by writing both speeches. Together, we created a warm home for one another, and I am grateful to them to this day.

53

Nixon could see how little I still knew. Fortunately, he was a born teacher and took me in hand, just as he had so many others who worked for him. He spent enormous amounts of time molding his team, helping them to understand modern politics. In speechwriting, he said, you need to learn that a torrent of words pours out of every White House in the name of the president—as many as 5 million words a year in speeches, written statements, proclamations, letters, etc. Nearly all of them wash over the public. They are dull, gray prose, eminently forgettable. The key to effective communication is to break through the babble, sinking your message into the public consciousness.

Let's try this exercise, he suggested. Each time you send me a final draft, underline the three sentences in the speech that you think the press will quote. We will check the television networks and the papers to see whether they quote those same sentences. At first, I was hopelessly off, but over time, I came to understand what "breaks through," the line that not only snaps but advances the story. Advancing a story is like advancing a conversation; you keep finding new ways to push forward.

To ensure that the television networks picked up the sound bite he wanted, Nixon insisted that we limit many of his public pronouncements to one hundred words. He would march into the pressroom, read the statement, and march out, answering no questions. The reporters were furious (rightly), but he forced their hand. Nixon believed that, in general, a public leader should say less and that in public communications less is usually more. Don't appear too often in the family living room and when you do make it memorable—that was his view. And remember, he told his speechwriters, the power of repetition. Just when you have written the same phrase for me so many times you want to throw up, people out there will be hearing it for the first time. Through David Parker in scheduling, Nixon also decided that no public event would go on his calendar unless we could say what would then appear as the headline, picture, caption, and quote. Strange as it may seem, that system was a helpful approach to scheduling. The Nixon White House also became well known for originating the "line of the day" concept, an orchestrated effort to ensure that every possible spokesman for the President—from press secretary to cabinet to friendly members of Congress—echoed the same points during the same twenty-four-hour news cycle. Nixon also taught his staff to stay on the offensive, framing and guiding public arguments.

There is no doubt that we went too far in the Nixon administra-

54

tion in trying to manage the news. We on staff knew it was too much, but there seemed no way to rachet down the machine. In his memoirs, Kissinger laments that "the conviction that Nixon's standing depended less on his actions than on their presentation was a bane of his administration." Haldeman confided to his diaries about the image-making: "It would work a lot better if he would quit worrying about it and just be President." In the next chapter, we will examine how the excesses helped to derail his presidency.

For now, the point is to remember that one of Nixon's strengths as a leader was the way he served as a personal mentor for many of those who came to work for him. Long before I arrived, he had helped to shape the work of Price, Safire, and Buchanan, along with other advisers like Len Garment. He taught almost everyone around him about politics and power. Some of his lessons were the wrong ones, sure, but many served productive purposes. Far more than any president I have known since, Nixon thought that a role of a leader is to train his own team. To a striking degree, the lessons he passed on, as in stagecraft, shaped presidential staffs that followed, all the way through Clinton.

The Strategist at His Chessboard

In 1984, Nixon made a rare public appearance before the American Society of Newspaper Editors, men and women whose blood still ran cold from Watergate. By now seventy-one, shoulders hunched, bushy eyebrows graying, no longer introduced by trumpets, Nixon at first seemed a curiosity. He stood before his audience unshielded, without a podium or notes.

Then, for the next forty-five minutes, the old fellow took them on a journey into the future. Five great powers would rule the world in the next century, he said, and peace would depend on how well the United States structured its relations with each of the others. A newly emerging China, a revived Russia, a united Europe, a resurgent Japan, and the United States itself—he weighed each in turn, its interests, its historical path, the quality of its leadership.

Those who knew Nixon recognized that it was his classic "up to the mountaintop" speech—a *tour d'horizon* conducted from the lofty perch that he liked so much. But even cynics had to admire his return from exile to give the performance that was his trademark. As he finished, young and old stood and applauded. Nixon, even in decline, was still a master strategist—and that was his greatest gift.

55

Nixon knew that he was different, and he played upon that difference in his long period of rehabilitation. He wanted to go out erasing as much of Watergate as he could. In his remaining twenty years after he resigned, he wrote seven books, nearly all about foreign affairs. Three made the best-seller lists. He traveled to China and Russia three times, received numerous private delegations, and conferred quietly with his successors. From time to time, he entertained prominent young journalists for dinner, people he thought unencumbered by memories of his past and more willing to focus on the future. He hoped they would be more forgiving.

Unlike many in retirement, he also had an incessant hunger to know what was happening and kept back channels open. I was among those who visited him from time to time or talked with him by phone. The experience was always the same: he had better intelligence on what was happening than I did. He seemed to know exactly what the secretary of state was thinking, his relationship to the NSC, and how the President was responding. As the 1992 election approached, he would call and ask me to get out my electoral scorecard so we could compare notes, state by state. "Here's what I hear from Illinois," he might say. "What do you know?" His scorecard was always more complete. One felt in those final years that you were bidding farewell to the last of his kind.

Chic journalists ridiculed the notion that he had become "The Sage of Saddle River." A final, desperate search for acceptance, they hooted; the Trickster reaching for his last card. Their criticisms are off the mark. Over time, Nixon had become a source of knowledge and, yes, of wisdom. For years, he had walked through the foothills, studying, traveling, negotiating, so that gradually he worked his way up to an intellectual plain. There were a few others up there, most of them bitterly opposed to him—men like George Kennan, Paul Nitze, John McCloy, Dean Acheson. They had earned their places, too. Nixon, as it happened, was the only one who captured the White House.

One of the reasons Nixon's fatal flaws fascinate us is that the same man had such strengths. The quality that I most admire—and have saved for discussion until now—was his capacity to look out from the mountaintop, foresee the trend lines of the world's future, and bend history to serve American interests. He was the best strategist we have had in the Oval Office in the past three decades and, arguably, since Woodrow Wilson. No one else in recent years has come close.

That is not to say that Nixon was brilliant or successful in everything he did in foreign policy. There are serious and legitimate questions whether he mishandled Vietnam, deceiving the country and waiting too long to settle the war. We shall return briefly to those matters. But most observers, even those who are jaded, would grant that Nixon restructured American foreign policy in ways that helped to end the Cold War peacefully and enhanced the ability of the United States to maintain long-term stability.

The best measure of how much Nixon's farsightedness achieved comes from snapshots of world affairs before and after his presidency. Before he took office, the United States was negotiating but had never concluded an arms control agreement with the Soviet Union, and the two superpowers were locked in an increasingly dangerous and volatile Cold War. The United States and China had been implacable foes for nearly twenty years, so much so that an American secretary of state, John Foster Dulles, wouldn't even shake hands with Chou En-lai in 1954. When Nixon took office, the Chinese and Soviets seemed joined at the hip in their hostility toward the United States. Many thought the forces of history were on their side.

By the time Nixon left office in 1974, the United States and Soviet Union had approved not only the first treaty limiting strategic arms (SALT) but stacks of other agreements, including meaningful economic ties that gave the Soviets a self-interest in preserving peaceful relations with the West. Détente represented the turning point of the Cold War, opening the way toward further progress at Helsinki and the collapse of the Berlin Wall in 1989. Meanwhile, the United States had also negotiated an agreement with China that normalized the Sino-American relationship and protected the security of Taiwan, a longtime American friend. Equally important, a Sino-Soviet split had ended the Communist alliance, thereby erasing what had been the most important threat to U.S. security. The status quo was broken. The United States had replaced the old two-power standoff with a triangular diplomacy that allowed it to play off one Communist power against the other.

Those accomplishments flowed from Nixon's capacity to plot out moves on the chessboard far in advance and then make the "big play," as he called it. As early as his vice presidency in the 1950s, he was talking of visiting Mainland China. By 1966, he told Leonard Garment in some detail about building bridges to Peking, then isolated and seemingly in the firm embrace of the Soviet Union. In October of 1967, a year before his election, he wrote a piece on Asia in *Foreign Affairs,* arguing for closer ties with China. The article drew little attention because hardly anyone thought that Nixon, the

57

staunch anti-Communist, would ever hold out a true olive branch to "Red China."

Maintaining that public fiction, he went to Asia early in the first year of his presidency, ostensibly to visit major allies and assess the situation in Vietnam. In truth, he was discreetly opening lines to China, working through President Yahya Khan of Pakistan, and then, on the way home, through a visit with President Nicolae Ceauşescu of Romania. Both men had personal channels to the Chinese. His overtures soon paid off, and Henry Kissinger had the famous case of indigestion in Pakistan that allowed him to venture secretly to Peking in 1971. The following year, Nixon made the most celebrated trip of his presidency, a journey to the Chinese capital that captivated millions of television viewers across the world.

Kissinger has said that as Nixon stepped off Air Force One onto Chinese soil, his first words to his hosts captured the essence of his foreign policy leadership: "I come here in the interests of the United States." Nixon obviously wanted to milk the trip for his own political gain. Dwight Chapin had spent months mapping out the choreography, making sure that The Boss would return on live prime time television, his helicopter landing dramatically on the grounds of the Capitol moments before an address to Congress. It was Chapin's masterpiece, and it came seven months before the President's reelection. But Nixon saw the opening to China as first and foremost a critical way to advance America's long-term interests; if he could also benefit politically, so much the better.

Drawing China closer to the United States, he knew, allowed it to slip out of its yoke to the Soviet Union. Instead of two against one, the United States was splitting its rivals apart and setting up a new game that favored the Americans. The Chinese had interests of their own. They thought that by creating a closer relationship with the United States they might benefit not only from trade and investment but also from a potential loosening of American ties with Japan, giving China more breathing room in Asia. Nixon recognized that possibility but thought that even if U.S. links to Tokyo diminished, the friendship with Japan would remain. He also believed that in the short term, talks with China would hasten an end to the Vietnam War. The North Vietnamese might lose some trust of friends to the north and become more willing to negotiate a settlement. Longer-range, Nixon understood that China, not Japan, would emerge as the dominant Asian power of the twenty-first century, and he and Kissinger were beginning to set up a balance of power favorable to the United States among the great Pacific nations of that time: China,

Russia, Japan, Korea, and the United States. Nixon, then, was playing an international chess game for big stakes—and he spent years mapping out his strategy.

He was not without critics as he pursued this course. Many wondered if he were engaged in new trickery. No one, after all, had scored more political points off the Red scare than Richard Nixon himself. He had crusaded against the Reds for twenty years, bringing down Alger Hiss, chastising his Senate opponent Helen Gahagan Douglas as the "pink lady," urging Ike to intervene in Dien Bien Phu, even wagging his finger at Khrushchev in their Moscow kitchen debate. On the Left, critics now gagged at his change of stripes. On the Right, old allies hated him for embracing the devil incarnate. Two years after Nixon left office, conservative Republicans forced Jerry Ford to accept a party platform that renounced détente and, implicitly, Henry Kissinger. Generally, however, historians have given Nixon credit for recognizing an opportunity to change the world, throwing off his ideological baggage, and helping the country get rid of its blinders, too. Leaders are often those who see fresh, historic opportunities and seize them, even at the expense of their own consistency.

People ask whether Nixon was the true brains behind his foreign policy. Especially after listening to him rant on some of the tapes, they think he could be awfully stupid—and they are right. So, maybe Kissinger was the mastermind, they say. I have never doubted that it was Nixon who was the chief strategist. While I did not sit in on any of his tête-à-têtes with Kissinger, I heard Nixon talk in dozens of private forums, saw him write out notes, and talked with him enough during and after his presidency. No one I have known in public life has exhibited as sure a grasp of the larger international picture, combined with an intricate understanding of the history, personalities, and political forces at play in other countries.

But it is equally clear that Kissinger was indispensable to Nixon. He provided the intellectual engagement Nixon needed, absorbed and diverted his wild jags, oversaw the execution of policy, and generally kept the President on a steadier course. Kissinger had his own idiosyncrasies, much publicized, and threatened to resign many times. Together, however, they made a good pair. Historians debate who the best teams were in foreign policy. Truman-Marshall-Acheson? Roosevelt-Hopkins? Wilson-House? Many give high marks to Eisenhower-Dulles, Reagan-Shultz, and Bush-Baker. Looking over modern history, Nixon-Kissinger fare well.

Vietnam remains the great, tragic question hanging over

59

Nixon's conduct of foreign policy. When he took office, some 530,000 American troops were posted to Vietnam, and there was no light at the end of the tunnel. The United States already counted over 200,000 casualties—more than 40,000 dead, 160,000 wounded. The last year of the Johnson presidency was the bloodiest yet, as 14,600 Americans lost their lives. At home, young people were protesting angrily in the streets and Congress was increasingly against the war. Nixon promised the country in his campaign that he would end the war—he implied he had a secret plan, which he didn't—but he had few options. Victory was never one of them. The country wouldn't stand for any more escalation. In 1973, four years after he took office, a peace agreement was finally signed and American troops came home. Two years later, Saigon fell to the North Vietnamese.

Were Nixon and Kissinger right in arguing that given the hand they were dealt, they did as well as they could, or are their critics right that they failed and needlessly wasted more American lives? The historical record is almost as much of a quagmire as the war itself. One can easily get lost among documents with conflicting tales of what happened, the misunderstandings, the mistakes. There was as much intrigue and plotting within the American government as there was at the bargaining table with the North Vietnamese. Memoirists have been trying to settle old scores and cover their fannies for years. Rivalries and tensions that started in Vietnam stretched even into the Clinton years, as Richard Holbrooke and Tony Lake sometimes crossed swords.

William Bundy, Melvin Small, Tad Szulc, and other authors assert that Nixon needlessly prolonged the war by dragging out the negotiations for four years. Better to have withdrawn immediately—a cousin of the "Aiken solution," which called for the United States to declare victory and come home. That, of course, is easy to say in retrospect, when we now see that the South Vietnamese were unable to pull themselves together by the time the Americans left, and the United States no longer had the will to help them.

But looking at Nixon's inheritance, the situation seems quite different. When he took office in 1969, he believed that a precipitous American withdrawal would not only topple the dominoes in Southeast Asia but also inflict serious damage upon America's reputation for steadfastness. As it turned out, the dominoes did not fall as expected, but there is little doubt that if the United States had "cut and run," as Nixon called it, his hand would have been weakened dramatically vis-à-vis the other great powers. He could not have negotiated from strength with either the Soviets or the Chinese. Was the trade-off worth it? Why not gamble and see if he could work out a reasonable deal in South Vietnam, giving himself an opportunity meanwhile to construct détente with the Soviet Union and open the door to China? That was his reasoning. That his gamble failed in Vietnam is obvious. But the rest of the gamble paid off richly. In preserving his negotiating strength, Nixon achieved breakthroughs in superpower relations that have kept the United States out of major wars since. On balance, Nixon was right not to withdraw precipitously.

By contrast, a second criticism of Nixon's handling of the war has merit. Writes Melvin Small: "The devious and deceitful ways that he and Henry Kissinger planned and executed their Southeast Asia policies were all too characteristic of their penchant for ignoring the fact that they were operating in a democracy." Tad Szulc: "Nixon's foreign policy, representing his greatest claim to glory, also carried the seeds of his own destruction. His obsession with secrecy and his inclination toward deception led him to exclude most of the government from participating in policy formulation. This exclusion was accompanied by a paranoid fear of news 'leaks' and a miasmatic conspiratorial climate at the White House."

In fact, Nixon wasn't straight with the country about Vietnam, violating the trust that a democratic people place in their leader. The Johnson administration had already told the country a pack of lies about Vietnam, but that did not justify the continued deceptions of the Nixon years. Secret bombings of Cambodia in 1969 and 1970 should have been revealed to both the Congress and the people. They were certainly no secret to the Cambodians and ultimately contributed to the rise of the murderous Khmer Rouge, practically destroying that once beautiful country. Nixon, of course, spoke frequently to the nation about Vietnam in Oval Office addresses, as he should have, but he never fully entrusted the public or the Congress with hard truths of what the country faced in Indochina and what he was trying to achieve. He never had a plan to end the war when he came into office, as he suggested in his campaign, and he kept vital facts out of the hands of others who deserved to have them—including his own defense secretary Melvin Laird and key members of the Joint Chiefs of Staff. While the price cannot be measured in lives, there was something precious lost. The lying and deceptions in Vietnam by two administrations, along with Watergate, seriously undermined public confidence in government and have handicapped 61 presidents ever since.

One can also draw a direct line from Vietnam to Watergate. The obsession with secrecy and stopping the flow of leaks led first to wiretapping of journalists and administration officials and then to the formation of the "Plumbers." Nixon was justifiably angry at the leaks in national security, but in setting up his own internal police unit and allowing them to break into the office of Daniel Ellsberg's psychiatrist, he wrote out his political death warrant. Approaching the 1972 campaign, Howard Hunt was reassigned from national security break-ins to political break-ins, and when he and the Watergate burglars were arrested, the warrant came due. He needed a cover-up of Watergate to keep the lid on the Plumbers and a range of other nefarious operations. It's a long, bitter tale that we will pick up later. The point here is that Watergate is rooted in Vietnam—and Nixon bears responsibility.

Does the Vietnam record change one's conclusions about Nixon as a master strategist? I don't think so. His legacy of a "structure of peace"—détente with the Soviet Union, an opening to China, the enhancement of the United States as the dominant superpower—remains a substantial accomplishment. He did have the capacity to see farther ahead. He did indeed bend history to favor America's long-term interests. But those of us who worked for him and continue to see him as a strong leader in international affairs must recognize that his darker side became twisted up in Vietnam. That is part of his legacy as well.

AT THE DEDICATION of his library in 1990, Nixon pulled me aside and said he wanted to show me some of the exhibits. To my surprise, he guided us straight into those rooms extolling his domestic initiatives. "In the long run," he said, "I believe these will be as well remembered as what we did in foreign affairs." That hasn't happened, at least not yet.

But there is little doubt that in the domestic arena, he exhibited the same sense of long-range vision that was characteristic of his foreign policy. Drawing from two early counselors at the White House, Daniel Patrick Moynihan and Arthur Burns, as well as advisers like George Shultz, he set forth ideas on domestic policy that were well ahead of his time, breaking out of orthodox thinking and blending the compassion of the Left with the hard-headed realism of the Right.

Nixon was the first president in 120 years who came into office with both chambers of Congress in the hands of the opposition. Not surprisingly, some of his most far-reaching domestic proposals died at the hands of congressional Democrats, who could not bear the idea of Nixon upstaging them. But Nixon's Family Assistance Plan was the first serious attempt to change welfare to "workfare," a notion later embraced and enacted into law with support from both parties. The more radical idea embedded in the Family Assistance Plan was to build an income floor beneath all Americans willing to work. Had FAP been enacted, it is estimated that 60 percent of the nation's poor would have moved above the poverty line. The Earned Income Tax Credit, put into effect in the Reagan years, is a variant of that approach.

Nixon's other radical idea that failed was to overhaul the health care system, requiring employers to insure their employees and providing insurance coverage to others through regional insurance pools. Variants of both ideas reappeared in the Clinton health proposals of 1994. Not only were these notions ahead of their time, but they set him at odds with his own party. Chief economics adviser Herbert Stein explained why Nixon was not eager to embrace traditionally conservative economic policies: "He always believed in throwing the long bomb. . . . He thought great presidents were activist presidents."

Nixon had more concrete success in other domestic arenas. He was the first president to deal seriously with environmental dangers, creating the Environmental Protection Agency and putting Bill Ruckelshaus in charge. While it remains controversial among some industrialists, the EPA has presided over impressive changes: emissions of lead have declined by 98 percent since 1970; sewage treatment has been upgraded for 73 million people; and U.S. production of chlorofluorocarbons has been cut by more than 60 percent in more recent years. Both air and water are much cleaner today. Nixon also made important changes in Social Security, tying increases in benefits to annual rises in the cost of living and removing them from the control of politicians. He also pushed toward giving state and local government more power, returned the nation to an all-volunteer military force, launched a major research campaign to overcome cancer, and granted Native American tribes significantly greater authority over their lands and resources.

But his greatest domestic achievement is perhaps his least understood: the desegregation of southern schools. Critics assail him for his political appeals to Wallace voters, his so-called southern strategy that helped him win by a landslide in 1972. But they ignore the fact that in dropping the confrontational stance that Democratic Justice Departments had taken toward the South, Nixon was ac-

63

tually able to gain more progress in desegregation through subtle, behind-the-scenes pressure. In 1968, some 68 percent of African-American children in the South attended all-black schools; by 1974, only 8 percent did. Writes Tom Wicker, a southern liberal, in his sympathetic biography of Nixon, *One of Us:* "The indisputable fact is that he got the job done—the dismantling of dual schools—when no one else had been able to do it."

Early on, choosing a code name for Richard Nixon, Secret Service agents decided to call him "Searchlight." They were more prescient than they knew. Nixon, who enjoyed operating in the shadows, had a gift for shining a beam out over the horizon, cutting through the murky darkness, recognizing danger or an opportunity—and then redirecting the nation's course. That capacity of seeing far ahead is important for the chief executive of any organization, but it is especially valuable in the presidency. A few others in the twentieth century were similarly gifted: the two Roosevelts, for example, as well as Wilson and Eisenhower, had a keen sense of how history was unfolding and could act on it. Nixon—for all his flaws, and they are grievous—is among those presidents who understood the forces of change and moved them in a favorable direction. He said he wanted to "nudge history," and he did.

If only that were the whole story . . .

3

Why He Fell

DICK NIXON may have read a copy of the Constitution, snapped Harry Truman one day, "but if he has, he doesn't understand it." Nixon, in fact, took justifiable pride in his knowledge of the Constitution. Sadly, however, Truman had him pegged: he often acted as if he didn't understand it. For all of the intelligence and tough-mindedness he brought to the presidency, there were fires burning within him that were not well suited to the demands of leadership in our democratic system.

The story of what brought him down is complex. Even though I was working on his staff and saw him regularly in his second term, I didn't understand most of it at first. Nor did my friends there. The cover-up worked better inside the White House than anywhere else. Only in the years that followed did we begin to piece it together. But the story should be an essential part of the education of every future leader.

One of my earliest memories comes from July 16, 1973.

Poking my Volkswagen "bug" past the White House guards and into a parking place near the Old Executive Office Building, I couldn't understand why so many aides were already scurrying back and forth to the West Wing next door. "What's going on?" I asked. "Not sure," said a friend, "apparently something's happening later today." At midmorning, my phone rang. "Alex Butterfield is testifying this afternoon at two o'clock at the Watergate hearings. A bunch of us are going to be watching down in Ken Clawson's office. Why don't you come join us?" "Okay," I said.

Clawson had a large, splendid office in the northeast corner of the Old EOB, where he worked with the communications director Herb Klein and with Chuck Colson, the President's Mr. Fixit. Ken was a former reporter for the *Washington Post*, and his willingness to slug it out with the press had made him a Nixon favorite. He also radiated an earthiness that drew others to him. I wandered in around two and was surprised to see an open bar, and some colleagues already pouring drinks. "Why so early?" I wondered. "Just wait and see," came the reply.

We didn't wait long. Shortly after Butterfield took the stand, an investigator for the committee asked him whether the White House had any means of recording conversations in the Oval Office. His answer was astonishing. Yes, came his response, and he calmly described an elaborate taping system that he had helped install for the President in both the Oval Office and in his hideaway office just down the hall from us in the EOB. His revelation set off a clamor in the room. We were all stunned that Nixon had been taping his conversations since at least 1971. But we were sharply divided on what that meant.

Personally, I was elated because I thought the President could finally vindicate himself. For weeks, we had been trying to prove a negative—that he had not known in advance about the Watergate break-in the previous summer and had not participated in the subsequent cover-up. But we had nothing to back us up other than his personal denials and those of Haldeman, Ehrlichman, and others of the inner circle. Now, with the tapes in hand, we at last had hard evidence that would surely prove his innocence! A number of people in the room agreed with me—nearly all from elite schools and cloistered suburbs. We left that afternoon pumped up for the battle ahead.

I couldn't help but notice, however, that some others in the room—people from the rougher, less privileged edges of life—reached a totally different conclusion. It's over, they said. It's only a matter of time before he's thrown out. They got drunk. If the rest of us had seen as clearly, we would have, too. The kids who grew up playing stickball seemed to understand life a lot better than those of us who tried lacrosse.

The march of events that followed in 1973 and 1974 gradually drummed out my own naïveté and I gradually awakened to the dark underbelly of Nixon's politics. The man I had watched with so much respect in the cabinet room, out in the Rose Garden, sometimes in the Oval Office or the hideaway was not the full picture. Only part of him was showing. The rest now came tumbling out into full public

66

view, destroying him politically and bewildering many of us around him who had believed in his rectitude.

The Cover-up Inside the White House

Inside the White House, there was a faint glimmer that something was amiss among the higher-ups but it was no more than that. On the morning after the break-in at the Democratic headquarters in June 1972—about four and a half months before the election—I read the police story in the *Washington Post* and told my wife, Anne, that we might be heading toward trouble in the campaign. The story had an eerie feel, reminiscent of other tales that made their way around Washington about mysterious "black bag" jobs when the home of a prominent political figure might be quietly entered late at night, his papers searched, and nothing of value taken. I doubted it was just a "third-rate burglary," as our press secretary Ron Ziegler called it at first. It sounded as if some crazed idiot over at the reelection committee had tried to pull off this stunt. Who could say for sure?

But in the days and months that followed, those of us on the lower tiers of the staff were continually reassured that neither Nixon nor anyone high up in the White House had done anything wrong. Nixon told us that directly, and Haldeman and others did so in the most adamant terms. With most reporters calling it a "caper," the issue never took off in the 1972 campaign, and I went merrily along into the second term, assuming Watergate would one day disappear.

Early in 1973, the story began to mushroom as Judge John Sirica cracked open the case in his courtroom and reporters Bob Woodward and Carl Bernstein started heading down the money trail. "Follow the money," Deep Throat reportedly told Woodward—an instruction now classic for investigative reporters. He and his partner did just that, and soon found a path leading from the burglars straight into the White House. It was obvious the wrongdoing went higher than many of us on staff thought, but we held tight to our belief that whatever the shenanigans of his team, Richard Nixon himself was innocent and so were the people in his inner circle. In politics, there is a will to believe in your man, especially if he is elected to the presidency, and even more so if you are working for him in the White House. It's a natural human tendency, strongest among the young, to idealize your leader, persuaded that you are part of some larger crusade for good and ignoring evidence to the

67

contrary. Your wagon is hitched to a star, and you resent those on the outside who tarnish the adventure.

The Nixon hierarchy kept the staff in the dark by building a fortress around the evidence relating to Watergate and leaving us on the outside. Stay focused on your job, Haldeman said, and things will turn out okay. Their denials ringing in our ears, we would see the President, Haldeman, and Ehrlichman hard at work every day, seeming to perform with integrity. I had never had a colleague or friend who had gone to jail, and it was just hard to believe that one of these men would wind up in the slammer. It was much easier to believe Chuck Colson or Ken Clawson when they tore into the biases of the *Washington Post*, then seen as a liberal flagship, and insisted that publisher Kay Graham had it in for the President. Only years later, as I came to know—and greatly admire—Katharine Graham, did I realize just how outrageous their arguments were.

Like several others, I had my own personal experiences that strongly reinforced my belief in Nixon's innocence. Ray Price, I was informed, would work directly with Nixon on all speeches and public statements regarding Watergate itself, and the rest of us would stay out. But there were several peripheral charges also being investigated by Congress and causing political headaches. The President wanted to publish "white papers" on each of these side issues— lengthy documents examining the evidence and trying to prove that all allegations of misdeeds were false. As the new chief of his writing and research team, I was asked to work with lawyers, accountants, and others and to serve as the principal drafter of the white papers.

On December 31, 1973, for example, I was summoned back from a family holiday in North Carolina to work on one of those white papers. With snow falling outside, I spent an unforgettable and lonely New Year's Eve immersed in the private records of the President of the United States.

One of my major projects was to work with tax lawyers and accountants from Coopers & Lybrand on allegations surrounding Nixon's personal income taxes. What we found was evidence of chintziness and highly questionable deductions (to some ballyhoo, Nixon had earlier announced his own generous gift to the White House of a new table for the cabinet room; his tax records revealed that he had promptly taken a sizable charitable deduction). Eventually, the IRS disallowed many deductions and concluded that Nixon owed substantial back taxes ($435,000 plus interest), but the agency did not find the corruption that had been widely rumored.

68

As it turned out, his critics had also accused Nixon falsely of ripping off taxpayers when the Secret Service installed security protections around his new home in San Clemente. The allegation was that he had improperly used the Secret Service to make various improvements on his properties that increased their commercial value. I spent dozens of hours on a team conducting an internal investigation and we then drafted a white paper that made clear that most (not all) of the improvements were necessary for security. Other stories alleged that Nixon was in cahoots with Treasury Secretary John Connally over a $10,000 bribe, popularly referred to as "the milk money" in Washington, that milk dealers had supposedly paid Connally. By that time, the White House taping system had been revealed, and I was asked to sift through the tapes, have them transcribed, and help draw up a public report. To the best of my knowledge, this was the first time anyone on the general staff had tried to go through the tapes. They were so scratchy I could barely make out the words, but Janice Barbieri of my office gamely sat for hours figuring them out. Again, the evidence showed Nixon (as well as Connally) innocent of serious charges.

Admittedly, these side issues were minor compared to Watergate, but if he were falsely accused here—as I thought he was—it seemed reasonable that the serious charges were baloney, too. Or so I believed until the final days.

The Shadow of Deep Throat

Sometime in 1973—I can't place when they started—Bob Woodward of the *Washington Post* metro staff began placing calls to my office, usually in the evening when I would still be working. Bob had graduated from Yale a couple of years after I did in 1963, and while neither of us can remember meeting there, friends had introduced us at a Washington party in 1970. Shortly before we met, the *Post* had farmed Bob out to the *Montgomery County Sentinel* in Maryland, where he could gain some reporting experience, and I was on the final leg of naval service. He followed up after the party with a couple of calls regarding the reform of Selective Service, on which I was working, and I helped him out before we lost touch.

By the time Bob called again, he and Carl Bernstein had risen to prominence as prime investigators of the White House, and I was trying to manage a boisterous lot of speechwriters from within. Ordinarily, I didn't talk much to the press in those days, but Bob was someone I knew, and his first incoming message had an insistence that made me pay attention. "We have a story that is very important to this president," he said in effect. "Ziegler won't talk to us nor will anybody else, and we don't feel right about putting it into the paper without somebody over there telling us your perspective. You won't like the story and maybe you can steer us off it, but at least you'll have a chance to tell our readers your views."

He was handing me a stick of dynamite, and I knew so little about Watergate that I couldn't tell how long the fuse was. I sought out two other people inside: press secretary Ron Ziegler and presidential adviser Leonard Garment. They thought I should bring Woodward into the EOB surreptitiously and deposit him with Garment, where the two of them could talk alone. Bob showed up at a side door a little later and had his conversation with Len.

I can't even remember what that particular story was, but we didn't stop it. The dynamite blew up the next day on the front page of the *Post*, raining more destruction on the administration. At least Len was able to insert a defense and explanation from the White House. He and I and Ziegler, so far as I could tell, thought the Woodward visit was worth it. They thought I should talk to him if he checked in again.

Thereafter, Bob would call from time to time when he had something "hot," and I might plug him into Ron, Len, or somebody else. We talked on background about the torment that members of the staff were feeling—my anguish was obvious—and I would try to scope out where he and his newspaper were heading so I could tell others inside. He provided a different take on what was going on around me at the White House, and I discovered how easy it is to learn at least as much from a reporter as you give out. He was young and idealistic, too, and we shared a deepening concern that the pillars of the presidency were crumbling. Bob didn't really care about Nixon personally—that wasn't his job as a reporter—but he seemed to care genuinely about the institution. I also found over time that, contrary to what I was hearing inside, his reporting on Watergate was usually right on the money. He was telling it to me straighter than my own superiors were!

It wasn't the last time I found a reporter to be my best source of what was truly happening within the government. A White House aide, just like a president, had better keep his antennae as well tuned outside the building as inside or he will be swamped with information that is misleading or wrong.

After Nixon left office, Bob and I became better acquainted and over the years I have gained respect for his work and his integrity. He is so seductive and reassuring that he can coax information out of the most hardened official; people almost *want* to confide in him. I don't accept everything he writes as gospel—he can get details wrong—but, generally, his accounts in both his books and in the *Post* are remarkably reliable and demand serious attention. I am convinced he writes only what he believes to be true or has been reliably told to be true. And he is certainly a force for keeping the government honest.

After the Nixon presidency collapsed, one of Washington's favorite parlor games was to guess the identity of Deep Throat, the famous source who Woodward said had met him secretly in a Washington garage and supplied the critical missing pieces to his reporting puzzle. A gathering of all those who have since been "named" as Deep Throat would almost fill Yankee Stadium—everyone from Al Haig to Haldeman himself.

At first, I was merely amused when my name also popped up. My amusement vanished when John Dean, the former White House counsel at the center of the cover-up, began suggesting me. He didn't have any evidence, only a conjecture based on the fact that Woodward and I had gone to the same college. In diplomatic parlance, I hold John Dean in "minimal high regard"; "First he betrayed his country," as someone once said, "then he betrayed his friends." Nora Ephron, married at the time to Carl Bernstein, knocked him down smartly; everyone knew, she wrote, that, at 6'5", I was too tall to meet in garages.

She might have added what other friends also knew: I had zero access to the kind of secret intelligence about campaign moneys inside the Committee to Re-elect the President and detailed FBI reports that Deep Throat apparently had. Even more convincing for my friends was the fact I was living in northern Virginia. It was inconceivable that as a slow starter in the morning, I would hoist myself out of bed at 5:00 A.M. or so and make my way into D.C. where I could leave out the first edition of the *New York Times* as a signal to Woodward.

Even so, the rumor recurs from time to time that I was Deep Throat. As late as 1998, Tom Brokaw reported on NBC that I was still among the "suspects." Sorry, Tom, an empty rabbit hole. I wasn't the man. My back channel to Woodward never carried highly secretive information and, as noted, was not only known but also blessed by key White House figures. On one of the tape transcripts, I was interested to read Nixon instructing Ron Ziegler: "Have Gergen tell

71

Woodward . . ." Even the President apparently knew and approved of our conversations.

Along with many others, I have long wondered who the mystery party might be. I'm not positive there was a single Deep Throat. Perhaps he was indeed a composite figure of all of Woodward's sources, conjured up to throw people off the scent. More likely, though, he was a single individual, as Woodward and Bernstein have said all along. If so, he most likely came out of the investigative or intelligence fields—from Justice, the FBI, CIA, or Pentagon. To provide that kind of rich, inside information, he had to meet two criteria: one, be in the flow of paperwork from others who were investigating Watergate (the FBI, say), and, two, have a motive (there is abundant evidence that agents of the military and CIA were engaged in covert warfare with Nixon over Vietnam, Cuba, and even the assassination of John Kennedy). Woodward has said that he and Bernstein will unveil Deep Throat's identity after he dies, which suggests he is an older fellow (as I suspect); alternatively, they will reveal his identity if he releases them from the pledge of secrecy.

The more interesting question is how to assess Deep Throat's character. Was he a hero or a bum? Deserving of a pat on the back or a kick in the rear? An argument can be made that he was the ultimate whistle blower and helped to save the country from even worse depredations. Perhaps, but I come down on the other side. If he were honorable, he should have first taken his information about crimes directly to legal authorities, not the press. Then, if his position were compromised, he should have resigned from government. That, it seems to me, is the duty we ask of those who work in government. He would also have avoided becoming a spy within the ranks, a quality that has delivered lesser men to the firing squad, and always troubled me about Deep Throat. There's only one caveat: What if he believed that the President and his men had so corrupted the judicial system that if he reported them legally, his report would have been "deep-sixed"—and, perhaps, so would he? A chilling possibility, but, in that hell storm, not inconceivable. Even so, I'm no fan of Deep Throat.

The Final Days As I Saw Them

72   The last few months of the Nixon presidency, as the noose tightened, were surreal. Strange things kept happening—and not just in Watergate.

In June 1974, two months before the President resigned, he was heading off to the Middle East and the Soviet Union when his phlebitis attack occurred, a foreshadowing of things to come. After stopping in Salzburg, we were off to Cairo, where President Anwar Sadat had organized a massive welcome. More than a million people poured out on the streets. Few presidents had seen such crowds. And some of them were unruly, jumping up on the roof of our staff bus, pounding on the windows, screaming wildly. Huddled inside, we weren't sure whether to wave or dive under the seats.

But even that moment of fear did not match the next one. After stopping in Saudi Arabia, we flew on to Syria, the stronghold of Hafez al-Assad and a country whose relations with the United States had been so strained that no American president had visited before. Aboard Air Force One, I was sitting about a third of the way back, next to one of our most experienced diplomats, Roy Atherton, who was explaining to me the intricacies of Middle Eastern politics.

Looking out the window, he suddenly spotted a Syrian fighter off our right wing; turning the other way, we saw a second Syrian jet off our left wing. What in hell were they doing there? Our pilot, Ralph Albertazzi, obviously wondered the same thing and put Air Force One into a steep dive. Roy and I were thrown on the floor, along with others. I asked him how far away we were from the Sixth Fleet. Too far to get there, he said. I don't think we're going to make it, he said grimly. Here we were, flying in a lumbering passenger plane with the American president on board, two Soviet-made MIGs in chase, the U.S. Air Force miles away. Horrible visions flashed.

Within minutes—or was it seconds?—word came to our pilots that there had been a huge mix-up on the ground. Assad had dispatched his jets as a welcoming committee to escort us into Damascus but apparently failed to tell our advance party of his plans. That was sweet, Hafez. Air Force One leveled off and we proceeded smoothly to the red carpet down below, but I always look back on our journey as a lasting symbol of that summer of '74. For the next several weeks, Richard Nixon twisted, turned, and tried to evade his pursuers until he crashed on August 9.

As special prosecutor Leon Jaworski closed in and the White House cover-up unraveled, the President crept into a shell so that few of us saw him for more than a glimpse at a time. The man to whom the country owes a continuing debt of gratitude for his contribution during those months is Alexander Haig, the Army general who had become White House chief of staff after Nixon forced Haldeman to resign in late April. Later on, as Reagan's first secretary

73

of state, Haig became a controversial figure, but during Nixon's final months, I found him to be a rock of stability, keeping the government on course during a time of constitutional crisis, steadying the President and the staff, and pushing toward a just resolution. Haig has never fully recounted what happened behind the scenes, but my impression is that once he understood the full extent of Nixon's culpability, he began to engineer what he believed was in the country's best interest: the President's resignation.

In addition to large morning staff meetings, Haig would periodically ask a smaller group of us, mostly department heads, to come to his office where he could update us on the legal wrangling. Just as Nixon finally ended his constitutional confrontation by relenting to a Supreme Court order to turn over his tape recordings to Jaworski, Haig summoned us for another briefing. It was a hot summer afternoon in August. "Gentlemen," he said as we all took our seats, "are your sphincters tight?"

He then revealed to us for the first time the contents of the Nixon tape from June 23, 1972, in which the President directed Haldeman to instruct the CIA to call off the FBI investigation of the Watergate burglary six days earlier. The President is "guilty as hell," some of us remember Haig saying. That June 23 tape was the famous "smoking gun" and it was now pointed directly at the White House. The President, it was clear, had been at the center of an illegal operation and would not survive politically. My feelings raced between devastation and betrayal. How could he possibly . . . ?

I didn't see the President again until the morning of his departure. As had been his custom on Watergate speeches and was fitting for his last hurrah, he called in only Ray Price to work with him. Ray conferred with his young assistant, Tex Lezar, and perhaps one or two others but wisely kept mum with everyone else. The rest of us weren't certain whether Nixon would resign or keep fighting. Only when a group of us gathered that evening in my office in the EOB did we realize the curtain was coming down swiftly and dramatically. He was resigning immediately.

A few moments after the speech ended, when people were sitting quietly, some crying, Haig called me. "We need an official resignation letter," he said. "Can you draft one he can sign in the morning?"

Sure, I replied, but what should it say and to whom does a president of the United States resign? Haig said he didn't know either—get it done. Since the President had already delivered his thoughts directly to the country, I decided it should be a single, simple sen-

74

tence. Where to send it was harder. The Speaker of the House, third in line to the presidency? The Senate president pro tem? The secretary of state? God?

I drafted three letters with different addresses, and took them to the lawyers for advice. Fred Fielding, Dean's successor in the general counsel's office, decided that pursuant to an obscure law passed by Congress in 1792, the President should sign the one addressed to the secretary of state. Nixon did the next morning and it now hangs in the National Archives: "Dear Mr. Secretary: I hereby resign the office of President of the United States. Sincerely, Richard Nixon." It is initialed by Henry Kissinger.

That next morning opened bizarrely. The cabinet, friends, and those of us on staff gathered sorrowfully in the East Room for the President's farewell as the Marine band played cheery, upbeat music—Broadway show tunes, as I recall. The entrance of the President and his family instantly changed the atmosphere, and Nixon stood there in the East Room one last time, the dreams ending, his life in ruins. He was maudlin—oh, how he could be maudlin—but he was also valiant as he talked of his early life, his mother, and his daughters, what he had tried to be and do. Strangely, he never mentioned his wife, Pat.

The best moment came toward the end when he pulled from his jacket the famous quote from Teddy Roosevelt, praising "the man in the arena, whose face is marred by dust and sweat and blood"; Eisenhower had sent that quote to his campaign team in 1952, a friend sent it to Lyndon Johnson at a moment of crisis, and Nixon had always cherished it. It was a fitting close, as he said "au revoir" and we all headed out to the South Lawn and a moment best captured on film. With a final, defiant wave, he stepped into the helicopter and permanent exile.

It was both inevitable and right that Richard Nixon was forced to resign. Twenty-five people were sent to prison because of the abuses of his administration, and many others faced indictments, including two attorneys general of the United States and several top officials of the White House. The Justice Department, FBI, CIA, and the White House itself were corrupted in the Watergate cover-up attempt. Investigations brought to light a string of other criminal activities, including illegal break-ins, money laundering, perjury, obstruction of justice, abuse of power, conspiracy, and wiretapping. Watergate represented staggering abuses of power. In the accompanying furor, the institution of the presidency itself was further weakened by a series of corrective laws in the years that followed and people's faith in

75

government was dealt yet another body blow from which it has never fully recovered. Richard Nixon had no choice but to resign.

There is one bit of good news here: megascandals are extremely rare in American politics. As political scientist Larry Sabato has pointed out, they seem to come along about fifty years apart. Crédit Mobilier swamped the Grant administration in the 1870s, Teapot Dome destroyed Warren Harding's reputation in the 1920s, and then Watergate burst in the 1970s. All of which suggests, as Sabato says, that we may be spared another whopper until 2020 or so.

But we have had a string of lesser scandals in the years since Nixon. In at least two of them—the Iran-contra scandal of the Reagan years and the continuous scandals of the Clinton years—it is apparent that the principals were shockingly unaware of what Watergate was all about. They may have known the fuzzy details, but they acted as if they did not understand any of the deeper lessons. If they had just paid attention, they could have stayed out of trouble that almost forced two other presidents from office. That's why the story of Watergate should be required reading—and *understanding*—for future leaders. It's a case study of what not to do.

The received wisdom is that Watergate teaches us two basic rules about politics. One, never elect a man of low character to high office. Two, if a president and his team do make an egregious mistake, a cover-up is always worse than the crime. Both of those rules are valid and should be emblazoned across our political landscape. But they do not adequately convey the larger story of why Nixon fell.

On March 21, 1973, meeting privately in the Old EOB, where Nixon kept an office hideaway, John Dean famously told him, "I think that there's no doubt about the seriousness of the problem we've got. We have a cancer—within, close to the presidency, that's growing. It's growing daily. It's compounding, it grows geometrically now because it compounds itself."

Scientists tell us that each of our bodies contains cells that can become cancerous. The mystery they are trying to uncover is what triggers them to turn into cancer cells. For those who wish to understand leadership, that is the essential inquiry we need to pursue about Nixon. What caused a cancer to grow and destroy his presidency? What are the telltale signs that others need to watch for in government that foretell trouble ahead? What must future presidents learn to avoid?

Looking back, I believe we can identify many of the basic causes of the Watergate break-in and the cover-up that followed. At the time, they were not so clear; with the passage of almost thirty years, they are becoming more obvious. In fact, we can see that some of these same forces have been at work as recently as the Clinton presidency. In Nixon's case, they were a deadly combination. We'll take them one by one.

The Demons Within

Hardworking, patriotic, and raised in a Quaker tradition, Richard Nixon sincerely wanted to be a model president. In private notes for himself that he kept at the White House, he once wrote, "I have decided my major role is moral leadership. I cannot exercise this adequately unless I speak out more often and more eloquently." His friend Billy Graham has written that Nixon "held high standards of ethics and morality for the nation. 'The hope of America,' he once told me, 'is the working people.' Furthermore, he held a high view of the presidency as a public trust."

Those sentiments bubbled to the surface at odd moments. One of the most poignant was the middle of the night on a Saturday in May 1970. Knots of students were gathering around Washington for a massive protest against the Vietnam War later that day. Nixon awoke at 4:00 A.M. and, accompanied by Manolo Sanchez, went to the Lincoln Memorial where he knew some of the protesters were hanging out. He wanted to share their thoughts about the war but was fumbling and eventually talked about college football. His staff never understood why he went there, and the press called it a publicity stunt.

But as biographer Herbert Parmet writes in *Richard Nixon and His America,* the Memorial visit actually revealed a more genuine, caring streak in Nixon. Parmet draws from a plaintive eight-page memorandum Nixon wrote just after the event, expressing frustration to Haldeman that no one on his own staff caught what he was trying to communicate to the protesters and what his deeper values were. "I am afraid that most of the members of our staff, to their credit, are enormously interested in material things and what we accomplish in our record, etc., etc, but that very few seem to have any interest and, therefore, have no ability to communicate on those matters that are infinitely more important—qualities of spirit, emotion, of the depth and mystery of life which this whole visit was all about."

He had talked with the students about the war, he explained,

77

saying he, too, had once been a pacifist who thought Churchill was a madman but had later come to see him as a protector of peace. He talked as well about the oppression of Indians, blacks, and Mexican Americans in the United States and the character of peoples overseas. He moved on to the environment and the importance of removing ugly blotches from the face of the earth. Then, in a rare moment for him, baring his soul to strangers, he recalls telling them, "You must remember that something that is completely clean can also be completely sterile and without spirit. What we all must think about is why we are here." To Haldeman, he added, "I just wanted to be sure that all of them realized that ending the war and cleaning up the streets and the air and the water was not going to solve spiritual hunger which all of us have and which, of course, has been the great mystery of life from the beginning of time." Until the end of his life, he carried that spiritual hunger with him, hidden from public view.

Yet, as is so often the case in human nature, Nixon's behavior as president fell grievously short of his own standards. Coexisting with the better angels in his nature were demons from a darker hell. These two sides—the bright and the dark—did not seem locked in mortal combat with each other; if anything, Nixon seemed content to let each quietly support him in his quest for power. But when he let those demons gain ascendance and perpetrate misdeeds against his enemies, they served to destroy him. Ultimately, his dark side did him in. Nixon's downfall was living proof of a cardinal rule: leadership starts from within.

Nixon would talk cheerily about American ideals in the Rose Garden—and mean it—but returning to the privacy of his office, he seethed at his enemies and would twist a knife into them by whatever means necessary. As a lawyer, some of his proudest moments had come arguing cases before the Supreme Court and he took pride in his legal training. But as the most famous tape from Watergate shows—the "smoking gun" from June 23, 1972—he had no hesitation ordering Haldeman to have the CIA impede the FBI's investigation of Watergate. He knew he was obstructing justice. When he went before the country repeatedly to deny any White House involvement in Watergate, he knew he was lying. When he directed Colson to infiltrate the Brookings Institution, he knew that national security was a false justification. When he ordered up wiretaps on journalists, his own aides, and even a favorite speechwriter, Bill Safire, he knew he was going too far. He had a tendency to use raw power to overcome problems, rather than the normal tools of democratic governance.

He knew as well that men acting in his behalf had been wantonly violating the rights of others. While his concerns about protecting national security secrets were legitimate, he willingly carried them to places governments are not supposed to go. Even as he campaigned for office as a candidate of law and order, he acted and encouraged others around him to violate both the law and the customs he was supposedly upholding. He knew all these things were wrong—but he went ahead, letting his worst instincts play out.

In their memoirs, Bob Haldeman, John Ehrlichman, and Ray Price all single out Chuck Colson as the true villain, the man who preyed upon Nixon's resentments, goaded him into swiping at his enemies, and then carried out Nixon's wildest instructions without alerting others on staff. Instinctively, upon hearing about the Watergate break-in, they wondered whether Colson was involved.

It is a mark of just how compartmentalized the Nixon White House was that Colson kept his nefarious side hidden from most of the younger staff, just as the President did. I sat through hours of meetings in Colson's office and never saw anything untoward. As the 1972 elections approached, he chaired a daily "attack" group at 9:15 A.M., orchestrating efforts in the administration and on Capitol Hill to punch holes in the Democratic campaign. Ray Price asked me to attend on behalf of the speechwriters; Pat Buchanan and Ken Khachigian were also there. The only idea I can remember that bordered on the illegal—and was also in bad taste—arose when some wiseacre suggested calling local fire departments to show up at a gay pride rally at the farm of Sargent Shriver, the Democratic nominee for vice president. The stunt never came off. Everything else was aboveboard and pretty harmless. After the campaign, Colson gave each of us cuff links inscribed "9:15," and I kept them, an emblem that I had for the first time been at the center of a national political campaign—or so I thought.

What most of us didn't realize was that Colson was meeting privately with Nixon and hatching up all manner of sleazy undertakings. Haldeman and Ehrlichman tried to quash a number of Colson's initiatives, not always with success, and no doubt they signed off on others. The record isn't entirely clear who had his fingerprints on some of the abuses.

Even so, it is clear where the responsibility lies: yes, with Colson but ultimately with the President. So what if Colson were seductive? Nixon should have had the inner strength to say no to him. But we have to recognize that Nixon *wanted* Colson around and *wanted* him to serve his darker side. As much as those who worked for Nixon believe that he accomplished great things as a leader, we can't fob off his mistakes on others. Harry Truman was right: the buck stops in the Oval Office.

Nixon obviously felt that to succeed in politics—to exercise and hold on to power—one must often be mean and manipulative. FDR sometimes played rough, and so did most of his successors. But Nixon's insecurities and anger could drive him beyond the pale. Working for him, one had a sense that he was at his best when he was down, fighting back, and at his worst when he was up. Just after he rolled to his landside reelection, for example, he was ready to squash whoever and whatever was in his way to the point that he was damaging his own capacity for governance. I wondered, as did others, whether he felt he wasn't good enough to be on top. Perhaps he harbored some sort of self-loathing that triggered a compulsion for self-destruction. I am not qualified to offer a psychological analysis. What I saw was a man who did not relate well to others and who seemed to deny softer, emotional feelings, choosing instead to face the world with a harsh steeliness that could get him into deep political trouble.

No one has ever located the wellsprings of Nixon's dark temperament. Psychologists focus on his childhood, when he grew up in meager surroundings, saw two brothers die young, and faced periodic rejection. The family had some terrible luck: shortly after his father sold the family store, oil was discovered beneath the plot of land there. Somebody may have done something terrible to him when he was young, as Bryce Harlow observed. Even winning Pat's hand wasn't easy. As a young man, he had a job in which he drove around while she sat in the backseat with her date.

Talking with him, my sense was that his early years as an adult and then as a politician also left painful, open wounds. To work his way through Duke Law School, only to be turned down for a job by prestigious law firms in New York and by the FBI, was a searing humiliation. His early experiences in politics were brutal affairs, too. Journalists tend to recall only how hard he slashed at his opponents but forget how viciously he was himself attacked, especially when he ran for the Senate against Helen Gahagan Douglas in 1950. He said she was "pink right down to her underwear." In effect, he was calling her a Communist. But she and her opponents struck at him with vengeance as well. And the label she pinned on him stuck for life: "Tricky Dick."

80   Yet, Nixon thought the real breaking point came when he single-handedly exposed the Alger Hiss case in the late 1940s, helping to reveal a Communist pillar of the liberal establishment. His ene-

mies in the press and elsewhere could never forgive him for being right about Hiss. They looked for every opportunity to crucify him, and in Watergate, they found what they wanted.

Nixon, then, had reason to see politics as the law of the jungle and to detest his enemies. They treated him horribly, and he gave back as good as he got—sometimes a lot more. But the mark of an effective leader is one who absorbs the punishment without surrendering his soul. Lincoln was vilified at least as much as Nixon and kept his inner composure. Jefferson suffered emotionally from the vicious attacks that came his way and rarely let it drive him off course. Andy Jackson thought the attacks of his enemies had sent his beloved wife to her grave. Embittered, he still soldiered on. Nixon let his demons take the upper hand, and they wrecked his presidency.

Confusing Power with Leadership

If Nixon had replaced Metternich in early nineteenth-century Austria, he would have been a statesman of the first order. If he had stepped in for Bismarck in late nineteenth-century Germany, he would have shaped European history. Indeed, if he had served in the place of Lee Kuan Yew in twentieth-century Singapore, he would have been one of the architects of a New Asia. But he lived in a very different context in a country with very different traditions—and he seemed not to have noticed.

Through much of history, societies have mostly been authoritarian and top-down. The men who have mattered have been those who knew how to exercise raw power with talent, courage, and will. They scrambled hard to get to the top and once there they had to be shrewd enough to use power well and ruthless enough to keep it. Nixon studied them closely, admired what they accomplished, and patterned himself after them more than he should have.

One of the books Nixon wrote after leaving the White House, *Leaders*, contains a revealing essay on the lessons of leadership he learned over a lifetime. He opens with a quote from de Gaulle: "Nothing great is done without great men, and these are great because they willed it." He goes on: "Just as F. Scott Fitzgerald pointed out that the very rich are different, I have found that those who hold great power are different. It takes a particular kind of person to win the struggle for power. Having won, the power itself creates a further difference. Power is not for the nice guy down the street or for the man next door."

81

Woven through the essay are other passages that capture Nixon himself. A leader, he writes, "has to bring to his work a cold, impersonal calculation." "Once he has the reins, he relishes their use." "History has had its share of despots who craved power for its own sake. But most leaders who rise to the top—certainly most of those whom we would call great leaders—want power for what they can do with it, believing that they can put it to better use than others can." "In evaluating a leader, the key question about his behavioral traits is not whether they are attractive or unattractive, but whether they are useful. Guile, vanity, dissembling—in other circumstances these might be unattractive habits, but to the leader they can be essential." Approvingly, he quotes from Max Lerner's introduction to a new edition of Machiavelli: "Let us be clear about one thing: ideals and ethics are important in politics as norms, but they are scarcely effective as techniques."

No one of these passages is wholly wrong about leadership; Nixon, as always, is perceptive. But together they reveal a mind-set that would undermine his presidency. Nixon at his core believed that leadership consists in the exercise of power by a singular figure—the great man—standing at the pinnacle, seeing what others do not have the wits to see, confronting the forces of history, and acting unilaterally on behalf of his followers. His relationship with his followers is of secondary concern: the leader informs them what he thinks they need to know in order to go along with him but he may also choose to conceal or lie to them as he wishes. Nor is he seriously accountable to other institutions. In his twenty-five-page essay on leadership, he mentions Congress only in passing. He speaks of the press but only in derogatory terms. The portrait is of a leader who is benevolent, yes, but also isolated, tough, and cunning. The leader is the man who exercises power by imposing his own will.

The American tradition, however, is quite different. Ours has always been a bottom-up society in which leaders draw their power not from themselves or even their office but from the people. "We the people," begins the Constitution. "A government of the people, by the people and for the people," said Lincoln. Thomas Jefferson divided leaders into two camps: those who distrust the people and think they know better and those who believe the people are the wisest guide to the public interest. The exercise of leadership and the exercise of power are obviously related ideas, but, within a democratic society, they are not the same. Unfortunately, Nixon confused them.

Nixon had great respect for Middle America, but he thought of himself as living on a higher plane, as he imagined other leaders did.

Average Americans, he told Haldeman, live a "humdrum existence." In an interview with Garnett Horner that appeared in the *Washington Star* shortly after his reelection in 1972, Nixon said that "the average American is just like the child in the family." His comment caused a stir. His comments seem reasonable if read in context —he was trying to explain that if pampered with government benefits, people will become dependent and spoiled—but many read them as one more sign that as president he thought he was above the crowd. And, in fact, he did. Another passage from his book puts his view succinctly: "Because the leader is busy, because he has a large ego, because he resents intrusions and distractions, because he considers himself superior, he may have little patience with those he perceives as his inferiors. The trouble with this inability to 'tolerate fools' is threefold. First, the leader needs followers—and a lot of those he needs have ideas he would consider foolish. Second, the man he is tempted to dismiss as a fool may not be. Third, even if he is, the leader might learn from him. Leadership requires a sort of mystical bond between the leader and the people; if the leader appears to show disdain for the people, that bond is likely to snap. *However, one must always remember that leaders are uncommon men* [italics added]. They should not try to appear common. If they do try, they will come across as unnatural—not only phony, but condescending."

As a result, Nixon never truly placed his trust in the nation's people. He told them what he thought they needed to know in order to rally their support on key issues, as he did in his appeal to the Silent Majority when he asked the public to be patient about Vietnam. But he hid the Cambodian invasion from them, and he never confided that the war had been lost. Brilliant strategist though he was, he thought that diplomacy should be conducted mostly in private by great men—and only when the deal was done should curtains be parted for the masses to see. Had Nixon been willing to trust the public's judgment, he would have come forward in June 1972 to explain the terrible mistakes that led to the Watergate break-in. Had he cleansed the stable then, he would have been badly hurt in the 1972 elections but he would almost certainly have won anyway— and then served out his full second term. Instead, he chose to mislead and lie about Watergate for more than two years. When the evidence finally came tumbling out, a historian went back to a television address Nixon had given on Watergate and found no less than seven major lies.

One of the most important exercises of public accountability by

83

a president is an open press conference. There are no other occasions when his constituents can hear him answer questions posed by independent monitors. The frequency of presidential press conferences had been declining since FDR, but under Nixon they fell to a new low. He averaged eight per year during his first term and five per year in his second. As historian Melvin Small notes, Nixon had "the fewest number of press conferences of any president from Hoover through Carter."

Standing so far outside the democratic tradition, it is not surprising that Nixon also had little regard for another major responsibility of an American president: moral leadership. Let's go back to basics for a moment. More than two thousand years ago, Aristotle asserted that the central purpose of the state is to enable its citizens to lead a good life—one of moderation, virtue, and contemplation. Each polis, he thought, should decide for itself what form of government to adopt, whether an oligarchy, a democracy, or a combination, but regardless of its form, the purpose of that government remains the same. Toward that end, as he argued in *Politics,* the role of the political leader is to teach "the spirit of their constitution" to the people. "What the Statesman is most anxious to produce is a certain moral character in his fellow citizens, namely a disposition to virtue and the performance of virtuous actions." Through his leadership, he must rally the moral spirit of the people.

Interpreting Aristotle today, presidential scholar Erwin C. Hargrove argues that a president must be a moral leader in the sense that he sets an example and encourages people to remember their highest values—not that he tries to impose a moral code on them. "The statesman does not invoke moral absolutes to cowed or deferential citizens. Rather, he must evoke those values and beliefs that citizens implicitly hold and apply them to the solution of particular problems."

Throughout most of American history, our best presidents have intuitively understood that same imperative: they have bent their efforts toward establishing a set of laws and customs that would embody the highest ideals of the republic. George Washington's presidency was devoted to that end. After struggling for years to establish his own sterling character, he said upon the winning of the Revolutionary War that "now it is time to form the character of the nation." In 1800, Jefferson eagerly sought the presidency because he thought the Federalists had lost sight of the purposes of the original Revolution; his was to be a second revolution to restore the values of the Declaration of Independence. Lincoln stood squarely in the same stream of thought. His purpose was not just to save the Union but to preserve the spirit of the Union—something Aristotle would have heartily endorsed.

Nixon could speak in moral terms, as he did at the Lincoln Memorial with the protestors, but he did not bring a moral framework to politics. He did not see his role as one of teaching people "the spirit of their constitution," nor did he see that he should encourage "a disposition to virtue and the performance of virtuous actions." He was much too fascinated by the exercise of raw power and left the preservation of democratic traditions to others.

At War with the Leadership Class

To understand Nixon's downfall, it is essential to recognize his own perspective on events. Nixon has offered various explanations, but a man who has explained his views better than he has himself is Ray Price, his loyal assistant throughout his presidency and friend for three decades. Ray, as we have seen, was head of Nixon's speech-writing team and then house philosopher.

Nixon, Ray wrote in 1987, was an embattled president who faced unique circumstances. "In domestic terms, the 1960s was the second most disastrous decade in U.S. history, following only the 1860s, ravaged by an actual civil war. It was Mr. Nixon's lot to inherit those passions: the verbal and physical violence, the escalation of hate, the riots and assassinations, the burning cities and bombed campuses. And he did so in the midst of a bitterly unpopular war, faced with an opposition Congress, at a time when 'adversary journalism' was reaching the zenith of its fashionable acceptance and the nadir of its professional standards. In a real sense, the battle that brought Mr. Nixon down was the final struggle of that tortured era."

Nixon, Ray is arguing, made grievous errors, but it was the hatreds and passions of his times that did him in. In another era in history, he would have survived; people would have understood that his misdeeds were no worse than those of other presidents and that he was the victim of a vicious double standard. This argument is at heart what I believe Nixon himself believed. One can almost hear him in that passage from his faithful friend.

But neither he nor the rest of us around him appreciated how different the administration looked to people on the other side of the gates. Even in the best of times, the White House can be closed off to reality; in the worst of times, it is a bunker. Certainly, as the incoming shells landed closer by the day, those of us who worked for Nixon felt under siege during the early 1970s. It was only when the war was over and we came out that we saw more clearly why it had become so fierce. There was lots of blame on the other side, as Ray has written—but there was blame on our side, too, I'm afraid. It's that which future leaders must understand.

Since the day he entered politics, Nixon hadn't liked people much, and they in turn didn't like him. By the time he was elected president, he had a legion of sworn enemies. No one drew as much venom until Bill Clinton was elected in 1992. Trying to make sense of the hatred toward Nixon and Clinton, one is reminded of the old ditty by Thomas Brown: "I do not love thee, Doctor Fell; the reason why I cannot tell. But this alone I know full well, I do not love thee, Doctor Fell."

Even so, Nixon—not unlike Clinton—made a manageable problem infinitely worse by assuming he had more enemies than he did. For every individual who hated him, there were two or three others who were simply adversaries. They didn't particularly like him or his politics, but respected his office and would go along with him, particularly on issues serving the national good, if he would appeal to their better instincts. They were open to persuasion. The administration didn't do that; it went to war with them.

Among the public at large, Nixon brought over a great many skeptics and adversaries. In 1968, some 31.7 million people voted for him for president; four years later, 47.1 million gave him their votes—an increase of over 15 million. Nixon kept most of his early voters, brought in large chunks of the George Wallace constituency, and reached beyond to hard hats and ethnics once in the Democratic column. His performance won them over.

But Nixon's experience with the political elite—what one might call the leadership class of the country—was exactly the opposite. Through most of his life, he felt rejected by Wall Street, the press, universities, the civil service, and others. Even as vice president, he never felt part of "the establishment" that Richard Rovere wrote of in those days. The salons of Georgetown were closed to him, and he dismissed them with a thumb of the nose.

Vietnam was his breaking point. He thought the liberal Left had gotten the country into war, sending working-class kids to fight, and had then turned tail and run, leaving soldiers face down in the mud. Even those of us on the middle rungs of the staff heard him rail time and again about a growing rot in the establishment. As much as he disliked labor bosses, he loved the rank and file because he thought they were the only ones principled enough to stand firm on drugs, crime, national defense, and a strong America. Hard hats were his kinds of patriots. Show me a man with a silver spoon and an Ivy League diploma, he thought, and I'll show you a man without a spine. The leadership class was failing the country, in his view.

Nixon tried occasional dialogues with the other side and came away feeling abused—not without reason. He invited in leaders on civil rights—an issue on which he was progressive—and as they left, they denounced him in front of cameras on the White House lawn. He asked university presidents for advice and felt they kicked him in the head. He was fed up, too, with the press, protesters, and peaceniks, all products of an amorphous evil he saw as "the establishment."

The first newly elected president of the century to find a Congress in opposition hands, Nixon appointed three veterans of Capitol Hill to serve as his liaisons: Bryce Harlow, Ken Belieu, and Bill Timmons. That was a formidable team. But a president cannot rely upon staff to do the heavy lifting; he must do much of it himself by cultivating personal relationships. Nixon wasn't much interested, and the Democrats weren't either. Relations, already testy, fell apart when Senate Democrats in 1970 rejected his Supreme Court nominee and Nixon sent up a second nominee who was widely seen as unqualified. "What a strange man was Richard Nixon," wrote biographer Stephen Ambrose. "Subtle and skillful in his approach to the Chinese, he was stubborn and spiteful in his approach to the Senate." The Senate called his bluff, rejecting the second nominee, too. One controversy after another followed—the Family Assistance Plan, Cambodia, impoundment. Over the course of six and a half years, Nixon did manage to get major legislation passed, but Democrats couldn't wait to hang him in Watergate.

Even though he attracted men and women of high caliber to his cabinet, Nixon treated a good many of them shabbily. Secretary of State Bill Rogers, a longtime friend from Eisenhower days, was continuously undercut. Secretary of Defense Melvin Laird was not only bypassed but found that the White House was tapping into his phone conversations with a Pentagon confidant. Attorney General Richardson and his deputy Bill Ruckelshaus felt compelled to resign rather than carry out Nixon's order to fire Archibald Cox.

Nixon failed to employ his cabinet well because he did not trust the hundreds of thousands of people who worked for them. He had checked, he told his cabinet in 1971, and found that 96 percent of the civil service were against the administration. "They're bastards who

87

are here to screw us," he reportedly said. Civil servants have never been loyal to the White House, he argued, but they're worse in our case because they are New Deal Democrats. "We have yet to fire any one of these people. From now on Haldeman is the lord high executioner . . ." Ironically, a president so interested in the exercise of power did not understand how much more powerful he could have been if he had properly used men like Laird and Richardson to bring along their departments.

When John Dean testified before the Ervin Committee in the Watergate hearings, he caused a storm when he revealed that the White House had also kept an "enemies list." On it were the names of some three hundred prominent Americans. Chuck Colson, whose office compiled it, insisted that it was merely the names of people who were to be excluded from White House social events. But Dean himself had once written a memorandum about the list that asked, "How can we use the available federal machinery to screw our political enemies?" And, according to Dean's testimony, Haldeman designated about twenty names on the list for harassment by the IRS.

There is something fundamentally unhealthy about all this. Psychiatrists think of paranoia as a serious personality disorder, and I am not qualified to say whether Nixon suffered from it. But there is no question that he adopted an "us versus them" mentality, and it spread to his staff. That is the most dangerous pose a White House can take toward the outside world. It invites trouble.

Perhaps Nixon saw the world more clearly than I give him credit for. As Alan Arkin put it in *Catch-22*, "Just because you're paranoid doesn't mean they aren't after you." There is no question that scores of enemies wanted to bring him down from the day he put away Alger Hiss. But in swatting at every adversary, real and imagined, his White House multiplied the scores into an army. A political crisis was sure to follow.

Savage Combat with the Press

Every president has run into trouble with the press, and a few have gotten into brawls. Reporters went after Lyndon Johnson with a vengeance over Vietnam. The administration lied so notoriously, reporters said, that it didn't have a credibility gap—it had a canyon. Jimmy Carter's press secretary, Jody Powell, thought the press was so mean that by the end, they blamed the President every time it rained in Washington. Bill Clinton has had a running feud with the press since the New Hampshire primary of 1992. But no modern president has surpassed Nixon in the fury stirred up in the press corps.

During the height of the Watergate crisis, I sometimes slipped into the White House briefing room to watch the interplay between press secretary Ron Ziegler and reporters. It was a scene of animalistic intensity, as each side ripped away at the other. Reporters were sometimes screaming, eager to tear out Ziegler's throat. They thought the men working in the White House were akin to Nazi storm troopers working for a neo-Führer. They wanted the whole kit and caboodle out. Those scenes are burned into the memory of all who witnessed them, reminders of what can come when a savage war breaks out between the government and the press.

The origins of that war, of course, stretch back into Nixon's past—from his hard-fought campaigns in California to the Alger Hiss case to the Checkers speech in 1952. One of the worst moments in his public career came in 1962, when angry, sleepless, and reportedly hung over after his defeat in the California governor's race, he finally sent press secretary Herb Klein down to the pressroom to give a concession statement. Then, without warning, Nixon burst into Klein's briefing and blurted out, "You won't have Nixon to kick around anymore because, gentlemen, this is my last press conference." It almost was.

Studies have shown that the press treated Nixon with reasonable fairness in his 1968 campaign. In fact, 634 newspapers endorsed him, compared to 146 supporting Hubert Humphrey and 12 in favor of George Wallace. Both sides seemed to want a solid working relationship as his presidency began. After Nixon's election, Herb Block of the *Washington Post* published a memorable cartoon showing Nixon in a barber's chair without his famous five o'clock shadow and inscribed: "This shop gives to every new President of the United States a free shave.—H. Block, Proprietor."

The mood was not to last. Reporters by this time had become cynics about government, and they weren't about to give Nixon the benefit of any doubt. Many of them were looking for ways to cut him up, he felt, and he was determined to have more than a shield. He wanted ways to strike back. As Bill Safire has written, Nixon wanted the press "to be hated and beaten" because it was "another power center . . . unelected and unrepresentative." Nixon once again was more interested in the exercise of his own power than working within a democratic system of multiple power centers. Safire again: "In his indulgence of his most combative and abrasive instincts

89

against [the press] . . . lay Nixon's greatest personal and political weakness and the cause of his downfall."

Nixon at first struck a Faustian bargain with the White House press corps. Until his administration, they were allowed to lounge around the main reception area on the main floor of the West Wing, easily intercepting visitors to the White House, but their filing space was confined to a room in the northeast corner of the building (now the office of the national security adviser). Except for fast-breaking stories, most had to return to their regular offices to write, an inconvenience. Nixon wanted reporters out of the West Wing so he could have more privacy, visitors could come unobserved, and—he thought—the place would look less slovenly.

How to do it? Offer them a deal: he would close down the indoor swimming pool between the West Wing and residence (where JFK liked to frolic and LBJ swam nude with ambassadors and staff). Over the top of the pool, he would build a pressroom and large filing spaces. In exchange, the press would leave the West Wing reception area and be restricted to their new quarters, except when escorted into the West Wing itself. The press corps agreed. In one respect, correspondents won out because they gained better quarters. But they also paid a price: they were corralled and, ever since, their access to White House officials and visitors has diminished. Looking back, that move was a symbol of how hard Nixon and successive presidents have tried to manage and control the press—with decidedly mixed results for their own leadership and the democracy.

If Nixon had wanted good relations, Herb Klein would have been the natural choice for press secretary. He was a former newsman, had served Nixon as press secretary in earlier days, and enjoyed the respect of reporters. He could have become another Jim Hagerty, who served Ike superbly. But from Nixon's view, Klein was too friendly. That's why he named him the first communications director and appointed a young Haldeman protégé from the advertising world, Ron Ziegler, to the press position. Ron was a decent man and on foreign policy became one of the best-informed press secretaries in recent times. But Nixon, Haldeman & Co. saw him as their tool, someone they could program to say whatever they wanted, regardless of the truth.

Down that road lay trouble. The prevailing view at the top, as I and others elsewhere on staff found out late in the game, was to see the press podium as a propaganda weapon. It was not a place for a free give-and-take between men and women seeking truth. How could it be, the White House command asked, if self-centered, Left-

90

leaning, intellectually arrogant reporters were out there looking for ways to bloody the President? In briefing the press, Nixon said to advisers, tell them what you want them to hear, not what they want to know. Control the story. Put a rosy face on everything, no matter what you may think. "The press is the enemy," Nixon told his top advisers over and over in private meetings.

Worst of all, Nixon had no compunction about lying to the press. Lyndon Johnson had done it to a fare-thee-well, he thought, and rarely paid a price. When Watergate hit, Ziegler was given daily marching orders to make announcements that weren't true. So far as I can tell, Ziegler himself didn't fully understand until too late that he was being set up. He no doubt suspected, but had as much difficulty penetrating the story as did almost everyone else on staff. Nixon and Haldeman continually exploited him. One of the lowest moments in press history came on April 17, 1973, days after John Dean had resigned. With walls closing in, Nixon read a statement that all members of the staff would be allowed to talk with prosecutors and be held accountable. Ziegler was instructed to say that Nixon's announcement was the "operative statement." Under prodding from R. W. Apple of the *Times*, Ziegler was then forced to concede that all of his own former statements on Watergate were "inoperative." Translation: we have been lying from the start. Ziegler's briefings descended to a hell hole after that.

Beyond the podium in the pressroom, Nixon had two other stratagems to control press coverage. One was to cut off unrestricted flows of information—leaks. They drove him as crazy as they did Johnson, and, like Johnson, he thought the answer was wiretapping. In May 1969—less than four months after the inauguration—William Beecher reported in the *New York Times* that the United States was secretly bombing Cambodia. Widely respected for his enterprising journalism, Beecher by his own accout had patiently pulled together facts, mosaic-like, until he saw the whole picture and then confronted sources within the administration. Nixon and Kissinger came unglued. Together, they ordered up seventeen taps that were carried out by the FBI. Four were on newsmen (including Beecher), most on administration officials (including Anthony Lake, later Clinton's first national security adviser). One tap was on Nixon's own brother, Don. Nixon believed they were legal, based on the Crime Control Act of 1968; the Supreme Court ruled in 1972 they were illegal. But as Stephen Ambrose points out, Nixon knew that a subsequent tap he ordered on columnist Joseph Kraft was illegal. The FBI refused to carry it out, and Haldeman had a retired New York City cop install it.

The wiretaps never identified leakers, but they helped to set the administration on the trail toward bigger scandals.

Another stratagem at the White House was to apply a government strong-arm against the press. In the summer of 1970, Jeb Stuart Magruder wrote a memorandum to Haldeman, copied to communications director Herb Klein, that contained a sinister proposal. Among other antipress maneuvers, Magruder recommended that the White House arrange for the Federal Communications Commission (FCC) chairman to attack the media's objectivity and prompt a senator or representative to write a letter to the FCC *recommending that individual reporters be licensed by the Federal Communications Commission!*

While Justice officials always claimed they were acting independently of the White House, it is more than curious that in April 1972 they filed antitrust suits against the three networks, ABC, CBS, and NBC. CBS soon complained of unlawful plans by the government to restrain, intimidate, and inhibit criticism of the President and his appointees. A tape of a conversation on September 15, 1972, finds Nixon telling John Dean and Haldeman that when a television station owned by the *Washington Post* came up for license renewal by the FCC, "it's going to be goddamned active there." Early in 1973, allies of the President, denying they were prompted by the White House, challenged the licenses of two television stations owned by the *Post* in Florida. Again denying any White House pressure, the Justice Department in late 1973 asked the FCC to deny license renewals for television and radio stations owned by four regional newspapers, three of which had often attacked Nixon. The pattern of governmental agencies suddenly springing into action against hostile news organizations sent an obvious, chilling message.

Fortunately, the legal challenges never went far, just as the wiretaps and other abuses had not. Most of us on staff were also unaware of them. While obviously they were related, they were also separate and apart from our efforts at stagecraft, described earlier. But the private war that Nixon was waging on the press—and he felt they were conducting against him—eventually burst into the open, not only crippling his government but wounding the presidency itself for years thereafter. With due respect for Bill Safire, it was not the only cause of Nixon's downfall—but it was certainly one of the major ones.

92   It also wounded the presidency itself. With Vietnam and Watergate coming back to back, the government's credibility suffered grievously. Those two seminal events represent the darkest chapters

in twentieth-century relations between press and government, "making it perfectly clear"—as Nixon liked to say—that a president's capacity to lead rests squarely upon a reputation for openness and candor.

A Reign of Fear Within

Much of what I have just described I did not personally witness. I was too junior and many decisions were made behind closed doors at high levels. Like most others, I learned later. But there were other elements of Nixon's dark side that I did see—and contained warnings of the danger that lurked within.

When I first met Dwight Chapin, he was a twenty-nine-year old "wunderkind." He had graduated from the University of Southern California, taken a job at J. Walter Thompson, the advertising firm, and had then been recruited to the 1968 Nixon campaign by Bob Haldeman, another alumnus of J. Walter. By 1971, when I joined up, Dwight was regarded as the creative impresario of the White House, a young man who could dream up wonderfully imaginative events that would showcase Richard Nixon at his best on American television.

Months before Nixon's trip to China, Dwight disappeared from sight into the basement of the White House residence to draw up detailed plans for the journey and for a dramatic return to the United States. It was a masterpiece of choreography, drawing Dwight many other choice assignments. Not until Mike Deaver was anyone as effective at the White House. Dwight also struck me as a fine human being.

Leaving the Nixon White House, Dwight Chapin went to jail. With a clank of the bars, his political life ended, and he became just another of several young men whose lives were mangled by working for or around the President of the United States. Dwight's sin was to hire Donald Segretti for a series of dirty tricks in the 1972 campaign and then to lie about it to a grand jury. He spent six months in a federal prison. When he came out, some of the President's pals helped him with jobs for a while and he went on to other successes, but he has since vanished from national politics. While in the Reagan White House, I asked Dwight and a few other Nixon alumni to come to the Roosevelt Room one afternoon to give us some advice, where they were immediately spotted, of course. Some of Reagan's confidants warned me never to make that "mistake" again. They didn't like

Dwight or the baggage he carried with him and didn't want the press to see him on the premises. How cruel and senseless it all seemed.

Dwight no more deserved his fate than many of the other young men who paid such a high price for working for Nixon—fellows like Egil "Bud" Krogh, Jeb Magruder, and Donald Segretti, all of whom went to prison. I believe they would never have taken that course had it not been for an atmosphere of intimidation that was created in that White House and that demanded the total loyalty of its underlings. The reign of fear started from the top and was enforced through the office of the chief of staff, the "lord high executioner." Perhaps if you were an older veteran, you could ignore orders from above, but not if you were young and down the line. When Haldeman's office called, you jumped. Action was demanded now, no questions asked. Even—as it was for Dwight—if it was illegal.

I don't know how things got so out of hand. The Bob Haldeman I came to know a little better after he had been forced out in 1973 was very different from the man I had learned to fear. He was caring and courteous; he was a good father with an adoring family; and he was a devoted Christian Scientist. After I joined up with Clinton, Bob graciously sent me a letter volunteering to help in any way he could, and we talked warmly.

I also found out later that as chief of staff he had often deflected or ignored Nixon's craziest orders; he knew they were just a product of frustration and if he waited for The Boss to settle down, Nixon would change his mind. He resented Chuck Colson in large measure because Colson would not only pump up Nixon's anger but, then, when the crazy order came, as it would, Colson would cheerily carry it out—and never give Haldeman a chance to intervene. After his career was ruined by Watergate, Haldeman had every reason to be bitter toward Nixon, but he mostly held his tongue in his memoirs and drifted quietly out of the Nixon orbit. (Note that Colson has since transformed his life, dedicating himself to a prison ministry that has helped many others in trouble.)

At the dedication of the President's library in July 1990, I stood next to Haldeman as the two men greeted each other—and saw that for a moment, Nixon didn't recognize him! What in the world had ever happened back in the 1960s to turn a decent man like Haldeman into a martinet at the White House? I'm not sure, but politics can twist people, especially when it is ferociously played. Whether it was Nixon's doing or his own, Haldeman certainly took it to heart that as chief of staff, his job was to be the President's SOB.

At first, I was impressed by the efficiency of the Haldeman ap-

94

proach. I had learned in the Navy to answer for every minute, but this crowd wanted you to answer for each second. A red tag on an incoming memo meant it should go to the top of your stack and be looked at promptly; a double red tag meant to drop everything else and give it immediate attention. Red tags poured into the office every day. Directives from the President also came over regularly in the form of Haldeman memos; our job was to carry out the orders, don't ask questions, just get it done. No paper went to the President without going first to Bruce Kehrli, the staff secretary, and he in turn would circulate them to others for comment—a "chop"—before sending them to the President. If a paper was due that night to the President, it had better be in his reading pouch late in the afternoon—or you should have a reason why. You arrived promptly in the morning, you stayed until the work was done, and you came back the next day for more. Meetings should be brief, to the point, and no one should leave without a clear understanding of his or her responsibility. No major speech should go to the President without carrying a chop from the policy staff, and they shouldn't send the President proposed remarks for a public event without a sign-off from the writers.

Haldeman's young lieutenants were called "the beaver patrol." They arrived at your office unannounced, demanding the paper you were supposed to produce yesterday or an explanation for what you had done on Action Item 413 on their list. Only if you were senior enough could you afford to throw them out. Sometimes, the beavers tried to chew on the wrong log. Early in the administration, as folklore had it, Kehrli appeared at Pat Buchanan's door with a draft presidential statement and a request from the President that Pat spice it up and return it quickly. Bruce should have understood that Pat was not to be toyed with: Buchanan had joined Nixon in the wilderness and by now enjoyed the President's total confidence. But Bruce belonged to the beaver patrol. Instead of leaving, he hung around the office, waiting for Pat, who was unamused, to work through the draft and give him the changes. Looking over the revisions, Bruce sniffed, "I guess these will do." The explosion from Buchanan could be heard in offices far down the hall, as he ordered Kehrli never to darken his door again. As far as I know, he didn't.

But if you lacked Buchanan's status (and a boyhood reputation for knowing how to throw a punch), you clicked your heels to Haldeman's orders. I have to say one thing in favor of this approach: while there were glitches, missed deadlines, and the like, the Nixon White House was the most efficient and thorough I have ever seen. Since then, a good many presidents—especially Clinton in his early

95

years—would have been more effective if their staffs had been more disciplined.

But like so much else in the Nixon operation, the zeal to win, to control every detail, to make the trains run on time, went completely overboard. It wasn't just efficient—which would have been fine—but was turned into a Marine boot camp. The system worked from the top down and brooked no dissent from the bottom up. If you didn't like it, there's the door. But how many young striplings will walk away from a job at the White House?

Nixon prided himself on hiring the youngest White House staff in history. But if one hires good young people, the president and his top staff must recognize their innocence, not exploit it. A young man in his twenties, given a chance to work in one of the most glamorous places in the world, will do damn near anything to stay and get ahead. I was certainly puffed up in those days, overly ambitious, looking too much for the "main chance." It's a wonder that family and friends stuck with me through those early years.

But I was also lucky. No one ever asked me to do anything illegal or unethical; maybe they thought I wouldn't or that I was too soft. The poisoned chalice just never passed my way. Others, like Chapin and Krogh, fine, upstanding men, got sucked in because they were asked to do things that were shady and they complied, thinking that must be the way the game is played. And they wound up in prison. There's no doubt that Chapin would never have engaged in dirty tricks or perjured himself unless he thought that's what his superiors wanted. Loyalty to the team, that's what was demanded, not fidelity to the law.

By nature, politics stirs up more passion than a corporate job or hanging out a law shingle. Those who play at it, especially in the upper reaches, know it can be rough. "Welcome to the NFL," we used to tell new recruits to the Nixon White House. An old pro who has been on the field long enough knows what the rules are and will avoid pulling a face mask or piling on after the whistle. He can keep himself out of trouble. But rookies don't know any better. That's why it is reprehensible for their coaches to send them into a game and direct them to rabbit punch or gouge the opposing quarterback, knowing full well they may get tossed out. Yet that is exactly what happened in the Nixon years and why a Chapin and a Krogh went to the slammer.

96   Nixon was not the last president who was reckless with the lives of his young assistants; Bill Clinton has certainly been guilty of the same thing. But one of Nixon's worst sins was to create a reign of in-

timidation and a culture of expectation that his finest young men should march over a cliff for him. It was more than Nixon's presidency that was wrecked. Innocent lives were also crushed.

A Rogue White House

For more than a quarter century, investigators and journalists alike have zealously pursued the question of whether Nixon directed or had prior knowledge of the Watergate break-in during June 1972. He always denied it and no one has proven otherwise. The question, however, is beside the point. Whether or not Nixon knew, he bears personal responsibility for the break-in because he created an atmosphere in which his subordinates would logically assume this was what he expected from them.

Had he not created a rogue White House and unleashed a war on his enemies, real and imagined, there would have been no Watergate break-in and no cover-up. For a small circle of those to whom he entrusted such matters, "dirty tricks" were part of their job descriptions. To him and to them, that's the way the game was played—and you should do it to your enemy before he does it to you. Their view of Watergate was the same as the Victorians' view of adultery: the sin was not in the doing of it but in getting caught.

Even now, after all of the revelations about the cover-up, it is stunning for me to read Haldeman's diaries, published posthumously in 1994, which record a steady stream of shameful orders from the President to his chief of staff. Sadly, only a tiny fraction of those working for Nixon knew anything about these orders. Had a George Shultz found out, he would have put a stop to them or resigned; he showed that later on in the Iran-contra scandal during the Reagan years. But Nixon had a private loop so that, at most, good people like Shultz, Garment, Price, Safire, and Moynihan might be suspicious but never knew anything for sure. Moynihan said at the end of Nixon's first term that it had been "damned good government."

For Haldeman, whom I found to be a straight arrow, some of the orders must have been wrenching. Consider this abbreviated summary of entries from his diary, recording conversations with the President:

> July 21, 1969—RN orders up a "dirty tricks" team to engage in "general campaign activity of harassment and needling of the opposition, planting spies in their camp, etc."

November 3, 1969—On the night he speaks successfully to the country on Vietnam, RN directs that "100 vicious dirty calls" be placed to the *New York Times* and the *Washington Post* about their editorials, even before they are printed.

March 4, 1970—RN orders "Operation O'Brien," an effort to dig up dirt against the new chairman of the Democratic Party, Larry O'Brien. Two years later, the Watergate break-in centers on phone taps of O'Brien.

March 10, 1970—RN tells Haldeman he wants a new attack group "to be sure we are doing an all-out hatchet job on the Democrat leaders, through IRS, etc."

April 9, 1970—RN wants two gumshoes reporting to Ehrlichman to "get dope" on senators opposing his Supreme Court nominee, especially Kennedy, Muskie, Bayh, and Proxmire. Both investigators are former New York City policemen. One had earlier put a tap on columnist Joe Kraft; both show up later as Watergate figures, delivering hush money to the burglars.

July 25, 1970—RN demands that his staff "destroy" television anchor Chet Huntley; he believes it would have a good effect on other commentators.

September 12, 1970—With midterm elections on his mind, RN orders an infiltration of John Gardner's Common Cause, trying to push it left, and the establishment of a fake far-left organization that can praise the liberal records of Democratic candidates, driving up their "radiclib" ratings.

November 25, 1970—RN wants a fake liberal front group to send out pro-Muskie letters that would deeply offend voters in the South.

December 5, 1970—RN is pleased with photos produced by Colson, who had a private detective follow Senator Kennedy in Paris, taking pictures of him with women and leaking them to the press and Congress.

May 28, 1971—Looking ahead to the 1972 election, RN wants "permanent tails" on Kennedy, Muskie, and Humphrey, covering "the kinds of things that they hit us on in '62; personal finances, family, and so forth."

98   June 23, 1971—RN wants to pull the tax files and order full field audits of Clark Clifford and top supporters of antiwar doves.

September 13, 1971—After hearing that the IRS has investigated his friend Billy Graham, RN wants his team to have big Democratic contributors and celebrities investigated by the IRS, too.

Notably, Haldeman's diary does not record other, more nefarious operations that came before the Watergate break-in. One was a famous letter falsely accusing Senator Edmund Muskie of racial slurs against an ethnic group shortly before the New Hampshire primary. Muskie had been running ahead of Nixon in the polls for the 1972 election. Muskie made an emotional denial of the slur and, as snow fell upon him, seemed to cry. The "crying scene" is thought to have cost him the primary and the nomination, leaving Nixon with a much weaker opponent in George McGovern. The Haldeman diary also pays little attention to Donald Segretti, a young man recruited by the White House to carry out a string of stupid acts of political sabotage and spying. Exposed by the *Washington Post*, Segretti eventually went to jail.

More central still, Haldeman does not fully address a wholesale invasion of citizens' civil liberties in the name of national security. The White House began its journey down a slippery path with the wiretaps of national security staff and journalists, noted earlier. On June 13, 1971, the day after his daughter Tricia was married, Nixon awoke to read a front-page *New York Times* account of a secret Pentagon study showing how the United States had become involved in Vietnam. The period covered was pre-Nixon, and the President was initially unperturbed. But Kissinger, according to Stephen Ambrose, convinced him the leak was a dangerous breach of security that could imperil back channels to China and the North Vietnamese negotiators. Kissinger also fingered Dr. Daniel Ellsberg as the chief culprit and said Nixon could not sit passively: "It shows you're a weakling, Mr. President," an argument certain to provoke him.

Nixon swiftly ordered an FBI investigation of Ellsberg, a government lawsuit to prevent further publication, lie detector tests of civil servants who might be implicated in the leak, reports on McGeorge Bundy and others on the outside who might still have security clearances, and operations to get the papers back from the Brookings Institution, where they were thought to be stored. "I want that goddamn . . . material [from Brookings] and I don't care how you get it," he told Haldeman.

When the FBI refused to investigate Ellsberg, a seething Nixon told Ehrlichman, "If we can't get anyone in this damn government to do something about [leaks], then, by God, we'll do it ourselves. I want you to set up a little group right here in the White House. Have them get off their tails and find out what's going on and figure out how to stop it." That July, Ehrlichman gave the assignment to two young men, Bud Krogh and David Young. They set up shop in the basement of the Old EOB with a sign on the door: "Plumbers." They were the men who would stop the leaks. (Young was the only one of the Plumbers who was never implicated in illegal acts.)

Nixon had thus established a government within a government—a rogue operation at the White House that would have far-reaching consequences. Later in 1971, the Plumbers sent a team to break into the office of a psychiatrist in California to photograph the medical records of Daniel Ellsberg. Nixon had approved of that break-in—or at least thought he might have—and even though he would justify it in the name of national security, he knew he might now be vulnerable to a future impeachment for committing "high crimes and misdemeanors." He also had his own off-the-shelf domestic intelligence operations—something we were not to see again until Oliver North and John Poindexter burst onto the public scene during the Iran-contra scancal.

The Plumbers had an insidious influence inside the Nixon camp. Almost imperceptibly, as the 1972 campaign heated up, the men first recruited to carry out "black bag" jobs in national security were redirected toward political dirty tricks. Among those arrested for the Watergate break-in were Howard Hunt, G. Gordon Liddy, and three Cubans, all of whom participated in the Ellsberg break-in a year earlier. Indeed, there is considerable evidence that Nixon wanted to curtail investigations of Watergate so that he could keep the national security operations concealed. His desperation to keep the whole bag of tricks out of public view sent him over the precipice.

As Leonard Garment has pointed out, a link thus runs directly from Vietnam to Nixon's downfall. The war itself stirred up the fierce opposition of Daniel Ellsberg and others at the Pentagon; Ellsberg & Co. decided to take the law into their own hands by stealing and then publishing the secret Pentagon Papers; Nixon set up the Plumbers to secretly investigate Ellsberg; and the Plumbers then became a political arm for White House dirty tricks, breaking into the Watergate. "So this is the spine that really connects the presidency from beginning to end, another casualty of Vietnam," argues Garment, "and the spine was broken in the end by Nixon's impeachment and resignation."

In defense of Nixon, some of his former lieutenants have advanced two arguments. Vietnam, they say, divided the nation more

100

sharply than any conflict since the Civil War, sending hundreds of thousands into the streets and signaling to the North Vietnamese that the United States was too fractured to stay in the fight. Antigovernment sentiments were complicating delicate U.S. attempts to wind down the Cold War with the Soviet Union, as leaks of national security information turned into a torrent. If Lincoln was justified in suspending habeas corpus during the Civil War, as many historians believe he was, why was Nixon—as commander in chief—not justified in bending lesser laws to protect the country's security during the Vietnam War? It's a fair question and one that frequently arises in national emergencies.

Obviously, I am sympathetic to Nixon and believe he had every reason to "get tough" in protecting national security secrets. Even so, the analogy to Lincoln is too much of a stretch. Lincoln limited his suspensions of rights, acted openly, and promised to restore full liberties upon the conclusion of the war. Nixon set no apparent limits, acted surreptitiously, and set in motion various illegal events that were increasingly disconnected from the war.

The other rationalization offered on behalf of illegal dirty tricks is that his opponents in the Democratic Party had been doing the same things for years. There are mountains of evidence to support this contention. Victor Lasky, a conservative writer, collected much of it in his book *It Didn't Start with Watergate*. The mainstream press has never given Lasky a fair shake. In fact, distinguished historians have found many of the same things as Lasky: presidents such as Franklin Roosevelt and Lyndon Johnson ordered their aides to check out the tax records of their opponents; Bobby Kennedy ordered the bugging of Martin Luther King, Jr., and it was during the Johnson years that J. Edgar Hoover's FBI sent to King a tape recording of his liaisons with other women and implied that he should kill himself. Nixon's own 1968 campaign was bugged, his doctor's office was broken into during the 1972 campaign, and Nixon had also faced a history of Democratic operatives, like the prankster Dick Tuck, sabotaging his campaign tours. And, undoubtedly, if we were privy to all the private conversations of other presidents in the White House, as we were privy to Nixon's tapes, our view of several of them would be tarnished as well.

While at the Nixon White House, I constantly heard from others on the staff how dirty the other side had been. There was a running assumption that whatever our fellows might be doing—and we assumed they were staying within the law—the other fellows were doing something far worse to us. Moreover, as suggested earlier, I noticed a suspicious pattern during the 1970s of "black bag" jobs occurring in the Washington area long after Nixon left office. A prominent journalist might find his home burglarized, his papers rustled, and nothing else missing; a political activist might report some of his materials had been taken; others in the private sector felt sure they were wiretapped. Something organized was afoot, of that I am virtually certain, but no one has ever pinned it down. Like many others, I have also wondered who was listening in on the telephone whenever I used a government phone; sometimes the line has been so weak that there may have been multiple taps.

There were, then, mitigating circumstances surrounding Nixon. He was convinced he was playing by the same rules as his opponents, and he could point to his own experiences as proof. But that doesn't get him off the hook for the massive abuses of power perpetrated in his name. Even if his predecessors had acted improperly, he took his own oath to uphold the Constitution, a document that charges in Article II, Section 3, that a president "shall take Care that the laws be faithfully executed." Or as English author Henry de Bracton famously put it, "The King must be under no man but God and the law, for the law makes the King."

Especially after campaigning as a law-and-order candidate, Nixon had an obligation to run a clean White House. By setting off a chain of dirty tricks against his opponents, allowing rogue investigators on the White House payroll, and unleashing the Plumbers, he virtually ensured that his men would run roughshod over the laws and customs he publicly extolled. Trouble was inevitable. Dirty tricks didn't start with Watergate nor did they stop there, but had he not charged down that slope, he would have served two full terms as president.

WHAT WE SEE, THEN, is that the "cancer on the presidency" that John Dean described to Nixon did not grow spontaneously. There were underlying causes—a president who was unable to control the demons within, his confusion of power versus leadership, the breakdown of relations with other centers of democratic power, a savage war with the press, a reign of fear among young White House aides, and the creation of rogue operations within the White House itself. The cancer grew and then metastasized out of this environment. A scandal was just waiting to happen. If it had not occurred in the break-in, it would have come in another form on another day. A Watergate was inevitable.

102

Most books about leadership tell us what a person *ought* to do to become effective and powerful. Few tell us what to *avoid*. But the latter may be even more valuable because many people on the road to success are tripped up by their mistakes and weaknesses.

Nixon's sins were not his alone. It is troubling that other presidents have committed one or more of them, too. His grievous error was to commit all of them and to do so in a way that put him far beyond the pale of acceptable behavior. It amounted to a political suicide. How one wishes he might have exorcised those demons within, to put down that shadow side so that his bright side could emerge triumphant. What a different president he would have become. But he was convinced that only by being tough and often mean could he survive. He thought of himself as a better person than was commonly understood, which added to his frustration, but he also knew how vengeful he could be. In the flap over the Pentagon Papers, he told his cabinet, "I get a lot of advice on PR and personality and how I've got to put on my nice-guy hat and dance at the White House, so I did it, but let me make it clear that's not my nature."

As complex as he was, Nixon left behind some simple lessons about leadership. It isn't hard to see how a man of his incredible strengths could climb to the mountaintop, nor how a man of his glaring weaknesses could tumble into the valley. The challenge for future leaders is to learn equally well from both adventures.

WHEN AL HAIG CALLED IN senior staff that afternoon in August 1974 and told us about the contents of Nixon's conversation with Haldeman two years earlier—the famous tape of June 23, 1972—I have never been angrier. Now we knew. Nixon had betrayed the country, the institution of the presidency, his family, the Congress, the press, everyone. And, yes, I felt personally betrayed, too. The "smoking gun" had flattened us all. Resignation was now inevitable; forget impeachment, please just go. It was horrible.

Until that time, there had been debates within the staff whether one should tender a quiet letter of resignation. A few did go early because they didn't believe in him anymore and couldn't continue. Most of us stayed, however, because we felt that it was wrong to kick him while he was down. To depart while the evidence was incomplete would send a public signal that we had lost confidence in him—a signal that would be unfair to him and to friends still there.

But now the evidence was in and it was conclusive. What to do?

103

To everyone in speechwriting, the answer was obvious: only a rat left a sinking ship. We stayed.

After Nixon waved from the helicopter his final morning in office, I wasn't sure whether I could ever forgive him for Watergate. The wounds were too deep. But as soon as he fell ill and nearly died from phlebitis in San Clemente a few months later, I found that he tugged at my emotions again. He didn't deserve to die so soon, and maybe he could help us all understand what had happened a little better. As time passed, I was disappointed that he never did unravel the full story—it was obviously too painful for him—but he did turn his energies to writing again, and I found as that side of him reappeared, my respect for his intellectual strengths grew again, even as memories of Watergate were still fresh.

Bill Simon had remained friends with Nixon and a year or more after the resignation asked me to come along when he paid a visit in California. Nixon greeted me more warmly than I had expected and fixed all of us his favorite martini before we sat down for an extended conversation about world affairs. Thereafter, I had a chance to visit and talk with Nixon on a more regular basis, and increasingly I began to see conversations with him as a privilege. My wounds were healing by now, and I looked forward to learning his insights into world events.

He had distinctly mixed feelings, I knew, about my signing up with Bill Clinton in 1993 but, at least in our private conversations, seemed to give his blessing—and he had a good many pieces of advice for my new boss, most of them printable. To the end, he remained a riveting figure. What was good in him—and what was bad—was deep, rich, and real.

When Nixon died in 1994, President Clinton asked me in for private counsel on whether he should go to the funeral, whom he should take along, and, importantly, what he should say. I was pleased that he accepted my suggestions. These were not easy decisions for Clinton: many of his closest supporters still detested Nixon and would have been much happier if Clinton stayed home or at least avoided a eulogy. But Clinton respected the former president and courageously insisted upon attending and accepted the invitation to speak. His eulogy was one of his finest moments, and it captured what I believe:

"Today is a day for his family, his friends, and his nation to remember President Nixon's life in totality. To them, let us say, may the day of judging President Nixon on anything less than his entire career come to a close."

Gerald Ford

4

A Man of Character

A FEW MONTHS after Gerald Ford retired from the White House, one of his assistants called to say the former president had a personal request. He was scheduled to give a major speech soon and wondered if I would look over a draft. That afternoon his office faxed a copy with an understanding that he would call me at home that night.

The speech that came buzzing across the wires was a gem. Its ideas were thoughtful and complex, its sentences hung together nicely, and it employed a rich, evocative vocabulary. Words of two, three, and even four syllables leapt off the pages. There was only one problem: after serving him for over a year in the White House, I could not imagine Jerry Ford speaking from a text so unlike anything he had given as president. What if his audience thought he was trying to reinvent himself? What if he stumbled over one of those jawbreaking words? Obviously, he was calling because he wanted a rewrite.

"Well," he said that night, and I could almost see him puffing on his pipe. "I am curious to know what you think of the draft, Dave."

"Mr. President, this is an excellent speech. Someone has written a first-rate draft for you." I began to stammer, not sure how to phrase the next words. "But some of this may not be quite what you like. Would you like me, sir, to smooth it out and put it in your style?"

Pause . . .

I realized I had crawled out on a limb but not how far. I also knew he knew I was suggesting he might be more comfortable with a simpler speech, full of the monosyllables I and others had dished up to him when he was in office.

A chuckle came on his end. "No," he responded slowly. "I just wanted to see whether you liked it as is. This is the first time in years that I have had a chance to sit down and write my own speech, saying things the way I would like to say them. I just wanted to try it out on you."

It's hard to talk after your jaw hits the floor. I mumbled something and we talked on a bit until he said good-bye. What an idiot I had been at the White House, I thought to myself, encouraging this good man to be less than himself. Why had we fed him all that pablum to regurgitate before public audiences? And why had he accepted it? Throughout his presidency, many who served him—me included—never twigged to his interest in addressing people on a more sophisticated plane. Maybe, having never aspired to the presidency, he even underestimated himself.

Yet, with the passage of time, Jerry Ford looks better and better. Recognition is spreading that the character and quality of his leadership more closely fit the needs of the country than was seen when he held office. He was a healer in a full sense. As we have lived through scandals since, especially during the Clinton era, Ford's honesty also reminds us of what we want our leaders to be. "Gerald Ford was our most underrated modern president," says Reagan biographer Edmund Morris.

Consider the change of heart by journalist Richard Reeves. In the fall of 1974, Reeves followed the new president around in the final days of the congressional campaigns and wrote a scathing article for *New York* magazine. Its cover ran a fake photo of Bozo the Clown sitting in the Oval Office with the headline "Ladies and Gentlemen, the President of the United States." Reeves wrote, "It is not a question of saying the emperor has no clothes—there is a question of whether there is an emperor." A year later, Reeves expanded his critique into a full-length book, asserting that "Ford is slow. He is also unimaginative and not very articulate."

In explaining Ford's ascent, Reeves even invoked Lord Bryce, who had come to these shores in the late nineteenth century and observed why so many mediocrities served as president: "When the choice is between a brilliant man and a safe man, the safe man is preferred." Reeves knew that Nixon had preferred John Connally as vice president but chose Ford as the man whose confirmation was safe in Congress. The portrait in the magazine soon became indelible in the public mind. In his biography of Ford, John Robert Greene wrote, "No journalist did more to popularize the image of Ford as inept than did Richard Reeves."

But as Reeves has watched history unfold since, he has recanted. Writing in *American Heritage* in 1997, under the headline "I'm Sorry, Mr. President," he laments the deterioration of politics and journalism in the intervening years, especially the media's penchant for trashing public figures, and manfully admits that his own pieces about Ford contributed to the growing negativism of the press. With the advantage of hindsight, he says that Ford did "a better job than I had predicted or imagined . . . he did his best and did what he thought he had to do: You have my respect and thanks, Mr. President."

While he was in office, that image of Ford as a bumbler, someone who meant well but, as Lyndon Johnson once said, couldn't walk straight and chew gum at the same time, took deep root in public thinking. (Actually, Reeves claims the real quote was "couldn't fart and chew gum at the same time"; LBJ's aides have cleaned up the story over the years.) It was an unfair characterization, but something journalists like Reeves and many others readily popularized, as did Ford's critics on the Democratic side of the aisle. Those of us around him in the government knew that he was more intelligent and more physically graceful than the press said (after all, he had been offered a contract to play professional football), and we struggled to help people see the man we worked for each day. But, in retrospect, most of us inside did not take the full measure of the man, either. We should have. I wish I had.

Jerry Ford served as president only 895 days, the shortest tenure in the twentieth century. Even in that brief twinkle, he left important lessons about presidential leadership that endure today. Some of the lessons grew out of mistakes. He showed how essential it is to success that an elected leader demonstrate a mastery of his job in his early weeks in office, especially during the first hundred days. As we see repeatedly, those weeks are more important than any other. While he need not be FDR, he must take great care to build the trust and confidence of the public, and Ford fell down on that one. It is equally essential, especially in a large organization, that someone take charge of the troops. If the leader does not have the temperament to crack the whip, he must empower someone else who will— and fast. Once word spreads that a leader and his team do not have a 109 firm grip, a belief takes hold that he is not up to the job, and it then becomes devilishly difficult to reverse that narrative. On those fronts, too, Ford had trouble, largely because he had been thrust into the presidency without benefit of preparation.

What is truly remarkable about Ford, however, is that he survived bad stumbles early on and emerged with the respect and gratitude of the country. So, his leadership offered positive lessons, too. First and foremost, he reaffirmed the importance of honesty among our elected leaders. "Truth is the glue," he said upon taking office, and he proved it every day. Because he followed the old adage "Take your job seriously, not yourself," Ford also surrounded himself with topflight people in his cabinet. He did not always manage them as successfully as he might, but he wound up with the best cabinet in modern times. The person who helped him the most, however, was not in a department. She was upstairs in the residence—"First Mama," as she came to be affectionately known. We will visit each of these lessons in the pages ahead.

Was there a single key to Jerry Ford's leadership? I have always thought him the most decent man I have known in the presidency. But there was perhaps something else that mattered even more. Emotionally, he was the healthiest president we have had since Eisenhower and Truman. He knew who he was, was at peace with life, and liked people. He trusted the public, Congress, and the press, and they in turn largely trusted him. Eventually, voters turned him out of office for Jimmy Carter, and, for a while, Ford and Carter had a bitter relationship. But, over time, even they made peace.

A Personal Odyssey

My relationship with Jerry Ford was almost as accidental as with Richard Nixon. As Republican minority leader in the House, he came to the White House from time to time for leadership meetings with Nixon, and I might occupy a back bench. Nixon and he had known each other since Ford was elected to Congress in 1948, and saw each other as rising powers in Republican ranks, though Ford's ambition stretched to the Speaker's office in the House, while Nixon always had his eye on a larger prize.

As president, Nixon saw Ford as a valuable lieutenant in Congress, a Republican loyalist ready and able to line up the troops on his behalf. More reliable, thought Nixon, than Hugh Scott, a renegade leader of GOP senators. Still, to a young fellow like me on the back row who didn't know Congress well and had not seen him in

110

action, Ford hardly set off sparks: he looked like a great companion on the golf course, not a man to shape the destiny of a great nation. Arrogant lot that we were, many of us on the Nixon staff were blind to his strengths as a legislator.

His selection as vice president did not change my evaluation. I was preoccupied with saving Nixon's presidency and didn't want to think about his successor. Many on the staff Ford brought with him from Capitol Hill were also like porcupines, prickly to anyone associated with Nixon. Had it not been for Ford's own warmth and openness when I visited him occasionally, I would have been stewing with suspicion that some of his subordinates were just waiting for Nixon to get the boot so they could take over themselves. It was an eerie, uneasy time.

My feelings toward Ford began to change during two moments shortly after he rose to the presidency. The first came as he and his wife, Betty, escorted the Nixons to the helicopter on the South Lawn, bade them farewell, and walked slowly back to the White House. Halfway, without speaking, Ford reached out to clasp his wife's hand. His humanness was instantly clear. And so was his relationship with his wife. Then and after, I had a sense that the two were both well grounded.

A second moment came when I listened to his brief inaugural address that day in the East Room. Declaring that "our long national nightmare is over," he spoke with a humility and directness that recalled a similar moment eleven years earlier when Lyndon Johnson first talked to the nation after the Kennedy assassination. Just as one's heart went out to Johnson then, so, too, with Ford. Somehow the country seemed blessed that a man of Ford's solid, reassuring midwestern character was there in the wings, just when we needed him. As his adviser and biographer James Cannon put it, "more than any other man in American public life at that moment, Gerald Ford personified what Richard Nixon was not."

I wasn't sure if there would be a place on the Ford team for Nixon holdovers like me and doubted there should be. Maybe "they" would want some help for a few weeks until settled in, but presumably they would then take a broom to the old White House staff. Had I been in their place, I would have. The country needed a fresh start. But only in recent years, as I turned to the memoirs of one of Ford's most intimate advisers, Robert Hartmann, did I understand how much some of Ford's congressional team despised the Nixon staff. Hartmann was gruff by nature and apparently felt insulted by the insolence of the Nixon staff during the transition. Fo-

111

cusing on Al Haig, Hartmann pejoratively tagged us "the new Praetorian Guard," men so inflated with self-importance that in the tradition of the Roman Praetorians, we tried to rule our own rulers. No doubt, there were times when we threw our weight around too much, but Hartmann was always quick to condemn anything associated with Nixon.

What he also failed to see was that many of us were no longer puffed up with our positions. We were wholly deflated. The final days with Nixon had been traumatic, our president had resigned in disgrace, and we thought we were through as well. Several players for the Chicago "Black Sox" of 1919 were banned from baseball forever after they threw the World Series. Why wouldn't we be banned from politics, our service forever blackening our names? What possible standing would we have? As I discovered, America is a forgiving nation, so that the men and women who were innocent in their work for Nixon—and even some of the wrongdoers—went on to higher glories in life. But it was touch and go for a while.

For me, it was go. A couple of weeks after the new president was sworn in, I was still formally in charge of the White House speechwriting shop, trying to integrate the old Nixonites with the tiny group that Ford brought with him from the vice president's office. In a strike out of the blue, Ford's new press secretary, Jerry terHorst, announced one morning that Paul Theiss had been appointed the new head of White House speechwriting. Wham! That was it. No one on the new team had given advance warning, either to me or to Al Haig, still the chief of staff. Al was as angry as I was, but there was nothing to be done. It was their White House, not ours, and they were entitled to put their own people in charge, no matter how brusquely. A veteran of Capitol Hill, Paul Theiss turned out to be a lovely man and, over time, I came to like both him and many of those he recruited. But when he offered me a chance to stick around in a senior writing position, I said no thanks.

There was one man in the cabinet who had captured my attention. William Simon had swept into Washington like a tornado in 1973, serving as Nixon's first energy czar when OPEC began squeezing international oil supplies, and after the crisis died down he became secretary of the treasury in May 1974. I had grown up with a strong, demanding, and yet caring father, and as a result admired men who exercised a firm grip. Bill certainly did that. Many were terrified of him. With the economy careening up and down, he was also at the center of action, exactly where a young man likes to be. I called him the day of my ouster from speechwriting and said I was looking for a temporary perch. By sundown, we had a deal: I would come over and draft his public statements and advise him on politics, while he and his team would teach me economics. For me it was a great trade—the Treasury team taught me all about free markets and fiscal discipline.

The year I spent with Bill Simon convinced me that early in a public career, a young person should either sign up with a bright, shining star who can serve as a mentor—in effect, become a tail to someone else's kite—or join a highly professional, dynamic organization that hones one's skills. In Simon and the Treasury Department, I was fortunate to have both. He was a supremely tough executive, who drove himself and everyone around him at breakneck pace. Coming from Salomon Brothers, the New York investment house, he was also accustomed to taking risks and making decisions with only about 20 percent of the information others like to have. In the investment world, a couple of dry holes won't hurt as long as you hit a gusher every so often, and Simon had a sixth sense of knowing where money would flow. In the arena of public policy, intuitive decision-making can be more dangerous, but he self-corrected so fast that his tenure proved to be highly successful.

Bill's temper was on hair trigger in those days. He was famous for barking at people and breaking pencils. One of my assistants found him so intimidating that one afternoon, when his office called, she went running down the hall to deliver a speech draft, slipped on the marble floor, and broke her ankle. Had she not been of good cheer, she could have caused a hell of a row. But Bill could also be fatherly, and he became another important force in my development. A treasury secretary in those days made at least one around-the-world journey while in office. When Bill planned visits to remote corners of Russia, India, and Sri Lanka, I eagerly tagged along on a ten-day adventure with him and his wife, Carol. Public leaders today think themselves too busy—and are so scared that opponents will accuse them of junketing—that they no longer take time to explore foreign cultures. More is the shame; they wind up impoverished intellectually. Simon was one of the last who knew how to travel. I look back upon Bill Simon as an exceptional boss. He expected the most, set the highest standards, and was the soul of integrity, qualities too rare among leaders today. Every young person could profit from a year in a harness like that.

I thought I had left the White House altogether, but I hadn't. As Simon returned from meetings there with hair-raising tales of internal strife, my phone began ringing with clandestine calls from for-

113

mer associates now working for Ford, asking for secret help on his speeches.

Ford was having a hard time putting together a smooth management team. His original crew from Capitol Hill was obviously not sufficient to run the White House, and much of the Nixon guard had left. He had no choice but to reach out for fresh reinforcements, usually culled from his extensive friendships on Capitol Hill. The results were mixed. Among the most impressive recruits were Don Rumsfeld, brought back from a NATO ambassadorship to serve as an informal chief of staff, and Rumsfeld's deputy, Dick Cheney. But the two of them were soon butting heads with Hartmann and his own growing phalanx of appointees.

Hartmann thought Rummy and Cheney smelled too much of Nixon. Even though they had established reputations on their own, they had once worked in the executive branch under Nixon, which put them beyond the pale. Hartmann saw them as the new ringleaders of the Praetorian Guard and tried to wall them out of everything he could, especially Ford's speeches, which he regarded as his own province. To Rumsfeld and Cheney, it was impossibly difficult to work with Hartmann, and a few of his newly hired minions were hacks, barely good enough to play in Division II college ball, let alone the NFL.

A story quickly made the rounds to prove the point about the Hartmann recruits. One of the writers he brought in was installed in a cavernous office in the EOB. It seems the fellow came to work each day in a suit and then changed into old trousers—"my writing pants," he said. Just before lunch, he changed back, after lunch he returned to his writing breeches, and at dusk, he was back into his suit. No one cared about his eccentricities until a cleaning woman was in his office vacuuming late one afternoon, and he hopped up and changed trousers smack in front of her. She dashed out the door. The next afternoon, returning gingerly, she was back in the office with her vacuum when he rose again and mooned her. "I declare," she told him, "the men here have always been gentlemen." Out she stomped, refusing to return. I don't know what happened to that fellow, but, thankfully, he soon disappeared from the White House.

Hartmann himself could turn out gifted prose. His draft of Ford's inaugural speech was a singular contribution to that presidency. But he had an uneven eye for talent and as he hired men in writing pants, he zealously protected their work from the remaining Praetorians. Frustrated with the results, Rumsfeld, Cheney, or an ally would call me and ask if I could write an alternative draft for an

114

upcoming event that they could slip surreptitiously to the President. It wasn't long, of course, before Hartmann caught on and saw me as another charter member of the guard.

Nor was the process always productive for Ford. In fact, one of my early drafts landed him in a pile of trouble. At the time, the finances of New York City were spiraling downward, and New York officials were pressing for a bailout from Washington. The administration was opposed, and Ford decided to tell them so in a speech in the city in October 1975. The Hartmann forces whipped up one address, and I was quietly put to work crafting another. I wrote a hard-hitting draft, expecting that if it ever came close to acceptance, I would have a chance to sit down with key players in the White House, tempering the language and strengthening the analysis—typical steps in the preparation of presidential materials. But our secrecy kept me outside the White House gates, and, to my surprise, some of my unedited paragraphs were plopped into the final text, rough and tough. It was a doozy of a speech, and the next day's *New York Daily News* carried a screaming headline: "Ford to City: Drop Dead." That headline horrified Ford's political advisers, and, sure enough, the Democrats exploited it in their advertising against Ford in the 1976 campaign. Jimmy Carter wound up carrying New York that fall, and its electoral votes were pivotal to his election. It was never clear how much that headline mattered, but it sure didn't help.

Late in 1975, Ford shook up his administration, sending Rumsfeld over to run the Pentagon and elevating Cheney to be White House chief of staff. That also ended my game of hide-and-seek, as Cheney invited me to come back in a general advisory role and to set up a small communications shop, focusing on television. Bill Simon gave his blessing, and I thus returned for a second tour in the White House. Inflation affected everything then, including job titles, and I was given one more glorious than deserved: Special Counsel to the President.

The fourteen months that followed were among my happiest in government. Jerry Ford's decency made everyone feel welcome on his team. His stance on public issues—hard-line in international affairs, fiscally conservative in economic matters, moderate to liberal on social issues—was also four-square with my own beliefs. A member of the staff need not agree with everything a president believes, but a basic compatibility is infinitely desirable. Philosophically, I happened to be more on Ford's wavelength—and, indeed, Nixon's—than those of either Reagan or Clinton, so I soon felt right at home. With some notable exceptions, the men and women Ford

115

had assembled around him were also public-spirited, honorable people who worked hard to restore the integrity and moral authority of the presidency. For all of its internal strife, the Ford White House was a good place to be.

Cautionary Tales from His Early Days

When I returned to the White House, Ford was still suffering from a tumultuous, rocky start to his presidency. There is nothing more important to the success of an actor, it is said, than his performance in his first scene and in his last. One shapes his character for the entire play, the other the memories that the audience carries from the theater. The same applies in politics and in other fields of leadership.

That was certainly what Gerald Ford experienced in his presidency. For a brief, ethereal moment, the country fell in love with him. His inaugural address was a welcome relief to a people torn apart by scandal, war, and a deteriorating economy. His quiet dignity and lack of pretense provided exactly the stabilizing force that people sought. One morning, the press watched him making breakfast for his wife, Betty, and he became the boy next door. Columnists invented an "English muffin theory of history"—the idea that any man good enough to make English muffins for his wife in the morning must be good enough to run a country.

Americans like straight talk and old-fashioned values in their president, and that's exactly what they saw now. There was an air of Harry Truman about him as he talked plainly to the country and brought a down-home feel to the White House. The Truman parallel ran deep. Both men became president amidst a national crisis; both had to make excruciating decisions; both were simple men from the Midwest, devoted to family; in both cases, their honesty and integrity comforted the nation. Despite great uncertainty about their abilities and intelligence, each of them then saw his approval ratings shoot into the stratosphere in the first days in office, only to fall sharply thereafter.

There, sadly, the parallel stops. Truman went on to that incredible comeback victory in 1948; after Ford's star dimmed, he could never quite regain its full luster. Within his first three months, in fact, he lost the chance to win the presidency in his own right. His First Hundred Days were his first scene on the national stage, and they shaped his public reputation for the rest of his time in office.

What happened to Ford? Why did his presidency go off the

116

tracks so quickly? And why could he never fully recover? There are three tales here, interconnected, and each serves as a caution for future leaders.

1. THE SUNDAY SURPRISE

On Sunday morning, September 8, 1974, exactly thirty days after Ford took office, the White House summoned reporters for a mysterious announcement by the President. He had carefully limited internal discussions of his decision to six trusted advisers, so the press lacked even a hint of what was coming. At eight o'clock that morning, he had taken communion at St. John's Episcopal Church, a traditional place of worship for presidents just across Lafayette Park. He had returned to the White House to begin calling leaders of Congress about his statement, and a few minutes before ten, his press secretary Jerry terHorst had slipped into the Oval Office with an agonized personal letter that caught him by surprise. But his secret still held.

At 11:00 A.M. sharp, with church bells still tolling in the distance, Ford made the most fateful announcement of his presidency to an unsuspecting public: "Ladies and gentlemen, I have come to a decision which I felt I should tell you and all of my fellow American citizens as soon as I was certain in my own mind and in my own conscience that it is the right thing to do. . . . I, Gerard R. Ford, President of the United States, pursuant to the pardon power conferred upon me by Article II, Section 2, of the Constitution, have granted and by these presents do grant a full, free, and absolute pardon unto Richard Nixon for all offenses against the United States which he, Richard Nixon, has committed or may have committed or taken part in . . ."

Moments after Ford signed formal papers, Richard Nixon released a statement from San Clemente accepting the pardon. Conspicuously, Nixon conceded only that he had mishandled Watergate but did not admit, as Ford's advisers had hoped, that he had violated the law or directed a cover-up. Nixon had gotten everything his lawyers wanted—a full and complete pardon, no admission of guilt, and a lengthy period of control over his tapes and records.

Still, Ford's mind was at ease and he left the office for an afternoon of golf at Burning Tree Country Club. Before he reached the first tee, he must have heard the thunderclap that rolled across the land. Americans weren't just dumbstruck by the pardon; they were 117 outraged. For most, with the Saturday Night Massacre still fresh in their minds, Ford's "Sunday Morning Surprise" reeked of Nixonian secrecy and backroom political treachery. Even as his White House counsel, Phil Buchen, was briefing the press within an hour after the announcement, calls and wires were plastering the White House. One of terHorst's assistants checked the White House switchboard and whispered to him during Buchen's briefing, "This one is going to be tough; reaction is running eight to one against."

Later in the day, the tumult mounted as the contents of ter-Horst's letter were revealed. After a night of soul-searching, the press secretary had written the President that he was resigning immediately, only a month after starting the job. "I cannot in good conscience support your decision to pardon former President Nixon even before he has been charged with the commission of any crime. As your spokesman, I do not know how I could credibly defend that action in the absence of a like decision to grant absolute pardon to the young men who evaded Vietnam military services as a matter of conscience and the absence of pardons for former aides and associates of Mr. Nixon who have been charged with crimes—and imprisoned—stemming from the same Watergate situation."

In that brief instant of the pardon, Ford had severed the gossamer thread of trust that ties the people to a presidency. In Pittsburgh the next day, he was booed for the first time. Some demonstrators shouted, "Jail Ford, jail Ford!" and a worker standing by the airport fence told reporters, "Oh, it was all fixed. He said to Nixon, 'You give me the job, I'll give you the pardon.' " The next day in Pinehurst, North Carolina, he was greeted with derisive, homemade signs: "Ford's Pardon Defies Justice," "Foxy Ford," and the like. The *New York Times* sent the Gallup team into the field and found that Ford's popularity had dropped overnight from a lofty 71 percent to 49 percent.

A venomous fury, not seen since the worst days of Watergate, returned to the press corps. TerHorst's resignation gave reporters added ammunition, allowing them to argue that if the President had only half the conscience of his own press secretary, he would not have acted so wickedly. As reporter Louis Thompson explained, "What we were going through at that time was one of the strangest periods between the White House and the press, having come off of Watergate and Vietnam. There was extreme doubt about the veracity of official statements. And an attitude due to the way the Nixon people had treated the press. We were really caught in the aftermath of that." Reporters demanded to know of any "secret deal" between

118

Nixon and Ford and quickly learned that, indeed, Nixon's chief of staff Al Haig had talked over a possible pardon with then–Vice President Ford. That was a bombshell. What was said between Ford and Haig remains unclear to this day, but conspiracy theorists are no more convinced that Ford acted alone on the pardon than they are that Lee Harvey Oswald acted alone in Dallas.

Ford argued persuasively that he had never agreed to anything with Haig on a Nixon pardon and that once president, he acted out of conscience and the best interests of the country. To allay criticism, he also took a step no other president had braved since Lincoln: he voluntarily went before a congressional committee and testified under oath that his actions were aboveboard. That was an important step in rebuilding White House relations with Congress, so tattered after Nixon. His friends and advisers—I am among them—believed Ford's account absolutely. It is inconceivable to us that Jerry Ford cut a private deal with Al Haig. Even if it were in Ford's nature, and it isn't, there was never any need for a deal. Ford could see that one day events would drive Nixon from office. Nothing would have been served by a secret deal with Haig.

Even so, the pardon rippled through politics for the rest of Ford's tenure, drastically weakening his presidency. Less than two months after his announcement, voters voted overwhelmingly for Democratic candidates in the 1974 congressional elections. Whatever faint hopes Republican candidates had after Nixon's resignation were doused by the pardon. The famous "Watergate class of '74" also brought a fresh burst of liberal energy to the Capitol— among its new members were Gary Hart, Tim Wirth, Dale Bumpers, John Glenn, Chris Dodd, Paul Simon, Tom Harkin, Paul Tsongas, Max Baucus, Pat Leahy, and Jim Florio.

With a wind at their back and a lopsided 291 to 144 majority in the House, the new Democratic Congress made legislative life a misery for Ford. Congress had already begun to strike back against the "Imperial Presidency" of Richard Nixon, and now it moved even more forcefully to assert control over economic, social, and foreign policy. More than once, Congress muscled Ford into reversing course on policy and repeatedly it passed up opportunities for compromise. Ford decided that his best weapon was the veto, and he exercised it more than any other modern president—sixty-six vetoes in two years and five months. Congress overrode twelve of them, and on the rest, there was mostly stalemate. While some voters gave Ford 119 credit for standing up to Congress, many more criticized him for an inability to govern. Nor was the pardon forgotten. As the 1976 elections loomed, Jimmy Carter and Ronald Reagan both gained traction against Ford by reviving the issue. That summer, Ford emerged from the Republican convention so hopelessly behind that despite a first-rate campaign, he could never catch up.

From the inside, it seemed that during twenty-eight of his twenty-nine months in office, Ford tried to run the country with heavy weights tied to his ankles. The fresh lease on life that he had given to Richard Nixon wound up shortening his own political life.

What does this episode tell us about leadership?

Conventional wisdom is wrong. Most observers argue that Ford was woefully misguided, even stupid, to have issued the pardon. At a minimum, they say, he should have waited until Nixon was indicted and admitted his criminal behavior. Even better would be no mercy at all.

Not so. As both a moral and practical matter, Ford's decision to pardon Nixon served the interests of the nation. "For God's sake, enough is enough," said Senator Hugh Scott. "[Nixon's] been hung, and it doesn't seem to me that in addition, he should be drawn and quartered." Ford also saw that if Nixon were prosecuted criminally, lawyers would fight over access to his tapes and papers, drawing out the process for years. It wasn't just a matter of sparing the old president but, of greater importance, allowing the new president to get on with the business of governing.

In the few short weeks since the resignation, the Ford White House staff was already being sucked into the morass of Watergate. Just after their boss departed, some Nixon folk tried to spirit away the bulk of his papers and tapes, and Hartmann had wisely put a stop to their efforts. By necessity, however, it was now up to Ford to decide himself what should be done with the Nixon documents, and if he gave any leeway toward his predecessor, he would stand accused of favoritism. Down the road of prosecution inevitably lay more and more such complications that would preoccupy him personally, stir up both the press and Congress, and paralyze his White House. As Ford explained to congressional leaders in his phone calls that Sunday morning, a pardon was the surest way to cut the Gordian knot.

Ford also concluded that neither he nor most other Americans wanted to put Nixon in jail. If prosecutors won a conviction, he would have to intervene anyway. Why wait through the turmoil of a trial? Why not act sooner, rather than later, especially since Nixon's health had deteriorated badly? Once Ford had made up his mind that a pardon was inevitable, his conscience told him to grant it immediately. His greatest hope as president was to heal the nation, and he saw the pardon as a surgical necessity. In all of these matters, his judgment was sound; the pardon was the right thing for him to do.

It was in the execution of his decision—not the decision itself—that the new president stumbled. As his press assistant, John Hushen, said, "It was delivered to the country like Pearl Harbor." Still learning his way as a leader, Ford had done nothing to prepare the public for the most controversial, most emotionally charged act of his presidency. In fact, he had steered the press and the public in just the opposite direction. During his confirmation hearings to become vice president, Ford had been asked whether Nixon's successor would have the power to prevent a criminal investigation or prosecution of the former president. "I do not think the public would stand for it," he responded.

As far as the public was concerned, that's where the matter still stood until August 25, when Nelson Rockefeller, later selected as Ford's vice president, told *Meet the Press* that, in his view, Richard Nixon had suffered enough and should be immune to prosecution. Ford's first press conference as president came three days later, and reporter Helen Thomas of UPI asked him straightaway whether he agreed with Rockefeller. Ford said that he had "asked for prayers for guidance on this very important point." But, he added, "There have been no charges made, there has been no action taken by any jury, and until any legal process has been undertaken, I think it is unwise and untimely for me to make any commitment." Translation: I may consider a pardon someday but not now; this issue won't be on the table unless and until Nixon is indicted. While Ford had cracked open the door for eventual action, consideration of a pardon seemed months away, both to the public and to his own circle.

Privately, however, Ford was changing his mind. Two days later, he revealed to three of his intimates—Hartmann, Buchen, and Jack Marsh—that he was considering an immediate pardon. They were thunderstruck. Why had he signaled so many times just the opposite? And what should they do now? In hindsight, they have said they would have tried to talk him out of it, but his mind already seemed 99 percent made up and they knew how stubborn he tended to be when that far along. "Outwardly, nobody was wildly enthusiastic, but neither did anyone violently object," writes Hartmann. Apparently, only Haig had anticipated the possibility of an early intervention, but the record indicates that he opted out of the discussions.

If even the President's closest advisers had no inkling of what was in store, one can imagine the surprise elsewhere when Ford went on the air that Sunday morning at a time when millions of Americans were at church. TerHorst's immediate resignation as press secretary, it was widely understood, was spurred in part by the way even he was kept in the dark until thirty-six hours before the announcement, and then informed. Everyone down the line was equally taken aback. Just as I can vividly remember coming out of a restaurant in downtown Washington when word hit of Nixon's Saturday Night Massacre, I can recall careening off a back road in Virginia when our car radio reported on the pardon. His appointees, the Congress, the press, the public—all were bewildered and, in most cases, deeply angry.

There are some instances in a democracy when a political leader can uncork a surprise and win public acclaim: Ike's trip to Korea after his first election, Kennedy's appeal for putting a man on the moon, Nixon's trip to China. They all reveled in the drama of their announcements. But their news was good, and the surprise gave it a special effervescence. Ford's announcement fell into a different category. When a White House decision will be controversial or require national sacrifice, our most effective presidents have carefully laid the groundwork over a period of weeks or months so that the public is psychologically prepared to accept it.

In the most famous instance, Lincoln decided in the summer of 1862 to issue the Emancipation Proclamation but kept it locked in his desk until Union forces could win a significant victory in the field, giving him enough political capital to hold the Union together. Meanwhile, he dropped a series of public hints, including a well-publicized letter to Horace Greeley, foreshadowing his announcement. Massive Confederate casualties at Antietam gave him the moment he had been awaiting, and he finally went public with his decision in September. Even then, he waited until January 1 to sign the Proclamation, giving the country three additional months to ready itself. A man of extraordinary insight into public psychology, Lincoln was always patient, allowing issues to ripen and events to move in his direction before he moved.

In that same spirit, Franklin Roosevelt foresaw as early as 1937 that the United States would very likely be drawn into war in Europe. But he didn't issue a series of presidential decrees or seek bold initiatives because he knew the country was sleeping under a blanket of isolationist sentiment and would resist being jerked out of bed. Instead, he slowly awakened the public mind to the dangers outside and prepared it for eventual sacrifice. His critics accuse him of misleading and lying to the nation, so that the public would follow his direction, and he himself later admitted as much. But most historians rightly believe that one of FDR's greatest achievements was to arouse the country out of isolationism gradually, preparing it psychologically and militarily for a fight. When the Japanese struck, America was ready to mobilize quickly and its enormous explosion of energy soon changed the course of the war.

Had Ford been willing to follow a similar course, it wasn't difficult to think through a public strategy. For example, he could have taken an opportunity in his September press conference to say that Nixon's future was weighing heavily on him, but he had not yet decided what to do. He could then have given three principal reasons why an immediate pardon would serve the nation and two or three arguments the other way. That disclosure would have set off a national debate. No doubt, newspapers such as the *New York Times* and *Washington Post* would have severely attacked the idea and polls would have shown public sentiment running against it. But the President would have taken the lead in framing the debate, and the arguments in favor of a pardon would have become familiar, even reasonable. A significant minority, probably including some southern Democrats, would have urged him to go ahead. Vice President Rockefeller was willing to argue the case, and so would others. In that political environment, an announcement of a pardon would have still been unpopular, maybe even set off a brush fire, but certainly not the firestorm that crippled him. Ford would thus have reached the same eventual goal, but he would have taken a more circuitous path that not only would have prepared the public mind but, I believe, might have saved his presidency. Lincoln and Roosevelt would have understood well.

Unfortunately, the rush to announcement also robbed the White House of time for thinking through its public rationales for the pardon. Nowhere did Ford offer listeners the central compelling reason that he gave privately to others—that a pardon would give everyone, especially him, a chance to get on with urgent business. As Ford has since explained in open forum, problems were piled high on his desk when he became president, "but I was spending 25 percent of my time each day listening to lawyers from the White House and Justice on what I should do with Nixon's tapes and papers." Ford went into that first press conference expecting reporters to ask him mostly about troubles gripping the economy and about his upcoming summit in Vladivostok with Leonid Brezhnev. "Nine out of 10 questions were about Nixon. As I walked back to the Oval Office, I

123

thought, 'That's not fair. I should be spending 100 percent of my time worrying about the problems of 250 million people, not 25 percent of my time on the problems of one person.' I immediately asked for an investigation of the pardon."

But instead of advancing that argument—which was sound— he chose in his announcement to put forward two other, less persuasive reasons for his action: to protect Nixon's health ("serious allegations and accusations hang like a sword over our former President's head, threatening his health as he tries to reshape his life") and to head off continuing litigation, which would further polarize the country for months, even years. Worse still, Ford was not even wedded to the two rationales he had just given in his public statement. Statements were put together haphazardly. When Buchen briefed the White House press corps that the President acted out of compassion—which his speech certainly implied—Ford put out the word that Buchen had misunderstood him. In his memoirs, Ford argues specifically that the pardon "had nothing to do with any sympathy I might feel for Nixon personally or any concern I might have for the state of his health."

Such were the conflicting statements—and from a White House that no longer had its press secretary—that neither the press, the public, nor his staff had a clear sense of why the President had acted. That was fallow ground in which his critics could easily plant seeds of suspicion that a "fix" had been in place from the start. And Ford's credibility took a nosedive. He and his team, finding their way, had fallen into one of the oldest traps in political life—not taking extra time, even at the risk of a leak, to think through a dramatic initiative before springing it on the public. Had they taken just two or three more days to clarify their thinking, putting the arguments pro and con on paper, arguing them back and forth, reaching a hard consensus, they would have issued statements that were well considered, coherent, and persuasive. Instead, the pardon appeared incomprehensible, possibly corrupt, and certainly impulsive.

The saddest part of this tale is that Ford acted out of honorable motives. There is no serious evidence that the pardon was anything more than a decision for legitimate public purposes. But the failure to prepare the public and the failure to marshal the arguments behind the decision turned it into a catastrophe. Both mistakes sprang from inexperience, not malevolence. But the new President had now
124 sunk into the bog of Watergate and over the next two years would never escape its embrace.

2. CREATING THE WRONG PUBLIC NARRATIVE

One of the first jobs of a new president is to clean up messes left behind by his predecessor. Resolving the Nixon crisis had been Ford's first order of business, and now he turned to a second. But his handling of that went awry as well, and the damage to his reputation was almost as severe. In the public mind, the tales became intertwined.

As the *New York Times* noted, Ford inherited "the worst inflation in the country's peacetime history, the highest interest rates in a century, the consequent severe slump in housing, sinking and utterly demoralized securities markets, a stagnant economy with large-scale unemployment in prospect and a worsening international trade and payments position." Stagflation seemed an utterly new phenomenon. The country had experienced skyrocketing inflation before and dropping employment, but rarely both together.

At first it appeared that spiraling inflation was the chief threat to national well-being, and the Ford team was eager to tamp it down. It was soaring at 12 percent, wholesale prices had increased by 20 percent in the previous year, and the trade deficit was heading up. Wage and price controls clearly weren't the answer. They had been tried in 1971–1972 and, while they worked for a while, had turned into a disaster. In fact, the uncapping of the controls was largely responsible for the inflation that besieged Nixon in his final days and now bedeviled the new president.

Lacking policy tools to tame the beast, Ford opted for public exhortation—a series of appeals to the consumers and industry to hold down their demands. Once again, however, inexperience crippled his White House. Instead of a well-considered attempt at jawboning, the new team tried to launch a jazzy public relations effort—a volunteer citizens campaign called "Whip Inflation Now" (WIN). Ford and members of his cabinet were soon sporting WIN buttons in their lapels. They were supposed to be emblematic of the Blue Eagle insignia of the New Deal, when stores all over the country put Blue Eagle posters in their windows to demonstrate support for Roosevelt's National Recovery Administration.

On October 15—only five weeks after the pardon—Ford flew to Kansas City to pitch his WIN campaign to the Future Farmers of America. Ron Nessen, the new press secretary who had replaced Jerry terHorst, called the television networks to request that they 125 cover the speech live during prime time. When they were reluctant, Nessen insisted and promised Ford would make plenty of news. The strong arm tactics worked—or at least that's what the White House thought—because the networks agreed to carry him live.

The speech, however, was a dud, a parody of a fireside chat. There were no new policy initiatives and no apparent reason why the President should be addressing the nation in prime time. Critics dubbed it the "clean-your-plate speech" because his call to action included an unforgettable admonition: "Take all you want, but eat all you take. The first words I can remember in my dad's house were very simple but very direct: Clean up your plate before you get up from the table. And that is still pretty good advice." Where was the news we were promised, the networks screamed. They were so furious with Nessen and the new White House that Walter Cronkite canceled an interview with the President in protest and the networks became resistant to putting him on prime time again. Political cartoonists had a field day, and the public shrugged off the WIN buttons.

Worse trouble soon struck. Later in October, the President went before Congress with a series of proposals for economic action, including a temporary tax surcharge of 5 percent. Continuing to lament inflation, a Republican president was asking for a *tax increase* to slow down demand. A Republican pushing for a tax increase was bad enough. But in a matter of just a few weeks, the economy tipped in just the opposite direction—it went into a tailspin. Suddenly, it was no longer inflation that scared the White House but recession— the worst since the Great Depression.

By November, the administration had shifted gears, so that the WIN program was abandoned and the President began to call for *tax cuts!* To the public, the reason why conditions changed so rapidly— that inflation and high interest rates had apparently thrown the economy into a downturn—did not matter. What mattered was that their new president didn't seem to know what he was doing: he was flip-flopping. One month he was warning against inflation and trying to slow the economy with tax increases, the next month he threw away his WIN button and was trying to stimulate growth with tax cuts. Public confidence was slipping fast.

Inevitably, his policy troubles brought on press troubles, too. One of the worst habits in the press is to build up a fresh public figure and then tear him down. It's the "King of the Rock" phenomenon that presidential scholar James MacGregor Burns has described in writing about the challenges of political leadership. Until he spared Nixon, Ford enjoyed an outburst of media admiration. But after the pardon and the WIN campaign, the press turned on him

126

with ridicule that was severe and merciless. Now he was the man who played too many football games without his helmet, the president who bumped his head when he turned to wave from his helicopter.

Those images of bumbling shadowed Ford for the duration of his presidency. Throughout 1975, the press seized upon every verbal or physical miscue and magnified it beyond all bounds. A scene from Ford's arrival in Japan as he walked down the steps from Air Force One and stumbled at the bottom was shown over and over. In a single news broadcast, one network showed it twelve times! The fact that an aide left behind Ford's tuxedo and the President showed up at a dinner in Tokyo with trousers two inches too short caused merriment as well, as did his occasional falls on the ski slopes of Colorado. In truth, Ford was a heck of a lot smarter than nearly all of the journalists who covered him—he was a good student at both Michigan and the Yale Law School—and could ski circles around most of them. But the story line was set and nothing that Ron Nessen or anyone else might do could change it.

We tried. In early 1976, after watching Ford prepare the federal budget, some of us came up with a public relations idea. Presidents in recent years had been visibly unfamiliar with the intricacies of their own budgets; there were just too many curlicues buried away. Unveiling a new budget to the press corps, a president would thus read a statement and hurry away, leaving his budget director and treasury secretary to answer questions. Not since Truman had a president remained at the podium, fielding hard ones. Since Truman, the budget had grown roughly eight times in size, not to mention complexity.

In budget preparations, it was obvious that Ford, from his long years on House Appropriations, knew the contours as well as any man alive. So we recommended that he surprise the press by doing the budget briefing by himself. He readily accepted the challenge, and at a briefing held at the State Department, held forth for an hour with élan. I would swear that was the first time reporters understood that Ford was a bright man—much brighter than they imagined— and for a while, they seemed to treat him with respect. Still, it wasn't enough to change the basic impression of Ford that had formed early in his presidency.

Given the fact that Ford became steadily better in the Oval Office and that the results of his economic and diplomatic efforts were especially good in his final year, the conclusion is inescapable: he could never fully dig himself out of the hole he created during his

127

early months. That points to a larger truth about presidential leadership. Ever since the New Deal, White House advisers have generally assumed that an incoming president should emulate FDR, overwhelming Congress and spellbinding the country with a flurry of legislative proposals during the First Hundred Days. But as we have now learned from a series of presidents, the importance of the First Hundred Days is not in how many legislative achievements or how much razzle-dazzle a new White House can produce. Jimmy Carter would send forth a blizzard of legislative proposals and new regulations, but neither the press nor the public could make sense of his priorities. The effort backfired. By contrast, as we shall see, Ronald Reagan had a limited, more focused agenda that, combined with other factors, built a much stronger foundation for his presidency.

Recent history suggests that the true significance of the First Hundred Days is this: they are the most precious time in the life of a president to define who he is and what he is seeking to achieve through his leadership. In those fourteen weeks, more than any other time in his presidency, he sets the stage for his entire stewardship. Before he reaches the White House, both the public and the press have been able to judge him only as an aspiring politician. They judge him on his past. Once he takes the oath, they must take his measure afresh—what is he actually like as president? They judge him on what he will be like in their future. That assessment can only begin after he raises his right hand and formally assumes the mantle of leadership. The public's judgment forms in a matter of weeks and, once formed, soon calcifies. It's a matter of public psychology.

In effect, both the press and the public begin writing a *narrative* in their minds about a new president: the journey he is undertaking, his character, and the roles of other characters around him in the story. It is in the nature of the press and of the public to think of reality as a series of unfolding stories. We collect enormous amounts of information early on, try to sort through it and form opinions that give shape and meaning to the narrative. By the end of the First Hundred Days, the story of a new president takes shape in the public mind and it tends to remain in that same shape for a long time thereafter. Very rarely is he able to reinvent himself later.

In the case of Jerry Ford, the shock over the pardon and the flip-flops of those opening months not only dissipated the goodwill of his first hours in office, but also created a public narrative that plagued him for the remainder of his presidency. The press repeatedly described him as a nice man who seemed in over his head, a postscript to Nixon, a caretaker until America elected a real president. His political opponents repeated those themes. The public bought into them, and Ford became trapped by them.

No matter how effective he might become in office—and the record shows a substantial improvement—a single verbal slip would revive old feelings. Ford discovered that with a vengeance more than two years into his presidency when he engaged in a presidential debate with Jimmy Carter in the fall of 1976. That was the famous moment when, asked about Poland, Ford declared that it was a free nation not under the domination of the Soviet Union. His questioner, Max Frankel of the *New York Times,* was so surprised that he reasked the question, giving the President a chance to correct himself, but Ford stubbornly stuck to his answer. He explained afterward that he wasn't rattled. Rather, he was trying to send a signal to the Soviets not to regard Poland as a permanent colony.

His explanation didn't matter. It was a campaign disaster—*Time* deemed it "the blooper heard round the world." At first, the public didn't notice and initial polls showed people thought Ford had won the debate. But the press was apoplectic and reported ad nauseam that poor old Jerry Ford couldn't keep his facts straight and in his latest blunder had liberated Poland. Instantly, the early narrative about Ford sprang back to life.

As Americans listened to press reports, they began changing their minds. The morning after the debate, our hearts sank at the White House as Bob Teeter, a chief strategist, reported that, hour by hour, his private polls showed growing numbers thought Ford had blown it. By noon, the public reversal was complete: Jimmy Carter was seen as the debate winner, enhancing his claim that he was ready to be president. If the public had assumed all along that Ford was an authority on foreign policy, his mistake would have been brushed aside, but given his vulnerability, it turned into a huge whopper. His campaign momentum slowed noticeably and when he fell just short of catching Carter at the wire, some thought that mistake was the difference.

In truth, what cost him a chance to serve in his own right were the mistakes of his First Hundred Days, starting with the pardon and extending beyond. At a time when he was least prepared to lead, he made a series of missteps—innocent in nature—that he would not have made later. But coming when they did, they helped to create a public narrative about his presidency that never fundamentally 129 changed. Those opening days are indeed precious to leadership.

3. OVERREACTING TO NIXON

A few days before Gerald Ford left office, a group of his advisers threw a good-bye celebration for Dick Cheney, his widely admired chief of staff. Among the gifts that night was a gnarled bicycle tire, rim twisted, its spokes broken and bent. Cheney instantly understood and we enjoyed a good laugh.

Our thoughts raced back to the early days of the administration. At the start, Ford's Old Gang from Capitol Hill didn't want anybody to run the White House with a firm hand. It was too Nixonian. Ford writes in his memoirs, "I did not want to have a powerful chief of staff. Wilson had his Colonel House, Eisenhower his Sherman Adams, Nixon his Haldeman, and I was aware of the trouble those top assistants had caused my predecessors. I was determined to be my own chief of staff." Memories of Haldeman were particularly bitter among Ford's advisers like Hartmann. They detested everything about Nixon, starting with Haldeman, whom they blamed for much of Watergate.

To sweep the place clean, the Ford team jettisoned the hierarchical staffing arrangement of the Nixon and Eisenhower days and put in its place something earlier Democratic White Houses had employed: a "spokes of the wheel" system. The idea was that the president would be at the center of action and roughly a dozen advisers would have individual access to him. He would be the hub, they the spokes. Ford would be his own chief of staff.

By Ford's admission, it was a horrible failure. As a new president, especially one with so little time to prepare, he had to scramble just to get on top of major issues and had no time to run down the details or to coordinate everyone around him. And no one else was in charge, either. As a result, advisers were stepping all over each other, uncertain what their marching orders were, playing by the seat of their pants. Conflict and confusion reigned. If a strong chief of staff had been in place from the start, the pardon decision would surely have been better executed.

Six weeks after taking office, Ford summoned Rumsfeld from Europe, asking him to assume the responsibilities of a chief of staff—but without the title or a portfolio of power. Rumsfeld at first demurred, saying he didn't think anyone could do the job as long as the spokes-in-the-wheel existed. "It projects the openness you want. In practice, however, it won't work," he said. "I know you don't want a Haldeman-type chief of staff, but someone has to fill that role, and unless I can have that authority, I won't be able to serve you effectively."

Ford persuaded Rumsfeld that he would have sufficient power and Rumsfeld signed up, but, like so many presidents, Ford was not yet ready to abandon his original instincts. He still didn't want a new Haldeman, and was never willing to give Rumsfeld enough authority to run the staff. A new organizational chart, released in December 1975, showed nine advisers reporting directly to the President, not through the chief of staff. Rumsfeld was "first among equals," coordinating but not running. The difference may sound small, but in practice in a large, complex organization it is immense. There were still too many spokes. At a crucial moment, Ford also overruled Rumsfeld by allowing Vice President Rockefeller to take control of the domestic policy operations, a continuing source of friction between the two men. The only operations over which the chief of staff had direct control were scheduling, the staff secretariat, and personnel.

An excellent administrator, Rumsfeld could have converted the Ford White House into a highly professional operation, but with one hand tied behind his back, he never pulled it off. A year later, when Rumsfeld was named secretary of defense and Cheney moved up, the problem of White House management still wasn't fixed.

I officially rejoined the staff in December of 1975 and became an instant fan of Dick Cheney. While our paths had crossed in college days and earlier in government, I knew him mostly by reputation. He had been a deputy to Rumsfeld at two agencies before joining him at the White House. Cheney was a first-class talent, one of the best public servants of recent years and, over time, a man who became qualified to serve as president in his own right.

With no more authority than Rumsfeld had and still in his early thirties, however, Dick faced a difficult struggle in convincing elements of the Ford staff and the cabinet departments to follow his directions. Four of Ford's intimates, Jack Marsh, Brent Scowcroft, Jim Cannon, and Bill Seidman, were constructive peacemakers, but not many others. Dick organized an inside team of about a half-dozen aggressive, upper-level managers to help him—among them Jerry Jones, Jim Connor, Jim Cavanaugh, Mike Duval, Terry O'Donnell, Red Cavaney, and me. Most of us would gather each night to talk and watch the news in Dick's office. Joining us was Alan Greenspan, then head of the Council of Economic Advisers and a canny student of politics. Alan was suffering from a bad back and would frequently

131

watch the news lying down on Cheney's rug. That never seemed to stop him from dishing out advice or wisecracks. After the shows ended, most of us—not Greenspan—would camp out in Jerry Jones's small, interior office across the hall for two hours or more of intense planning and coordination for the next day. Those evening sessions gradually became the nerve center of the Ford White House.

Jerry Ford had a mind of his own about what he wanted—and, as president, he was certainly entitled—but I wished he would give Cheney the power of a full chief of staff. Heading toward a crucial State of the Union address in January 1976—the last opportunity to speak to a national audience before a bruising Republican primary season—the President ordered up a draft from Hartmann. It came in as a laundry list of dreary, warmed-over legislative proposals for the coming year. To Cheney & Co., the draft fell desperately short of what we wanted: a thematic and visionary address vigorously projecting the direction the country should take for the remainder of the decade. That speech, we hoped, would rocket Ford toward nomination and election. Dick talked privately with the President and persuaded him to allow our camp to prepare an alternative draft. Greenspan and I were tapped to write it, receiving plenty of help from others.

One night shortly before the State of the Union, Ford assembled some of us to consider the opposing drafts. After we debated, Ford asked each of us to state a personal preference: did we want him to go with the Hartmann draft or the alternative? As I recall, he went slowly around the room and, to a person, everyone preferred the alternative except two men, Hartmann and the President. The vote was about 15 to 2. The President said he wanted to think about it some more, thanked us, and we moved out. In the end, of course, he gave the Hartmann speech, adopting only bits of ours. Hartmann was reminded of a vote Lincoln once took among his cabinet. Everyone voted no except Lincoln. "The ayes have it," he announced.

There were times when some of us were driven to distraction by the rivalries and uncertainties of those days. As a graduate of the Haldeman school, I longed for an operational system in which someone had a grip on the administrative reins. Why would the President give his chief of staff responsibility for running things but not the authority? How else could one ever combat the insurgency arising in the West—the campaign of Ronald Reagan that Ford later admitted he never took seriously enough?

For me, frustrations boiled over most often in the speechwriting process. In my experience in the Nixon White House, the writing team would crank up a draft based on guidance from the President or his policy advisers. Frequently, Kissinger's national security team would even provide a first cut at a foreign policy address, and it would always be of high caliber. After the writing shop reworked it, adding texture and sparkle as best we could, the draft would be circulated to key policy and political players, and their comments would then be incorporated into successive versions. Finally, the speech would be ready to go forward to Nixon—always in his overnight reading, so that he could dictate changes or order a new direction. If the speech were sufficiently important, he would pick up a pen and rewrite large sections on his yellow legal pads. Back and forth a speech might go, sometimes stretching through a dozen drafts until it was polished. I am not saying we produced poetry, but the process was tightly disciplined, hours of time were devoted to finding the right nuance, and, at the end, his speeches had both depth and a long shelf life. That was the system to which I had become accustomed—and which I respected.

Imagine the surprise when I joined the Ford staff and was invited to attend the weekly meetings the speechwriters had with him in the Oval Office. The fact that they had regular, face-to-face conversations was, to be sure, a great improvement over the Nixon process, but the meetings themselves must have been a special form of hell for Jerry Ford. They began as Hartmann or one of the full-time writers would remind the President of an appearance he had five days hence with, say, the American Legion. The writers would then give Ford a draft they had prepared and pass them out to the other ten or twelve people in the room.

Many of us, starting with the man who was to deliver the speech, had never seen any draft before. Collectively, we would have a moment of silence while everyone read page one. Ford would then ask for comments on that page, talk them over, and order up amendments. Page two: another pause for reading, more discussion, more changes scratched in. Page three, etc. What was going on here? I asked myself. Why hadn't anyone shown us the speech and collected our comments before we ever sat down? Without knowing where the whole speech was heading or how it hung together, how could we offer constructive comments on page two or three about logic and structure? Were we only there to suggest stylistic changes and point out typos? Moreover, the meetings could drag on for more than two hours, chewing up the most precious asset a president has: time. Ford was too good-natured to put a stop to things, and, at first,

133

neither Cheney nor anyone else had the muscle to do it for him. It was so frustrating that I eventually did something I had never done before: asked to be excused from a meeting with the President of the United States. What they were doing to the President was unbearable.

Yet even that was trifling compared to the damage of another day. Under our crazy system, a cabinet officer could meet with the President privately about a policy matter without anyone from the White House staff sitting in. After all, Ford was still the center of the wheel—his own chief of staff. John Dunlop, a highly regarded labor secretary, anxiously sought out Ford one day in 1976 to seek his support for a common situs picketing bill intended to resolve a long-standing dispute between management and labor over secondary boycotts. Seeking a resolution was an extremely delicate economic question, one that required a great deal of thought by others in the cabinet and by the White House staff before a presidential decision. And it was also politically explosive, especially as it appeared that the powerful head of the AFL-CIO's Building and Construction Trades Department, Robert Georgine, might be persuaded to support Ford in the 1976 general elections. In short, Labor Secretary Dunlop should have had a chance to make his case—but only in the presence of a chief of staff and after a great deal of legwork. Nonetheless, under "spokes of the wheel" government, the President agreed to see him alone and without benefit of advance deliberation. It was an invitation to disaster—and that's exactly what happened.

Dunlop walked out of his tête-à-tête believing he had Ford's unconditional support for a common situs bill. Ford thought he had made it conditional on management agreeing to the bill. After Dunlop announced Ford's support, Congress passed the bill but, in a brewing storm, management suddenly opposed the measure. Some 700,000 cards and letters flooded the White House from local builders, mostly in fierce opposition. No other presidential action—not even the pardon—stimulated as much mail. The rest of the cabinet urged the President to veto the measure on policy grounds and, after soul-searching, he did. Having signaled Dunlop and labor that he would support the measure, he had reversed himself. It was the right call, but it came at an enormous price. Dunlop resigned and Georgine dropped his political support. There could no longer be any doubt that our system was broken.

134   It was Cheney who gradually won the growing confidence of the President and secured more power over the organization of the government. With Ronald Reagan breathing fire at him in the Re-

publican primaries, Ford realized that he had to tighten up White House operations if he was to survive politically. By the summer of 1976, Cheney eventually became a chief of staff in the classic Republican mold and Ford at last had a White House that was hitting on all cylinders. As he recruited campaign veterans like Stuart Spencer and Bob Teeter, along with media strategists Doug Bailey and John Deardourff, Ford was ready to run the race of his life—and he almost pulled off a Harry Truman upset. What helped him more than any of the Old Guard would admit was letting Dick Cheney run the place in a neo-Haldeman style—absent the clicking of heels and abuses of power.

To me, there were two central lessons for leadership here.

The most obvious is the importance of a well-run, disciplined organization. Eisenhower was right: it won't guarantee success, but its absence can ruin you. Ford learned that too late, and so did Clinton, as we shall see. Ford had strong reasons to take the approach he did. Roger B. Porter pointed out later, "The principal virtue of the spokes-of-the-wheel concept is that it projected an aura of openness and accessibility, a perception that was essential to Ford's desire to establish the distinctive characteristics of his administration. Moreover, it also emphasized the president's personal role in assuming control of the executive branch."

Historical experience makes clear, however, that one of the first requirements of a president is to assert control over his own household. The White House has become a sprawling political organization—even with a 10 percent cut under Ford, there were 485 people on his staff—and, typically, the top people compete hungrily over turf, policy, and prestige. Somebody must crack the whip and monitor operations closely, and it can't be the president—he is too busy struggling with a messy outside world. That's why he must invest a chief of staff with full authority. Indeed, the decision of who should serve as chief of staff and what skills he or she should bring to the job turns out to be as important to a president as his selection of vice president.

As Cheney showed toward the end of the Ford presidency, an effective chief of staff need not be a second Haldeman. It's the president who sets the tone. Had Nixon not demanded seclusion and secrecy, Haldeman would never have become a Teutonic chief himself. As for openness and accessibility, which are also important, a president with a strong chief can still achieve those goals by throwing open the doors for policy discussions. In his economic policy-making, as Porter points out, Ford did just that with considerable

135

success. His Economic Policy Board, which had Secretary Simon as chair and Bill Seidman of the White House staff as vice chair, ensured that Ford received economic advice from a wide array of sources—a "multiple advocacy process," as it was called. The EPB held 520 meetings at the cabinet level—an average of almost five a week. By increasing the cabinet's authority and diminishing that of the White House staff, it also began reversing a trend that had grown dangerous under Nixon. There is nothing inconsistent between that approach in policy-making and a strong chief of staff. They fit together.

The other lesson from Ford's struggles over management is how tempting it is for a president to overreact to the mistakes of his immediate predecessor. It is essential, of course, to learn from the past and make course corrections. George W. Bush, for instance, must put in place safeguards against the abuses of the Clinton years. But it is equally important that he not throw out what worked. For Bush to abandon wholesale Clinton's economic management would be foolish.

As a Nixon alumnus, I was no doubt biased, but I felt that some leaders of the Ford team made a serious error in trying to eradicate everything associated with Nixon, regardless of merit. The mention that Nixon approached his scheduling in a certain way meant that Ford must do it differently. If papers only went to Nixon after extensive review by staff, papers must flow to Ford without inhibition. If anyone worked for Nixon, he could not be loyal now. Ford himself didn't agree with all this; he knew that some Nixonites were trying to serve him well and kept them on board.

In the early months, however, it was as if the new Ford appointees were sacking an enemy city as they demolished everything that Nixon had built—every structure and practice. No one seemed ready to make distinctions and wise government usually comes down to just that: distinctions. In my judgment, Ford would have had a more successful beginning if some of his advisers had kept their perspective—and kept the best of Nixon, even as they rightly threw out the worst.

A political leader, then, must be informed by history—it is essential to know how people have chosen directions in the past—but it is equally important not to become a hostage to history. The Ford White House was not unique in overreacting to the past and paying a price. Jimmy Carter's White House would overreact to the strong staffing system of Nixon, and it, too, would be weakened for months on end by internal disorder and discord. George Bush was so of-

136

fended personally by what he considered the overscripting of Ronald Reagan by his staff that he refused for a long while to accept even modest stage coaching—and his public appearances wound up as herky-jerky affairs that hurt him. "The use of history can stimulate imagination: Seeing the past can help one envision alternative futures," Richard Neustadt and Ernest May remind us in their classic book, *Thinking in Time*. But, as they hasten to add, one must learn to apply the lessons of history within one's own political context.

By the summer of 1976, the Ford White House had finally adopted structures and practices that bore a striking resemblance to the best of the Nixon and Eisenhower years. Dick Cheney was there as a strong chief of staff, atop a pyramidal system—just as Sherman Adams and Bob Haldeman had been in their heydays. The whole system was humming again. That's why Dick smiled the night we presented him with a gnarled bicycle tire, its rim twisted, its spokes bent and broken.

Why His Stature Grows

If that were all of the Jerry Ford story, his presidency would have long ago faded from mind. He would be seen as a footnote, a man who filled an interregnum. But, in fact, his stature has been growing in recent years as longtime political reporters and historians recall him now with warmth and nostalgia. It's a relief for me personally to focus at last on why I came to admire him.

After the stumbles in those early months, his leadership matured and took hold. Over the course of the presidency, he tamped down the flames from all three fires he had inherited: Watergate, stagflation, and the war. While millions never forgave him for the pardon, his integrity began to restore public trust in government. The men and women he appointed to the cabinet did as much as the White House itself to repair the breach. He also worked with Congress to put in place new safeguards against governmental abuses, including measures to regulate campaigns and to monitor the CIA. Much remained to be done, but Ford had made a start.

On the economic front, he began moving the country slowly toward greater independence from Middle East oil producers—though the bulk of the work was left to Carter—and his string of vetoes helped to hold down fiscal deficits. Inflation had dropped from 11 percent in 1974 to 5.8 percent by 1976 and 4 million jobs had been added since the depth of the recession.

137

He was far less successful in protecting South Vietnam from the North, but it is hard to blame Ford for the fiasco there. By the time he took over, the peace of 1973 was already imperiled and there was no will left in the United States to prop up the South again. When the Saigon forces began to crumble against the pressure from North Vietnamese troops, Congress refused Ford's request to provide transitional assistance to the South and Saigon's defenses were soon overrun. Even if Congress had come to financial rescue, it is doubtful that the South Vietnamese government could have survived. The war was lost. What Ford could and did do was to offer conditional clemency to the fifty thousand Americans who had ducked or run from the war. His amnesty did not go as far as they would have liked—nor was it as generous as the pardon he gave Nixon—but it helped to end the agony. The fire at home at last began to die.

The rest of his record is mixed. Because he never had the normal preparations for the presidency, he didn't have a mandate or an agenda. Many policy decisions were buffeted by cross pressures from a revived Democratic Congress and conservative Republicans gathering behind the Reagan banner. With the Republican Right in full cry against Kissinger, historians say Ford allowed détente to lose some of its momentum. They have a point. Ford, however, deserves more credit than he gets for the Helsinki agreement he negotiated with Leonid Brezhnev in his first summit conference. Helsinki was the first serious crack in the Iron Curtain. It put Soviet policy in Eastern Europe on a new, more liberal course that became irreversible in the decade that followed. The Cold War might not have ended as it did had not Ford and Kissinger worked well together.

While he had not achieved all he hoped, Ford could still be proud. In December 1974, he told a business audience, "Leadership, in my opinion, is based on results. If you have the right kind of people giving you advice, the odds are that you'll make good decisions. If you make good decisions, you'll get results. And leadership is the product of results." Two years later, he had some significant notches on his belt.

But the most lasting impressions from Ford rest not in his accomplishments. Rather they are in the quality of the man himself and the people he gathered around him. As critic Richard Reeves has argued, we have seen so much deterioration in our politics since the mid-1970s that, in retrospect, Jerry Ford's approach to governance deserves fresh attention. Along with Truman and Eisenhower, Ford stands among the presidents of highest character to have served in modern times. He may not have moved mountains in his twenty-

138

nine months, but he upheld standards that people are thirsting to see again.

"Truth Is the Glue"

The most important lesson Jerry Ford taught me is that trust is still the coin of the realm in politics.

In 1973, when the Senate was considering his nomination to become vice president, Ford's opening statement captured the essence of his philosophy. Referring to his "good friends in the Congress," it went on, "I have never misled them when they might have wanted to hear something gentler than the truth. Truth is the glue that holds government together, and not only government but civilization itself." In classic Ford fashion, he also stumbled a bit, misreading the line to say, "Truth is the glue on the bond that holds government together." While destroying the sound bite, he managed to preserve the phrase "Truth is the glue," and that remains the best memory of his presidency.

His friends in Congress came from both parties and they had learned that however deep the disagreements, they could trust him. "You could take his word to the bank," as the old saying went. Even his old nemesis LBJ, after many disparaging remarks behind closed doors, told Ford, "You and I have had a lot of head-to-head confrontations, but I never doubted your integrity."

Trust on the other side of the political aisle was, in fact, what propelled him into the presidency. Biographer and adviser James Cannon points out that Nixon had first wanted the vice presidency to be filled by John Connally, the former Texas governor who had just switched parties to become a Republican. Democratic and Republican leaders alike told Nixon that Connally would not be confirmed. Anxious to move quickly, Nixon on the afternoon of Agnew's resignation invited in the top Democratic leaders, Senate Majority Leader Mike Mansfield and House Speaker Carl Albert.

Both men thought Nixon would soon be forced out and they were thus selecting the next president. Nixon thought there was at least a 50 percent chance of that, too. So, who should it be? Albert suggested only one man, Jerry Ford, and Mansfield seconded the idea. "We gave Nixon no choice but Ford," said Albert later. "Congress made Jerry Ford President." Qualities of leadership, experience, character—that's what counted to his peers on Capitol Hill.

139

In today's politics, we tend to focus almost exclusively upon a president's image and polls as a measure of his effectiveness. There is no doubt that public approval is important to a president. While necessary, however, it is not sufficient. As Richard Neustadt instructed, presidential power also rests upon a good personal reputation among his colleagues in the political system. Jerry Ford was Bill Clinton's opposite: he lacked the skills to stir public support, but inside Washington his integrity served him well.

In my experience over the past thirty years, every White House—save one—has on occasion willfully misled or lied to the press. Some have done it promiscuously. The lies haven't always come from the president himself, but there has always been at least one senior aide, serving at his pleasure, who has knowingly provided false information. A White House press secretary these days must often play investigative reporter, figuring out whether a colleague is peddling a false story inside. Unless the spokesperson carefully gains independent verification, she or he can be used as a vehicle to pass it on. When the truth outs, the press secretary is dead.

The exception to the rule was, of course, the Ford White House. More than one of our modern presidents has been a congenital liar; Jerry Ford was a congenital truth-teller. And his staff took their cues from him. While internecine war often broke out among us, we were still candid with each other and with the public. I cannot remember a single conversation in which Ford's aides connived to put together a statement for him or the press secretary that would intentionally mislead. It just didn't occur to people. Of course we engaged in puffery, but never the blatant distortions that have become routine in recent years.

His philosophy animated his policy decisions, too—and influenced me in a way that later got me in hot water. As a conservative on fiscal policies, Ford was appalled by federal deficits and was also eager to lighten tax burdens. But he wasn't willing to push for across-the-board tax cuts because he worried they would increase the deficits. To solve the problem, Ford proposed in October 1975 a "one-for-one" approach: he asked Congress to reduce taxes by one dollar for each dollar it also agreed to cut in anticipated spending (overall a reduction of $28 billion in complementary cuts). Democrats turned him down, but he convinced me that his approach was right. In effect, he was saying no dessert until you eat your spinach. It was a straightforward, midwestern kind of answer. Later on, when I signed aboard with the Reagan administration, I was still a believer in the Ford approach. That view made me a bête noire of supply-side

140

conservatives who said—with justification—that I wasn't fully on board with their philosophy.

A Well-Centered Man

Unlike Richard Nixon, it was apparent from the start that Jerry Ford didn't need to be president to be happy with his life's arc. He wanted to be a leader in the House, and that was enough. After the Goldwater debacle of 1964, a group of Young Turks in the House plotted the overthrow of GOP minority leader Charlie Halleck and put Ford in his place. There he waited patiently for a GOP takeover of the House. In 1972, he hoped that a Nixon landslide would produce it, but, alas, Democrats clung to their majority. Disappointed and now fifty-nine years old, Ford promised his wife, Betty, that he would retire from politics altogether before the 1976 campaign—a vow that she ardently welcomed.

Only when the presidency fell in his lap did Ford decide to seek the office on his own, but even then he didn't need it to satisfy his inner soul. That, I have learned, is a major virtue in a president. It is one that Ford shared with Truman, Eisenhower, and Reagan—and it made all of them better leaders. Ambition is healthy in a president, but when it turns into a hunger that can only be sated by winning office, it becomes destructive. Johnson, Nixon, and Clinton needed to win too much, and that gnawing anxiety drove them to extremes that sucked the dignity out of their presidencies.

One could see the difference in Ford the moment he took office. Theretofore, the chairs around the table in the cabinet room were the same size except for the president's. Its back was about two inches higher. At the very first cabinet meeting, I noticed that Ford's chair was now the same size as the rest. Tiny signals tell the whole government what kind of man is now at the helm.

The ripple effects were immense. Because he was comfortable with himself, Ford was comfortable having men and women around him who might be brighter or more talented in their area and might also be outspoken in public. That didn't matter to him as long as they could perform well. Not that he was relinquishing power over final decisions or would stand for insolence. He decided to fire one of the brightest lights in Washington, Defense Secretary James Schlesinger, for alleged insubordination and because he didn't like Jim's lectures on how to handle Congress. As a twenty-five-year veteran of the House, he didn't think he needed that.

141

But he had a deep streak of humility. In his confirmation hearings to become vice president, he said straightaway that he was "a Ford, not a Lincoln." As president, he wasn't troubled by the stardom of a Henry Kissinger, as Nixon had been. He happily supported Henry, even to the point of suffering erosion among conservatives. Bill Simon, as treasury secretary, was also a hard-hitting, take-charge kind of cabinet member whose pronouncements would ultimately have rankled the Nixon staff but were quietly accepted by Ford. That embrace paid rich dividends: Simon not only did a fine job but also shored up Ford's support on Wall Street and among some conservatives.

Within months of taking office, Ford named new secretaries to seven of the eleven cabinet departments. By the time he was through, he had assembled the finest cabinet in the past thirty years. Among its members were Kissinger at State, Simon at Treasury, Rumsfeld at Defense, Ed Levi at Justice, Jim Lynn and Paul O'Neill at the Office of Management and Budget, George Bush at the CIA, William Coleman at Transportation, Carla Hills at HUD, Elliot Richardson at Commerce, and David Mathews at HEW. And under his wings at the White House, he had Cheney growing into a full chief of staff, Brent Scowcroft as national security adviser, Alan Greenspan as chief economist, along with Bill Seidman, Jack Marsh, and Jim Cannon as domestic advisers. They all served him well and over the course of their careers have earned national reputations. To this day, they also remain loyal fans. Not one has written a mean book about him, a record matched only by the loyalty of Lyndon Johnson's team.

Ford also took advice from any quarter, as long as it was helpful. Typically, the White House photographer is seen and never heard. Not David Kennerly, a wisecracking young photo ace from *Time* magazine with a good eye for politics. Ford had taken a shine to him while he was vice president and upon entering the White House asked him to join up. It was an auspicious choice: Kennerly not only produced some of the best White House pictures in years but became a confidant who cut through the timid advice often given a president. David had been on assignment in Vietnam, seen its harsh face, and wanted the war to end. He put it on the line to Ford. The President also loved David's irreverent humor along with that of two others who helped out with speeches, Don Penny and Bob Orben. Those three men helped Ford to remain centered.

142

Ford's goodwill did not save him from personnel mistakes. Upon taking office, he made a daring choice of Nelson Rockefeller to become vice president, knowing that the Right would be displeased. Rocky served him faithfully and never upstaged him, but in the heat of the 1976 primaries against Reagan, Ford caved in to conservatives, dumping Rockefeller from the 1976 ticket. The former New York governor never flinched and worked to deliver New York and other moderate delegates to Ford at the convention. Ford later admitted it was "the biggest political mistake of my life" and "one of the few cowardly things I did." Along with that headline in the *Daily News*, it also helped to cost him New York in the general election (lost by 829,000 votes). The shabby treatment of Rockefeller recalled an incident in the Eisenhower campaign of 1952, when a fear of Joe McCarthy prompted Ike to drop from a speech in Wisconsin some flattering words about his old mentor, George Marshall. In later years, Ike cringed at the memory of how he had treated one of the best men in his life. That's how Ford felt about his treatment of Rocky. In both cases, their mistakes marred but did not erase otherwise high standards of public service.

One measure of Ford's character was in his friendships across the spectrum. Hearing about Nixon's enemies list that John Dean had compiled, Ford had remarked that anybody who couldn't keep his enemies in his head had too many enemies. The interesting point is that Ford left public office with an even larger reservoir of goodwill—something that infrequently happens. Tip O'Neill, as partisan a Democrat as Ford was a Republican, regarded him as a friend until he died. Among recent presidents, only Ford has returned every year since he left office for a reunion of his old team in Washington, and, to this day, every cabinet officer and staff member who can make it is there. So are some reporters from days gone by.

Historian Michael P. Riccards argues that Ford was too nice to be a strong president. "Throughout his career, Ford conveyed a sense of personal openness and honesty, exactly the traits the successor to Nixon needed." But after reviewing his difficulties in cracking heads and pushing an agenda forward, Riccards adds, "Trained in the passive ways of Congress with its emphasis on debate and consensus, Ford at times did not provide the type of tough leadership that good presidents must exhibit." The point is well taken. If he had been elected in his own right in 1976, I expect he would have imposed more discipline upon his staff and cabinet. Even so, and especially with the passage of time, Ford's straightforward ways and his humanity seem more appealing than ever.

143

His Port in the Storm

A year after Ford took office, correspondent Morley Safer of *60 Minutes* sat down with the First Lady of the United States for an interview. Where did she stand on ERA? Solidly for it, she said. What about legalized abortion? For that, too. Had her children ever experimented with anything like marijuana? Probably had. After all, it was as common as beer and if she were young again, she would try it herself. Did she condemn premarital sex? Actually, it probably decreases the divorce rate. What about your own children? "Wouldn't be a bit surprised" if eighteen-year-old Susan had had an affair. "I think she's a perfectly normal human being, like all young girls; if she wanted to continue it, I would certainly counsel and advise her on the subject. And I'd want to know pretty much about the young man."

That Monday, all hell broke loose. In New Hampshire, where Ford would soon be in a tough primary, the conservative flagship, the *Manchester Union-Leader,* called the First Lady "a disgrace to the White House." President Ford said when he heard it, "I thought I'd lost 10 million votes. . . . When I read it in the paper the next morning, I raised it to 20 million." But a short time later, the public rallied to her side as people saluted her candor. After hearing the interview himself, Don Rumsfeld told Ford that it would earn him 30 million votes, which the Harris polls confirmed. Later on, showing her own humor, Mrs. Ford sent Safer a picture with an inscription, "Dear Morley, if there are any questions you forgot to ask—I'm grateful."

That was quintessential Betty Ford, a woman who insisted upon being herself as First Lady—and wound up as one of her husband's prized assets. An editorialist gave her the title "An Honest Woman." On staff, one didn't see much of Mrs. Ford (that's what most of us called her) because she stayed out of politics and out of the West Wing. But there was no doubt she struck a balance in her life that preserved her independence while advancing her husband's interests. In her youth, she had trained as a dancer and was mentored by Martha Graham. Yet, in marriage, she quietly shifted direction, staying home and raising children. Ford was an inveterate traveler as a congressman, so that many a night passed with him on the road and her left at home. If she complained, the record doesn't show it. Yet she never gave up her gaiety. At the White House, her lightheartedness carried her onto the set of *The Mary Tyler Moore Show* and she bought her own CB radio, very popular at the time, so she could talk

144

to truckers around the country. They gave her a radio name that stuck, "First Mama."

Even more than in the 1960s, the women's rights movement caught fire in the 1970s. Women began to move from the home to the workforce in the greatest numbers in history, and the Equal Rights Amendment became a symbol of liberation. Betty Ford spanned the divide between the new and the traditional as well as any First Lady in modern times, including Lady Bird Johnson, who has always struck me as a model in the White House. Mrs. Ford believed in the advancement of women and she directed her influence toward that end. When her husband was still vice president, she told Barbara Walters on television that *Roe v. Wade* was a good decision and that it was time to bring abortion "out of the backwoods and put it in hospitals where it belonged."

Quietly championing women's rights inside the East Wing— "pillow talk" was real to her—she lobbied for the appointment of more women to federal posts, helping to open the door to Anne Armstrong as ambassador to Great Britain and Carla Hills as HUD secretary. At her urging, Ford signed an executive order establishing a National Commission on the Observance of International Women's Year. She also lost some rounds: When William Douglas retired from the Court, she pushed for a woman and the seat went instead to John Paul Stevens. She traveled the country on behalf of the Equal Rights Amendment, buttonholing legislators in key states and persuading her husband to back it, but she was unable to secure passage. Along the way, she made a distinction that is revealing: the role of the First Lady, she said, is to serve as "the heart of the nation" while her husband serves as its "mind." Eros and logos: a good balance.

Yet she was neither strident nor polarizing when she spoke out about women's rights because she also voiced respect for traditional female roles. "Being ladylike does not require silence," she said once of the ERA. "I spoke out on this issue because of my deep personal conviction. Why should my husband's job or yours prevent us from being ourselves?" But she went on to speak directly to homemakers: "We must take the 'just' out of 'just a housewife' and show our pride in having made the home and family our life's work. Downgrading this work has been part of the pattern in our society that downgrades women's talents in all areas." As reporter John Pope wrote, "Mrs. Ford became the most outspoken First Lady since Eleanor Roosevelt." And she did it without stirring national hackles against her husband or seeming to live off his power.

145

One of the greatest threats to the Republican Party, then as now, is that it become monolithic in its public philosophy, that different voices are squelched rather than encouraged. In particular, it would be suicidal for Republicans to become branded as a party of old white males marching in lockstep. Betty Ford was a tonic to the party, sending a message to women and minorities that the welcome mat was out. No one else in the administration did that as well. In 1975, *Time* magazine named her one of the Women of the Year, the first time for a First Lady. Her husband was the first president since Herbert Hoover never to be named Man of the Year. In typical fashion, he took both in stride.

Her candor, of course, extended far beyond her feminist views. Shortly after the inauguration, doctors found that Betty Ford had breast cancer. They immediately performed a radical mastectomy, removing her right breast and lymph nodes in her armpit. She then had to undergo chemotherapy. Hearing the news, Ford sat at his desk and cried, later describing it as "the lowest and loneliest moment" of his White House days.

At first, the Fords kept her disease a secret. But, as Mrs. Ford said, "lying in the hospital, thinking of all those women going for cancer check-ups because of me, I'd come to realize more clearly the power of the woman in the White House. Not my power, but the power of the position, a power which could be used to help." So she went public and became a national spokeswoman for breast cancer exams. Her crusade persuaded hundreds of thousands to get check-ups, including Mrs. Rockefeller, who was later diagnosed with cancer.

Some of us on staff suspected there was more wrong with her health than breast cancer. Behind the happy, supportive exterior she showed in public, we could see that Mrs. Ford periodically withdrew, seemed slow of movement and speech, and was even later than usual to appointments. What we didn't know—or at least most of us on the President's side of the house—was how much she was suffering from depression, drugs, and alcohol. She had pinched a nerve years before and took painkillers for the injury. As she describes in her memoirs, she became addicted to the painkillers, which eased the many moments when her husband was on the road and her children grew independent. Her growing consumption of alcohol and pills caused her to slur her words, which some, including her press secretary, Sheila Rabb Weidenfeld, noticed in the 1976 campaign, but it remained an intensely private concern. After the loss in 1976, however, her husband was on the road even more fre-

146

quently, hitting the lecture and golf circuits, and she increased both her medication and alcohol consumption. Her family finally convinced her to seek treatment.

Again, she decided to lift the veil of secrecy and confronted the issue in public. With friends' help, she also opened the Betty Ford Center in Rancho Mirage, chaired the board, and personally counseled patients. It was a culmination of her long efforts to champion controversial causes and to provide a support system for American women. That courage and social concern remain her most important legacy.

But there was something more central to her relationship with him: especially in the early days of his presidency, Ford was trying to stay calm on a heaving deck. She was there, steady, tethering. It's one of the most vital supports a president needs—a safe port in the storm—and she was always that for him despite her own struggles. His character and hers were in the end intertwined. Betty Ford was certainly not alone among First Ladies who have provided a haven for their man—Bess Truman and Lady Bird Johnson come instantly to mind—but no one has done it any better.

IN THE FIRST HOURS after his inauguration, Jerry Ford went into the cabinet room with his new counselor, Bob Hartmann, for an important presidential ritual: selecting three predecessors whose portraits the new man wants to have peering down from the cabinet walls. Those choices are a telling signal about the models a new president has in mind. Nixon had chosen Eisenhower, Teddy Roosevelt, and Woodrow Wilson—each providing an obvious link to his own dreams.

Standing there alone with his longtime friend, Ford pondered for a moment and decided to keep Ike and to bring down Teddy Roosevelt, replacing him with Lincoln. "The other might be a Democrat," Hartmann recalls saying. "How about Andy Jackson?" "No, Harry Truman," Ford answered, remembering how fate had drawn Truman to the White House and he had proven to be an inspired choice.

Searching for words, Hartmann said, "You are going to be a great President."

"Thanks, Bob," Ford responded. "I don't know about that. But I want to be a *good* President."

Among historians, Ford has never made it into the hall of greatness but, over time, he did fulfill his own dream. For all his fumbles,

147

especially those in the First Hundred Days that cost him a national election, he turned out to be a good chief executive. He helped to repair the breach left by Watergate and Vietnam, guided the nation out of recession, began to crack open the Iron Curtain, and turned over to Jimmy Carter reins that were once again taut. In the most basic test of presidential fitness, Ford succeeded: the country and the presidency were in better shape than he had found them thirty months earlier.

More fundamentally, Jerry Ford knew that goodness of another kind had been lost in Vietnam and Watergate, and he restored that to the White House. Lies gave way to truth; disillusionment to a modicum of trust. Jimmy Carter, to his credit, pursued that same path as a candidate and president, but it was Ford who began the march. He may have been too nice to play in a tough racket; that's a fair critique. Nor was he able to lead the nation fully out of the mire; the public's faith in government and politics never regained its earlier peaks. Still, Jerry Ford set a standard of decency, openness, and honesty that, as a new century begins, is a flame of hope that somehow politics can once again become a noble calling.

Tip O'Neill, the Democratic Speaker of the House, put it well about his friend in his memoirs: "God has been good to America, especially during difficult times. At the time of the Civil War, he gave us Abraham Lincoln. And at the time of Watergate, he gave us Gerald Ford—the right man at the right time who was able to put our nation back together again. Nothing like Watergate had ever happened before in our history, but we came out of it strong and free, and the transition from Nixon's administration to Ford's was a thing of awe and dignity."

Ronald Reagan

5

The Natural

Ronald Reagan taught me more about leadership than anyone I've ever known—usually through a surprise.

In the third year of his presidency, it was Reagan's turn to serve as host of the annual economic summit of industrialized nations. He chose Williamsburg, Virginia, as the site, and the leaders were lodged comfortably in colonial homes near the square. Their staffs were also well looked after—except for the French, whom we packed off to motels in East Jesus in retaliation for their high-handedness toward the American delegation when they had been hosts a year earlier.

From our perspective, the G-7 summit posed a major test for Reagan. For the first time, he had to act as chair of the group, guiding intricate discussions of world economics and politics. As president, he was also expected to have one-on-one talks with each of the other leaders—"bilaterals," as they are called in the trade—a requirement shared by no other chief executive. The world press, skeptical of Reagan's grasp of world issues, would be digging in hard to see whether he could juggle so many conversations.

Midway through the summit, Reagan had a particularly rugged day ahead. There were to be plenary sessions, and bilaterals were on tap with Margaret Thatcher, François Mitterrand, Helmut Kohl, and perhaps one or two others. For each meeting, the staff of the National Security Council, the scheduling office, and others prepared lengthy background papers for the President to study the night before. Be-

151

cause there were such a large number of meetings, the briefing book looked like a telephone directory.

Here was the dilemma: when he was in Hollywood, Reagan made a practice of committing what he read to memory—he had a steel-trap mind for such things—but as a result, he also read very slowly. We had learned, just as his aides did when he was governor of California, not to give him too much to read at night because he would stay up too late. The next morning he would be exhausted—and worse, Nancy would be on the warpath. On the other hand, this summit would put him on display before the world. Surely, he had to walk into every single meeting stuffed to the gills with details. How could we not give him this monstrous briefing book?

With some trepidation, as I recall, chief of staff Jim Baker gave him the book: "Mr. President, try to go over this material quickly. Please, please don't stay up late reading it."

At our 7:30 A.M. staff breakfast the next day, Reagan walked in late and looked as if he had been run over by a Mack truck. His eyes were puffy, his gait slow. "My God," I thought to myself, "he stayed up half the night with that damn briefing book. Where is Nancy? This is going to be a horrible day."

About twenty minutes into his eggs, Reagan gave us that aw-shucks look and said, "Fellas, I've got a confession to make. Last night, I sat down with your briefing book, which was good. But around nine o'clock I turned on the TV, and *The Sound of Music* was playing. Well, that's one of my favorite movies, so I watched. It went on pretty late, and I'm sorry I never got through the briefing papers."

Instantly, Nancy disappeared from my thoughts. She couldn't blame us for his lack of sleep!

But fear shot up on the other side: how would he get through all these meetings? Where would he be without our elaborate staff briefings? Were we going to be murdered by the international press?

That's when the surprise came. Fortified with breakfast and a few laughs, Reagan was as good that day as he had ever been in meetings. He stayed above the forest of facts we had provided and focused on the larger goals he wanted to pursue. Though tired, he was also relaxed. His visitors enjoyed the easy flow of conversation. It was a boffo performance, and the other leaders—as well as the dragons of the press—were suitably persuaded. As for those of us on staff, it was a good warning not to take ourselves or our briefing papers so seriously.

152

Reagan wasn't just comfortable in his own skin. He was serene.

And he had a clear sense of what he was trying to accomplish. Those were among his greatest strengths as a leader. Nobody had to tell him those things. He knew where he wanted to go and how he might get there. Instead of trying to treat him like a marionette, as we did sometimes, the best thing we could do on staff was to help clear the obstacles from his path.

Bernard Malamud once wrote a novel about a baseball player called *The Natural*. Not many have read it, but millions have watched Robert Redford play the protagonist in a film. He glides through life, never works as hard as his teammates, and in the climactic moment, smacks the ball out of the park. Ronald Reagan was one of the naturals in politics, the rare men like Teddy Roosevelt and Franklin Roosevelt who seem blessed with instincts and intuitions that set them apart as leaders. Like them, Reagan had a magic that came easily and made others seem plodding.

Goodness knows, Reagan wasn't perfect. He could be so dreamy and inattentive to detail that he allowed dramatic mistakes to occur. He had less curiosity about public policy than any president since perhaps the 1920s. He depended too much on staff for day-to-day operations and that eventually landed him in deep trouble. His critics always provide a long list of other flaws, and we'll consider them soon. But fair-minded observers—even those who did not agree with all of his policies (and I was never as conservative as he was)—would have to agree that on balance, he was a highly effective president. In my view, he was the best leader in the White House since Franklin Roosevelt.

Measures of His Success

The Reagan story wasn't supposed to turn out that way—at least to most smart people along the Eastern Seaboard. When he came riding in from the hinterlands in the early 1980s, sophisticates thought he was a cowboy, the president least likely to succeed since Hoover. They snickered knowingly when Clark Clifford told friends at a Washington dinner party that Reagan was an "amiable dunce." Reagan himself had once said he was the "Errol Flynn of the B's," and the establishment saw no reason to disagree. He was the washed-up actor who had become the Willy Loman of General Electric, a traveling salesman with "a smile and a shoeshine," and then made it to Sacramento by changing scripts and attacking kids at Berkeley. Peo-

153

ple who "mattered" weren't sure whether they were more horrified by his conservatism or his broad popular appeal. But surely he wouldn't succeed. They shorted the stock.

The country was also in a funk. An end to the war in Vietnam and the integrity of both Gerald Ford and Jimmy Carter had not erased the pain of recent times. Instead, what most Americans thought of as they looked back over nearly twenty years was a string of assassinations, a lost war, political scandals, economic turmoil at home, embarrassment overseas, and uneven responses in Washington.

In the summer of 1979, President Carter looked over a batch of polls from his adviser Patrick Caddell showing that for the first time on record, a majority of Americans thought the present was worse than the past and the future would be worse still. Alarmed, Carter retreated to Camp David for ten days to commune with intellectuals and policy-makers. Coming down from his mountaintop, Carter delivered a speech that haunted him long thereafter, declaring that the country was facing a "crisis of confidence . . . threatening to destroy [our] social and . . . political fabric." Among a people who have believed in progress, he sermonized, "too many of us now tend to worship self-indulgence and consumption." He talked of national "paralysis and stagnation and drift. . . . We simply must have faith in each other. Faith in our ability to govern ourselves and faith in the future of this nation. Restoring that faith and that confidence to America is now the most important task we face." He was right, but people no longer thought Carter was the man to do it. Nor did he help himself when he fired four cabinet officers the day after his speech.

The economy Carter handed over to Reagan was in even lousier shape than the one Nixon left to Ford. In his winning campaign of 1976, Carter had invented a "misery index" to measure economic conditions—it was the combination of the inflation and unemployment rates. When Carter ran that year, the misery index stood at 13.5; Carter beat Ford over the head with that statistic. By the time Carter ran for reelection against Reagan, the misery index had climbed to 20.6, a punishing high. (By contrast, the misery index over the course of 1999 stood at less than 8.) When interest rates skyrocketed, wags said Carter was the first president in history whose popularity was below the prime. An oil cartel nobody had heard of a few years earlier had the country by the throat, and American industry seemed 154 unable to compete with rising powers in Asia. Middle-class families were hurting, and those hardest hit were the poor. Inflation in the 1970s cut the real value of welfare benefits by a third.

As if that weren't enough, the nation's power was visibly deteriorating overseas. In the years since they won in Vietnam, the Marxists had raised their flags over the capitals of seven more countries—five on Carter's watch alone. The United States military was reeling from its defeat in Asian jungles. A third of our ships could not get under way at sea, a quarter of the planes in the Air Force were out of service, and drugs were rampant among the troops. Nothing disturbed the electorate more than the graphic ordeal of Americans held hostage for 444 days by mobs in Tehran. When Carter sent in a rescue team that lost its way in the desert, humiliation seemed complete.

Carter did not bear responsibility for everything going wrong. Four presidents in a row were popularly seen as failing. Something deeper was amiss, and serious people worried about the state of government itself. James MacGregor Burns wrote about government living in a cobblestone era. Seymour Martin Lipset and William Schneider described a collapse of confidence in the federal government. Carter's general counsel, Lloyd Cutler, wrote trenchant pieces arguing that the political system needed a thorough overhaul. He and others organized study groups to discuss constitutional changes that would turn American government into a quasi-parliamentary system.

Could anyone lead anymore? Maybe not—and certainly not Ronald Reagan, they said.

It did not take long before he changed people's minds. The economy had slid into a painful recession early in his first year, as unemployment climbed to over 10 percent. It was the sharpest downturn since the Great Depression. But, in 1983, the economy bounced straight up and kept climbing. "Seven fat years," as Robert Bartley called them in a book by that title, following the seven lean years that had begun in the mid-seventies. Inflation was down, jobs were up, and the stock market jumped more than ten times in value. OPEC no longer had the nation in its grasp, and American producers were making rapid strides against foreign competitors. Not everything came up roses: federal deficits had quadrupled, income gaps were widening, and people at the bottom felt stuck. But the country was beginning to build an "enterprise culture" that was to become the driving force behind the economic boom of the 1990s.

On the day of Reagan's inauguration, the Iranians released the American hostages in Tehran—to spite Carter and possibly to ward off an attack from the new president. In the eight years that followed, the Communists took no more territory. As money and support 155 flowed in, the American military was rebuilt. Enlistments went up and so did morale. Ten months after Reagan left the White House, jubilant Germans tore down the Berlin Wall and the Soviet empire collapsed.

With prosperity returning and their homes safer from missiles, Americans were feeling better about themselves and even about government. One of the rich ironies of the 1980s is that public confidence in the federal government stopped a fifteen-year slide under the most conservative president since Calvin Coolidge. By the time of the 1984 Olympics in Los Angeles, where fans waved the flag and cheered lustily for the nation's athletes, it was obvious that the pessimism of Pat Caddell's polls had given way to a buoyant national pride. "It's morning again in America," Reagan's ads proclaimed that year, and voters responded by giving him victories in every state but Minnesota and the District of Columbia, the biggest sweep of the electoral college since FDR lost only Maine and Vermont in 1936.

Reagan certainly does not deserve the entire credit for the comeback of the 1980s, nor would he claim it. One of America's oldest strengths is its natural resilience, its capacity to adjust to hard times and snap back. In this case, Federal Reserve chairman Paul Volcker did more to break the back of inflation than anyone else. The cuts in taxes and regulations under Reagan would never have occurred without the support of a remarkably united Republican Party, joined by southern Democrats in Congress. From Boston to Detroit to Silicon Valley, private entrepreneurs were giving the economy an edge. America's research universities churned out discoveries in science and technology, women poured into the workforce, and companies changed their management styles to give employees a larger voice. Prosperity came from many hands, not one alone.

Mikhail Gorbachev, more than Reagan, dismantled the Soviet empire. He saw the game was up and moved courageously to put his country on a new course. Had he not stayed the hand of the Red army, posted nearby, the scenes at the Berlin Wall in November 1989 would have made Tiananmen Square look like a Sunday picnic. From Britain, Margaret Thatcher also put some much-needed backbone in the Western Alliance, and Chancellor Helmut Kohl was masterful in steering both Germany and Europe toward unification.

So, Reagan did not stand on the pinnacle alone. But is there any doubt who became the chief architect of the 1980s? In her memoirs after serving as FDR's labor secretary, Frances Perkins wrote that she was biased in favor of Roosevelt because she had worked for him and had ties of affection. I feel the same way about Reagan. From my

156

vantage point, he more than anyone else in public life unleashed the innate forces of the American economy, beginning the Long Boom. He more than any other public leader believed the answer to the Soviet threat was to challenge them to a race they could not win. Yes, they were crumbling from within, and, yes, Gorbachev was heroic. But it was Reagan who called the Soviets' bluff. He forced them to sue for peace, and then it was over. A half century of unstinting pressure by the West, paid for in blood and treasure, supported by Democratic as well as Republican presidents, ended the Cold War without a shot. It was the most complete triumph since World War II. No wonder Americans felt better.

Reagan also changed our minds—about government and about ourselves. Franklin Roosevelt had convinced a majority of Americans that the federal government is the most important instrument we have for achieving social justice, economic progress, and international peace. Reagan displaced one set of political beliefs with another. In his book, *The Politics Presidents Make*, political scientist Stephen Skowronek writes that our most significant presidents have been those who knocked down the props of an old political regime and began erecting a new one in its place. Jefferson, Jackson, Lincoln, and Franklin Roosevelt each created a new political philosophy that shaped succeeding presidencies. Reagan, says Skowronek, did much the same, albeit not to the extent of FDR.

Reagan believed that government was creeping into too many areas of domestic life, smothering other forces in civil society. He wanted to restore the central role of the family, church, and other mediating institutions. By reducing tax rates and lifting regulations, he thought he would do more than revive the economy. People would also reclaim personal freedom and self-reliance. And, over time, they would rebuild confidence in themselves. Reagan was an evangelist for a new civil religion. In the 1960s and 1970s, he was a voice in the wilderness; in the early 1990s, he was still seen as a reactionary; by the late 1990s, his ideas were ascendant. When a Democratic president, Bill Clinton, declared in his 1996 State of the Union address that "the era of big government is over," it was clear that Reagan had introduced a new political regime.

The measure of a leader, it is said, is the shadow he leaves behind. A president who ushered in a New Economy, helped to end the Cold War, changed the country's mind about its government and itself—who else since Roosevelt has cast so long a shadow? 157

Reagan himself wondered whether it was possible to change things. One of his favorite stories was of a baseball manager watching a young rookie commit a string of errors in center field. Charging onto the field with glove in hand, the manager yelled, "Here, Jones, let me show you how to play that position."

The next batter sent a scorching grounder over second base and it went through the manager's legs. Another one hit a line drive that bounced off the manager's glove. A third popped up and the ball landed on the manager's head.

"Jones," the manager bellowed, "you've got center field so screwed up, nobody can play it anymore!"

Reagan sometimes thought that about the presidents who preceded him in office. They had screwed it up so badly that maybe nobody could play president anymore. But somehow he did.

How did Reagan do it? What were the lessons behind his leadership? Obviously, he was a first-class communicator. Even now, those who wish to diminish him say that's all he was; worse, they claim he was a puppet dancing on the strings managed by others. As his first director of communications, I saw his talents firsthand and, more to the point, can assure he was nobody's puppet. But I also learned that there was far more to his leadership than his skill in moving an audience. He built upon far sturdier foundations.

Solid Grounding as a Politician

During the past century, there have been better politicians in the White House than Reagan. The two Roosevelts were in a class by themselves. Woodrow Wilson, at least in his first term, was a model in building public support and passing progressive legislation. In the face of a Republican takeover of Congress, one can only marvel at the legislative victories Harry Truman chalked up in 1947–1948, starting with the Marshall Plan. And in the mid-1960s, Lyndon Johnson was a master of the craft, rolling up the biggest landslide and passing more bills than any president since FDR.

Ronald Reagan pretended to be a nonpolitician, a citizen who had happened to run for office, a Mr. Smith Come to Washington. But behind that thin veneer, he was pretty darn good at politics, too, and that was an important—no, an *indispensable*—ingredient in his leadership. As Joseph Alsop once observed about the presidency, "Rule I, at any rate in America, is that you have to be a good politician in order to get the chance to be a great statesman."

Reagan began to hone his skills in the late 1940s and early 1950s when he was elected six times as president of the Screen Actors

Guild in Hollywood. He became so caught up with the union that a rift developed with his first wife, Jane Wyman, and contributed to his divorce. The toughest part of the job was to represent the actors in negotiations with the film companies, and he learned how to bluff and deal with the sharks. "You got to know when to hold 'em and when to fold 'em," he used to say later on, quoting the Kenny Rogers song "The Gambler." When he left the film industry, his long years on the mashed potato circuit not only shaped his capacity as a public speaker—more on that later—but also exposed him to the wide diversity of voices and interests that every politician should know before running for office.

But his best training ground for Washington was in Sacramento. Sophisticates back East should have appreciated the importance of that job but didn't. If the twentieth century taught us anything about the preparation of a president, it is surely the fact that men who have served as governors of large, complex states are far better groomed for the White House than men from small, one-party states. Think of the presidents who came from the governor's chair in the big states: Teddy Roosevelt from New York, Wilson from New Jersey, Franklin Roosevelt from New York, Reagan from California. Compare their performances in the White House to the two men who came from the smaller states of Georgia and Arkansas. It's a much bigger leap to the White House from Little Rock than from Sacramento.

In his eight years as governor, Reagan had to persuade a predominantly Democratic legislature to pass controversial legislation, joust with a sophisticated press corps, manage the largest state government in the country, keep campuses like Berkeley from flying apart during the student rebellions of the sixties, and appeal to a population exploding in size and diversity. Anyone who can emerge from that cauldron knows a thing or two about politics. Carter and Clinton had to learn on the job much of what Reagan already knew before he became president.

Two trial runs for the Republican nomination sharpened Reagan even further. After he was elected governor of California in 1966, he made a last-minute feint to win the Republican nomination in 1968, but Richard Nixon quickly squelched him. In his run against Ford in 1976, he came within a whisker of seizing the nomination, something no one had ever done before to a sitting president. While he lost, the experience itself was invaluable training, giving him a chance to learn the track before he made his real run for the roses in 1980. 159

Those of us watching from afar did not fully appreciate, as well, how much political strength Reagan gained from building the conservative movement. During the 1950s, as he moved away from the Democratic Party and toward Republicans, Reagan often thought of himself as a lonely voice. His nationally televised speech on behalf of Barry Goldwater in 1964 changed that. In the debris following the election that year, the Taft-Goldwater wing of the party gravitated heavily toward Reagan as its New Hope. But still, the conservative movement then was in rough shape, beaten down by LBJ and, it thought, by the liberal media. When Nixon ran and won in 1968, he portrayed himself more as a moderate, and over the next eight years of Republican reign, conservatives often felt aggrieved. It was Reagan who had their hearts and Reagan who turned the movement into a tidal wave by the late 1970s.

Reagan, then, had a thorough grounding as a politician before he took on Jimmy Carter in 1980. He had entered elective politics relatively late—at fifty-five, he was older when he entered his first public office than Bill Clinton will be when he leaves his last—and his background was anything but orthodox. But he was ready for the rough-and-tumble of a national campaign.

Winning a Mandate to Govern

The 1980 contest for the White House was the last truly good one the country has had because all three candidates—Carter, Anderson, and Reagan—provided clear choices for the electorate. They said exactly what courses they intended to pursue if elected, didn't blur their differences, held down the mud-slinging, and didn't sell their souls to their pollsters and handlers. Each man ran as the genuine article, and people knew what they were getting. Sadly, that has not been the case since—even Reagan's own reelection campaign of 1984 was mostly about the past, not about choices for the future.

As it turned out, the way Reagan conducted the 1980 campaign also helped him enormously in governing. It was one of the few elections that has transformed a presidency—and was another revealing demonstration of his political skills.

That campaign was also my introduction to the governor. When the primaries opened, I wasn't persuaded Reagan ought to be president and favored George Bush. In my view, Bush had all the credentials to serve in the Oval Office, and I liked his centrism. In 1979, at his request, I happily signed up as a Bush volunteer and went off to New Hampshire to help him with preparations for two debates. He

160

had just upset Reagan in the Iowa caucuses. With assistance from Hugh Gregg, the former governor and father of the current senator, Bush easily won the first debate. The second was scheduled to be a one-on-one between Bush and Reagan, and after our debate preparations were done, I went home to Washington to listen on radio. My presence would not have changed anything, but I felt I had let our side down by not being around when the Reagan forces outfoxed us. They insisted at the last minute that the other Republican candidates be invited to join the fray, and as the proceedings opened, the moderator, Jon Breen, publicly refused. He also tried to shush up Reagan.

Reagan turned scarlet with anger and exploded, "I'm paying for this microphone, Mr. Green [sic]!" The line was straight out of an old movie, *State of the Union,* where Spencer Tracy said, "Don't you shut me off! I'm paying for this broadcast." While Bush sat there flat-footed, Reagan hijacked the affections of the audience, turned around his campaign in New Hampshire, and swept on to victories there and across the country.

He was obviously impressive. The press might still call Reagan a lightweight, but I was reminded of a comment that Lincoln's fellow lawyer, Leonard Swett, once made about his days in a courtroom: "Any man who took Lincoln for a simple-minded man would very soon wake up with his back in a ditch."

Reagan's chief speechwriter, Peter Hannaford, asked me to come to the convention that summer to help out in drafting some speeches. On a couple of other occasions in the late seventies, he had requested me to write speeches for Reagan, which I had done. I did not meet Reagan in that process but did go over to hear him deliver one of the products at the National Press Club. It was a pedestrian effort, but Reagan made it sing in ways that startled. I also liked Hannaford and decided to accept his invitation for the convention in Detroit. I was high up in the convention hall with another Bush ally, Dick Fairbanks, when word came that Reagan had selected Bush as his vice presidential choice. We were ecstatic and rushed over to his hotel suite to salute him in the celebrations there.

Soon Reagan had another surprise. After consulting his kitchen cabinet—successful businessmen in California—the most conservative Republican nominee in half a century decided he wanted moderates on his campaign team, even in starring roles. His most important personnel decision was to ask Jim Baker, who had worked for George Bush, to join him at the top of his campaign structure. It was the first time the campaign chief of an opponent was given such elevated rank. Up there with two longtime Reaganauts, William Casey and Edwin Meese, Baker was to offer campaign advice and to direct preparations for debates that fall with President Carter and Illinois congressman John Anderson, a Republican maverick running as an independent. He also had carte blanche to bring in any assistants he wanted.

Baker quickly reached out to a number of moderates from the Bush ranks, asking us to help with the debates. He recruited me to prepare the debate briefing books for Reagan, a part-time job where I worked in close harmony with another Baker man, Frank Hodsoll. Public policy experts sent us stashes of materials, which we massaged and placed in a series of books. The first book I gave to Reagan was quite thick. He passed it off with a joke but I noticed Nancy looking daggers. I made sure the next book was drastically shorter.

The weeks following began my education about leadership, Reagan-style. He proposed a three-way debate that Carter declined, apparently worried that Anderson would siphon votes from him. I thought Carter was wrong: standing between Anderson on his left and Reagan on his right, he might have emerged as the candidate of sweet reason. As it was, he looked as if he were ducking. Reagan accepted an invitation from Anderson for a one-on-one. It was to be the first debate of the fall season.

Anderson was a smart fellow who could be dangerous, so we took him seriously. We needed more than briefing books; we needed a good sparring partner. I had never met Congressman David Stockman, a rising young member of the House, but, through Karlyn Keene at the American Enterprise Institute, had been introduced to his writings and was impressed. Since David had also worked as a staff assistant to John Anderson, I thought he would be a perfect stand-in for Anderson and recommended him to Baker. Congressman Jack Kemp also weighed in on Stockman's behalf, advice that meant a lot to Baker.

Stockman showed up for the first practice debate primed for action. Reagan ambled in, stood at an opposite podium, and we posed mock questions. Stockman decked him. Reagan's answers were tentative and short, and Stockman pummeled him with endless facts and clever one-liners. I shuddered. Reagan wanted a rematch the next day, and by that time, he had studied up. Round two was a draw. Would Reagan now say he was ready? I wondered. Nope, he wanted round three. I still don't know what he did overnight, but 162 this time he was in full command of his arguments and funny rejoinders. As strong as Stockman was, Reagan knocked him out of the ring. He clearly knew how to gear himself up when it counted.

As it turned out, Stockman was better at arguing the Anderson case than Anderson was himself. Reagan won the actual debate in a breeze. As for Stockman, he had won favor in Reagan's eyes: David was on his way to becoming budget director.

Soon after, Reagan engaged in a single debate with Carter that sealed his election victory. Stockman had returned as a sparring partner in the warm-ups, and Reagan had little trouble manhandling him. It was obvious that Reagan would perform well in the finals, once again upsetting a press corps that underrated his abilities (as I had earlier). Reagan pressed his case against Carter's stewardship with passion and clear arguments—skills that served him well in his presidency. He also brought a bag full of one-liners to sprinkle through the night, keeping Carter off guard and the audience laughing. As a practiced orator, he knew how to deflect an opponent while winning points, and he did so memorably when Carter bore in with an attack. "There you go again," responded Reagan, sloughing him off. Some of his one-liners weren't part of the debate prep, so I assumed that Reagan dreamed them up.

Observers have given me too much credit for crafting one of Reagan's most telling lines. Heading into the Carter debate, Baker asked Dick Wirthlin and me to draft a short statement that Reagan could use for his closing remarks. Wirthlin, the campaign's master strategist, told me that over the years Reagan had shown that asking rhetorical questions could be a powerful weapon with audiences. Our draft included one that Reagan seized upon. "Ask yourself," he said in his peroration, "are you better off today than you were four years ago?" The line was withering because it captured the essence of the campaign against Carter: millions of Americans thought the country had in fact drifted downhill and they wanted a change. Some thought that Reagan's question clinched the election.

What the episode reveals is how a team can work magically together in politics—as in other fields. It was Reagan who had demonstrated the power of rhetorical questions through long years of practice. It was Wirthlin who had observed him closely and was smart enough to know we should go to that well now. I had the understanding of how then to distill the thought into a question that defined the reality so many Americans were experiencing. Each of us—Reagan, Wirthlin, and I—benefited from the talents of the others. One savors moments like that in politics.

A week later, Reagan racked up a smashing victory, pulling in 50.75 percent of the popular vote in the three-way race and winning forty-four states. Reagan swept the megastates on both coasts, the

163

Midwest, and nearly all of the Sunbelt. Carter won only Georgia, Maryland, West Virginia, Rhode Island, Minnesota, Hawaii, and the District of Columbia. He was the first elected president to be ousted since Hoover.

Reagan's political savvy in that campaign paid off in another way for his presidency. He didn't run aloof from his party, as Nixon did in 1972; nor did he separate out from his party, as Clinton did with his "triangulation strategy" in 1996. Instead, he campaigned as a partner with other Republicans, joining them on the hustings and trying to help them win, too. His themes were the same as many of theirs. As a result, he extended his coattails farther than any winning presidential candidate in the past thirty-five years. Republicans swept up twelve additional seats in the Senate, enough to gain control for the first time since 1954, and thirty-three seats in the House. That wasn't enough to gain control in the House, but it was enough to create a working coalition. Among modern presidents, only Lyndon Johnson in 1964 and Franklin Roosevelt in 1932 have had longer coattails.

Moreover, Reagan ran ahead of scores of House members in their own districts, giving him enormous bargaining leverage in the months that followed. Every single one of the new Republicans owed a debt to Reagan that he could collect as president, and many others in Congress, especially southern Democrats, knew he was more popular in their districts than they were—a popularity that translated into supportive votes for his agenda.

Equally important to his capacity to govern was a campaign decision he had made long before the debates. Soon after capturing the nomination, he commissioned one of his best advisers, Martin Anderson, to draw up an economic agenda for his first term. Marty huddled with Alan Greenspan, then running his own economic consulting firm in New York, along with others to draft a speech that Reagan gave in Pittsburgh in September 1980. The speech set the course for Reagan's first four years in office: it pledged a 30 percent cut in income tax rates, a reduction in social spending, an increase in defense, a paring back of government regulations, and a balanced budget.

Once he became president, some changes were made as his plan for a tax cut was modestly scaled back and defense spending was sharply increased. Most of his economic plan was highly successful. Only one plank fell apart—painfully—and that was the promise of a balanced budget. Ironically, FDR had gone to Pittsburgh in his cam-

164

paign of 1932 to promise a balanced budget, and his pledge later haunted him, too.

Reagan's Pittsburgh speech and its many repetitions during the campaign told voters in advance where he was going if elected. Three out of ten told exit pollsters they voted for Reagan because he wasn't Carter. But other voters were drawn to him by his agenda. Because he had been so crystal clear about his plan, Reagan could credibly claim an election mandate. The morning after the election, Ed Meese told a press conference that the people had spoken—and they had spoken not only in favor of Reagan but what he proposed. The press agreed and soon the public did, too.

A mandate is magical in politics, and it made all the difference for Reagan in his early presidency. Throughout the transition and then in office, Reagan could proclaim that he was the only person in America elected by all the people, the people had embraced his agenda, and now Congress owed it to the people to enact it. Mandate in hand and a Congress ready to work with him, Reagan was exquisitely poised to lead in the months that followed. His political skills were paying off.

Putting Together an Early Action Plan

He wasted no time getting ready for the presidency. The day after he won, he began moving swiftly.

Reagan named Jim Baker his incoming chief of staff, and Baker in turn invited a number of us in Washington to sign up for the transition and for early duty in the administration. As I took up my assignment at the transition, it was readily apparent that Reagan's campaign gave us two immediate advantages. First, neither he nor his staff had to spend transition time trying to figure out his main substantive agenda. That was mostly done, rooted in the plan laid out in Pittsburgh. The staff could thus concentrate on ways he could quickly take charge the moment he was inaugurated. Second, he could work with a small group of trusted advisers to focus on personnel selection—a subject we will turn to in a moment.

In order to hit the ground running, Reagan needed his own budget that would flesh out the details of his overall plan. If he were slow on that front, Jimmy Carter would send his own budget to the Hill as he was leaving office and that would shape congressional action for months. Reagan could not afford to wait; he had to make his

165

imprint fast. Early in the transition, he appointed Stockman as his budget director and gave him leeway to move. Stockman took up the spending shears with relish, pruning back every Great Society program he could get his hands on. Reagan had signed off on a raft of spending cuts before most new cabinet officers were on board. Many of them screamed—they had been deballed before they even put their pants on—but they had to go along. The Stockman plan, to which Dick Darman also contributed significantly, was an aggressive exercise of power, but it gave Reagan a head start as president.

My task in the transition was to work with Richard Wirthlin in co-drafting an "Early Action Plan" for the First Hundred Days of the Reagan presidency. Dick, a Ph.D., provided most of the conceptual framework for the plan that emerged. We were both helped by one of his assistants, Richard Beale, along with a team of young researchers.

The researchers assisted me in pulling together a study of the First Hundred Days of the past five presidents who had been freshly elected, just like Reagan: Roosevelt in 1933, Eisenhower in 1953, Kennedy in 1961, Nixon in 1969, and Carter in 1977. Given the hallowed reputation of FDR's First Hundred Days, we felt it important to plot out precisely what each man had done during each of his days—his legislative proposals, executive orders, symbolic gestures, meetings with Congress, introductions to the Supreme Court, speeches, press conferences, trips, and the rest. We then reviewed the press clips and historical accounts that appeared after each "new beginning," assessing what seemed to work and what didn't. From there, we could begin to map out how Reagan might successfully master his own moment.

I drew three conclusions from that study of the past:

First, the public makes a fresh evaluation of a president the day he takes office. Until then, people have known him only as a candidate. Now he finally holds the reins for the first time, and people must judge anew: Is he really up to the job? Can we trust him? Does he know where he wants to go? Do we want to go there, too? Does he have a central focus? In short, do we like what we see—or suffer from buyer's remorse?

Carter's experience convinced us that focus is essential for a new president. Taking over in 1977, he had tried to emulate Roosevelt by sending up stacks of legislative proposals in his early months. But his ideas had no internal coherence and, in the absence of crisis, struck many observers as hurly-burly. By the end of Carter's First Hundred Days, puzzled reporters wrote they couldn't

166

make sense of what he was trying to accomplish. "He seems to stand for everything and believe in nothing," was their basic story line. Obviously, we weren't going there.

Second, those early months provide an opportunity for a president to put a firm thematic stamp upon his entire administration. Roosevelt had become "Doctor New Deal," as he called himself, helping a sick patient recover. Eisenhower slipped away from reporters and flew off to the Korean War front during his transition, becoming a president in search of peace. While Nixon spoke in his inaugural address as a man who wanted to "Bring Us Together" at home, he showed quickly that his attentions were elsewhere as he flew off to Europe. People soon realized that he would mostly be a foreign policy president. At the end of a Hundred Days, Americans were less sure what Kennedy was all about, though they liked and admired him, and even less certain about Carter, who left them scratching their heads. Clearly, Reagan had to put his own stamp on his presidency.

Third, it was obvious that the First Hundred Days were also a time of great peril, when presidents made some of their biggest mistakes. Kennedy had his Bay of Pigs in the First Hundred Days; Ford had his pardon of Nixon; Carter had a small disaster over a proposal to cut water projects and a bigger one with announcement of his energy plan.

Because Carter was still so fresh in our minds, his presidency was particularly instructive: he had promised during his 1976 campaign to make the United States "energy independent," but his ideas were vague. They lacked the specificity that might have allowed him to claim a mandate. Taking office, he called in one of Washington's smartest men, Jim Schlesinger, and instructed him to come up with an energy plan within ninety days. His work was to be secret. Schlesinger obediently pulled down the shades, ignored the Congress, and, with a few aides, produced a comprehensive energy proposal. On the merits, the Schlesinger plan had much that was ingenious, but the process had so shut out Congress and the lobbyists that they were steaming mad. They refused to sign on quickly. Appearing in cardigan sweater by a log fire in the Oval Office (another mistake, in my judgment, since presidents in their early days are still trying to identify themselves with the dignity of the office), Carter unveiled the plan. It hit with a thud. As the late-night shows said, Carter gave his first fireside chat—and the fire died.

Reagan looked over all this history, reviewed our recommendations, and soaked up some additional thoughts from Wirthlin. When

167

he and Nancy came to Washington for a transition visit, we gathered at the Blair House where he gave his blessing to the Early Action Plan. Once in the White House, Reagan did not try to follow it to the letter, but it proved to be an important road map for his first weeks in office. It is important to reiterate that a plan for those early days in office would not have been possible had not Reagan—along with Meese, Anderson, and other policy advisers—first worked out a substantive agenda for his presidency long before he was elected. We could build on their foundation.

The Early Action Plan was also but a piece of a much larger organizational effort during the transition. Dozens of men and women, many of them veterans of the Nixon and Ford years, joined in teams to study each of the departments inside out and make recommendations for changes in policy, process, and personnel. Another large group planned out the inauguration. Still another group planned the physical move into the White House. I was particularly proud because a wonderful young man who had worked with me over the years, John F. W. Rogers, had risen in the ranks and was now helping to plan the physical takeover.

Putting Together a Strong Team

In his days as governor and then in his campaign, Reagan had relied heavily upon longtime loyalists as his inner circle, and, with few exceptions, they served him well. Coming to the White House, he wanted those same men to be at the core of his administration, and they were: Ed Meese, Mike Deaver, Lyn Nofziger, Martin Anderson, Cap Weinberger, Bill Clark, Ed Rollins, Craig Fuller—all from California—along with Dick Allen and Bill Casey from Washington. Hovering inside the circle but outside the White House staff was Wirthlin, the pollster and strategist. All of these men had earned a favored place at the table. Most of them were keepers of the conservative flame. They also knew him well—his instincts, moods, and rhythms. Without them, he would not have succeeded in Washington.

But unlike most presidents, Reagan also realized that most of his inner circle was inexperienced in national government and didn't run with the Washington crowd. That's why he integrated into his staff a sizable band of experienced hands who tended to be allied with the more moderate Ford-Bush wing of the party. Jim Baker was our leader.

168

Putting together a White House staff, Jim reached out to many veterans from Nixon and Ford days. Among them were Dick Darman, who became deputy chief of staff; Max Friedersdorf, to run congressional relations; Ken Duberstein, to organize links to the House; Elizabeth Dole, to serve as head of outreach efforts; Jim Brady, to serve as press secretary; and Lee Atwater, to work with Ed Rollins in political affairs. I was one of those recruits, brought in early on with an anomalous title, White House Director. I helped out wherever Baker wanted, usually on public communications. To a person, we were seen as moderates. On the right, we were derisively called "pragmatists"; we preferred to think of ourselves as the "realists."

Conservatives never forgave Reagan for that decision. "People are policy," they argued, worrying that we would hijack his administration. Whenever he veered slightly toward the center, they blamed us—and not entirely without reason. We thought he could govern more effectively there. Yet, history will show that Reagan was wiser than his friends thought. The coalition government that he created at the White House in his early years was one of the strongest teams in the past forty years. Jack Kennedy and Lyndon Johnson had equally strong operations but, so far as I can tell, no other recent president. As a man who liked to delegate, Reagan needed an effective group around him, and that first team he assembled in the White House squabbled too much and leaked too much, but it got the job done.

More to the point—a point conservatives have never appreciated—the moderates weren't calling the policy shots in those early days. Those had all been decided in the campaign before we arrived. Just as important, we felt we had to prove ourselves in our first months on the job, and the way to do that was not by questioning the tax and spending cut proposals but by working like hell to get them enacted in Congress. That's what we did.

Privately, I admired Reagan for welcoming so many moderates aboard. Had George Bush won the election, I am virtually certain his moderate supporters would not have rolled out a red carpet to as many conservatives. Indeed, when Bush eventually did win the presidency in his own right, his team forced so many Reaganauts out of office that there was bad blood. The Bush folks didn't seem to mind. "They've had their time in the sandbox," one Bush intimate told me dismissively. Reagan was more magnanimous—and smarter.

Less noticed but important to Reagan's early success was a personnel operation under a professional headhunter, Pendleton James.

169

Most presidential candidates wait until after the election and sometimes after the inauguration to begin identifying candidates for the cabinet and subcabinet. Reagan, recognizing the importance of getting an early jump, began moving on recruitment during the campaign. He directed James to assemble a small team and round up names. It was too early to sound them out, but résumés could be collected and preliminary checks made.

Pen was thoroughly prepared. When a new member of the cabinet was named during the transition, Pen was there on his or her doorstep the next morning with a bound notebook containing the names of several potential candidates for major subcabinet positions. "Start here," he said in effect. "These are candidates we think might be good. See if you agree. If not, come back and we'll talk." Those notebooks and the accompanying message helped to fill the government with people who arrived early and stayed loyal to the president who brought them there. To my knowledge, no other modern president has had such a well-oiled personnel machine in place during the transition.

Reagan knew something about management as well as politics, and it was the combination of forces that came together in those eleven weeks. Looking back, scholars generally agree that he ran the best transition in the past half century—a model even now.

Hitting the Ground Running

At the split second of twelve noon on Inaugural Day, John F. W. Rogers had a line of trucks at the South West Gate to the West Wing, ready to move boxes into offices. As the parade started, pictures of the Reagans were going up on the walls. By the end of the day, all was in readiness for work to begin promptly at 7:30 the next morning. A PBS team followed the process and later produced a documentary so complimentary that viewers must have dropped their dinner forks.

The quick start was no accident. After his landslide election victory a decade before, in 1964, Lyndon Johnson warned his staff that each day, his strength would slip away in Congress. They had to move fast, fast, fast. "You've got to give it all you can, that first year. Doesn't matter what kind of majority you come in with. You've got just one year when they treat you right."

Johnson appreciated that time works cruelly against presidents. They tend to have a honeymoon in Washington that may last until

170

August of the first year and perhaps to the end of the year. But, as Steve Hess once wrote, their power declines in Year Two and then, with rare exceptions (FDR in 1934), their party loses seats in the first congressional elections. Having lost strength on the Hill, presidents often concentrate on foreign affairs in Year Three before seeking re-election in Year Four. If strong enough to win the job again, their strength bounces back for just a while, though never as high as in the first honeymoon. Newly reelected presidents also tend to suffer from hubris (witness FDR in 1937, Nixon in 1973, Clinton in 1997), and suddenly they slip into trouble. Domestically, second terms are often a gentle ride downward, hitting bottom in the off-year elections and then bumping along at low levels until shortly before the end, when a wave of public nostalgia may give a retiring president a pleasant send-off. Not surprisingly, many presidents spend more of their second terms on affairs overseas than at home.

In corporations, a CEO who succeeds in the early months can continue to build stature and power within the company for many years to come. So can a university president or the head of most other organizations. But the cycle of power for a president of the United States is unique: freshly elected, he has only the briefest time to make his mark. He must strike immediately and must strike hard if he wants to achieve significant domestic change. Armed with his mandate and strengthened by his transition, Reagan was ready to move from Day One. "We didn't come here just to fiddle with the controls," he told us. "We came to change the direction of the ship."

We also went to school on the failures of the previous administration. After Carter's inaugural parade, his aides drifted into the White House and gathered in the Roosevelt Room, just across from the Oval Office. For a while, they chatted amiably, not sure who was in charge. In the film *The Candidate*, Robert Redford wins election and famously asks, "What do we do now?" Eventually, one of the Carterites piped up with the same question. Robert Lipshutz, the general counsel, realized he was the oldest person in the room and volunteered to run the meeting. Frank Moore, the new liaison to Congress, was asked how they would approach the Hill. "It's just like Georgia ham, you remember Senator. . . ." And so on.

We had seen, too, how Carter had lost traction in his early days. He sent a blizzard of legislative proposals to Capitol Hill, but seemed to lack focus. No one knew what his priorities were. When Reagan raised the issue of priorities in his transition, Baker re- 171 sponded that we would have three: the economy, the economy, and the economy. We stuck relentlessly to that game plan.

Inside the White House, we were tracking Reagan's standing with the public through nightly tracking polls undertaken by Dick Wirthlin. On staff, Frank Ursumorso was simultaneously tracking television coverage on the nightly news, so we could match the polls against what people were seeing on the air. So long as Reagan continued to talk about the economy, his numbers seemed to stay up in the stratosphere. But if we went off message, he dropped.

One day early in the administration, Secretary of State Al Haig testified on Capitol Hill about new information showing the Soviets infiltrating more guns into Central America through Cuba. The United States cannot stand by idly, warned Haig. We may have to "go to the source," he said.

Journalists were already wondering whether Reagan was trigger-happy, so the Haig comment set off a storm. That night, the networks led with stories darkly suggesting that Reagan might use military force to strike at Castro. As the controversy grew over the next couple of days, we watched glumly as Reagan's popularity dropped sharply. His whole reform program could be jeopardized, we thought.

Alarmed, Baker went to Reagan and with his permission called Haig. In essence, he said, "Al, we agree with you that this gun running is dangerous, and we wish you well. But would you please get the hell off television?" It wasn't said that gently, and the reply was anything but. Later, in his memoirs, Haig complained bitterly about the politicos at the White House interfering with foreign policy and identified that incident as one of the seeds of his eventual resignation. As one of the few in the Reagan White House who admired Haig's record—I had seen his contribution to the nation during Watergate —I regretted that dustup. But I also thought Baker was right: it was essential to Reagan's success that we focus unremittingly on the economic agenda.

Throughout those opening weeks, Reagan moved with dispatch to send his tax and spending legislation to Capitol Hill, seeking large-scale victories before the year was up.

Defining Moments

Most Americans took an instant liking to Reagan. He had a warm, sunny disposition, his speeches sang, and he seemed to know where he was going. But in those opening days, they were still hesitant about him as president, uncertain whether he had "the right stuff" to take the country with him. They weren't quite certain what was at his core. If a political figure is not well known on the national stage, it takes more than a single campaign and a few weeks in office to seal his bonds with the public.

By early March, less than eight weeks after he took office, we began to see slippage in Reagan's standing. Try as we might to stay on message, the honeymoon might be fading. I was seriously worried that his economic program might go down, too.

All that changed on March 30, 1981—a defining moment that forever changed the Reagan presidency.

That afternoon, the President had a speech at the Washington Hilton, a dozen blocks from the White House. I had planned to go with him, but seeing that Mike Deaver and Jim Brady were already going and we had plenty of staff support, I decided to hang back for a meeting in the Roosevelt Room.

When Lincoln was shot, it took seven days for word to reach London. When Reagan was shot, a British journalist posted in Washington learned about it within minutes when his editor, sitting in London, saw it on the telly and called him with the news. The ricochet within the White House was even more instantaneous and startling.

The President was SHOT! Would he make it? Would the Reagan candle be snuffed out? Should we invoke the Twenty-fifth amendment, which elevates the vice president when the president is temporarily incapacitated? And what about our friend Jim Brady and the Secret Service man who had been shot?

About a dozen of us gathered in the chief of staff's office and then hastened to the Situation Room, a small, wood-paneled, windowless conference room in the West Wing basement. The "Sit Room" belongs to the NSC staff and is the only space in the West Wing—outside the Oval Office—that is fully secure against foreign intelligence. It is also hooked up electronically to key government sites around the world.

Baker, Meese, and Deaver were at the hospital with the President. Haig soon arrived at the White House from the State Department, Weinberger from Defense, Regan from Treasury, Casey from the CIA. Ordinarily, the vice president would be in charge, but he was on a flight toward Texas; a message went out asking him to turn around and head back. He was due in several hours.

There we sat, nervously monitoring calls from the hospital, Se-

173

cret Service messages, and network television. The early information suggested that the President had not been hit badly. He was in surgery but should be all right.

But who was John Hinckley, the attempted assassin? And why had he shot the President? Were foreign nations involved? Would the Soviets take quick advantage of our situation, moving their military forces somewhere? Haig and Weinberger, never close, began sparring over the defense preparedness of American forces. Weinberger had put them on higher alert; Haig wanted to avoid roiling the international waters. Haig was informally trying to chair our meeting. "The helm is right here in this chair," one participant remembers him saying.

Larry Speakes, the deputy press secretary, returned to the White House from the hospital shortly after 4:00 P.M. and, without knowing of the tensions downstairs, walked into the pressroom, where reporters were thundering with questions. He was reassuring about the President's prospects, but when they zoned in on how the government would operate with the President under anesthesia, he wavered, anxious to avoid a mistake. Surprised that he was even on the air, we watched him closely on television and when he sounded uncertain, Haig exploded.

"We've got to get him off," he insisted, and bolted out of the Situation Room, down the hallways, and up the stairs to the pressroom. Dick Allen and I ran after him. I could see Haig was perspiring freely and wondered whether his heart bypass operation had left him even more breathless than we were. He should have composed himself, but in the rush, burst into the pressroom. It was like walking into a lion's den with lights and questions burning into him.

Al meant to calm things down by his presence. His agitation and perspiration did just the opposite. And so, I am afraid, did his answers. After answering many questions flawlessly, he fumbled. "Constitutionally, gentlemen, you have the president, the vice president, and the secretary of state in that order, and should the President decide he wants to transfer the helm, he will do so. He has not done that. As of now, I am in control here, in the White House, pending return of the Vice President . . ." He was trying to say that the government was continuing to run smoothly and the meeting downstairs was under good control—his own—but his demeanor and words created the jarring impression that the White House was in the hands of someone out of control. It didn't help that he had also mangled the legal line of succession.

Overwrought and out of breath after running up those stairs,

174

Haig paid dearly for his mistake. That phrase, "I am in control here," hung like an albatross, destroying whatever hopes he had to be elected president after Reagan. One slip of the tongue offset nearly three decades of meritorious service. That was a cruel price—and underscored once again how easily a public official can fall off a high wire, especially during a moment of crisis. Ironically, it was Haig who had maintained the coolest head in the Nixon White House and held the government together. He has always deserved more public gratitude than he has received.

Our fear that afternoon soon focused on Jim Brady. A bullet had entered his brain and almost killed him on the spot. At one point, the Secret Service passed information to Secretary Regan that he had died and ABC reported the same thing on television. We were devastated. Dick Allen asked for silent prayer. Moments later, Frank Reynolds reported on ABC that he had been misinformed. We shared his relief as well as his anger.

For hours, we labored inside the White House under the illusion that the President himself had not been gravely wounded. Only later, did we begin to piece together the story of what truly happened—and realize that the shooting transformed his presidency.

As his limousine raced toward George Washington Hospital with Secret Service man Jerry Parr piled on top of him, Reagan himself didn't fully understand that he had been shot. He knew he was hurting but thought maybe Parr had cracked his rib.

Climbing out of the car, he waved off help. Instinctively, he buttoned his suit jacket—a small but telling gesture about his sense of the presidency. As long as the public could see him, he walked upright. Just inside the door of the hospital, he collapsed. A bullet was lodged within an inch of his heart.

In his hours of peril, Reagan maintained a flow of humor that many can recite by heart now. As he was wheeled toward the operating room, he looked up at the doctors and said, "I hope you're all Republicans." To wife Nancy, he said, "Honey, I forgot to duck." That was a quip attributed to Jack Dempsey when Gene Tunney took the heavyweight boxing title from him in 1926. That night, after surgery, he scribbled out a note: "All in all, I'd rather be in Philadelphia." He was recycling an old movie line from W. C. Fields.

Reagan's bonhomie when he was hovering close to death was a "naked moment" in politics—one of those rare instances when people can see through to the core of a public figure. They catch a crucial glimpse of someone's character. There are no handlers around to help put a better face on things.

The cameras have caught people in similar moments over the years: Jackie Kennedy standing fragile but poised after her husband's assassination; Bull Connor unleashing his dogs on black marchers in Birmingham; John Lewis being clubbed on the bridge in Selma; Richard Nixon insisting, "I am not a crook"; Bill Clinton wagging his finger at the nation and denying he ever had sex with that woman. Those moments don't come very often, but they leave indelible impressions. Reagan's "naked moment" came in that hospital.

It was also the defining moment of his presidency. The public rallied to him, as one would expect, but there was now a different feeling about him. To a great many, especially working people, he was now the president who had taken a bullet—and smiled. He had guts. Whatever else one might say about his policies—and when recession hit a few months later, people had plenty of negative things to say—you could never take from him his new reputation as a man of courage who, in Hemingway's phrase, had shown "grace under pressure."

Reagan now stood on a pedestal and would remain there for most of his presidency. People understood his character and began to trust him as they never had before. By responding as he did to crisis, he overcame the opposition that was building up to his domestic program and went on to achieve the best start in the White House since Lyndon Johnson. What no one could plan, his display of courage, became indispensable to his leadership. It was the turning point of his presidency.

FIVE MONTHS LATER, a second incident occurred that was less dramatic but reinforced the belief that Reagan was strong, decisive, and consistent. On August 3, air traffic controllers across the nation declared a strike, threatening chaos in the airways.

Reagan knew where to find his cue. Early on, he had surprised the press corps when he installed a portrait of Calvin Coolidge in the cabinet room. Coolidge had enacted major tax cuts that spurred the economy. Coolidge also slept twelve hours a day, which Reagan liked, too. "It's true that hard work never killed anybody," Reagan quipped, "but I figure, why take a chance?" In 1919, when Coolidge was governor of Massachusetts, two-thirds of the patrolmen in Boston refused to work. He ordered out the National Guard to keep the peace, commenting, "There is no right to strike against the public safety by anybody, anywhere, anytime."

Reagan followed Coolidge now. Without waiting two or three days to test public opinion, he announced that any air traffic controller who wasn't back at work in twenty-four hours would be fired. He charged transportation secretary Drew Lewis with finding replacements to keep planes flying. Most controllers chose to defy Reagan and lost their jobs. But replacements streamed in and the airlines kept to schedules with a minimum of disruptions.

Americans had become accustomed to chief executives who ducked and dithered, trying to postpone hard decisions, looking for a middle ground that would leave no one mad—and no one happy. Reagan cut through that. What? Someone would take charge? Someone had enough conviction to lay down the law? His decisiveness carried the day.

Some believed that Reagan was trying to crush the union movement, just as Margaret Thatcher was doing in Britain. I never thought that. As a former president of the Screen Actors Guild, he was rather sympathetic to unions in the private sector. But public employees were a special category, and Reagan intended to block them from striking, whatever the consequences for his own popularity. Given the growing power of the public unions, he took a clear risk. That didn't seem to matter to him, and for that very reason, the public generally thought he had been gutsy. Along with his courage after the shooting, his crackdown on the controllers shaped Reagan's place in the public mind.

In his first seven months in office, then, he had solidified his hold upon the popular imagination and more through deeds than words. He had demonstrated that he was a man of character whom people could trust for consistency and strength. It was not just that he was happy being Ronald Reagan. That was obvious. But he had also shown that he had a tough inner core and that people could rely upon him. He had courage, and his words and deeds marched in lockstep. He was seen as a leader with conviction—an invaluable asset.

At the heart of leadership is the leader's relationship with followers. People will entrust their hopes and dreams to another person only if they think the other is a reliable vessel. The relationship is very similar to that of two lovers: they are tentative in their feelings until trust is built between them. The other's character—demonstrated through deeds as well as words—is at the heart of it. If over time, a person demonstrates character, trust begins to flow. So it is with leaders: their speeches may be musical, but until one sees them in action, the words may ring seductive but empty.

Reagan's effectiveness, then, depended upon far more than his capacity as a communicator. His speeches were obviously a strength. He was a grand communicator. But his words would have been pure confection, tinsel from Hollywood, had he not proven to people that beneath them was something durable—a character that inspired trust. It was a major building block of his leadership.

Drawing Upon His Staff

The shooting that March introduced dramatic changes within the White House, too. My own life was turned upside down, and the staff itself was challenged as never before. Our boss had lived but he was terribly frail and needed maximum support.

Permit a personal detour. During the transition after the election, Jim Baker had asked about my availability to help out in the new administration. I told him I was open—but with an important qualification. I had grown to admire Reagan and agreed with many of his conservative views, especially his hard-line on foreign policy. After four presidents in a row had been forced from office, I was also deeply worried about the presidency as an institution and wanted very much for him to succeed. But as a moderate on domestic issues—a pro-choice, high safety net man—I did not qualify as a Reaganaut.

It would be better all around, I told Jim, if I were not working in the White House itself. What I really hoped, I said, was to be considered for the directorship of the United States Information Agency, which I wanted to remodel along the lines of the BBC, an authoritative voice in international affairs. Baker and I compromised. At his request, I agreed to come to the White House for six months, helping to get things started, and he gave a gentleman's pledge that at an appropriate time down the road, he would explore with Reagan the possibility of my heading up the USIA. With that, I signed up.

On January 20, 1981, I was proud to take a chair on the inaugural platform, a few rows away from Reagan's swearing-in. Hours later, I could hardly believe that I was moving into an office on the first floor of the West Wing, one door away from the chief of staff, two doors away from the President himself. It was a far cry from the Old Executive Office Building, where I had lodged in two earlier presidencies. The Reaganites were treating me with incredible graciousness.

True to his word, Baker went to Reagan a few weeks after the in-

178

auguration to talk about the USIA job. As it turned out, Reagan during the transition had already asked his old pal, Charlie Wick, to run the agency. Even though I was enjoying my post, I was disappointed. How about the deputy's job at USIA? Jim asked. Maybe Wick won't want to stay long. Let's arrange a meal with Wick, we agreed. So, at a corner table in the White House mess, both of us hesitant, I asked Charlie, "How long do you expect to be around at the USIA?" He looked mischievous. "Well, I haven't decided what I will do during Reagan's second term," he said. At that, we both roared with laughter, knowing I would never wait around that long in the deputy slot. He could now look for his own deputy, as he wanted, and I could look elsewhere. While controversial, Charlie Wick hauled the USIA into the television age and was one of its best directors.

Two months into Reagan's term, I was starting to look for a graceful exit from government. John Hinckley's bullets intervened. With Brady horribly wounded, there was no prospect of him returning as press secretary any time soon. Baker, securing Reagan's blessing, reorganized some of the staff. He asked Larry Speakes to step up as "acting" press secretary, and he created a new post of communications director, asking me to fill it. I was to have oversight of all the administration's external communications—press, speechwriting, relations with the press outside Washington, and coordination of the public affairs units within the departments and agencies. I accepted and remained in the post until leaving the government on December 31, 1983—essentially three years into the first term.

Wise men tell you to take your work seriously, but not yourself. I learned that soon enough. Accompanying Reagan to the Far East, I was among a small group selected for the "official party." We were the ones who followed the President down the ramp at the front of Air Force One, went through the receiving line along the red carpet, were invited to meetings and dinners and had the best rooms. Glittery stuff. I strutted among the best—for a while. Coming into an East Asian capital, the Secret Service had clamped on tight security and word passed there might be snipers about. As we prepared to leave the plane, I noted that the Secret Service agents were quietly passing out bulletproof jackets. There were ten of us in the official party and five jackets. Guess who didn't get one. Guess who stopped strutting.

The shooting of Reagan changed far more than my role; it dramatically affected all of us at the White House. We had to pull together as never before. Fortunately, the rest of the staff arrangements had settled into place so that we had a clearer chain of command than in the early days. The staff was also strong in almost every position. It was a terrific team.

At first, no one in Washington—or in the White House—was certain whether the Baker-Meese-Deaver combination—the "troika"—would work. It had the appearance of a shotgun marriage to some, with Baker representing the moderates, Meese the conservatives, and Deaver the swing. On paper, the troika was a lousy idea. No White House could be run by a committee, especially a White House bent upon change.

What saved it was the emergence of a pecking order among the three. At first, Meese was the dominant player. He had been the heavyweight in Sacramento, so the press assumed he would become Reagan's "prime minister" in Washington, calling the shots for a figurehead in the Oval Office. But Meese didn't have the instinct for the jugular or a fingertip feel for Washington. He was more at home sitting with Reagan at the table, shaping policy directions.

Baker, suave and savvy, was a master of the Washington game. In his first conversations with Meese, he proposed a division of labor. Baker would be in charge of political management and would have direct control of all outreach, including Congress, communications, interest groups, and political groups. Meese would be in charge of policy management: both the domestic policy staff and the national security staff would report to the President through him. Mike Deaver would be "in charge of the body" (the President's schedule as well as all the teams, such as the advance team, that moved him from place to place). He would also be chief choreographer and the main link to Mrs. Reagan. Meese agreed to sign a paper formalizing his arrangements with Baker, and Baker carefully preserved it in his safe. Within months, as he had foreseen, power gravitated into his hands. For most purposes, he became *primus inter pares*—first among equals.

Jim never tried to become "prime minister." Rather, he fit the more traditional role of a strong White House chief of staff, keeping assignments straight, knocking heads, and serving as the major point man on the outside. As it turned out, he was ideally suited for the job and, over the course of the first term, emerged as the best chief of staff in the modern presidency.

From his long association with the Reagans in California, Deaver knew both of them more intimately than anyone else on staff and seemed practically a son. Certainly, he gave them filial devotion. Deaver had also spent years with Meese, Nofziger, and other conservatives from California so that he had natural friendships with them.

180

Yet, Deaver at heart was more of a moderate, and he bonded immediately with Baker. As a result, he often served as an honest broker between both sides, though conservatives came to think he joined the natives. Deaver was also a black belt in public relations, and we shall see more of him in that role.

Every morning, Nancy Reagan spoke to Mike by phone so that he could hear how her husband was doing that day and could convey her wishes to Baker or Meese. To the extent that this extraordinarily private president confided his dreams and frustrations to anyone, it was Nancy. No other president I have known has had such a singular relationship with the First Lady, shutting out almost everyone else from his inner thoughts. She was First Friend, and so far as I could see, no one else came close as Second Friend. Thus, her pipeline to Deaver was important in managing the White House.

At first, Nancy stayed out of policy, but she cracked down hard when we overscheduled her husband and she closely monitored his staff for loyalty, compatibility, and effectiveness. Reagan hated to fire people; she didn't. I remembered Nixon's favorite quote from Gladstone: "Every prime minister must be a good butcher." He was right; somebody has to be the disciplinarian, and in the Reagan White House, Nancy played that role. It didn't help her in press reviews nor with those who were fired. After he lost his job as chief of staff with barely a thank-you for the considerable service he had given over six full years, an enraged Don Regan went after her in his memoirs. But even Regan would admit that in most instances, Nancy was valuable as First Friend and as The Enforcer.

But in the day-to-day operations of the White House, it was the troika who pulled the administration together. They met for breakfast every morning at seven-thirty, comparing notes and preparing items for a larger staff meeting at 8:00 A.M. and a private meeting with the President at nine. They might also confer during the day as events warranted. When Reagan traveled, one of them was always at his side. They also gave him a smooth flow of information upward and tight management of his team below—exactly what a president needs.

That system alone might have sufficed, but it was an innovation introduced by Richard Darman that became crucial: the formation of a Legislative Strategy Group. The LSG expanded the troika to include other players key to enactment of the President's agenda, including the deputy chief of staff and staff secretary (Darman); cabinet secretary (Fuller); OMB director (Stockman); congressional

181

liaison (Duberstein); public liaison (Elizabeth Dole); communications chief (Gergen); press secretary (Speakes); and, as appropriate, policy heavyweights like Anderson or Treasury Secretary Don Regan.

That group met for hour after hour around the conference table in Baker's office, hammering out details of how to get key legislation teed up and then passed on Capitol Hill. Who needed to be stroked in Congress? How? With what arguments? What interest groups must be mobilized? To pressure whom? How should the issue be framed in the press? What columnists need special attention? How about the anchors? What must the President do? How can members of the cabinet take some of the load? If we can't get what we want from Congress, what's our backup plan? The LSG integrated every facet of White House operations so that all came to exert pressure on the important point in the system, giving the President maximum leverage.

Darman created the agenda for our meetings and ensured follow-up. On policy decisions, he was always the best in the room at looking down the street, around the corner, and anticipating what danger might lurk there. While the two of us sometimes sparred, I came to see that his dedication and commitment to public service lifted the quality of the entire government. The LSG should also become a model for every White House to come. Many conservatives always resented Darman's presence—they saw him as a black prince of centrism—but, in truth, he proved to be a pillar of Reagan's success.

On staff, tensions remained high between the conservatives and moderates. There was one point on which conservatives were justifiably rankled: we moderates tended to get too much of the credit for Reagan's successes. In effect, the way the system worked was that the conservatives quietly made the snowballs and the moderates got to throw them, always more eye-catching. Conservative thinkers like Marty Anderson worked for years fashioning policy proposals for candidate Reagan. His work was at the heart of the Reagan campaign and, as noted, formed the basis of his economic agenda. But once Reagan reached Washington, people like Baker, Stockman, Darman, Friedersdorf, and Duberstein did much of the negotiating on the Hill; others like Jim Brady, Larry Speakes, and me did much of the talking to the press, and still others on staff like Elizabeth Dole, Ed Rollins, and Lee Atwater were prominent in working with outside groups. With the exception of Rollins, none of us was a hardcore Reaganaut. Nor had we battled on behalf of Reagan in California or even in the New Hampshire primary.

182

Yet we all began showing up in the news. In every legislative battle, the press prefers to write about the politics rather than the substance of legislation, so the negotiators, organizers, and communicators were paraded out front. Many of the moderates deserved every bit of praise they got, starting with Baker, but the record should show that Reagan's success as president also rested heavily upon conservatives like Meese, Anderson, and Nofziger.

I doubt that Reagan cared who was up or down in the press. He had a sign on his desk: "There is no limit to what a man can do or where he can go if he doesn't mind who gets the credit." What he wanted were results, and those he got.

A half century earlier, FDR frequently pitted his aides against each other in drawing up policies and speeches. The tensions between them set off sparks, making his White House more creative. Whether Reagan was consciously copying the Roosevelt model, I'm not sure, but the system he set up had much the same effect. There was a continual jockeying for power and for Reagan's ear. Each side frequently leaked self-serving information or stories that might be damaging to the other. Machiavelli would have felt right at home. The quarrels were intense, and I tried to keep my back snugly to the wall. Knives could come from anywhere. To my surprise, I learned that some others felt I carried a switchblade, too. That was discouraging. While I didn't mind promoting friends to the press, I tried to avoid saying harsh things about anyone. And I didn't like infighting, probably because I wasn't good at it.

Even so, the tensions Reagan introduced within his team had at least one positive result: they turned his senior staff into toughened professionals ready to take on the outside world. We might not like each other very much, but, to a person, we wanted to win for the Gipper. I had always heard that Kennedy and Johnson inspired fierce loyalties among their troops; now I saw it firsthand with Reagan. It is a powerful force for a president.

Reagan could count on the conservatives on staff to keep the administration heading in the right direction; he could count on the moderates to help clear the path and to strike compromises where necessary. The conservatives liked to ensure that Reagan carried bold colors into battle; the moderates said fine, but let's make sure that when the smoke clears, he still has a victory. The conservatives believed Reagan's strength lay in the heartland, which was true; the moderates said it was also true that to govern, he had to make the 183 system work inside Washington. Inevitably, our views clashed. Reagan didn't seem to care, and, indeed, he stayed out of the fights. He let us settle them outside the Oval Office, usually in Baker's office down the hall. Because of the loyalty people felt toward him, the system worked: we came up with battle plans that served his interests, took them to him for reworking and approval, and then swung into action. Once we got going, we were hard to beat.

Are there lessons here for future leaders about the organization of the White House? I think so. Every president—just like every CEO—must fashion a supporting team that fits his or her own personality. The troika that Reagan had was unique; it would probably not work for another. But the Reagan experience did point to some universal truths about White House operations:

- Every president needs a strong team, starting with a strong, compatible chief of staff.
- The team should include a mix. People who have known the president a long time to keep the flame alive; veterans of Washington to make sure the flame burns effectively. Youngsters to give the team energy; gray hairs to give it wisdom.
- Within the staff, lines of authority should run up and down. They shouldn't run sideways, in a circle, or look like a plate of spaghetti.
- A White House these days, like other organizations, must be able to adjust at lightning speed to new events, but someone still has to manage the team from the top.
- The team should hammer out as many questions as they can out of earshot of the president. They should always keep him informed—no surprises—but should take to him only those questions they cannot or should not resolve among themselves. Don't overload him.
- The president needs an enforcer—someone who can make sure others toe the line.
- And the president needs a best friend—someone with whom he can talk after hours and who won't talk with Bob Woodward.

Working with the Press

Of the six presidents I have known, all but one have felt battered, even brutalized, by the press. Nixon thought the media were instrumental in driving him from office; Bush felt the press never gave credit for the economic recovery that began late in his term; Clinton thought the press denied him a honeymoon and drove him into the arms of Ken Starr. Reagan stands out as the exception.

"He handles the media better than anyone since Franklin Roosevelt, even Jack Kennedy," growled House Speaker Tip O'Neill in late 1981. "We have been kinder to President Reagan than any president that I can remember since I've been at the *Post*," executive editor Benjamin C. Bradlee said in 1984. At ABC, vice president David Burke, who had once worked for a Democratic governor of New York, told Mark Hertsgaard, "I don't know how to explain why he hasn't been as vulnerable to the onslaught as some American presidents; it's a hard subject for me. . . . It isn't because he intimidates us. It isn't that he blows us away with logic. So what the hell is it?"

Most of the answer, as usual, was in Reagan's approach. He treated reporters with respect, and they returned it. That was critical. As frustrated as they grew with his vague, sometimes loopy responses to their questions, they liked him. The "aw shucks" manner got to them. He was a gentleman and, a rarity among politicians, didn't have a mean bone. Like the two Roosevelts, he also provided colorful copy, not just in his one-liners but in his physical appearance, the ruddy complexion, and barrel chest. He could be exasperating to cover, was frequently unavailable, and some of his policies went off track—with results that could be harsh—but the press continued to provide balanced, measured coverage. Even he thought so.

The other part of the equation is that Reagan assembled a strong team and worked with them in launching an offensive in communications. As he did elsewhere in the White House, he integrated two streams of people—advisers like Deaver, Wirthlin, Nofziger, and Fuller who had been with him in California and Baker, Brady, Darman, Speakes, and me, who had worked with the press in Washington.

With the help of our Hundred Days Plan, we were off and running in those opening months. Or was it off and spinning, controlling, elbowing, and manipulating? It may depend on one's perspective. Deaver, Speakes, and Marlin Fitzwater—along with reporters Helen Thomas, Ken Walsh, Sam Donaldson, and Lesley Stahl—have all written lively accounts that provide a range of views.

I was convinced that Reagan had to be on the offensive in his communications. Since Kennedy's time, the White House had gradually abandoned the bully pulpit to the television networks. Executive producers in New York had become the arbiters of what

Americans heard and saw of their president, and what was coming through diminished both the voice and stature of the only person elected by voters to lead the nation. A more aggressive, cynical press corps was making it too difficult to govern. It was time to take the pulpit back.

Our strategy was to focus relentlessly on Reagan's priorities as president. White Houses are tempted to step into every event or minicrisis that arises, but it is a temptation to be resisted. A leader must focus on what's important, not on small issues that pop up randomly. Reagan's repeated emphasis on his economic program served to intensify pressure on Congress, and when he won, magnified his reputation as a leader. We were also thematic in approach, which is not the ordinary inclination of presidents. They assume that the public is hanging on their every word, so that if they make a single pronouncement, word is out. History teaches that almost nothing a leader says is heard if spoken only once. We also spent enormous time paying attention to details and coordinating within the government. Deaver went on foreign advances because we wanted the perfect visual, not just one that would do.

Trust is the coin of the realm in working with the press, just as it is with Congress. There were occasions when someone on staff lied—as we did when John Poindexter of the NSC staff misled Speakes about an invasion of Grenada—but we tried hard to keep those outbreaks under control. Baker was a stickler for truth (one of the reasons why he was extraordinarily effective) and, to my knowledge, Reagan never intentionally lied or misled the press. Having a reserve of credibility in the bank with reporters also helped us out of more than one jam. Trust and respect run both ways, of course, so we tried to sort out which journalists could be depended on to write straight stories. That's why Ann Devroy and Lou Cannon of the *Washington Post*, along with a few others, had such prime access. They would make you squirm with their questions but would always report fairly. Candor matters enormously for both government and the press.

Before returning to my account of his early months in office, let me take a longer view for a moment. If I were to direct a White House communications team today, I would keep about 80 percent of the Reagan playbook and change the rest. We did many things well, and, after airing their complaints, most reporters paid grudging respect. But we also made mistakes. I certainly made my share. In particular, I find it painful how some of the initiatives I helped to launch, have become exaggerated and misshapen in current politics.

186

I worked hard under Reagan to persuade the press corps that he was on the right track, often calling television correspondents just before they went on the air to make sure our views were represented in their stories. Reporters began calling it "the spin patrol." Those efforts were fair, in my judgment, but in the years since, spin has become a twisted form of propaganda.

I also wish that we had had regular press conferences in Washington, as Reagan did in Sacramento. Some on the White House staff were afraid to put him in front of baying reporters and wanted him to stick to speeches in the Oval Office. Their cries reached a fever pitch when he made a series of gaffes in afternoon press conferences in his third year. The networks painted him as a ninny, and some inside wanted to cancel press conferences altogether. Baker, Darman, and I (and perhaps Deaver) prevailed with an alternative idea: schedule his press conferences in prime time and let a giant audience judge for themselves. Reagan agreed and turned those evenings into a success. He still made slips, but his message and good nature drowned them out.

Regular press conferences by a president are the best vehicle we have for ensuring responsible government, and they serve as a stiff disciplinary force upon policy-making within the executive branch. If Reagan had been answering questions from the press regularly after he dispatched Marines to Lebanon in the early 1980s, he would have become so agitated by the lack of clear answers from his own advisers that he would have changed his policies earlier. In Reagan's final year in office, Marvin Kalb of the Kennedy School convened a working group to examine what might be done about the poor state of presidential press conferences (I was a member). The group urged that presidents hold daytime conferences twice a month and six evening conferences a year. I agreed then and now with those recommendations. If anything, I would prefer a daytime session once a week. FDR, after all, averaged almost two press conferences a week in the midst of depression and war. Regular and frequent meetings with the press, as he knew, are indispensable to modern leadership.

Looking back now, I think that Reagan overall did strike a healthier balance with the press corps than most other presidents—and that was part of his success. While he was not available as much as he should have been, he responded to questions with a high standard of honesty. Members of his staff were also accessible, and many of us went out of our way to talk regularly with the press. At the same time, we worked hard to carry his message to the public so that he could govern effectively.

187

Long after I had gone, Reagan demonstrated one other lesson about working with the press—the importance of good damage control. He had botched the Iran-contra affair late in his administration and knew it. That scandal was one of the worst stains on his escutcheon. But what he did thereafter was a model of damage control. He took a series of major steps, first ordering Attorney General Ed Meese to conduct a quick, inside investigation to find out what had happened. He then cleaned house inside, firing or letting go key players like Oliver North and John Poindexter. Opening the door to Congress, he waived all claims of executive privilege and made all relevant documents available. He set up a bipartisan outside commission to look at what had happened and come up with recommendations for tightening up NSC operations, which he then carried out. At first he dodged, but then he took full and personal responsibility for what happened. Finally, he brought an outstanding new team to the White House, headed up by former senator Howard Baker (as incoming chief of staff), Colin Powell, Ken Duberstein, J. B. Culvahouse, Jim Cannon, and David Abshire, who was his counselor in straightening out the mess. When the Iran-contra scandal broke, there had been serious talk of impeachment among congressional Democrats. Dick Wirthlin found that public confidence in Reagan was shattered. By meeting the crisis head-on, especially in the press, Reagan gradually rearranged the political landscape so he could govern again. The following year, he and the Congress were able to work out a sweeping overhaul of the tax system, a feat few thought possible, and Reagan pushed forward in relations with Gorbachev. When one considers how Clinton's handling of the Monica scandal and the resulting fight poisoned the rest of his second term, the wisdom of how Reagan handled Iran-contra becomes all the more important.

A Congressional Touch

Space does not permit a full accounting of Reagan's political skills as president. The story here is intended to highlight what we can learn from his leadership, not serve as an exhaustive retelling. But one cannot understand Reagan's success in Washington unless we see how he dealt with other power centers in the city.

188   Even though Reagan campaigned as an outsider, he understood Washington well enough that he began courting the inside power structure as soon as he was elected. On his first visit to the city dur-

ing the transition, he and his wife supped in Georgetown with Katharine Graham of the *Washington Post*—the very symbols of Washington power that Richard Nixon both envied and hated. The city's elite could have become Reagan's enemies, too, but they never did. He and Nancy told Kay Graham and others that they wanted to be good neighbors, and they were. The Deavers and Bakers built bridges as well, and, over time, so did the Meeses. The Deavers and Meeses still make their homes in Washington.

The relationships that formed did not stop the *Post* or anyone else from knocking Reagan on his conservative policies, but they sucked the venom from the system. Washington, as it has been for much of its history, seemed a civil place to work and dine. People could still enjoy each other's company despite political differences. Those days almost seem quaint in the Washington of recent times, where distrust and disdain have run deep. But the way Reagan reached out, his charm, his political sensibility, made it much easier for him to lead.

Reagan also reached out to Congress, and that paid off even more. A Democratic member told me that over four years of the Carter administration he had had two contacts with the President's chief congressional liaison. The first was a letter saying how much the White House looked forward to working with him. The second was a letter at the end of the term saying how much the White House had enjoyed working with him. Nothing in between. The Democrats' top man in the House, Tip O'Neill, was still smarting from an invitation to Carter's inaugural that placed him out in Siberia. O'Neill started calling Hamilton Jordan, Carter's chief of staff, "Hannibal Jerkin." And these were the memories of Carter's allies!

Lou Cannon, whose account of the Reagan presidency remains the definitive work, writes that Reagan "told me after he was elected in 1980 that the most enduring lesson of his governorship for the presidency was the realization that he could work successfully with the legislature. During the first hundred days of his presidency, Reagan held sixty-nine meetings with 467 members of Congress, prompting some of them to say that they had seen more of Reagan in four months than they had of Carter in four years."

Reagan knew when he had a good act to follow, and he recruited one of the finest congressional staffs since LBJ. Jim Baker was his chief negotiator on substantive issues, while Max Friedersdorf headed up the full-time congressional team, bringing his talents as 189 an old pro who was well liked on the Hill. Ken Duberstein followed Friedersdorf as the chief and was so successful that he eventually became Reagan's chief of staff and remains close to the family to this day. Duberstein, as a Republican, had closer ties to Democrat Danny Rostenkowski, powerful head of Ways and Means, than did the Clinton White House.

But, again, it was largely Reagan who provided the glue, as only a president can. He had an ability to hold together the Republican side in a way no one since Eisenhower had done. In the House, where Bob Michel was the minority leader, Republicans backed Reagan at levels of 90 percent or better on key votes. The press and the Democratic leadership called them "Reagan Robots." In the Senate, Howard Baker and then Bob Dole usually had similar results. Even among Democrats, while every vote was tough, Reagan achieved results that in today's dank partisanship seem impressive.

What accounted for his success in Congress? In part, he was a savvy negotiator. Drawing upon his days with the Screen Actors Guild, he would say "No" at first and the other side would often make a concession. Another "No"; another concession. Finally, he would say "Yes," and they would leap. Then, a year later, he would return for more. Speaker Tip O'Neill thought Reagan knew how to get 60 percent of the loaf the first time and come back for the rest later.

Reagan also had strength in Congress because he could arouse grassroots support at a moment's notice. His years traveling the country had created a small army of supporters. Advisers like Elizabeth Dole, Nofziger, Rollins, and Atwater organized them into a network that came through time and again. Early one afternoon, the Democratic leadership in the House informed us they were moving up a key spending vote to the next day, completely surprising us. Baker called us to general quarters. Reagan was traveling in the West, and that afternoon he read a strong statement to the press on an airplane tarmac, urging congressional passage. It was the lead story that night on all the networks. More importantly, the grassroots team activated their system and by that morning, key members of the House had each heard from more than one hundred of their most influential constituents, urging passage, and that was before the Internet. The bill passed.

None of this would have worked had Reagan not built up personal relationships. He didn't know many members of Congress when he came to Washington, but, as with the press, he treated people there with respect and dignity. There were no enemies' lists, no "us versus them," that we saw with Nixon. From his days as governor, Reagan understood the importance of floating coalitions. Someone who fought you today might be your best friend tomorrow, so you kept your relationship up.

And everyone had a good yarn to swap. Reagan and Tip O'Neill scrapped like tigers during the day, but after 5:00 P.M., they were two Irishmen topping each other with jokes. In a recent biography, Adam Clymer writes that Senator Ted Kennedy's two favorite presidents have been Reagan and Clinton. Despite the chasm between them, Kennedy liked Reagan because he stood for what he believed, conducted himself with dignity, and was personally respectful to the Kennedy family.

His then–chief of staff at the White House, Ken Duberstein, recalls that toward the end of his presidency, when Nancy was on the road, Reagan loved a "stag's night" at the White House. Some of his buddies from the Hill would come down and after dinner, they would sit around over a drink telling each other funny stories, one bawdier than the last. I wasn't there by that time, but I still have memories of listening as Reagan related tall tales for hour after hour with anyone who could keep up. They saw him as a guy's guy.

Years ago, I didn't realize that camaraderie mattered much to leadership. I now think that a leader can barely survive without it. To Reagan, as to other presidents like Eisenhower, Johnson, and Ford, relationships with others were the oil that kept friction down and allowed their initiatives to move more smoothly through the system.

Looking Back with Satisfaction

That August of 1981, as the fog rolled in over his ranch while he sat signing the tax bill into law, Reagan could look back upon one of the most productive beginnings to any presidency since Franklin Roosevelt. Only LBJ in 1965, with huge Democratic majorities, got more major legislation through the Congress. On his big bills on Capitol Hill, Reagan was seven for seven. A Congress with a Democratic House had enacted all of the main features of the economic agenda and the defense increases on which he had campaigned in 1980. Reagan felt he had stopped the growth of the State and was turning the country in a new direction.

The building blocks of his success were clear, at least to those of us who were working for him: his early grounding in politics, a campaign that yielded a mandate, an effective transition, the recruitment 191 of a strong supporting team, the fast start out of the blocks, his decisiveness when crisis hit, the maturation of his staff, and his capacity to work with the press and Congress. Something new was in the air. The notion that no one could govern anymore was now shattered. As Henry Goddard Leach had written after FDR's opening days at the White House, "We have a leader."

There were shoals just ahead, and we couldn't see them that August. Only a few weeks later, the economy began sinking and soon it fell into the deepest hole since the Great Depression. Unemployment rocketed above 10 percent, and the pain was bitter. Even though his own economic programs had not yet taken hold, Reagan became the scapegoat. His popularity ratings plummeted in the spring of 1982. On the media front, I found myself battling back against Bill Moyers—a man I have always admired—for his harsh television portrayals of the hardships Reagan had supposedly brought. Inside, some advisers wanted Reagan to pressure the Fed into easing up on interest rates. Our back channels said Nancy was among them.

Reagan once again showed political courage, but this time he got little credit. As he arrived at the White House, Federal Reserve chairman Paul Volcker was trying to end runaway inflation. Volcker had started to apply the brakes during the Carter presidency, but his monetary policies first began to bite in the fall of Reagan's first year at the White House. That's when the economy went down.

Reagan must have been tempted to go after Volcker, but he knew that inflation had to be slain and he stood by the chairman. In fact, at the urging of Jim Baker and a few of the rest of us at the White House—and over the objection of Treasury Secretary Don Regan— Reagan reappointed Volcker to another term later on. Heading into the midterm elections that year, he even insisted on a campaign slogan: "Stay the Course." It was a tough call. A few political advisers like Lee Atwater thought Republicans might actually gain seats, but others foresaw the bloodbath that occurred: a loss of 27 Republican seats in the House. Chances of getting much done in the next two years were sharply diminished.

Reagan took it in stride: he thought the pain was worth it, even to his own standing, if inflation could be killed once and for all. In the end, he was vindicated.

As the economy came out of the depths in 1983 and Reagan was headed toward a comfortable reelection victory, I thought it was time to take my leave. It is always better to leave a staff when a president is up, not down. Over the course of the recession and various other frays, I knew I was also wearing out my welcome in some quarters. Some conservatives who had always thought I was too moderate were happy to see me go. The President himself gave me a

192

wonderful send-off in a public speech and a warm farewell that drew in my family. From the moment I met Reagan, until the last time I talked to him just before he slipped into his final illness, he was kind.

I looked back upon those early Reagan years with great satisfaction. Reagan had proven it possible for a president to lead again. The voters saw that, too. Lou Cannon points out that when voters went to the polls in 1984 to reelect Reagan, many of them told exit pollsters they liked his stand on government spending or said he would keep the country prosperous and militarily strong. "But 40 percent of these voters—nearly twice the number who cited any specific issues—said that what they liked most was that Reagan was 'a strong leader.' " The public perception rested in part on his identification with American values. "But the perception depended even more on congressional passage of his budget and tax bills in 1981. White House pollster Richard Wirthlin had observed at the time that most Americans, after years of stalemate between Congress and the White House, viewed congressional approval of administration programs as a sign that government was working. Voters consequently gave high leadership marks to Reagan whenever Congress passed portions of his program."

Jeffrey Alderman, ABC polling director, put it this way: "[This 1981] show of leadership was enough by itself to buy Reagan the time he needed. It allowed him to survive the worst recession since World War II with much of the public . . . the bottom held remarkably firm for Reagan throughout the recession." Just so.

6

A Rooseveltian Style

IN STYLE—THOUGH NOT IN SUBSTANCE—Ronald Reagan's role model was Franklin Roosevelt. At twenty-one, casting his first vote for president, he chose Roosevelt over Hoover. As a young radio announcer, he cheered Roosevelt through the streets of Des Moines during the 1936 campaign, and voted for him that year and in each of the two subsequent elections in which Roosevelt stood. FDR's impact upon his leadership style was profound.

Reagan was a New Deal Democrat for almost twenty years. In his memoirs, he even characterized himself as "a near-hopeless hemophilic liberal." His ideological migration finally began as his movie career ended and he began new relationships with General Electric and Nancy Davis. In 1950, he was opposed to Dick Nixon in the California Senate race; by 1960, he supported Richard Nixon in the presidential race. "I didn't desert my party," he would joke. "It deserted me." In truth, his views had changed more than he liked to admit.

But Reagan never lost his affection and respect for Roosevelt. When he was young, he had memorized passages from FDR's first inaugural and listened avidly to his fireside chats. During his years of experimenting with speeches during the 1950s, Teddy White has written, Reagan "learned new rhythms, the hesitation, the toss of the head, the style that he claimed had been inspired by watching Franklin D. Roosevelt." As president, he would recite lines of Roosevelt to us in the Oval Office. FDR was an unmistakable idol.

There are a number of parallels between Roosevelt and Reagan, but one story in particular helps to illuminate Reagan. Five days after taking the oath of office in 1933, FDR paid a surprise birthday visit to Oliver Wendell Holmes, who had just turned ninety-two and was barely a year into his retirement from the Supreme Court. As Geoffrey C. Ward relates in his biography of FDR, "No President ever had a greater sense of historical occasion than Franklin Roosevelt, and Justice Holmes embodied for him much of American history's sweep." Holmes had known Ralph Waldo Emerson, had been wounded three times in the Civil War, and, incredibly, had lived long enough to serve on the High Court for some three decades into the twentieth century. Roosevelt and Holmes talked for about an hour, and after the President took his leave, the Justice eased himself into his favorite chair.

"You know," he said to a companion, "his [Cousin] Ted appointed me to the court."

"Yes, Mr. Justice?"

Holmes considered for a moment and then rendered his verdict on the newest Roosevelt at the White House.

"A second-class mind. But a first-class temperament."

Holmes, continues Ward, "was a shrewd judge of men as well as laws. There were always wiser men and women than Franklin Roosevelt in American public life, people who were better informed, more consistent, less devious. But there were none whose power to inspire both love and loathing was so great, none whose political success or apparent self-assurance exceeded his."

Ronald Reagan did not share all of those qualities. He was not as devious as FDR nor did he inspire as much love or loathing (though he did scare people sometimes). But, like Roosevelt, he had a second-class mind and a first-class temperament—and the combination served him extraordinarily well as president.

Many of us have struggled to understand the qualities of Reagan's leadership. In the last chapter, we considered his political skills as he grasped the reins. In the next, we will look more closely at his capacity to stir the public through his speeches. But we need to examine the man, his instincts, and his values to see him whole.

Many observers come at Reagan asking, in effect, how is it possible that a man with so many gaping holes in his knowledge of the world became a world leader? Is there some part of his mental geography that we are missing? Biographer Edmund Morris puzzles 195 endlessly over that issue, probing to see if there's a there there. He winds up uncertain, dismissing him at one point as an "airhead" and praising him elsewhere for his insights. When Morris cannot locate the real Reagan, he turns to invention.

His frustration in trying to get inside Reagan's head is understandable. Those of us who worked for him found it difficult, too. Even those who had known him intimately for years confessed they couldn't quite make him out. He drew down a curtain to protect his interior and remained emotionally distant from everyone save Nancy.

I grew up believing that the first requirement of leadership is a first-class mind. The heroes of childhood legend, King Arthur, Roland, and Lincoln, were always wise. Didn't that mean they must be very bright, too? Didn't Plato teach us to believe in philosopher kings? And what about Franklin and Jefferson? Weren't they learned men? Didn't they prove that men who knew the most would also do the best?

By my late teens, I still believed that, but I came to see that the brightest minds can also be among the most erratic. Woodrow Wilson, it turned out, was the only Ph.D. who ever made it to the White House, and he went off the tracks in his second term. As historians have pointed out, Wilson was very high strung and arrogant; he was not willing to strike any middle ground. Vietnam reinforced that lesson: men with IQs in the stratosphere were sending blue-collar kids to die without a clue of how to win the war. The "best and brightest" could be dangerous.

I gradually came to think that in electing leaders, we should seek a man of intellectual strength but that we should not rely on brains alone. In the 1950s, Americans had to choose between Adlai Stevenson, an articulate intellectual, and Dwight Eisenhower, a reader of Westerns. My family always admired Stevenson, who was seen as brighter, but, in retrospect, it is clear that Ike was the better leader. It wasn't just a matter of his more centrist philosophy: he had more seasoned judgment and natural instincts for drawing people to him. As Garry Wills has written, "Stevenson was Roosevelt without the polio—and that made all the difference. Adlai remained the dilettante and ladies' man all his life. Franklin was a mama's boy who was forced to grow up."

Eisenhower was certainly a smart man—he planned out the most complicated military invasion in history and had been tested in the crucible of war. But, as president, he kept his keen intellect and political skills hidden from public view. He intentionally tried to appear above the political fray, trying to seem amiable rather than sophisticated, as Fred Greenstein has written in his trenchant analysis:

196

"On the assumption that a president who is predominantly viewed in term of his political prowess will lose public support by not appearing to be a proper chief of state, Eisenhower went to great lengths to conceal the political side of his leadership." According to Greenstein, Ike thought that his approach to leadership was an essential part of his success in ending the war in Korea.

But what was one to make of Reagan? Working for him, I saw he was no dullard, as his critics claimed. From his eight years as governor and his many other years of writing and speaking out, he had thought his way through most domestic issues and knew how to make a complex governmental structure work in his favor. In the first year of his presidency, I also saw him dive into the details of the federal revenue code and become an authority as he negotiated with Congress. When he wanted to focus, he had keen powers of concentration and could digest large bodies of information. He was also one of the most disciplined men I have seen in the presidency (much more so than Clinton, for example), so that he worked straight through the day, reading papers and checking off meetings on his list. At day's end, he headed off for a workout and would plow through more papers in the evening in the upstairs residence. He made the presidency look easy in part by keeping a strict regimen. He also had a retentive mind. After years of memorizing scripts in Hollywood, he could recall verbatim a lot of what he had read. He recited Robert Service poems as well as he did jokes.

Yet Reagan could be remarkably unaware of (and indifferent to) developments around him. If I were still working for him, I would probably pass it off as being "intellectually selective." But it's hard for anyone to argue that he knew as much as a president should about the state of the world. If a subject didn't interest him—many did not—he breezed by it. He knew about the tax code, the size of government, the threat of Communism, and the state of the military. Those mattered to him. As for the rest, he wanted to ensure that policy directions were consistent with his philosophy, but he left the details to others.

His inattention to details and hands-off stance could be dangerous for his leadership. His Republican allies in the Senate believed that because he did not pay close enough heed, he turned down a budget deal in 1985 that they had carefully crafted to cut the deficits. By their account, he didn't seem to understand the terms of the deal and let it slip through his fingers, accepting instead a House proposl. 197 Some Republicans thought that failure cost the party three of the eight Senate seats it lost in the election that fall, returning the chamber to Democratic control. Majority Leader Bob Dole was furious at the time.

Reagan wandered into an even deeper swamp later in his second term because he had blithely allowed Treasury Secretary Don Regan and White House chief of staff Jim Baker to swap jobs in late 1984. A president who had been a shrewd judge of personnel in his first term didn't think through what he needed in a second. With Meese and Deaver going out the door at the same time as Baker, the President surrounded himself with a considerably weaker team. His new chief had been a success as treasury secretary and as former CEO of Merrill Lynch, but he wasn't cut out to run the White House, especially with a president who heavily delegated power. Neither Reagan nor Regan tended the store as they should, giving a young Oliver North and his national security boss, John Poindexter, an opening for extraordinary mischief. The result was the Iran-contra affair, a scandal so serious that it stirred up impeachment efforts on Capitol Hill and badly impaired their capacity to govern.

In effect, there were three Reagan presidencies: Reagan I, when he had the troika; Reagan II, when Don Regan was staff chief; and Reagan III, the Baker-Duberstein era. The first and third were successes, but the second bordered on disaster. Together, they showed a president whose extensive delegation of authority and inattention to important details made him more dependent upon the quality of the people around him than is wise. In one instance, he paid dearly because he chose the wrong people. This experience suggests that Reagan was not a model in every respect. It is important for chief executives to have a firmer hand on the tiller than he had. He himself must have realized that the Iran-contra affair damaged him badly in the eyes of historians.

But the interesting point is how successful Reagan was despite his weaknesses. Even with his failings, he was a leader. Something about him obviously compensated—overcompensated, really—for the lack of a curious, penetrating mental ability that we normally associate with strong presidents. Biographer Lou Cannon points us toward the answer. "The riddle of Reagan's intelligence for a long time seemed insoluble," Cannon writes in his biography. "Then I came across the work of Howard Gardner, a Harvard psychologist who has pioneered in developing a theory of 'multiple intelligences.' ... In place of a single intelligence, Gardner postulates seven specific intelligences with distinctive characteristics. In Gardner's categorization, Reagan ranks high in a form of intelligence he calls 'interpersonal,' high in 'bodily-kinesthetic intelligence,' high in an aspect of 'language intelligence' and low in the 'logical-mathematical intelligence' at which lawyers and professors usually excel. . . . Gardner's analysis of the way Reagan functions intellectually produced in me the sense of discovery that a scientist or a detective must feel when a gigantic mystery abruptly becomes comprehensible."

Cannon continues: "Others who have struggled even longer to explain Reagan think this theory of intelligence makes sense. 'That's exactly right,' said Stuart Spencer, who understands Reagan as well as anyone I know. 'Exactly. I'm always asked to explain him, and I talk about him as intelligent but not intelligent in the way politicians are intelligent. This explains him."

Since the original publication of Cannon's biography in 1991, Daniel Goleman has written extensively about one element of multiple intelligence that most clearly fits Reagan—what Goleman calls "emotional intelligence." A person's "EQ" is his capacity to relate both to self and others. Goleman argues that there are five components to a person's emotional intelligence. Three measure relation to self: self-awareness, self-regulation, and personal motivation. The other two components are empathy for others and social skills, both measuring one's relationship to others.

The interesting point for our purposes is Goleman's research into corporate leaders. From his study of 188 companies, summarized in the *Harvard Business Review,* he concludes that the higher up one climbs in the corporate world, the more important emotional intelligence is to effective leadership. To gain a place on the corporate ladder, one needs reasonable brains and technical competence. Those are entry-level requirements. But as one acquires more responsibility, what distinguishes a leader who succeeds is increasingly his emotional intelligence. People who are only smart usually flame out. The leader most likely to succeed has perhaps only a relatively good mind but strong emotional intelligence. Goleman writes: "The higher the rank of a person considered to be a star performer, the more emotional intelligence capability showed up as the reason for his or her effectiveness. When I compared star performers with average ones in senior leadership positions, nearly 90 percent of the difference in their profiles was attributable to emotional intelligence factors rather than cognitive abilities."

The "emotional intelligence" Goleman describes seems to be exactly what we traditionally have called "temperament." Reagan exhibited all five of Goleman's characteristics. He was certainly self-aware, self-regulated, and self-motivated. Even more, he had an ability to read others and to inspire their trust. (Note how Clinton,

199

who is empathetic and has strong social skills, falls short on other elements of Goleman's scale.)

It was said of Reagan that he never had to take the pulse of the country; he *was* the pulse. He had a fingertip feel for the mood of the country that was as good as anyone we've had in the presidency, including Clinton. That's not to say polls were unimportant to him. He looked forward to his strategy sessions with Dick Wirthlin, who reviewed the latest numbers and offered political counsel. But he relied upon polls less for policy-making than for double-checking his instincts and sharpening his arguments.

Reagan could reach people with his speeches because he felt an emotional bond with them. They weren't "children" to him, as they were for Nixon; they were fellow Americans. He wasn't talking to them, as most leaders do; he was giving voice to them. When the shuttle carrying the astronauts exploded, Reagan spoke in a way that gave expression to what millions of Americans thought already. At the fortieth anniversary of D-day, he could put himself in the shoes of the men who had climbed up Pointe du Hoc and describe what they felt inside.

People who came into Reagan's presence felt protective about him. If he didn't pick up on an argument made in a cabinet meeting, a George Shultz would make everyone stop the proceedings, force the speaker to go over the point again, making sure Reagan had it. At Number 10 Downing Street, I watched Margaret Thatcher talk over issues with him as an equal. But just before they went out to see the press, she turned motherly. "Mr. President, can I suggest that you say this . . . and then I might say this . . ." And so on. People say she thought Reagan was incompetent, but I never saw a hint of condescension. Like Shultz, she was gentle and caring, trying to make sure he navigated safely. With a Clinton or Nixon, aides might snipe behind his back or roll their eyes if he went off half-cocked. Not here. I was reminded that in Japan, it is customary to designate special artists and craftsmen as Living National Treasures. Associates around Reagan treated him the same way. Eisenhower, say those who worked with him, inspired similar support.

Reagan changed my mind about the qualities we need in a president. We no more need an Einstein in the Oval Office than a Mother Teresa. What we need is someone who has a good grasp of public affairs and an excellent temperament. The United States experienced some of its best leadership under Franklin Roosevelt. And FDR turned out to be a good model for Reagan.

200

A Contagious Confidence

Reagan had a sunny confidence in the future that served him well, too. As George Will put it, he had "a talent for happiness." Biographers say it came from his early days in Dixon. What I saw of him persuaded me that, like so much else, it was also rooted in the Roosevelt era. Twice when he was a young man, he saw the country knocked flat—first in the Great Depression, and then at Pearl Harbor and the losses that followed in the Pacific. Each time, the nation picked itself up and came roaring back. Reagan came away with an indelible impression that America was a resilient nation, capable of achieving anything its people put their minds to doing.

He was struck by the way Roosevelt could rally people's spirits. Churchill once said Roosevelt was like an electric light who lit up everything around him. Reagan always remembered that glow from Hyde Park and set out to provide the same thing himself when he was in the White House. In 1981, preparing for the centennial celebration of Roosevelt's birth, David McCullough talked with former presidents and with Reagan. Of them, he found Reagan the most enthusiastic. "He gave confidence to the people. He never lost faith in this country for *one minute*," Reagan told McCullough. "I must say I think [FDR] was a great war leader . . . I remember him when he . . . said that he was going to ask for 50,000 planes a year, and I remember when the American press tore him to ribbons for that. . . . They said that, you know, that this was impossible. It couldn't happen. But when you look at what this country did starting from the low point of Pearl Harbor in 44 months—something like 350,000 planes and hundreds of thousands of tanks and of trucks and of every kind of weapon, we truly were the arsenal of democracy . . . I think his leadership in the war was great."

Reagan was by nature a dreamer who liked to dream of what the country could be. He wanted to raise people's expectations of what they could become if they would unite behind his banner. Some of his notions sounded corny. But he genuinely believed in them and persuaded others to believe in them, too.

Reagan was also lucky in following Jimmy Carter. The two men could hardly have been more different. Carter was a quiet, studious man who didn't try to fill a room. Reagan was a large, barrel-chested man who walked like John Wayne. Carter was inward-looking; Reagan loved to laugh and be "one of the fellas." Carter was Scotch-Irish; Reagan was all Irish. Wrongly, Carter struck some people as

201

prissy; Reagan was full of bluff. Most of all, Carter had confidence in himself but little confidence in other people; Reagan was brimming with confidence in both. To Reagan, the future always looked brighter than today, no matter what the polls were saying.

He had been proud of his record and his physique since his early years in the Middle West. It was not just the number of people he fished from the river where he was a lifeguard. He also took satisfaction in his good looks and the way girls gathered round. He took care of himself. When doctors opened him up after his shooting in 1981, so I was told, they found he had a younger body than press secretary Jim Brady, a man thirty years younger.

When I saw Reagan during his convalescence, he seemed smaller and frail, shriveled. But then he put himself on a workout regimen in a gym he built on the third floor of the White House. Within no time, it seemed, he had added an inch and three-quarters to his chest—pretty darn good for a man seventy years old! Months after the shooting, I went up with a small group to see him at Camp David. He was at poolside showing two young children how to do "jackknives," jumping off the board, touching his toes, then stretching himself out before knifing into the water. The kids were having trouble making it; to the old lifeguard, it was easy. Novelist Tom Clancy remarked after meeting Reagan, "This guy has a handshake like a lumberjack."

In 1983, an editor of *Parade* magazine called to ask for an interview with Reagan about his physical fitness regime. That was a story to die for, I thought; if we had proposed it, they might have said no, but here they were proposing it to us. "Well," I hemmed and hawed, "I'm not so sure he would want to do that. He might see it as an invasion of his privacy. But I'll tell you what: if you will also agree to run a cover picture of him working out, maybe we can talk him into it." They took the bait. "Oh yes, that sounds good to us. We weren't sure he would be up for a photo shoot. Why don't we try to do that." A few weeks later, the story itself drew little attention. But the cover picture of Reagan working out was a smash. More than 23 million people saw their president, age seventy-two and victim of a near-fatal wound, looking like a graying Tarzan. How could people not draw confidence from that?

Reagan didn't preen or put on airs. As proud as he was to be president, he regarded himself as a temporary occupant. This is "the people's house," he said, and he felt as he did growing up, "living above the store." He had a quiet assurance about life, so that he seemed to glide, serene in his belief that everything would turn out

202

for the better. People felt good being around him, as if everything would be all right for them, too. The contrast with other presidents was stark. With Nixon, for example, I was often in awe but usually on edge. With Clinton, the focus is typically on him—what he is feeling, whether he is angry or frustrated, and how he is mentally processing. Reagan directed attention away from himself because he was so comfortable with who he was.

Consciously or not, Reagan was following in a tradition set early in the century by Teddy Roosevelt and picked up by Woodrow Wilson in his first term, then by Franklin Roosevelt and John Kennedy. Each understood a fundamental lesson: that leaders must inspire people with confidence in the future. Only if he truly believes in the future himself will his followers make the leap and join him. Optimism is contagious.

A Reliance Upon Ideas and Instincts

Ronald Reagan never pretended to be an intellectual and never bothered to read much political philosophy. Yet his ideas probably changed the world as much as those of any other political leader in the late twentieth century. I was told Margaret Thatcher once said, "He only had five or six ideas, but all of them were big and all of them were good." While others may disagree about their quality, there is little doubt about their impact.

Few ideas in politics spring full-blown from the minds of politicians. Occasionally, a leader like FDR might take a few days away from the hurly-burly and come up with a creative plan for providing armaments to Great Britain, as he did. But most of Roosevelt's early agenda in the Depression was drawn from policy notions developed by liberals while they were out of national power and then from professors and others who streamed into Washington after his election. Roosevelt was wise enough to pick and choose from their menu. Similarly, Reagan was blessed as a leader because the conservative movement had generated a storehouse of policy solutions while it was out of power. Think tanks like the Hoover Institution, the American Enterprise Institute, and, increasingly, the Heritage Foundation and the Cato Institute had seized the intellectual offensive in policy debates during the late 1970s, and their scholars and other conservative thinkers provided a rich array of fresh ideas. Reagan, like Roosevelt, knew enough to draw heavily from his intellectual allies.

I saw one of those ideas take shape—and only later began to un-

203

derstand its power. It was the spring of 1983, two years after he took office, and Reagan was engaged in a fight with Congress over his call to increase defense spending once again. To marshal public support, Reagan wanted to speak to the country on prime time television.

Gearing up, our speechwriters gathered with defense experts around the government to produce a draft. As communications director, my job was to keep one eye on the drafting process while persuading the networks to carry the speech live.

During the Cold War, the networks traditionally opened their airwaves anytime a president wanted to talk about national security, but in this case, they resisted because Reagan's proposed speech sounded like a sales pitch for his defense budget. "Will he make any news?" the Washington bureau chiefs pushed me. "Otherwise, New York doesn't want to give up its entertainment shows with all those ad dollars just to give the president a free shot to lobby Congress."

Our draft so far didn't break any new ground, but Jim Baker told me a mysterious, last-minute insert would be coming from the NSC staff that would definitely make news. "I can't tell you now exactly what it will be." He winked. I had learned the networks would carry a Reagan speech if we not only promised them hard news, but also gave them an advance peek at the contents. We could trust the bureau chiefs not to tell their own correspondents what was coming, so the President would not be scooped. But that informal arrangement required us to show a little ankle. A mere promise of news would not be enough, I thought.

Sure enough, they balked. So I returned to Baker: "Look, Jim, you need to call them yourself and give an iron-clad guarantee that we will be making big news. They're not buying it from me; they're more likely to take it from you." He called and made a hard sell that the president's "surprise" would be big news. The networks agreed to carry it—and never regretted their decision.

Late in the morning of the speech, a group of us—Dick Darman, Ken Duberstein, Craig Fuller, Larry Speakes, and I—were called into the Situation Room where the NSC adviser, Bill Clark, and his deputy, Bud McFarlane, finally unveiled the mysterious, one-page insert. We were startled: seemingly out of the ether, without full debate in or out of the government, Reagan was calling for the United States to erect a missile defense shield that would cover the country.

Both the feasibility and costs of the Strategic Defense Initiative 204 were missing from that one-pager. Had anyone figured out the answers? Some of us were aghast that so grandiose a proposal was being launched without a thorough vetting inside the government.

We knew as well that congressional bulls like Senator Pete Domenici would be outraged because they had expected the speech to help settle the defense budget fight; SDI would pull the rug out from them. A surprised secretary of state, George Shultz, read a draft before delivery and reportedly commented, "We don't have the technology to say this." "We weren't ready to announce it yet—the necessary policy groundwork had not been laid," Admiral James Watkins of the Joint Chiefs said later.

But, for the moment, our second-guessing would have to wait. Now we had to hustle to ensure that Congress was properly notified, other agencies in government were alerted, foreign governments were told, White House briefings would be ready, press packets written, friends like Henry Kissinger contacted—the full nine yards. The President had made his decision; we needed to carry it out.

In the short run, the secrecy that enshrouded the birth of SDI came back to haunt us. Congress was indeed angry, the press was confused, and allies were aghast. We sprang the idea on the world with so little advance warning that scientists and nuclear strategists immediately attacked it as "Reagan's folly." A missile defense was years if not decades away, they said; even if we could build a miniversion one day, it would cost a gazillion dollars, destabilize the nuclear balance, and bring the world closer to the brink of a conflict with the Soviets.

Henry Kissinger had been scheduled to give a public briefing supporting Reagan's expected call for more defense spending. Now uncertain what to say about missile defense, he canceled. Commentators and cartoonists tore into us. This is a fantasy from Hollywood, they cried, Reagan's own Star Wars. Missile defense was in trouble on Capitol Hill from the moment of announcement.

But in one place, people were paying serious attention: Moscow. And that's what counted in the long run. A number of Soviet sources have since reported that their bosses in the Kremlin, starting with Mikhail Gorbachev, were thrown into turmoil by Reagan's idea. They were not sure the United States could make good on the idea, but they knew they could not. To them, whether SDI *would* work was less important than whether it *could* work. The United States had challenged them to a race they could not win. Rather than bankrupting themselves trying, they left the game.

Former Soviet foreign minister Aleksandr Bessmertnykh told a Princeton University conference in 1993 that SDI "made us realize we were in a very dangerous spot." The proposal, he said, accelerated the collapse of the Soviet Union. James Baker said in 1998 of Reagan,

205

"I think he saw SDI as a pressure the Soviet Union could not withstand, and I think he was right." Margaret Thatcher was more emphatic. She said later, "Reagan's decision to go ahead with SDI ended the arms race as we knew it; the Soviet Union couldn't match SDI." To her, SDI was the most important initiative of the Reagan presidency.

I doubt SDI would have gotten off the drawing boards under any chief executive other than Reagan. Another president would have vetted the idea within the government. The Pentagon and State Department would have strenuously opposed it, especially in the expansive form that Reagan proposed. The proposal would surely have leaked as well, and outside experts would have shot it full of holes. Reagan's chief conspirators inside, such as McFarlane and science adviser Jay Keyworth, understood and worked assiduously to keep its existence secret until the last minute. The President gave his blessing.

Were many within the administration stung by the secrecy and lack of advance scrubbing? Absolutely, and I was among them. It is an article of faith within public administration that before going public, every proposal must be studied six ways from Sunday. That remains the best approach to policy-making. But in this instance, were we better off that Reagan sprang his vision this way? In retrospect, I would have to say yes. With a by-the-book review, SDI would have been so watered down that it would never have had a bang in Moscow. The Cold War might have lingered for years to come.

What the SDI episode revealed was Reagan's deep reliance upon instinct and a faith in American ingenuity. As Hedrick Smith points out in his book *The Power Game: How Washington Works*, Reagan had a personal epiphany in 1979 when he and his domestic adviser, Martin Anderson, had a briefing at the North American Defense Command in Colorado. Reagan was struck by the fact that if the Soviets launched a missile strike, a president had only two options, both unacceptable to him: hit the button or do nothing. Nuclear physicist Edward Teller persuaded him a third option was possible: a missile defense. Reagan then engaged in a series of quiet conversations and briefings over time that convinced him to go forward with SDI. He was playing a hunch, as he knew, but his common sense told him it might just work and it was worth taking the risk. Controversy continues still. One day soon (hopefully), the United States will erect a limited missile shield, but experts still decry the feasibility, cost, and destabilizing effects of a robust system. Whatever shortcomings SDI may have as a military weapon, however, it surely worked as a diplomatic weapon.

A reliance upon instinct and a gambling spirit were integral to

Reagan's leadership. They gave him the confidence to embrace bold ideas and rally the country behind him. Sometimes he threw the dice and lost. Early on, at least, that appeared to happen in his economic plan. Cutting taxes more than spending, he hoped that a growing economy would bring in so much extra revenue the federal government would balance its books. Senator Howard Baker, later his chief of staff, called his plan "a riverboat gamble." The economy did grow, but the deficits exploded. Reagan, Bush, and Clinton were all forced to raise taxes (though rates remain much lower than when Reagan took office). Over the course of Reagan's two terms, the federal debt jumped from over $1 trillion to over $4 trillion. In 1999, Washington paid out over $300 billion in debt service, a scandalous figure. Those of us who worked in the Reagan White House should own up to our responsibilities. One of my greatest regrets from government service is in not fighting harder to hold down deficits.

Two points should be added. Democrats in Congress share responsibility for the deficits of the 1980s too, having refused to control entitlement spending. There is also great merit to the argument of Reagan economist Lawrence Kudlow, who says that Reagan's economic plan helped to ignite the economic boom of the 1980s and 1990s. The gamble that didn't work in the short run, then, has turned out considerably better over the long haul.

For students of leadership, there is an equally important lesson: leaders who advance large ideas are usually gambling with the future. Inevitably, some ideas fail, but the best leaders are not paralyzed by fear of what may go wrong. Roosevelt was a master gambler in the New Deal. Throughout his first term, he tried one thing after another until something worked. Two of his biggest initiatives, the NRA and AAA, failed. "I have no expectation of making a hit every time I come to bat," he said in his second fireside chat, and he went right on swinging. As long as he kept trying, he knew the public would invest hope in the future. Sometimes a leader doesn't solve a crisis; he helps followers get through a crisis. Lincoln felt he had no choice but to gamble in the Civil War. He kept on improvising on military strategy and finally, in Grant and Sherman, found generals who embraced his ideas for an unconditional victory.

That's not to say that recklessness in a leader is a good thing, nor is a willingness to fly by the seat of the pants. Decisions should obviously be thought through in advance, prudence should be shown, and plans should be made to figure out worst-case scenarios. But equally important are leaders who have sound instincts, solid values, a faith in the future—and the courage to act. What Reagan

207

lacked in the way of meticulous planning and policy knowledge he usually compensated for in his instincts, values, faith, and courage. There he was as surefooted as Roosevelt. Most of his leaps into the dark carried across the chasm and onto higher ground.

Steady in His Core Beliefs

Like most successful leaders, Reagan had developed a set of core beliefs long before he came to power. They were not in popular favor during the 1960s and much of the 1970s, but by the end of those turbulent decades, many Americans were ready to embrace them. As old-fashioned and as simple as they sounded, Reagan gave them new life.

It was also important that Reagan consistently stuck to his values while in office. One of the marks of a leader is whether he or she has a sense of conviction and can hold to it. The leader can be flexible in the means of getting there but should be firm about direction. Lincoln once compared his efforts to save the Union to his days as a young man when he was navigating a small boat on the Mississippi. His object was always the same, but to make it down the river he learned how to steer "from point to point." Reagan held firm to his direction throughout his eight years, even as he shifted course temporarily. His beliefs were his guide.

One can summarize them briefly:

America is a chosen nation with a special mission. To Reagan, religious and patriotic beliefs went deep and were so intertwined that one could barely distinguish them. To him, Americans were a "chosen" people who had to prepare the way for Armageddon. If he had an anthem, it came from John Winthrop's famous sermon in which he told Pilgrims aboard the *Arbella* that they should become a "city upon a hill." Lincoln had been right when he called America "the last, best hope of earth." Reagan did not feel a messianic urge to spread American ideas and culture to other countries, as did some of his predecessors. But he did think the country had to set an example and that it should nurture democracy and freedom in other lands.

His evangelism had a distinctly religious tone. Billy Graham has told me that religious beliefs were actually at the core of Reagan's presidential leadership. After he was shot in 1981, Reagan told Graham privately that he felt he had been spared by his Maker and that the rest of his time in the White House belonged to Him. He repeated that sentiment at a National Prayer Breakfast and in other forums.

America should be number one. Not second and not second to none. Number one, period. However enlightened Gorbachev might be, a Kremlin ruled by Communism was still an evil empire that threatened America's existence. Therefore, he refused to accept the notion popular in the late 1960s and 1970s, especially on the Left, that America could afford an equal co-existence with an enemy bristling with weapons. He thought it vital for the protection of freedom that the United States be the foremost military, economic, and political power in the world. And he wanted to see Communism destroyed, so that it would no longer threaten anyone. "Mr. Gorbachev, tear down this wall," he declared in perhaps his most influential speech.

Strength matters. Starting in Vietnam, Reagan believed, the United States had lowered its guard, letting its military strength deteriorate and practically inviting its enemies—from Moscow to Tehran—to advance. He was willing to spend whatever it took to rebuild the military, even if that drove up budget deficits. Only American strength would ensure peace.

Freedom matters. America would be strong at home only if it unleashed the energy and imagination of its people. Just as the United States had permitted its adversaries overseas to grow too powerful, it had permitted its government at home to become too burdensome. Not only that, but the experiment in Big Government wasn't working. "The government declared a war on poverty. And poverty won," he quipped. Long before he came to Washington, it was obvious that cutting taxes, cutting spending, and cutting regulations would be the centerpiece of his domestic agenda.

Values matter. The American experiment depends not only upon the preservation of individual freedom, but also on the cultivation of old-fashioned values. Growing up in the rural Midwest, Reagan had imbibed those values early and had clung to them even in Hollywood. But he thought they, too, were crumbling in modern life, and he set out to restore them.

One feels almost embarrassed trying to summarize Reagan's core ideas, so familiar are they. But it's important to recognize that in the context of the late 1970s, Americans were tired of rebellions and were looking for a restoration of old-fashioned values. Reagan was giving voice to ideas whose time had come again. Moreover, he voiced his beliefs so consistently that they became synonymous with who he was. His ideas and personality merged, and there is nothing more powerful than that for a leader. Reaganism was what Reagan was all about. We see the makings of a "Great Communicator." 209

7

Secrets of
the Great Communicator

THE MOST MEMORABLE PRESIDENTS of the twentieth century have
been excellent communicators. Teddy Roosevelt invented the bully
pulpit to drive the country forward. Woodrow Wilson's speeches are
some of the finest expressions of idealism and of democratic sentiment ever voiced by a political leader. Franklin Roosevelt gave hope
and light to millions of downtrodden Americans with his fireside
chats. John F. Kennedy, the first president elected through television,
turned it into a magic wand. And then there was Reagan.

One finds exceptions to every rule of leadership, of course. In
the first days of the Republic, Washington believed he should express himself more through actions than words. While eloquent with
a pen, a shy Thomas Jefferson gave only two public speeches during
his eight years in the presidency, his first and second inaugurals.
Neither Truman nor Eisenhower was noted for his oratory. So, it can
happen that great presidents are not excellent speakers. In the modern age, however, there is no weapon more powerful than persuasion by speech. As Winston Churchill once wrote, "Of all the talents
bestowed upon men, none is so precious as the gift of oratory. He
who enjoys it wields a power more durable than that of a great king.
He is an independent force in the world."

I was Reagan's first "director of communications" at the White
House. The title was a misnomer. He was director, producer, and star
210 all rolled into one—the "communicator in chief" from the beginning
to end of his presidency. The rest of us might think we were important, and there were moments when we were. But we were staff in

the true sense of the word: the President leaned on us when he wanted to. When the curtain went up, he stood at center stage alone.

While Reagan was a born storyteller, he worked hard to hone his skills. For more than half a century, he made his living by holding an audience. Signing on as a radio broadcaster just out of college, he built a reputation covering the Chicago Cubs and learning to describe the game through his imagination. In those days, minimal pitch-by-pitch accounts would come over a telegraph wire and Reagan, sitting in Des Moines, would reconstruct the game in colorful detail.

Of the six hundred games he re-created over radio, Reagan's favorite occurred on a day the telegraph failed and he had to fake the game until it went up again. "When the slip came through, it said, 'The wire's gone dead.' Well, I had the ball on the way to the plate," Reagan recalled at a White House luncheon for Hall of Famers in 1981. "I thought real quick, 'There's one thing that doesn't get in the scorebook,' so I had Billy [Jurges] foul one off . . . and I had him foul one back at third base and described the fighting between the two kids that were trying to get the ball . . . And I did set a world record for successive fouls, or for someone standing there, except that no one keeps records of that kind. I was beginning to sweat when Curley [in the control room] sat up straight and started typing . . . and the slip came through the window and I could hardly talk for laughing because it said, 'Jurges popped out on the first ball pitched.' " Is there any doubt where Reagan learned to embroider a story?

Young Walter Cronkite broke in about the same time, announcing news and games from KSMO radio in Kansas City. He was broadcasting a Notre Dame–Southern Cal football game when his wire went down for nearly a half hour. He still regales audiences with the plays that he invented to keep the teams rolling back and forth at midfield until the wire went up. Years later, Cronkite and Reagan loved to swap stories.

Dutch Reagan's honeyed voice helped him all the way to the White House. In 1937, three years after he broke into radio, he persuaded his station to let him go to Southern California to cover the Cubs' spring training (and to give him a chance to knock on doors in Hollywood). When Warner Brothers opened one just a crack, he jumped through and for thirty years—the prime of his life—he was an actor or a union representative of actors. "From the time of his first screen test until he went to Sacramento as governor of California in 1967, Reagan was Hollywood's child, citizen, spokesman, and defender," writes Lou Cannon. On the screen, he never matched idol

211

and near-look-alike Robert Taylor, as some hoped, but his acting was good enough and he built a national reputation. In fifty-two films, he was usually the good guy who sometimes got the girl—a reputation that helped in politics. Near the end of his presidency, David Brinkley asked whether anything he had learned in Hollywood had helped him in the White House. He grinned: "There have been times when I've wondered in this office how you could do this job if you hadn't been an actor." He knew what many of his predecessors also learned: every good leader is good on stage.

In the early 1950s, Reagan's acting career was fading, his presidency of the Screen Actors Guild ended, and Jane Wyman left their marriage. He might have come apart if new forces had not entered his life: Nancy Davis and General Electric. With one, he recovered his heart; with the other, his voice. Nancy, who married him in 1952, became his greatest source of strength. GE hired him to play host and occasional parts in a new weekly drama series on television. He was also expected to tour the country for ten weeks a year, plugging GE products and meeting employees. Nothing was said about delivering speeches, but after he gave his first one to plant employees, he was off and running. Over the eight years of his contract, he was out regularly, sometimes delivering as many as fourteen speeches a day. He was a white-knuckle flier, so trains carried him.

One cannot overestimate how much those speaking tours shaped him as an emerging political leader. Listening to average Americans talk of their lives, learning how to read an audience, watching sparks come into eyes of listeners as he made a telling point, Reagan evolved rhetorically and philosophically. He learned as much about public persuasion as any politician in the country, and he found his political voice. When the decade opened, he was a Roosevelt Democrat; by its end, he was a Goldwater Republican. Over time, he developed and repeatedly delivered a talk about the creeping dangers of governmental socialism in Washington. He would modify it to fit his audience and incorporate new facts, but the framework remained. In 1964, it became "The Speech," a thirty-minute television appeal on behalf of Goldwater that vaulted him into politics and into the governor's chair. It wasn't far from there to the top. For good reason, he was called "The Great Communicator" long before he was called "Mr. President."

Ever since Reagan left the White House, people have wanted to know the secrets to his success as a communicator. Former assistants like Mike Deaver and speechwriter Peggy Noonan, academic scholars like Kathleen Hall Jamieson and Paul D. Erickson, and journal-

212

ists like Lou Cannon and Ken Walsh have all written fine accounts. Yet the question persists. Audiences have asked me everywhere. Not just Republicans but Democrats have invited explanations. I am convinced that one reason Bill Clinton asked me to join him in the White House was to unlock the answers. For all their differences, Clinton wanted to know, "How would Reagan have handled this one?"

There is no step-by-step program to duplicate him, no off-the-shelf guide. As with other rhetorical leaders like Martin Luther King, Jr., and Franklin Roosevelt, Reagan was a man unique unto himself, effective in his time and place. No one can clone a leader from the past. Even so, there is much to gain by teasing out the different elements of his success. They shed light on some important questions. Why can some speakers mesmerize a crowd, while others bore? What makes them persuasive? Why do their thoughts linger in our minds?

In the pages that follow, I once again draw a sympathetic portrait of Reagan. As noted earlier, I recognize that he had his flaws and that many do not share his politics. But even for those who oppose his views, there is a lot to be learned from him about public communications.

His speeches, especially on television, were the staple of his presidency and the legend of his leadership. A buoyant Jack Kennedy told Pierre Salinger after his election victory in 1960, "We wouldn't have had a prayer without that gadget." Reagan not only won through that gadget, he also governed through it. Only he and Kennedy have turned television to its full advantage. Reagan knew how to capture a mass audience and to direct its energies toward achieving a shared vision. That is a substantial accomplishment for a president, and we need to understand how he managed it. He never wrote out his principles of communication, as did a twenty-four-year-old Winston Churchill, who wrote a valuable essay, "The Scaffolding of Rhetoric." But perhaps we can piece them together one by one.

Opening People's Ears to Listen

In April 1982, Reagan decided to deliver a prime time speech to the country in support of the economic programs he was sending to Congress. My role was to help with the choreography.

While the speechwriters were preparing a draft, I suggested to him that he use an easel and charts, drawing a thick red line to show

213

what would happen to the federal deficits if Congress did not enact his budget (little did we know what would happen if they did . . .). He agreed. We set the speech for 9:00 P.M. Eastern.

Even an experienced speaker, I thought, would need some prep time. After all, he would have to be reading from a TelePrompTer while sitting at his desk in the Oval Office, and then, on cue, stand up, walk over to the easel, and draw his red line, still reading from the prompter. "Mr. President," I said, "would you mind coming over about fifteen minutes early so that we can practice that part of the speech?" "No, I'll be there."

The rehearsal went flawlessly, Reagan reading the lines, walking over to the easel, drawing the line with a red felt tip pen, returning to his desk without a hitch. We were set—or so I thought.

As the speech opened, Reagan sailed along until he got up and went over to the easel. With horror, we realized we had made a mistake: after the rehearsal, we had forgotten to put the cap back on the red felt tip pen. Under the hot klieg lights of television, it had gone bone dry.

"Our original cuts totaled $101 billion. They (pause) I can't make a big enough mark to show you," the President said, drawing the pen across the chart.

"Screeeccch!" That was all that could be heard or seen. No line. An awful silence.

I was standing on the other side of the Oval Office, just behind the cameras . . . mentally updating my résumé.

Fortunately, our television producer, Mark Goode, had more foresight than I did. He had brought a second red pen with him, and as soon as he saw what was happening, he hit the floor and started crawling across the Oval Office. The Secret Service had conniptions, not knowing what to think about this man crawling toward the President. Reagan just looked puzzled.

Mark, dear Mark, made his way around the back of the desk to the Old Man's feet. He held up the second pen. A twinkle came into Reagan's eye. Reaching off camera and without missing a beat, he told his audience, "Now my pen is working." Magically, the line appeared. The night was saved!

I have long imagined that if Nixon had been giving that speech, he would have thrown us out the garden window, called off the speech, and had bombers flying over Hanoi the next morning.

214   I have told that story so many times, embroidering on a detail here and there, that I can no longer swear that's exactly what happened. That's certainly what I remember and, sadly, I can no longer

check it with Mark because he died in 1998. But it captures Reagan. He *was* The Natural—a man always at ease before a camera. That was one of the assets that made him an effective speaker.

By the time he reached the presidency, Reagan had talked before so many audiences and cameras that they were both his friends. He didn't really need their company. As a man, he was essentially a loner. But when they were around, he would light up, his juices flowing, eager to talk. "The only time I feel truly alive is when I walk the tight-rope," said one of the Wallendas. That was Reagan with speeches. He was the Old Trouper, always coming to life for the performance.

Audiences always wait to see if a politician is comfortable with himself and with them. Nixon, brow wet with perspiration, would set a television audience on edge as it shared his uneasiness. They wondered so much about him that they could lose track of what he was saying. On paper, Lyndon Johnson's speeches are among the most lyrical of any modern president. But with rare exceptions (his speech upon taking office was one, his moving and successful plea for voting rights in 1965 was another), Johnson generally made his audiences uncomfortable. Neither Carter nor Bush felt at ease talking most of the time, stirring anxieties among their listeners. Walter Mondale even blamed his tightness on television for his loss in 1984—an exaggeration but not without point.

The best memoirs by a presidential speechwriter are those by Judge Samuel Rosenman, who penned speeches for FDR and then wrote a warm, inspiring account, *Working with Roosevelt*. Rosenman recalls that in fireside chats, Roosevelt thought of himself talking with his country neighbors around a hearth. He was comfortable and so were they as he chatted away. Years later, Dick Moore introduced the Rosenman book to me and to others so we could be more helpful to our boss, Richard Nixon. It's a treasure that I still dip into today.

Reagan had the same geniality as his role model. And his ease served the same purpose: it made his listeners relax. They could stop worrying about the man they were hearing and pay attention to his words. Their minds opened to what he had to say.

Yet with Reagan, as with both Roosevelts and Wilson and Kennedy, it was more than ease as a speaker that made audiences pay attention. Something far more fundamental was at work. Speeches take place within a context, never in a vacuum. Listeners bring to the occasion not only their own dreams and frustrations, but also a range of questions about the speaker. Who is he down deep?

215

What does he stand for? Does he speak with authority? Does he care about people like me? Can I place my faith and trust in him? Does he have the capacity to make a difference? Who the speaker is speaks as loudly as anything he says.

This point, so central to leadership, is often lost by politicians and their staffs. I have drafted enough presidential speeches over the years to know the temptation to string together a series of sound bites, spice in a few facts, dress it up with quotes from a classic, and deliver it to the Oval Office—Domino's Speechwriting, guaranteed within thirty minutes. It doesn't take long to realize, however, that the best-written speech since Cicero will fall flat in the mouth of the wrong person. And sometimes vice versa. When he spoke out on behalf of a foreign initiative, a president like Eisenhower could move the needle of public opinion by more than twenty-five points, even though his speech might be pedestrian. That's because he was Ike, and people automatically trusted him. George Marshall's speech at the Harvard commencement in 1947, announcing the Marshall Plan, wasn't much of a talk, but it had enormous influence, in part because he was among the most respected men in the country. No one in public life in recent years has spoken with the authority of an Eisenhower or Marshall. But Reagan has come as close as any contemporary leader, and, as a result, people paid attention.

"Communicating Great Things"

In the best of circumstances, the man and the message meet—when a leader has gained the respect of his audience and also has something to say. Reagan, in his farewell address to the nation on January 11, 1989, offered this assessment: "I won a nickname, 'The Great Communicator.' But I never thought it was my style or the words I used that made a difference: It was the content. I wasn't a great communicator, but I communicated great things."

I quibble with Reagan on one point: the *way* he said things actually did matter. Style does count. But he is right on the larger point: *what* he said mattered a great deal more. In the politics of the late 1970s, when millions were disillusioned and worried that the country was on a slide, Reagan communicated a vital message: America could regain its glory if it found its core values, and he was the man who would lead the way.

216   Most politicians think the way to approach voters is to take a stand on individual issues: What should we do to fix the schools?

How about guns? Or Social Security? They work off talking points carefully prepared by staff, loaded with facts, statistics, and arguments. Increasingly, the talking points are dictated by polls: let's figure out what the people think so we can tell them we think the same thing. Partisans look for ways to score politically and shake money out of interest groups. After a steady barrage of arguments that grow stale, listeners hit the mute button. The issues are unresolved; the bickering goes on, as E. J. Dionne has argued.

Reagan did not avoid issues of the day. He had crusaded on them over the years and had his favored solutions. But he stood first and foremost for an idealized vision of America. Once people agreed with him on that, it was easier to persuade them on the issues. An issue is only a means to an end, not an end in itself. First, the leader paints a picture of the future he envisions; only then does he point to a path for getting there. For Reagan, the vision was of national renewal; the policies he supported were his strategy for getting there.

Woven into almost every speech Reagan gave, especially on memorable occasions, was an evocation of what America had been and could be again. Liberty, heroism, honor, a love of country, a love of God. Those were notions that sophisticates tend to dismiss as platitudes, or worse. But they went deep with Reagan, and as he had discovered from years on the speaking circuit, they went deep with most Americans. If one could recover the values of the past, the country could be great again.

As with most leaders, some values mattered to Reagan more than others. A tension has always existed in our democracy between those whose primary allegiance is to liberty versus equality, the individual versus the community. Reagan came down on the side of freedom and the individual. Equality and community were less compelling to him. Philosophically, he was closer to Jefferson, Paine, and Calhoun than to Lincoln and FDR. "Government," he said in his first inaugural, "is not the solution to our problem; government is the problem."

That commitment to conservatism was essential to his success. Building up his flock over the years, he had found that his conservative base was a large and durable foundation for governing. Dick Wirthlin estimated that Reagan's core constituency was roughly a third of the population. As long as he stayed true to his base, he could count on its unflagging support, even in the worst of times. A base equal to a third of the population may not sound like much, but in the modern presidency, it's a lot—more than other presidents have enjoyed in recent years.

217

Yet, in light of the political fights of the 1990s, it is also important to understand that Reagan's brand of conservatism was distinct from some other voices in the movement. American conservatives have been drifting toward a split that echoes a turn-of-the-century division among British Tories. The "Little Englanders" of that time were those who wanted to place more emphasis on England than on the British Empire. They had a cramped, neoisolationist view that was sharply opposed by others of a more expansive view of British greatness. The Little Englanders eventually lost the argument. Among conservatives in the United States, a similar argument would break into the open in the late 1990s when William Kristol and David Brooks wrote a series of articles in the *Weekly Standard* and elsewhere, denouncing a neoisolationist, "Little America" strain within the Republican Party. They argued that the GOP should embrace the more Olympian stance of a Teddy Roosevelt.

While those arguments were never as sharply posed in the 1980s, Reagan was firmly in the "Great America" camp. He was at heart an internationalist who believed that the United States was a linchpin of world peace, that it should exercise power overseas wherever it needed to combat Communism and encourage freedom. That stance won support for him far beyond traditional conservatives. Former Democrats who had become neoconservatives—people such as Jeane Kirkpatrick, Irving Kristol, and Ben Wattenberg—rallied to that banner. It was one of my own chief attractions to him. One didn't have to be a *National Review* conservative to believe in a vibrant America, and if Reagan would take us there, well, where do I sign up?

In his speeches, Reagan also tried to make *non*conservatives feel welcome. There was a place at his table whether you agreed with him or not. In the bright future he envisioned, you would no more be penalized if you weren't a conservative than you would be barred from heaven if you weren't a Christian. He wasn't lecturing people on how to live; he was inviting them to live in a more positive way. Evil existed in the world, but it was over there in the Soviet empire. People here might have lost their way, but they were still fundamentally good. Some conservatives today convey the opposite impression. They come across as avenging angels, painting those who disagree as the embodiment of evil. Reagan would have no truck with that. He wasn't a stern father sitting in judgment. He was the friendly uncle, trying to help.

If one paid close attention, Reagan's words and manner could actually seem feminine. He spoke in warm, velvety tones that enveloped listeners and made them feel good—about themselves *and* about him. He respected his opponents, even as he disagreed with them. He wasn't directing action from the top; he was suggesting. He talked softly, even gently at times. "What is most beautiful in virile men is something feminine," Susan Sontag has written. "What is most beautiful in women is something masculine." Reagan rode in like John Wayne and spoke like Jimmy Stewart.

Those additional messages that he communicated through his speeches—that he wanted to rebuild a strong, vibrant America and that everyone was welcome to his table—were crucial. They enabled him to reach beyond his conservative base. That base, as we have seen, propelled him into the White House and gave him a foundation for governing. With the base alone, however, Reagan would have remained a minority figure. By keeping conservatives with him while appealing beyond, he was able to stitch together a working majority.

Sizable swatches of the electorate still weren't buying, of course. Academics thought him a reactionary. Activists in civil rights, women's rights, the gay movement, and the environmental movement thought he threatened all that was dear. Most White House reporters voted Democratic. Many seniors worried he would take away their benefits. The coalition against him was large and diverse. Even so, Reagan through his speeches built a majority that would support the most significant changes in national direction in almost half a century. To Main Street, he was a "communicator of great things."

The Well-Chosen Story

In September of his second year in office, Reagan dispatched Marines to Lebanon. The administration, divided over whether they should be sent, did not define the mission well, and there the Marines sat for thirteen months, until a suicide squad one night blew up their barracks near the Beirut airport. Some 241 Marines died, the highest number of military casualties since Vietnam. It was an awful blow as well for U.S. prestige.

Even as the nation was mourning, Reagan sent a separate military operation to Grenada, a tiny Caribbean island threatened by a Marxist takeover. U.S. troops made short order of island resistance. "National honor" had thus been partially restored, but public pressure was mounting to yank the troops out of Lebanon. The President's national security advisers thought a precipitous withdrawal from Lebanon would be disastrous, so Reagan decided to make a prime time address on both Lebanon and Grenada. Maybe, he hoped, we could win public patience on Lebanon, allowing the troops to stay in place while diplomats tried again to end the fighting.

Since our policies were almost as convoluted as affairs within Lebanon itself, I asked Reagan how he wanted to explain what he was seeking there. "Let's tell a story," he responded. Walk the audience through from beginning to end—what was happening in Lebanon before we went there, why we sent in the Marines, what happened to them, and where we go now. In essence, he was saying, if people can see the problem as we first did and share our perspective as it unfolded, they will be more likely to agree with us on next steps.

That was useful guidance. Reagan went on the air to talk about Lebanon as well as Grenada in narrative form, and the speech was an immense success. Dick Wirthlin's opinion polls registered a twenty-point swing in public opinion on Lebanon, building a majority in support of the President's plan to stay there for the time being. That was one of the biggest changes in public opinion I had witnessed. It wasn't enough to guarantee permanent backing; within six months, support began to evaporate again.

But the speech bought something invaluable—more time to work things out. Winning extra time from the public is often one of the most important goals a leader has. In this case, the diplomats were still unable to achieve peace and the administration eventually brought the troops home, but the withdrawal was less damaging to U.S. credibility in the region than if the terrorists had chased us out earlier. Looking back, the intervention in Lebanon was a misguided venture, but Reagan's power of persuasion—especially the story he told—prevented it from becoming a full-scale disaster.

Storytelling—or narrative, as scholars now like to call it—was one of the most effective weapons in Reagan's repertoire. No doubt it was the Irish in him, for he loved to regale an audience with a story. If it were a public setting, it would usually be about heroism; if in private with "the fellas," an earthy story was never far away. He was also an accomplished mimic—elites, ethnics, gays, it didn't seem to matter much. After the 1980 primary in New Hampshire, when reporters prodded him into repeating a private, ethnic joke and then reported his indiscretion, he kept a tight rein on his public stories.*

220 *"How do you tell who the Polish fellow is at a cock fight? He's the one with the duck. How do you know who the Italian is at the cock fight? He's the one who bets on the duck. How do you know the Mafia was there? The duck wins."

But the storytelling went well beyond the anecdotes and jokes that so many speakers sprinkle into their speeches. They weren't simply a form of light entertainment. In his public speeches, Reagan was eager that his tales illustrate the larger American story as he believed in it. They were a critical part of his connection with his followers—as critical as the values he emphasized. The two went together: the values informed the stories and the stories brought the values to life.

Reagan was weaving a large tapestry for his listening public, one that told them who they were and what they could become. Each of his stories—about Jimmy Doolittle or Davy Crockett or General Custer—was a thread. Together, they framed a heroic past, stretching from the battlefields of the Revolution to Vietnam. Some stories were funny, some poignant, some tragic, but they were all uplifting. His point was to show that the country had been on a journey of over two hundred years in which people fought and died for liberty, and from that struggle had come a bounteous nation. Surely, he was suggesting, we must have the gumption to stay on that same road in our own generation so our grandchildren will enjoy even more freedom and well-being.

Far more than a pleasant diversion, his stories were a form of moral instruction. In his first inaugural, Reagan chose to stand on the west side of the Capitol—the first president sworn in there—and offer a sweeping panorama of what he could see in his mind, just as Martin Luther King, Jr., had at the steps of the Lincoln Memorial in 1963. Reagan talked of the memorials to Washington, Jefferson, and Lincoln that lay out across the Mall in front of him. Then he added his special touch:

"Beyond those monuments to heroism is the Potomac River, and on the far shore the sloping hills of Arlington National Cemetery with its row on row of simple white markers bearing crosses or Stars of David. They add up to only a tiny fraction of the price that has been paid for our freedom.

"Each one of those markers is a monument to the kinds of hero I spoke of earlier. Their lives ended in places called Belleau Wood, The Argonne, Omaha Beach, Salerno and halfway around the world on Guadalcanal, Tarawa, Pork Chop Hill, the Chosin Reservoir, and in a hundred rice paddies and jungles of a place called Vietnam.

"Under one such marker lies a young man—Martin Treptow—who left his job in a small town barber shop in 1917 to go to France with the famed Rainbow Division. There, on the western front, he 221 was killed trying to carry a message between battalions under heavy artillery fire.

"We are told that on his body was found a diary. On the flyleaf under the heading, 'My Pledge,' he had written these words: 'America must win this war. Therefore, I will work, I will save, I will sacrifice, I will endure, I will fight cheerfully and do my utmost, as if the issue of the whole struggle depended on me alone.'

"The crisis we are facing today does not require of us the kind of sacrifice that Martin Treptow and so many thousands of others were called upon to make. It does require, however, our best effort, and our willingness to believe in ourselves and to believe in our capacity to perform great deeds; to believe that together, with God's help, we can and will resolve the problems which now confront us."

Reading that passage again, one sees that Reagan employs few of the techniques of most orators. There is no alliteration, hyperbole, or anaphora. Nor are there analogies, similes, and metaphors, which are even more effective. William Leuchtenburg has written an entire essay on FDR's use of analogies to convince people the country had to mobilize in the Depression as they had during the Great War. James M. McPherson argues that Lincoln's employment of metaphors was crucial to his leadership during the Civil War. Reagan did not tend in that direction. For him, as for Lincoln, a story was an extended use of a metaphor, and just as effective.

Critics might dismiss Reagan's tales as sappy and sentimental, but he wasn't trying to please them. He was trying to overwhelm them. For too long, as he saw it, the dominant culture had been telling stories that denigrated the American experience and undermined public confidence. Listening to the Left, he believed, one might think that U.S. history was primarily a tale of white male brutality toward Native Americans, blacks, and women; that the Revolution of 1776 had more to do with economic self-interest of a small elite than personal freedom; that Jefferson and even Lincoln weren't serious about black rights; that the dropping of the atomic bomb on Hiroshima was a heinous act; that the Vietnam War was an act of American imperialism, and on and on. Not only did Reagan not believe those things, he wanted to persuade Americans to believe in a more heroic story. He was more successful than his critics expected.

His stories struck a resonant chord partly because he told them so vividly that audiences could picture the characters in their heads. But his audiences also related to them because many had grown up believing the things he believed. His remembrances were as familiar

222

as Bible stories. They may have been tucked away in the backs of minds, but Reagan revived them and put them up front again. He reminded people what had they believed as children, and they remembered. America has always been a creed as well as a place, and Reagan brought that creed out of mothballs, dusted it off, and made it a centerpiece of his presidency.

In his book *Leading Minds: An Anatomy of Leadership*, Howard Gardner describes narrative approach. "Leaders achieve their effectiveness through the stories they relate. . . . As a rule of thumb, creative artists, scientists, and experts in various disciplines lead indirectly, through their works; effective leaders of institutions and nations lead directly, through the stories and acts they address to an audience."

Studying eleven different leaders, from George C. Marshall and Eleanor Roosevelt to Pope John XXIII and Martin Luther King, Jr., Gardner found that they told stories "about themselves and their groups, about where they were coming from and where they were headed, about what was to be feared, struggled against, and dreamed about." Their stories have a dynamic perspective: more than a headline or snapshot, the leaders relate a drama that unfolds over time. Moreover, both the leader and the followers are principal characters in the story; they can control its ending. The most basic story, he goes on to say, is about *identity* of the group: who they are, why they are special, how they can be distinguished from other groups.

The audience, as Gardner points out, is not a blank slate, waiting for the first story to be etched on a bare tablet. Rather, they come equipped with many stories that have been told and retold in homes, schools, and elsewhere in society. The leader seeks to bring a favored narrative to the fore. "The stories of the leader—be they traditional or novel—must compete with many other extant stories; and if the new stories are to succeed, they must transplant, suppress, complement, or in some measure outweigh the earlier stories, as well as contemporary oppositional 'counterstories.' In a Darwinian sense, the 'memes'—a culture's version of genes—called stories compete with one another for favor, and only the most robust stand a chance of gaining ascendancy." Most people have never heard of memes—a recent idea originating with Richard Dawkins—and I'm sure Reagan hadn't either. But he understood the point.

Interestingly, Gardner thinks leaders are distinguished by the kinds of stories they tell. The *ordinary* leader, in his view, simply relates the traditional story of his or her group without trying to stretch 223 the consciousness of the audience; he puts Gerald Ford and French president Georges Pompidou in that group. The *visionary*, so rare in religion or politics that only one or two may appear in a century, creates a new story that is unknown to most individuals before. Confucius, Jesus, Buddha, Mohammed, and Gandhi would qualify. Somewhere between the ordinary and the visionary is the *innovative* leader, taking a story that has been latent in the population and bringing to it new attention or a fresh twist. "In recent world history," Gardner writes, "neither Thatcher nor de Gaulle nor Ronald Reagan created wholly novel stories. Rather, it was their particular genius to have identified stories or themes that already existed in the culture but had become muted or neglected over the years."

A postscript is in order: some of Reagan's stories weren't quite true, as his critics never tired of pointing out. One of his favorites, which he retold to a dinner celebrating Medal of Honor winners, involved a B-1 bomber flying a mission over Europe. German shrapnel hit the plane and it started going down. The men up front jumped for safety, but the rear gunner—a young kid—was pinned and couldn't get out. He sat terrified, awaiting death. He looked up and there joining him was the pilot, an older man. "Don't worry, son," said the pilot, "we'll ride this down together." A wonderful story, but there's no record of it anywhere in military annals. As best anyone can tell, it may come from a World War II movie, *Wing and a Prayer*, starring Dana Andrews, that Reagan had seen years earlier.

Columnist Mark Shields charms audiences today with memories of Reagan complaining in the 1980 presidential campaign about government imposing fifty taxes on a loaf of bread. "There aren't fifty taxes, of course," he tells listeners, "but one day Reagan went further and said trees emit more pollution than cars. It doesn't get any better than that, and we all rushed to the phones to file." The story hit the wires as Reagan was flying back to California to give a speech. He landed amidst heavy pollution and was driving along a freeway when reporters looked out and saw a sign a graduate student had tied to a tree: "Cut Me Down Before I Kill Again!"

Funny now, but back then, some members of the press took that stuff pretty seriously. They apparently thought that if they could expose Reagan's errors in his stories, people would think he was wrong on policy, too. Soon after he arrived in the White House, a drumbeat started up in the media about how many verbal mistakes he had made in his storytelling, stretching back to the campaign.

He directed me to check out the facts behind each of his alleged misstatements so we could defend him. Our research staff began dig-

224

ging and found that on several items, there was evidence to support him. Not conclusive, but good enough for politics. While Reagan was mixed up on his gases, there was actually some evidence that trees emit a slight pollutant (obviously not as dangerous as he had suggested). There was also evidence for his story of a "welfare queen" in Chicago who was collecting twenty-three different welfare checks. But some of his stories seemed to have no verifiable foundation. We never found fifty taxes on a loaf of bread, for example.

I was asked to defend Reagan in the press, and unable to think of a better explanation, I argued that his stories were in the nature of parables, their literal truth less important than the larger truths they captured. Theologians often make this argument about stories in the Bible—that they're not literally true but are instructive and edifying. I should have known that explanation would land me in hot water. I was scalded. James David Barber, a renowed presidential historian at Duke, wrote a sulfurous piece in the *New York Times* accusing me of fabrications. I survived and Barber later became a friend.

But looking back, I believe that "parables" fairly describes how Reagan's audiences received his stories. Some listeners were, of course, outraged. Most people knew there might be an embroidery here, a deletion there. While they would have preferred absolute accuracy—and so would I—they didn't see Reagan as manipulative or deliberately hiding something from them. Nor was he inventing stories to puff himself up, as we so often see today. Rather, they accepted the idea that he was trying to get at some of the verities of life. He was telling them fundamental truths about themselves and the country, truths that might otherwise be lost. That's why grassroots America responded to him—and why sophisticates never quite understood his appeal.

Embodying the Message

"The orator's first test is his ability to create heroes in response to his call. The orator's final test is his ability to create heroism in himself to match what he has been preaching," writes Garry Wills in his book on leadership, *Certain Trumpets.* Wills is describing the progress of Martin Luther King, Jr., in becoming an authentic leader. As the son and grandson of preachers, King was raised in an oratorical tradition that lifted others up. "Martin King, like Cicero's ideal orator, marshaled all his resources—his learning, vocal exercises, physical bearing, memorization—to the effective address of his chosen audience."

225

King did not see himself initially as an activist and thought others should take the lead in the streets. His own words forced his hand. "King's oratory urged others on to heroic tasks—and where they went he had to follow. His voice wielded him rather than vice versa. Reluctant to go to jail, he was shamed into going there after so many young people responded to his speeches and found themselves in danger. King had, progressively, to face imprisonment, threats, a stabbing, blackmail, FBI harassment, and a growing certitude that he would be murdered. All these pressures drove him deeper into his own religious motivation—back, that is, into the meaning of his own words."

King learned by practice what other leaders have found—that rhetoric alone will seem artificial to the audience unless the speaker embodies the message. All leaders must embody personal traits that appeal to their followers. But for leaders who rely heavily upon rhetoric, as King did, it is especially important that their lives match the stories they tell. Their stories and their example must reinforce each other. Howard Gardner puts it well: "It is a stroke of leadership genius when stories and embodiments appear to fuse, or to coalesce, as in a dream—when, as the poet William Butler Yeats would have it, one cannot tell the dancer from the dance."

Churchill first developed a public story about the need to maintain the glory of Great Britain, and he then exemplified that courage through his own presence during the Battle of Britain. George Patton's stirring calls to arms worked with his troops because he went to the front lines with them, linking his fate to theirs. By contrast, the Nixon presidency fell apart because he was a public champion of "law and order" and his administration then engaged in egregious acts of lawlessness. "I am not a crook," he said, and his words rang hollow.

There is no question that Reagan's speeches were more effective because audiences found his life consistent with his message. He talked about Boy Scout values, and he had lived a Boy Scout life. He spoke of people lifting themselves up from humble beginnings, and he had done exactly that. He spoke about the magic of freedom where one could live out his own dream, and he seemed to have done that in Hollywood. He recalled the values of another, more rugged era, and pictures appeared of him riding high in the saddle on a western range. He talked about the importance of citizens pitching in to run the affairs of the country—not leaving it to professional politicians and bureaucrats—and he seemed to personify Mr. Smith going to Washington, straight out of Frank Capra. He talked of the importance of hearth and home, as Nancy looked up at him with a starry gaze. On only one dimension did he seem deficient for many years: how could one say that his life lived up to the heroism he so often extolled in others? Especially after his military service in World War II was spent making training films in Culver City, some sixteen miles from Hollywood? That's why, again, his survival of the bullet that John Hinckley put in him in 1981 was a turning point in his presidential leadership.

Was hypocrisy lurking in his public rhetoric? Some journalists certainly thought so. Al Hunt, Jr., among others, criticized Reagan in 1984 because he frequently spoke about the importance of family and yet was distant from most of his children and seemed indifferent to his grandchildren. I don't know why he was that way; he just was. Trying to figure him out, Peggy Noonan turns to Janet Woititz's *Adult Children of Alcoholics,* in words that may apply to Clinton as well: "Adult children of alcoholics have difficulty with intimate relationships. Because they lacked reliable and consistent love from one or both of their parents, building a relationship with another person is very painful and complicated. Because they have been disappointed and manipulated, however subtly, many of them wind up with 'the colossal terror of being close.' " Noonan may be right, though his relationship with Nancy certainly makes clear he was capable of closeness. Nancy provided unconditional love, and we know that in other cases, that can be the key to making a child of an alcoholic feel "safe" psychologically. In any event, his followers never seemed to mind the strains within his family, even though the pattern was inconsistent with his public rhetoric.

The hypocrisy of the Iran-contra scandal cut more deeply into his leadership. Reagan had long pledged that the United States would never bargain with terrorists over the release of hostages. Forced by Congress, he also agreed not to aid the contras in Nicaragua. Even though the administration disclosed its own wrongdoing, the fact that Oliver North and others working for Reagan secretly violated his public promises had a devastating impact.

As Richard Wirthlin explained to me, Reagan during the first six years of his presidency had established a bond of trust with the public: people believed that his words and deeds were consistent. Their faith was the bedrock of his strength. The Iran-contra episode was a serious blow not because of the misdeeds themselves, wrong though they were, but because they snapped that bond. For the first time, 227 people saw the administration's private acts blatantly contradict Reagan's public rhetoric. Something precious shattered. Reagan had been recording approval ratings of over 60 percent for sixteen straight months during his second term. After the Iran-contra scandal hit in late 1986, his approval dropped to 47 percent and a Harris poll found that his "credibility" had plunged from 66 percent to 43 percent, one of the steepest drops on record. The same Harris poll found that 67 percent believed the Iranian arms deal was the worst mistake Reagan had made in his presidency. Though his efforts at damage control helped, his presidency never fully recovered. It was fortunate for Reagan that the Iran-contra scandal came as late in his tenure as it did. Had it come earlier, he would never have been able to forge the strong bonds of public belief that sustained him for six years. His presidency would have been crippled.

Keeping the Focus on Others

If you listen closely to many people in power, you realize they continually bring the conversation back to themselves: "Here's how I feel . . ." "Here's how I am processing this latest event in our national life . . ." "You may be interested in knowing more about my boyhood . . ." It is not surprising that politicians who spend years climbing the slippery pole become self-referential if they make it to the top. Not surprising, but also not effective. George Bush and especially Bill Clinton practically invited listeners to focus on their own personal journeys. At first they seemed interesting, but after a while, they were diminished as leaders, and the day came when critics said they were boring.

Reagan was not given to introspection and was even less interested in talking about his own feelings. Happily secure in himself, he thought and talked mostly about others. He was also determined to maintain a zone of privacy, so that he and Nancy intentionally erected barriers around their personal lives. He was outwardly a friendly president, but all of us on his staff stayed carefully on the other side of the mental fence and wondered who he really was inside. Lyndon Johnson would talk to his assistants while he was sitting on a toilet in the family living quarters; it was a rare day when Reagan's men even entered the quarters. We'll never know many of Reagan's inner thoughts because he didn't keep many notes, and other than Kennedy, he was the only president since Roosevelt who did not write serious memoirs about his time in the Oval Office. His book *An American Life* is more a life story than an account of his presidency.

228

The fact that Reagan refused to open himself up to Edmund Morris does not mean he was empty, as Morris concludes. Rather, it suggests that he was no more willing to reveal his hidden passages to his authorized biographer than he had to anyone else over the past seventy years. Even Nancy, who sometimes seemed to play the role of his mother as well as his wife, never saw everything. Whether there was something missing in his interior life, I do not know, but no one else ever is likely to, either. He will always be opaque. What we do know is that whatever he had inside, his personality worked within the context of his times. And he never tried to fake it; he never manufactured a mask to hide what wasn't there, as some politicians do. He was who he was, and people learned to trust him for that.

Morris evidently had little interest in Reagan the political leader. If he had searched there, he might have found more fertile soil. That's what is truly significant about Reagan anyway, and that's where Reagan himself focused. Over the course of a half century of acting and speaking, Reagan had learned what other leaders have discovered: he could relate to people better if he talked about them, not himself. His listeners were more likely to take a higher path if they thought about their own journey.

One of Reagan's favorite techniques for helping people think themselves capable of great deeds was to describe the heroes among them. Consider the symbolism he introduced in his State of the Union address in 1982. As he stood in the well of the House of Representatives, he pointed to a guest in the balcony, a young man then on everyone's minds. Days before, Lenny Skutnik had put his life at risk when he dove into a freezing Potomac to save a survivor from a commercial jet that had crashed. Television cameras had captured Skutnik's swim and replayed it frequently. He had become a folk hero. As Reagan revealed Skutnik's presence and recounted his deeds, the Congress rose to its feet and roared with approval. They clapped as well for one of their own whom Reagan singled out: Senator Jeremiah Denton, who had been a prisoner of war in Vietnam for over seven years.

No previous president had so effectively drawn his audience—and television cameras—to focus on individuals who had ennobled themselves through bravery. Reagan liked to call them "ordinary Americans." As I recall, the idea for placing heroes in the balcony that first time in 1982 originated in a staff discussion. Probably Mike Deaver suggested it. But the rest of us immediately supported the idea because it was vintage Reagan. He had long pointed to heroes as a way to retell the American story and illustrate the values he

229

thought precious. "Some days when life seems hard, and we reach for values to sustain us, or a friend to help us, we find a person who reminds us what it means to be an American," he once said.

By now, the "hero in the balcony" has become a cliché at a State of the Union address. For Reagan, the gesture worked because it was fresh and, more importantly, because he was so obviously genuine in his praise. He believed in the men and women he was talking about. His audience sensed that and believed with him. The speaker must first be credible.

In the years after I left the White House, the staging became even more elaborate. In 1985, for example, his staff planned the State of the Union address on Reagan's birthday. His "heroes in the balcony" were Jean Nguyen, a Vietnamese immigrant who was about to graduate from West Point, and Clara Hale, a seventy-nine-year-old black woman who ran a home for child drug addicts. At the end of the speech, Bob Michel led Congress in singing "Happy Birthday." Columnist Sandy Grady wrote in the *Seattle Times:* "Every 74-year-old president who has won a 49-state landslide deserves such a boffo finish. His staff did everything but shoot Tip O'Neill out of a cannon, rush Fritz Mondale down the aisle with a birthday cake, and fly F-16s through the House chamber."

By keeping the focus on others, Reagan also managed to avoid the worst sin in politics: to become boring. Even though his ideas didn't evolve much and his energies wore down, his audiences stayed with him. He always had a new tale to tell, a different hero to introduce. As commentator Chris Matthews pointed out, Reagan became "the nation's host." He left his audiences wanting more. He had found a way to connect with them emotionally. It did not escape notice that when he held up others for applause, the audience was clapping for the host, too. A president is known by the company he keeps.

Drawing Upon Communal Experience

In her book *Eloquence in an Electronic Age,* Kathleen Hall Jamieson highlights an element of Reagan's rhetoric that I didn't pay much attention to at the time. Nearly all of our communal experiences as a people now come from visual images we see on television and in movies. Consciously or not, Reagan was adept at evoking those common visual experiences in his speeches, bringing them back to life and stamping upon them his own interpretation. As director of communications, I just assumed as a matter of course that, given his background, Reagan enjoyed talking about what was on the screen; only with time—and with Jamieson's analysis—have I come to appreciate the full power of that approach. In effect, he became the interpreter-in-chief, the man who imprinted upon the public mind the meanings of large events.

Probably the most poignant example occurred in January 1986, when the space shuttle *Challenger* exploded shortly after lifting off from Cape Canaveral. Aboard were six astronauts and Christa McAuliffe, the first schoolteacher chosen for a space flight. McAuliffe had wanted to "humanize" space flight for children, and a CBS/*New York Times* poll found that 40 percent of schoolchildren surveyed had watched the launch on live television in their classrooms. The explosion, captured in extraordinary visual pictures, ignited intense feelings of national grief. Everyone in America could replay the scene of a single plume of white smoke ascending into the heavens.

"The moments in which words fail are precisely the moments in which words are most needed. This complex situation required presidential words of assurance," writes Jamieson. Working with a draft written by Peggy Noonan, the most gifted of his speechwriters, Reagan rose to the occasion. First, he consoled the children, helping them to reframe the event so that it wasn't senseless but meaningful: "I know it's hard to understand, but sometimes painful things like this happen. It's all part of the process of exploration and discovery. It's all part of taking a chance and expanding man's horizons. The future doesn't belong to the fainthearted. It belongs to the brave. The *Challenger* crew was pulling us into the future, and we'll continue to follow them."

As Jamieson points out, Reagan saved his best statement for the close. He could have recalled the image of the exploding shuttle but that would have left listeners thinking only of tragedy. Instead, he displaced that awful image with another one seen less often but offering an image of hope and heroism. "The crew of the space shuttle *Challenger*," he said, "honored us in the manner in which they lived their lives. We will never forget them nor the last time we saw them—this morning—as they prepared for their journey and waved good-bye, and slipped the surly bonds of Earth to touch the face of God." During the replay of Reagan's speech that night, NBC showed the picture of the waving astronauts throughout his closing words. By invoking that picture and weaving in words from "High Flight," John Gillespie Magee's poem about an American flier in combat, he immortalized the flight as a moment of human triumph. The leader gave meaning to the nation's grief.

231

In talking to the nation about the Marines killed in Lebanon in 1983, Reagan again turned to communal experiences to shape opinion. "The scenes of senseless tragedy in Beirut this week will remain etched in our memories forever," he told listeners. A different president might then have talked about all the rubble the networks had shown; Reagan chose to recall a different scene. "We will not forget the pictures of Ambassador Dillon and his staff, Lebanese as well as Americans, many of them swathed in bandages, bravely searching the devastated embassy for their colleagues and for other innocent victims." In one stroke, Reagan refashioned the meaning of the bombings from one of horror to heroism.

Continuing, he said, "We will not forget the image of young Marines gently draping our nation's flag over the broken body of one of their fallen comrades. We will not forget their courage and compassion, and we will not forget their willingness to sacrifice even their lives for the service of their country and the cause of peace." In fact, most of the Marines had died sleeping in their beds.

As Jamieson points out: "A set of images damaging to Reagan is being displaced by another: heroic soldiers willingly sacrificing their lives in place of vulnerable, inadequately protected soldiers dying in their sleep." She adds: "When visual images can communicate meaning instantaneously to individuals of different languages and faiths around the world, the function of words changes. In such a world, words contextualize pictures and specify desirable or practical courses of ensuing action."

A few months earlier, floods had struck the southern United States and television cameras had shown gripping pictures of men and women fighting back the water. In his radio address that Saturday, Reagan seized upon their efforts: "The entire nation has watched the volunteers who have been filling and stacking sandbags. You exemplify the concept of neighbor helping neighbor, which is the very basis of our way of life." Once again, he drew upon a communal experience to make a larger point about civic virtues, a continuing theme in his speeches.

He was equally at ease calling attention to still pictures and newspaper cartoons that reinforced his view of the world. Upon the death of Graham Washington Jackson, a seventy-nine-year-old black man who was once in the Navy, Reagan paid tribute in his Saturday radio talk. "You probably don't recognize his name," he said, "but 232 his face became familiar to millions of Americans when President Roosevelt died in Warm Springs, Georgia, in 1945. There's a very famous, very moving photo of Chief Petty Officer Jackson, tears streaming down his face while he played 'Going Home' on his accordion as FDR's body was borne away by train to Washington." Anyone who sees that picture never forgets it. The tribute that Saturday was deserving but also, as Jamieson notes, accomplished another purpose: "By tapping a memorable moment and speaking a few kind words, Reagan reminds us of our common humanity, a humanity even dog-driven Democrats share for this brief moment."

As a man who turned to the funny papers each morning soon after he scanned the news, Reagan relished newspaper cartoons. Under fire for spending so much on a defense buildup, he reminded reporters about a favorite—one he often talked about in the Oval Office, too: "I think [the situation] was summed up in a cartoon about the late Leonid Brezhnev when he was cartooned in one of your publications. The cartoonists had him speaking to a Russian general, and he said, 'I liked the arms race better when we were the only ones in it.' I think that you have to, if you're going to negotiate, you have to have some strength on your side."

I doubt Reagan was conscious of how often he turned to visual images to make rhetorical points. He had lived so long in a visual world that images populated his mind and flowed through his speeches. His private conversations were equally filled with references to film and television. Despite his fluid prose, Reagan didn't have an intense personal interest in the written word, as did Teddy Roosevelt, Wilson, and Kennedy. He didn't try to copy the eloquence of others, nor was he a serious reader. TR would poke his head in a book in every idle moment, even waiting for his next White House visitor, and he devoured as many as a book a day. No president has matched him since. Reagan watched the world go by more than he read about it. Pictures had a deep impact upon his thinking—and upon his policy.

Foreign policy experts worry about "the CNN effect"—whether television pictures from overseas drive policy makers in Washington. In my judgment, the effect is exaggerated. But Reagan reversed the CNN effect. He seized upon pictures as a way to drive public opinion.

Leavening Speeches with Humor

A photo often reprinted from the Reagan presidency was taken in 233 my White House office by Diana Walker, a prizewinning photographer. It shows Walter Cronkite and Reagan in the foreground, bending over with laughter, and six others of us laughing our fool heads off, too. George Bush, Jim Baker, and Ed Meese are there. I am tucked in the back, Jim Brady alongside. Cronkite had been in to interview the President in the Oval Office and afterward we had repaired to my office down the hall. Either Cronkite or Reagan told a ribald story, and we cracked up. Diana has since interviewed everyone in the picture, and no one can remember what was said or who said it. She sent me a copy with the inscription, "You don't remember the joke, either!"

True, yet everyone still associates Reagan with laughter. Just as the words of his speeches have been largely lost, but we remember the themes, we no longer remember his jokes but remember our own laughter. And that was a large part of his charm. After the anguish of Nixon and the sober days of Carter, Reagan made us smile again.

There was a Will Rogers quality to his humor. It was gentle with just a slight edge, never harsh or biting. Humor was the one place where Reagan might easily talk about himself. He was almost always self-deprecating, signaling that he understood his vulnerabilities. If tension was building, his humor could pop the bubble. During the 1984 campaign against Walter Mondale, Reagan appeared in their first debate looking horribly old. Afterward, the lead article in the *Wall Street Journal* carried this headline: "Fitness issue— New question in race: Is oldest U.S. president now showing his age? Reagan debate performance invites open speculation on his ability to serve." Voters wondered, too, and began moving toward the Democratic ticket.

The issue mushroomed, and in a second debate, Henry Trewhitt, a veteran correspondent from the *Baltimore Sun*, asked Reagan if he was too old to be president. He was waiting. "I will not make age an issue in this campaign. I am not going to exploit, for political purposes, my opponent's youth and inexperience." Pop!

Lincoln liked his funny stories to have a political or moral point. Reagan tended to humor that lightened a speech or defused an issue. Story was his preferred method for making a larger political point. But humor was a potent part of his armory. How could people not feel good about an older man who cracks about his age: "Middle age is when you're faced with two temptations and you choose the one that will get you home by nine o'clock." Humor relaxed his audiences and disarmed his critics.

234   Most of all, humor served Reagan's political purposes as a leader. Like FDR's tilt of his cigarette holder and broad smile, Reagan's quips told people that their president was full of good

cheer about the future. FDR understood how important optimism is in the Oval Office; so did RR. Conservatives want to throw old people into the snow, cried liberals, but there was Reagan, inviting you to warm yourself by his campfire.

Tricks of the Speech Trade

Paul D. Erickson, in his study *Reagan Speaks: The Making of an American Myth*, estimates that in traveling the country on behalf of General Electric, Reagan spent over four thousand hours appearing before factory workers, civic associations, and business groups. On average, that works out to be roughly ten hours a week for eight consecutive years. No one has ever counted how many additional talks he gave in the 1960s and 1970s, including his eight years in Sacramento, but one point is obvious: by the time he reached the White House in 1981, he knew every trick of the speech trade—and then some. Working for him in communications, one could see him employ a number of techniques that went beyond the broader points about his rhetoric made above. Here's a sampling:

• *Prepare carefully.* The speeches that appear the most effortless—and are also effective—are usually the ones that require the most preparation. Winging it can be disastrous. Winston Churchill learned his lesson early in life when he tried to speak extemporaneously in his maiden speech in Parliament as a young man. He didn't just lose his way; he damn near fainted. Thereafter, Churchill would spend hours carefully writing, rewriting, and practicing a speech before he delivered it. Even then, he always insisted upon keeping notes in front of him. In the midst of World War II, when his time was precious, Churchill spent as many as twelve hours in preparing and rehearsing a speech. His valet once heard him clamoring in his bath and rushed in to see if anything were wrong. What are you doing? he asked. "Giving a speech to Parliament," Churchill replied. The results, he thought, were worth it.

Reagan also believed that he should seriously engage in the preparation of his own speeches. While he rarely spent as many as twelve hours in drafting and rehearsal, he enjoyed the process of writing his own material or heavily editing what was prepared for him. He relied upon others to take the lead in developing policy choices but thought his special strength was oral persuasion, and he threw himself into it. Between his governorship and the White House, Reagan kept himself in the national eye in part by publishing 235 a newspaper column and delivering national radio commentaries. Pete Hannaford prepared both for him in draft form. Pete told me once that the newspaper columns would often come back without a scratch, but Reagan would rewrite the radio scripts to ensure that they were in his voice.

When he became president, several million words a year were published under his name. So, his speechwriting shop churned out drafts in a steady flow. Typically, the writers would deliver a major address to him two or three days in advance of delivery, and he would carefully work it over in the quiet of his study. Back would come his changes—usually written in chicken scratches—and the drafting would commence again. If the subject touched a nerve with him, as Social Security did (he hated it when opponents attacked him for "cutting" Social Security), he would write out speech inserts on long, yellow sheets and try them out with a few members of the staff the next day.

With all the infighting that took place, a conservative writer might surreptitiously slip a draft to him by a back door if the moderates had blocked a first knock on the front door. If Reagan liked the alternative, he would try to stitch the two speeches together. He hated internal fights, but he never seemed bothered by conflicting drafts: he generally knew long before what he wanted to say and how he wanted to say it. As hard as he labored over his speeches, his pen was fluid. Ken Khachigian drafted Reagan's inaugural address in 1981. Sitting down with Ken's suggestions along with some of his own work, Reagan rewrote the address in longhand. Looking at those yellow sheets, one sees that Reagan worked smoothly through, changing no more than a few words of what he first put on paper.

Once the final draft was ready, he studied it closely for delivery. I never fully understood the system he used for marking up his reading copy, but he would underline each word that needed dramatic emphasis and add two stick lines at the end of a phrase where he wanted to pause in the speech. By the time of delivery, he had almost memorized the text and he knew exactly how to make it sing. As Peggy Noonan put it, he was "the only American poet who can sing outdoors." Preparation paid off.

• *Keep it short.* Reagan liked to remind us on staff of a story. A young preacher came to church one Sunday to give his first sermon and found only one man sitting in the pews. "What do you think I should do?" the preacher asked. "Don't rightly know," said the fella, "I'm just a cowpoke, but if I went out in my field and found only one cow, I would feed it." So, the preacher climbed into the pulpit and

236

delivered a fiery sermon that went on . . . and on . . . and on. "What did ya' think?" he asked when it was over. "Don't rightly know," said the fella, "but if I went out in my field and found only one cow, I sure as hell wouldn't feed him the whole load!"

Twenty minutes max for a good speech, Reagan thought. No more than thirty minutes for a formal press conference. That leaves an audience remembering more—and wanting more. His most memorable speeches—his first inaugural, his address on the fortieth anniversary of D-day, his eulogy for the *Challenger* crew—were lean and to the point. At Gettysburg, after all, the famous orator Edward Everett talked for over an hour in a beautifully scripted piece that was soon forgotten; Lincoln spoke ten sentences.

• *Keep it brisk.* When one of his department heads droned on in a cabinet meeting with a litany of statistics and arcane arguments, the first person to nod off was the commander in chief. As his former chief of staff Ken Duberstein told me during the Monica affair, "I can remember when sleeping with the president meant going to a cabinet meeting with Ronald Reagan."

A speech should have more than a logical structure—*logos*. It should have passages that inspire—*ethos*. And it should have *rhythm*. A story, a surprise, an injection of humor when no one is expecting it—all these are meant to keep the audience engaged, relaxed, taking it in. His wake-me-ups in a speech were like the jelly beans he kept on the cabinet table and passed around from time to time: they broke the tension and gave listeners some sugar just when they needed it.

• *Use the language of the living room.* Through most of history, political orators in the West have chosen to use traditional, stylized forms of speech. They have drawn from the traditions of Demosthenes and Cicero, the Bible and Shakespeare. Americans have added their own idiom and have often been more robust, but the nineteenth-century speeches of Clay, Webster, Calhoun, along with Edward Everett and Frederick Douglass, all drew from those classical wells. Even into the television age, John F. Kennedy relied upon Theodore Sorensen for uplifting rhetoric that would have brought pride to Cicero.

Reagan was never like Kennedy as an orator. He preferred FDR's conversational style. There was, however, one significant difference: FDR tended to be more formal in his big public speeches; he left behind a litany of memorable lines. The *Bartlett's* of tomorrow will carry columns of quotes from FDR—"The only thing we have to fear is fear itself"; "This generation of Americans has a rendezvous with destiny"; "We must be the great arsenal of democracy." Even to 237 an editor of conservative bent, Reagan will have fewer entries. How much can one do with "Make my day"?

Reagan wasn't speaking for the history books. He was interested in his audiences in the here and now; he would leave history to others. He would stick to his television-style language. In his own time, it worked. We shall see how the historians remember his oratory a generation from now.

• *Look for catchy facts.* His critics had trouble believing it, but Reagan actually liked facts in his speeches. As one of his speechwriting chiefs, Ben Elliott, put it, Reagan thought specificity was the soul of credibility. Carefully chosen, pruned facts would show that the speaker knew what he was saying.

An unusual fact could make a speech. After one of his Saturday radio talks, Reagan told me that when he was speaking, he always envisioned a couple listening while they were out for a drive. What he wanted in his talk was at least one fact that would stir a conversation after: "Gee, honey, I didn't know that pigs fly. Did you?" In the communications field, the capacity of a listener or reader to recall a message is considered an important goal, and Reagan was always shooting for it. In a 1981 speech, for example, Reagan reported, "A few weeks ago I called such a figure, a trillion dollars, incomprehensible, and I've been trying ever since to think of a way to illustrate how big a trillion really is. And the best I could come up with is that if you had a stack of thousand-dollar bills in your hand only four inches high, you'd be a millionaire. A trillion dollars would be a stack of thousand-dollar bills sixty-seven miles high."

• *Use the occasional prop.* Long before Ross Perot came along with his charts, Reagan was trying out props and graphics in his televised speeches. They were another device to increase viewer engagement and help with pacing. We never had enough money in the White House budget to match the visual pyrotechnics of the networks, but for a president broadcasting from the Oval Office, it was a pretty good show.

The key was to keep the props simple and stimulating. Once that red felt tip pen worked, his budget chart of 1981 made an effective point. In his State of the Union address in 1984, he went up to Capitol Hill with a stack of IRS codes and regulations that he could barely lift. He wanted to show the public just how complex the tax rules had become and why reform was necessary. No one missed his point.

238   His best graphic was the one he didn't use but, as best I can tell, anticipated. When he surprised the nation with his proposal for a

Strategic Defense Initiative, we didn't have time inside the White House to prepare a graphic display of a missile defense shield. But the networks soon did it for us and, given their deep pockets, with more sophistication. Network producers had grown up on Buck Rogers, so that it took no stretch for them to imagine how the military might knock down an incoming Soviet missile with a laser beam. In fact, U.S. scientists were—and are—years away from figuring out how to make such a system work against a massive attack, but the graphics put on the air by the networks made Star Wars seem real. Every time the enemy might put a missile into the air, viewers could see the United States shoot it out of the sky.

• *Be positive.* Upbeat, that's the way Reagan lived and that's the way he wanted his speeches to sound. His speechwriting team is correctly given credit for his address after the *Challenger* exploded, but as Peggy Noonan acknowledges, their inspiration came from Reagan. He was talking off the record that day to a group of network anchors when he was told that the shuttle had blown up. Karna Small of the NSC staff kept notes. One asked, "What can you say to the children to help them understand?" Reagan answered, "Pioneers have always given their lives on the frontier. The problem is that it's more of a shock to all as we see it happening, not just hear about something miles away—but we must make it clear [to the children] that life goes on."

It was an article of faith among the early Reagan staff that one of Carter's worst blunders was that 1979 televised speech blaming the nation's troubles on the downbeat mood of its people. Reagan was determined to prove what Americans *could* do if challenged, not what they *couldn't* do, and he bent his language toward that end.

• *Anticipate the critics.* From his years on the political outskirts, Reagan understood that his conservative views were controversial and could draw withering criticism. At first, he was vulnerable to personal attacks. Lyn Nofziger recalls an incident in 1966 when Reagan and his opponents in the Republican primary were appearing together. Two of his opponents labeled him a racist, and Reagan lost his temper, storming out of the meeting while muttering in a loud stage whisper, "Sons of bitches." The press came down hard on him, especially cartoonist Paul Conrad in the *Los Angeles Times.* By his own account, Reagan learned not to "explode in response to attack on my personal integrity."

Later that year, Reagan put forward what the chairman of the 239 GOP in California called "The Eleventh Commandment: Thou shalt not speak ill of any fellow Republican." Reagan evangelized on behalf of that commandment for the rest of his life. It not only quieted his foes within the party but allowed him to play peacemaker between factions.

Fending off critics within his own party, however, was nothing compared to the broadsides from outside. Democrats attacked hammer and tongs because they thought Reagan such an obvious threat to their own agenda. He used two devices in his public appearances to suck out the bitterness. While he never shied away from an argument over policy, he tried to treat his opponents with personal respect. When they came at him hard, he responded with civility and, where he could, with humor. Ike had that same approach: he said he never wanted to get "in the gutter" with his opponents. By staying above *ad hominem* attacks, both presidents protected their reputations and found that their enemies treated him more civilly.

Reagan's other device was anticipation: in presenting a proposal, he tried to figure out what the other side would say in advance, tell his audience what was coming, and then answer it before the charge was made. "I know you're going to hear that my idea is cockeyed. They will tell you that your grandmother will starve. But let me explain why that isn't so." Since Reagan, as president, had a bigger megaphone than his opponents, that approach always helped. It inoculated him and allowed him to take the high ground early in the debate. It's an approach smart speakers have employed for centuries.

• *Have a good closer.* As age caught up with him late in his presidency, Reagan might wander off rhetorically toward the end of a speech, leaving his listeners baffled. But in his prime, Reagan usually ended his speeches with a "closer." A letter that tugged at the heart. A story that left mist in the eye. A quote that captured his meaning in amber. Those were his specialties. As a former actor, he wanted to leave his most memorable line to his exit.

Speechwriters in Tune with the Boss

The address at the fortieth anniversary of D-day, delivered on the bluffs of Pointe du Hoc, was the height of his presidential speechmaking. With veterans in front and the sea behind, he described the valor of the men who scaled those sheer, hundred-foot cliffs as German fire cut them to pieces. His audience was moved to tears, and clips will forever be shown in Reagan retrospectives. It was so powerful that at the fiftieth anniversary ten years later, Clinton and his

240

chief speechwriter, Don Baer, worked tirelessly to ensure that Clinton's speech would somehow come close to Reagan's. (It did.)

Now consider: Reagan's address was drafted by a young Peggy Noonan, who had come to the White House four months earlier *and had never talked to the President about that or any other speech!* I had left the Reagan team by the time Peggy arrived, so that I first learned that when I read her memoirs. Rarely does anything that happens at the White House shock me anymore, but that one did. In fact, as she reported it, the entire White House speechwriting team had never met with Reagan for an entire year when she was hired. Her first contact with him came after Pointe du Hoc—she wasn't even invited to the occasion—when he called to thank her.

What is one to make of this? For starters, it's a lousy way to run a White House. A speechwriter there or in any other organization needs regular contact with the principal, chewing over ideas, taking the boss's temperature, probing for ways to bring out inner thoughts. Nixon's speechwriters like Price, Safire, and Buchanan had frequent face-time. For all the clumsiness of the Ford operation, his writers talked to him regularly. Clinton knows his writers by first name. But Reagan was remote. Only a few writers over the years like Pete Hannaford, Ken Khachigian, and eventually Peggy Noonan had significant contact. At the White House, I doubt he knew more than one or two of his writers by sight.

Yet, the fact that Peggy Noonan was able to draft a Reaganesque speech for a man she had never met suggests two additional thoughts. Peggy knew her man because he had written out his views and spoken them so consistently for so many years that he left her a clear road map. When he first came to Washington, he sent his speechwriters a pile of his old speeches and instructed them to read carefully. Every member of his staff knew exactly what Reagan believed and how he had expressed his beliefs in the past; their task was to freshen up his words of the past to fit a new context. In an interview with scholar William K. Muir, Jr., one of Reagan's favorite writers, Tony Dolan, put it well: "I often say that writing speeches for this president is writing some things he has already said and giving them back to him to say again."

The second point that emerges from Noonan's experience is the importance of hiring speechwriters who are philosophically and culturally in tune with the boss. Soon after Reagan was elected, I had a hand in the appointment of Aram Bakshian, Jr., as the first head of the new White House speechwriting team. Aram is a splendid, fluid writer who had served well in the Nixon White House and certainly

241

qualified as a conservative. With blessings from on high, Aram hired a stable of other conservative writers such as Dolan. In the first months, the speechwriting team reported to Reagan through Jim Baker and, later, through me.

Baker was not seen as a staunch conservative, nor I, and we took periodic heat from fellow centrists for harboring so many red hots as speechwriters. Their drafts were often scorching, and flares would then go up around the administration. The National Security Council staff and the State Department were particularly apoplectic at the prospect of Reagan saying some of the things these writers drafted. But Baker and I and Darman thought it important that Reagan have writers who were in sync with his views. We could fight out policy choices and take disputes to the President, but if he were to govern in bold colors, as he said, his writers shouldn't compose in plaid.

In March 1983, Reagan wanted to address the nature of the Soviet threat at an evangelical forum in Orlando, Florida. Tony Dolan wrote a draft attacking the Soviet system in terms so strong it rattled the windows. Tony had won a Pulitzer Prize exposing organized crime in Connecticut. If the "prags" blocked his stuff at the front door, he was one who would slip it around the back. He was relentless. Sometimes, I wondered if even Reagan thought he could be a pain in the ass. But you had to give Tony high marks for devotion.

Tony's draft for Orlando might please the evangelicals, but we worried that it was at odds with Reagan's approach toward the Soviets. We asked him to water it down. Time was running short when Tony's revised version came in, still very tough. This time, I pulled NSC adviser Bud McFarlane from a security session with the President and said, "Bud, you've got to go over this." We moderated a few more sentences.

Eventually, with Tony angry at how much we had pulled it back, we sent it forward to Reagan—and he watered it down some more. Reagan had a good sense of where the edge was. But the draft was still plenty strong, and I kept wondering: Was it okay to leave in that phrase calling the Soviets the Evil Empire? Were we going to upset U.S. diplomacy? Tony insisted; I agreed, reluctantly.

I hate to admit it, but it's true: history has shown that Tony Dolan was right and I was wrong. That phrase, the Evil Empire, allowed Reagan to speak truth to totalitarianism. "A semantic infiltration," Tony called it in later years. "The secret is to give the world a cliché, a semantic infiltration. Now and forever the Soviet Union is an evil empire. . . . The Soviet Union itself can't let go of it. . . . The

242

'evil empire' is one of the few semantic victories the West has won. . . . In history it has always been thus. It was Churchill's rhetoric which made a difference in the World War. People respond to the truth. With 'evil empire,' people said, 'That's right. Cut out all the bull. The emperor has no clothes.' "

In retrospect, I'm glad Tony won. The conservative writers knew their boss and served him well.

Symbolism and a Theatrical Touch

Critics who lambaste Reagan for bringing a touch of Hollywood to the White House forget their history. Acting has been at the heart of leadership since the beginning of time.

In *The Mask of Command*, his survey of great military leaders, historian John Keegan records that during his conquests of Persia, Alexander the Great surprised the Greek world by sending spoils back to Athens, not Sparta. The Spartans were seen as far more likely allies for Alexander's Macedonia because they had long championed Greek liberty from Persia. Alexander saw that Athens, the greatest of the Greek states, might become an even better friend. Linking up with Athens and not with Sparta was "a calculated stroke of public relations . . . a brilliantly theatrical" move.

"But theatricality," Keegan observes, "was at the very heart of Alexander's style of leadership, as it perhaps must be of any leadership style. Throughout the Alexander story, acts of theatre occur at regular intervals." Alexander's entries onto the field of battle were dramatically staged, and he undertook elaborate rituals and ceremonies for public consumption. Taking his sword and cutting the Gordian knot was one. On another celebrated occasion, a general gave Alexander's father, Philip, a spirited and beautiful but wild horse, Bucephalus. The horse defied Philip, shying and stamping whenever approached. Alexander, still a lad, "announced that he would mount him, seized his halter, turned him and leapt into the saddle, to the applause of courtiers and his father's tears of joy. The son's trick was to have noticed that Bucephalus shied at his own shadow and to turn him towards the sun." Alexander "was in the strongest sense a brilliant theatrical performer."

Fast-forward some two thousand years to another general, George Washington. It is shortly after the battles ended in the American Revolution, but before a peace was negotiated. Washington stayed with his troops in Newburgh, New York, and over time they

243

grew restless because they hadn't been paid. His entreaties to the Continental Congress were to no avail. Some of his officers began organizing a rebellion and talked of marching on Philadelphia, the seat of the national government. With danger mounting, Washington made a surprise appearance before a gathering of the officers. After praising them for their service, he pulled from his pocket a copy of a speech he wished to read. But then he fumbled with the paper and finally reached for a set of reading glasses—glasses most of the men had never seen before. "I have already grown gray in the service of my country, and now I am going blind."

Historian Richard Norton Smith writes: "Instantly, rebellion melted into tears. It was a galvanizing moment, a brilliant piece of theater and a narrow escape for republican government. Never mind that Washington had used reading glasses for years.... [He] was rarely bashful about manipulating the emotions of an audience where the good of his country was concerned."

From Washington on, every effective president has understood that a theatrical touch is an essential part of leadership in a democracy. Washington often talked of public life as a stage, and loved the theater himself. Lincoln was a regular theatergoer and he, too, drew from what he saw. Perhaps the consummate actor was Franklin Roosevelt. After battling unsuccessfully for seven years against the ravages of polio, Roosevelt created an elaborate public illusion that he had conquered its effects. Hugh Gregory Gallagher wrote an entire book on the matter entitled *FDR's Splendid Deception*. With his head tilted up, framed in a smile, Roosevelt convinced his audiences he was walking across the stage when, in fact, his legs were in iron braces and he was clutching the arm of a companion as he swiveled toward the podium. Gallagher writes: "It is not surprising that he once told Orson Welles he considered the two of them to be the finest actors in America."

If anything, Reagan's career in Hollywood was almost as important in preparing him for Washington as his eight years in Sacramento. Both made him more effective as a leader. His stage presence added dramatic flair to every one of his television speeches. "The camera seldom lies," he told Mike Deaver, but he knew how to connect through it, how an inflection of the voice or a twinkle of the eye would communicate. If he were working from a TelePrompTer and wanted to tell the audience about a letter he had received, he would automatically return to the text in his hand, reading directly from it as if it were the letter. If the speech had an emotional close, his voice would crack, an eye might mist—not because he was acting, but because as an actor, he had learned to let himself go. His emotions were close to the surface, and he wasn't afraid to show them.

When Reagan sat down to give his Saturday radio addresses, he would sometimes make a wisecrack just before he started reading his text. One or two made it onto the airwaves because no one had told him that the mikes were on. "My fellow Americans," he announced once, "I'm pleased to tell you today that I've signed legislation that would outlaw Russia forever. We begin bombing in five minutes." He caused a miniuproar in the press, and we put out the word that he was joking, hadn't realized he was on the air, etc. After that I set up a red light on the desk that would go on when the mike was live. But when he repeated similar "mistakes" a couple of times, I decided he was being a wily old fox. I bet those wisecracks were a way for him to signal hard-line conservatives he was still one of them at heart, even if he had to be "presidential" in conducting national affairs.

Answering reporters' questions, Reagan always kept in mind that his real audience was on the other side of the camera. He spoke to them *through* reporters. In Hollywood, he had also seen how cameras made him look from different angles as he walked. From day one in the White House, every step was as commander in chief, shoulders thrown back, back ramrod straight, purposeful. And he loved it because the role so neatly fit.

As a former actor, he also understood the importance of symbolic communication. Memorable leaders usually have their trademarks: Churchill, flashing a V for Victory; Gandhi, in his loincloth, marching toward the sea; MacArthur, riding in the back of a jeep, his cap pulled down; Roosevelt, his head tilted. Those images reinforced their message. Reagan never had a single trademark that stood out so well, but he offered a steady stream of smaller gestures that also reinforced his message. His moments on a horse, looking like a Marlboro man without the cigarette; snapping off salutes to men in uniform; cupping his hand to his ear as he brushed past the press on the way to a waiting helicopter; the insistence that whenever he was working, he stay in coat and tie. Here, he was signaling, was a steadiness you could count on.

Communication by symbols is particularly important as a leader takes charge. Again, Franklin Roosevelt was the consummate model for Reagan. Before the campaign of 1932, presidential candidates were expected to stay away from their party's nominating convention. Roosevelt broke the tradition: when word came that he was officially over the top, he and Eleanor captured the nation's attention

245

as they flew in a small plane from Albany to Chicago. It was a long, slow journey through storms, and by the time FDR climbed to the podium to give his acceptance address, he had built a massive radio audience. The journey signaled that FDR was ready to bring forceful, innovative leadership to tackling the Depression.

Reagan's gestures never rivaled Roosevelt's. But from the moment of his election, he made clear he intended to be different from Carter, still the Washington outsider. The Reagans' first visit to Washington featured those dinners with the city's elite; they said, "We want to be good neighbors." Early on, visits began with Congress, too. The Supreme Court was invited to dinner, reestablishing an old White House tradition. Reagan was intent on being more than a neighbor. He wanted to govern.

Would he have been as effective with symbolic communication had he not been trained as an actor? Perhaps. Much of what he did as president flowed from his personal nature. But it is inconceivable to me that he would have brought the same theatrical touch without his earlier career. What kind of governor do you expect to be? he was asked before he took office in California. "I don't know," he replied. "I've never played a governor."

•   •   •

ARE THERE LESSONS HERE FOR OTHERS? I think there are. While Reagan was a natural, he had honed his talents as a speaker over many years of trial and error. As Lou Cannon, puts it, "If the voice is a gift, the delivery which sounds so natural is the result of hard work and careful preparation."

For Reagan, as we have seen, speaking was a way of bonding with his audience, aligning them behind his political agenda and mobilizing their support. As he said in his farewell address, he tried to be "a communicator of great things"—the values and the ideas that he thought would renew America's greatness. Stories were a means of bringing the values to life. He wove them into every speech. They were part of a broader narrative. He was seeking to retell the American story and to restore tradition. He was using his stories to remind people what they once believed and to encourage them to believe again. None of this would have worked had he not struck his audiences as authentic. Most people (not all) believed that the sentiments came from within, that the man embodied the message. He practiced the politics of conviction, and people saluted him for it.

Through experience, Reagan also knew that his audiences were more interested in hearing about themselves than about him. He kept the focus away from himself by identifying heroes among ordinary Americans such as Lenny Skutnik. He knew how important communal experiences were for a national audience, and he retold the stories of what people had seen on their television screens to shape the meaning and memory of events like the *Challenger* explosion. Audiences stayed with him, as well, because he laced his appearances with humor and knew how to give an appealing speech—brisk, pointed, well paced, well illustrated, and a strong closing line.

After he became president and could no longer write most speeches, he relied upon a stable of younger men and women for early drafts. That could have been dangerous, especially since he was so remote. But he had many thoughts on the public record from which they could borrow and they were in tune with him philosophically.

His critics liked to dismiss Reagan as Bonzo at the White House. He didn't seem to mind. His acting years, he came to realize, were almost as important as his political years in preparing him for the post. Indeed, men over the centuries have discovered that theatrical talent is indispensable to public leadership. What Reagan had—an engaging style, a guiding philosophy, an inspiring story, an enveloping humor, a theatrical touch—he put to good use.

Bill Clinton

8

Dreams and Disappointments

I'M IN TROUBLE. I need your help."

When Bill Clinton called me nineteen weeks into his presidency, I thought I knew who he was. A year and a half later, after working and talking with him almost every day, I was honored that he had asked, respected his accomplishments, and wanted him to succeed—but felt I no longer knew who he was.

To friend and foe, Bill Clinton is a mass of contradictions. He is one of the smartest men ever elected president and has done some of the dumbest things. He has a deeper knowledge of history than most of his predecessors and has used less of it. He genuinely wanted, as he pledged, to have "the most ethical administration in history," and enters history as the first elected president ever impeached. He is the first Democrat since Roosevelt to win a second term in the White House and the first since Truman to lose both houses of Congress. He is attached to his wife and needs her daily affirmation, yet he has wounded her repeatedly. Over the years, he has built a vast network of loyalists who worship him; he can be the most caring of friends. But he has a habit of using people and throwing them away.

Some of Clinton's contradictions have served him splendidly. He ran for office as a Main Street Democrat promising middle-class tax cuts, but once there was smart enough to embrace Wall Street economics, raising taxes and cutting spending. Those policies helped to fuel the longest boom in the history of the country. He believed, along with his advisers, that in reforming welfare the government should spend large additional sums on child care, training, transportation, and related supports. But when Republicans presented him with a welfare bill that left out the extra money, he signed it. Two years later, welfare rolls had been cut nearly in half.

It is hardly surprising that the country is split over Clinton. To many Americans, he has been a successful president who would have been even better had he not been pilloried by his enemies from the day he was elected. To others, he disgraced the office and deserves not a whit of credit for the economic boom. Still others are hopelessly ambivalent. As time was running out on his presidency, over 60 percent of Americans said they approved of his performance, and an equal number said they would not elect him to a third term.

Richard Nixon, as we have seen, had a dual nature—light and dark sides that were clearly distinguishable. Clinton's strengths and weaknesses are so intertwined that one can hardly look at one without seeing the other. The chocolate, vanilla, and a dozen other flavors are all swirled together. Nixon was the layer cake; Clinton, the marble. That's why everyone who knows Clinton has so much trouble sorting him out.

Franklin Roosevelt had many of the same personal qualities as Clinton and, if anything, was more devious. Yet he turned out to be the finest president of the century. John F. Kennedy—the man who once told British prime minister Harold Macmillan that he got a headache if he went more than three days without sex—was far more promiscuous at the White House. Yet he continues to be admired.

Clinton will always be our paradox. When he decamps and the dust settles, we will look back and see that despite the scandals, he left the country far better off than he found it. Economically, socially, even culturally, the nation made substantial gains during his stewardship. For America, the nineties turned out to be one of the brightest decades of the twentieth century, and Clinton was one of its prime movers. He will be remembered well for that. Yet, a sense of aching disappointment hangs over his presidency. How much more he could have achieved . . . how much went smash.

Winston Churchill once remarked that he expected to be well remembered in history because he intended to write it. Bill Clinton is capable of writing memoirs that could rival Churchill's in insight; he is that talented. No matter how thoughtfully he writes, however, history will always offer a mixed verdict on his years in the White House.

252   The mystery will remain. What happened to this man, so gifted and caring? How did he get so much right—and still get so much wrong? What lessons can we draw? What does the Clinton experi-

ence tell us about the qualities we should be seeking in future presidents?

That's the story I would like to tell here to the extent that I can. Much of it will be centered on the year and a half when I served him at the White House. It is only a piece of his presidency, but it is a time that helps us to understand this president at his best and see the roots of the trouble that came to haunt him. Part of it is also my own tale, joining up with a Democratic president after three tours with Republicans.

Clinton's Early Promise

As I considered his phone call in 1993, I thought back on the ten years or so since we had met. He was governor of Arkansas then, and I had come to know him as he undertook reforms in education and economic development, trying to lift a poor southern state up from the bottom. I admired him as a New Southerner, one like Terry Sanford, who had first inspired me to enter public service when he was governor of my native North Carolina. Both men had been courageous in tackling race, the most difficult issue of our region. Clinton was not only the youngest American elected governor in four decades, but the magazine I worked for, *U.S. News & World Report,* had recognized him as one of the best governors in the country. I thought one day he might make a fine president.

We talked many times over those years. The first time we met, he was reading a book about the Japanese economic system and he engaged in a long discourse about ways the Japanese trained and protected their workers versus our own, more entrepreneurial approach. He had come to visit the editors of *U.S. News,* where he blew us away with his wide-ranging knowledge. I had never met a governor who had a better grasp of domestic policy issues and whose commitment to reform was as compelling.

Over the New Year's holiday, he and Hillary usually attended Renaissance Weekends in Hilton Head, an event that began in the early 1980s as a small gathering of families, mostly from the South. Phil and Linda Lader, the organizers, called it a "Low Country House Party," and my wife and I were charter members. The Clintons came early, too. There, as the numbers grew, he built a coterie of fans who wanted him in the White House. He and I were often assigned to the same panels, and I learned never to speak after him. He was the hardest act I ever followed. He was a mesmerizing speaker,

253

and by the time I got the microphone, he had talked so long that it was usually past midnight. By the time of his 1992 campaign, reporters listed me as an "FOB"—Friend of Bill.

Before Renaissance started up, I was giving a talk at the Smithsonian one day when a woman at the back of the room asked a question about Reagan that pinned me to the wall. I struggled through an answer, and she came back with another zinger that I ducked. "Who in the devil was that?" I asked afterward. "Hillary Clinton," I was told. At Hilton Head, she and I got to know each other better and sometimes had a friendly joust. One argument turned pretty fierce when I praised business leaders for pushing education reform, and she insisted they ought to keep their mitts off the schools. I came to like her but was closer to her husband.

Clinton exuded an animal magnetism that drew both men and women. They loved to be around him, to hang on his words, and enjoy a hug. No man ever hugged more people than that fellow. I also began to see that his conversation with everyone he met, man or woman, was always a seduction. That was his modus operandi. The first time out, he just charmed you into liking him.

He was especially good with women, no matter what age. At Renaissance, he took a keen personal interest in my mom, then in her seventies. As long as she was alive, he inquired about her, greeted her as "Babs" when they met and, when she visited him in the Oval Office, treated her as a queen. How could you not like someone who liked your mom so much? She adored him.

I had heard plenty of rumors, of course, about his relationships over the years. As they say down South, he was a hard dog to keep on the porch. I didn't know what was true and what wasn't. It was obvious from the way women flocked around that he had had plenty of opportunities. People also wondered what other mistakes he may have made in life. But I also didn't care much. I didn't know any saints from the sixties generation, and I was not one myself. More to the point, I figured that if he ever ran for the White House, he would chain up his sexual appetites, just as Teddy Kennedy did when he ran against Carter. Clinton seemed too ambitious to trip himself up over a dalliance.

As our friendship blossomed, he and I often talked about politics. He wanted to know all about Reagan and other presidents, and he taught me a good deal about Democratic politics. It was clear
254 from the beginning that he wanted to run for president, but it was not clear when his moment would come. I was one of many he sought out to chew things over.

When Clinton finally announced his entry into the race in October 1991, he made a surprise call to my home about ten-thirty that same night. We talked for probably an hour or more about his prospects, even as people were leaving a festive party at his house, saying good-bye to him. At the time, he didn't think he had much of a chance for the Democratic nomination in 1992. The race was more of a warm-up for 1996, when he thought he might win. During the campaign, I went out to cover him a few times and we would talk when he was available. I also alerted viewers of *The MacNeil/Lehrer NewsHour*, where I was a political analyst, that I had a personal relationship with Clinton.

I had voted Republican in every presidential race for twenty years. In 1988, I voted for Bush, reflecting a decade of support for him and a devout hope for his success. As much as his conduct of foreign policy lived up to my expectations, however, I grew disappointed that he did not move aggressively to tackle the nation's domestic needs. He was becoming an "in-box" president, as William Schneider had argued. Since leaving Reagan and entering journalism, I had had an opportunity to travel the country, looking closely at the problems of schools, the growing wage gap, entrenched poverty, and cultural decay. In editorials for *U.S. News* and in television commentaries, I began speaking up for sweeping social reforms and urging Bush to embrace them. He undertook some important initiatives, such as deficit reductions. But the Republican Party was moving farther to the right, even as I was moving toward a new progressivism.

My emotional break with President Bush came in the aftermath of the Gulf War. With his popularity soaring to over 80 percent, he could have demanded anything he wanted from a Democratic Congress. In a dramatic appearance on Capitol Hill, he asked for virtually nothing. His cupboard of ideas seemed bare. There was to be no domestic Desert Storm, as I had hoped. I was crestfallen. While I admired Bush and was grateful for his past friendship, I sadly concluded he would not pursue a reform agenda. Early on in 1992, I had a long dinner with Ross Perot and wrote an enthusiastic piece about him. He later approached me about working in his campaign, and I declined. I wasn't looking for a job. But I was looking for a change in national direction.

That November, I voted for Bill Clinton. He was the best hope the country had, I thought, for a new era of progressive politics that would revive the spirit of Teddy Roosevelt and Woodrow Wilson. 255 That earlier movement not only overhauled many domestic institutions, making them more responsive to the needs of common folk, but also rebuilt public faith in democracy. And it was bipartisan, an enormous appeal to me. Surely an America that had just triumphed in the Cold War could now pour its energies into healing the breach at home, drawing us together as one people. Bill Clinton would carry that torch to the White House. His election raised my expectations that a new moment of reform was at hand.

An Election without a Bounce

As election results came in that November, it was apparent that Clinton would have a tough go at the White House. Barely 43 percent of voters cast their ballots for him, as 37 percent went for George Bush and 19 percent embraced Ross Perot, the highest number any third-party candidate had ever won. His native Arkansas gave Clinton more than half of its ballots; no other state did.

Only two other presidents in the twentieth century had come into office with such slim pluralities: Woodrow Wilson won in 1912 with 42 percent and Richard Nixon won in 1968 with 43 percent. In their cases, however, their parties picked up seats in Congress, giving them a modest amount of leverage. In Clinton's case, Democrats lost ten seats in the House in 1992 and in a special election a short while later fell back a seat in the Senate. He ran behind all but five members of the House. Republicans had nothing to fear and Democrats little to cheer: Clinton had neither a mandate nor coattails. He had won office but not power.

Nor could Clinton draw much encouragement from studies of the electorate's attitudes. As George C. Edwards has pointed out, "Much of the president's vote was anti-Bush rather than pro-Clinton, and exit polls found that 54 percent of the electorate preferred lower taxes and fewer services to higher taxes and more services, hardly the policy thrust of an activist Democratic president." In his analysis after the election, *Out of Order,* scholar Thomas Patterson found that Clinton, despite a press that treated him more favorably than Bush, emerged from the election with the highest negative ratings of any newly elected president in modern times.

Nor could he count on many allies in Washington. Beyond his campaign staff and network of personal friends, Clinton had few ties to the capital. In Congress, he could rely upon the loyalty of his Arkansas senators, David Pryor and Dale Bumpers, but not many others. After all, he had never spent much time in Washington, and as James MacGregor Burns and Georgia Sorenson point out in *Dead Center,* he had run a highly personalized campaign, distancing himself from Democratic regulars. The party's barons on Capitol Hill would wait and see about the new kid downtown. As for Republicans, they were spoiling for a fight. During the final years of Reagan and the four years of Bush, they thought Democrats had treated their presidents with arrogant disdain. It was payback time.

If Congress started piling on Clinton, the press wouldn't be far behind. While many of them had tilted in his direction during the campaign, that love affair had begun to sour. Journalists who had once gloried in him as a New Democrat were drifting away—among them influential commentators such as Joe Klein and Michael Kramer—while veteran columnists like David Broder weren't sure the truth was in him. As Patterson's study had found, the press corps as a whole was tougher and more judgmental.

Clinton had won an election without a bounce. Doubts about his character were planted deeply in the public mind, so he would have to be extra careful. One wrong step, and he could be chewed to pieces. Given how the odds were stacked against him, one might have thought that Clinton would have buckled down immediately after the election to plot out a serious, sustaining strategy for governing. Instead, he let the time slip away from him with consequences that went far beyond what he foresaw at the time. Future presidents should pay close heed.

Eleven Crucial Weeks . . . Lost

From a public perspective, the eleven weeks between Clinton's election and inauguration were a pleasant interlude. He seemed a fresh breeze, maybe even another Jack Kennedy. Working families still digging out from the recession of the late 1980s looked on approvingly as he called together a summit of CEOs, economists, and others to talk about improving the economy. No hard policy decisions emerged, but Clinton's public message was unmistakable: he cared. In the election, 43 percent voted for him; by the end of the transition, 58 percent approved of him.

Yet, as I covered his transition, I was perplexed. Beneath the smooth surface created by his public relations machine, a mess was building up. Those eleven weeks are crucial. Only if the transition is put to productive use will the honeymoon come after January 20. As we saw with Carter and Reagan, a newly elected president must 257 seize upon those intervening weeks to appoint his new team, map out policy and communications plans, build bridges to key constituencies, and—whenever he can—get some rest. It is the moment to put the campaign behind and focus on governing. But here was Clinton still in full campaign mode.

There is no doubt—even in his mind, I think—that his transition planted seeds that almost destroyed his presidency. For all their surface appeal, those were eleven lost weeks, a time irretrievably squandered. He made three fundamental mistakes:

First, he failed to create a team that could govern. Intellectually, Clinton understood that one of the hardest challenges for a new president is to have a functioning, effective government in place soon after he takes the oath. As Thomas Mann and Norman Ornstein have pointed out, "The task of staffing a new administration is staggering: more than 6,000 presidential appointments, including roughly 600 Senate-confirmed cabinet and subcabinet members. . . . If appointments are not made well before the inauguration, they can be delayed for months into the presidency, creating uncertainty in agencies and gaps in policymaking."

Clinton started out on the right foot. He put experienced people in charge of transition appointments, Warren Christopher and Vernon Jordan, and he and Gore met with them diligently to make cabinet selections. He also insisted on a cabinet that would "look like America," as he had promised in the campaign. While critics carped that he failed to recruit heavyweights, the cabinet that emerged was respectable and did fulfill his promise of diversity. For the first time in history, white males were in a minority.

But his obsessive demands for balance and the way he agonized over choices prolonged the process so much that few other jobs were properly filled. Most cabinet officers had no time to assemble a subcabinet. With vacancies riddling departments like Justice, much of the administration was an empty shell in the early, critical months after Clinton took office. By dangling and withdrawing job offers during the transition, Clinton also left many wounds among his top appointees.

Worse, Clinton waited until the last possible moment to think through a White House staff. Most of his people didn't know what they would be doing or where they would be sitting until the eve of the new administration. That was a horrible blunder, as he himself acknowledges. No one could plan out the early months of his administration, as we did with Reagan, and his staff arrived in Washington still breathless from Little Rock.

Inexplicably, Clinton also chose his top staff almost entirely from his campaign team. If anyone had paid attention to Reagan's success, they would have noted how much he gained from integrating campaign loyalists with Washington veterans. But people around Clinton seemed more interested in evening scores and keeping out—most dreaded of the dread—anyone who worked for Jimmy Carter! Stuart Eizenstat had signaled to Mack McLarty, the incoming chief of staff, that he would be willing to serve as Mack's deputy. Eizenstat would have been a stellar addition to the Clinton White House. But he was vetoed because he had been Carter's domestic adviser. It seemed odd to shut Carterites out of the White House when they were filling up the top jobs in foreign policy. But that's what happened. Eizenstat dutifully took a post on the diplomatic circuit, and in the second term shone in top posts at Treasury and State. Blackballs also kept Mike McCurry out of the early White House: he had committed the sin of working for Senator Bob Kerrey in the early days of the presidential campaign. A slew of other Washington veterans such as Tom Donilon were also prepared to join the White House, but invitations never came. Had Clinton reached out for veteran players for his White House as he had for his campaign, he would not have floundered in those early weeks in office.

The people who did come—George Stephanopoulos, Dee Dee Myers, Rahm Emanuel, Gene Sperling—were certainly talented. They had been the backbone of the first Democratic campaign to win the White House in sixteen years. But they were also young and inexperienced in governing. Dee Dee Myers had rarely been to Washington and never worked there. If she had first gained some seasoning as deputy press secretary, the number-two slot, she would have stepped up to number one and been outstanding. Instead, she was thrown immediately into the lions'den and had chunks taken out of her. Her job was doubly difficult because a male-dominated staff left her out of the loop too often and Hillary, worried about her ability, was frequently on the warpath against her. Through pluck and a good head on her shoulders, Dee Dee still managed to do a credible job. But she wasn't treated fairly.

Gene Sperling represented the alternative case. Young and smart, he was properly appointed to a deputy slot in economic policy under an older, more experienced Bob Rubin. After training there, Sperling eventually emerged in his own right and was a pillar of Clinton's second-term White House. But Sperling was the exception: most others his age who should have started as number twos

259

began their White House careers as number ones, an invitation for trouble. Responsibility for that rests at the top.

When Clinton asked his childhood friend to become his chief of staff, Mack McLarty at first demurred. As a CEO of a *Fortune* 500 natural gas company, he was willing to serve as a liaison to business—perhaps at Commerce or in the White House—but he felt his lack of Washington experience disqualified him as chief of staff. Under continuing pressure, he reluctantly agreed. Once again, the Clintons unwittingly stacked the deck against their own success. They not only nixed Eizenstat, the man McLarty wanted as his deputy, but filled many other slots and assigned office spaces without asking their new chief. Before McLarty even signed up, two of Hillary Clinton's partners from her law firm, Vince Foster and Bill Kennedy, were installed in the counsel's office with another of her former associates, Bernard Nussbaum, as general counsel. Despite that, McLarty was instrumental in helping the President score some of his most important legislative victories. He was also one of the finest people I met in the administration. But it was a constant, often losing battle for him to bring order out of the chaos he was handed. The president who most needed an organized White House ensured he would not have one.

Second, Clinton failed to use the transition to make elaborate plans for his first weeks in office and to mobilize congressional support behind him. He was handicapped in part because his campaign, while politically appealing, did not lay out clear, precise ideas for his presidency. "It's the economy, stupid," was a winning slogan, but it was not a policy. It left him without a mandate and his transition team without a road map. Through most of those eleven weeks, as Bob Woodward has detailed in *The Agenda*, his economic advisers clashed incessantly with his campaign chieftains over the course he should take. What little time they had together was also eaten away by the "economic summit" in Little Rock, the event that drew in plenty of CEOs and cameras but produced little policy.

Clinton did try to avoid an early Carter mistake by calling in Democratic congressional leaders for an early powwow, but even that went awry. In December, a delegation headed up by Senate Majority Leader George Mitchell and House Speaker Tom Foley descended on Little Rock for a private dinner with the president-elect and his wife. He asked for their support in reducing the deficit, overhauling health care, and enacting family and medical leave. They happily agreed. But they also had an agenda of their own. During the campaign, he had spoken out for campaign finance reform, the

260

line-item veto, and significant reductions in staff, including Hill staff. Would he agree to put both ideas on a back burner? Thinking he had to give in order to get, Clinton went along. According to his aides, he left the dinner thinking he had bonded with his new friends on Capitol Hill.

But sources told me some of his visitors came away with a different view: "This is a man who can be rolled." He had given in too easily for their taste. Members of Congress, like other key players in the system, try to size up a new president at the earliest opportunity. They want to know what kind of leader he will be: how tough, how trustworthy, how cooperative. They look for signs of weakness, and if they see any, they pounce. From their point of view, there is not enough power to go around in Washington. If the president grabs it all, they have little. But if he concedes even the tiniest fraction, they seize it for themselves. Democrats have no compunction about doing that to one of their own, nor do Republicans. It's not personal; that's just the way the game is played—and has been for all time.

Notably, Clinton did little to reach out to the Republican minority during the transition. By the time he reached Washington, he had a problem in both parties. Machiavelli wrote that a new prince must be loved or feared, and if he must choose, it is better to be feared. Clinton was neither. Over the next eight years, he won some significant victories but also suffered major defeats—and never became King of the Hill.

Third, he simply would not prepare himself physically for the ordeal ahead. At Renaissance that New Year's—eight weeks after the election—Clinton was still celebrating the victory and loved staying up half the night to laugh and talk with old friends. The next morning, he would be up at the crack to hit the beach for an early run or perhaps a game of touch football. David Maraniss writes in his biography, *First in His Class*, that Clinton had been sleeping only four to five hours a night since a professor said in college that many great leaders of the past had gotten by that way. Many of us at Hilton Head were familiar with his nocturnal habits and knew he was having a good time. Didn't he deserve it?

Even so, we worried that he seemed worn out, puffy, and hyper. His attention span was so brief that it was difficult to have a serious conversation of more than a few minutes. By contrast, Hillary was turning in early every night, getting a solid sleep, and in conversations each day was focused on what was coming after inauguration. I began to think of her then as far more of his anchor than I had understood, and we had a couple of good talks. In a short encounter

261

with Clinton, I tried to say gently that the presidency is a marathon, not a hundred-yard dash, and I hoped he would have a chance for some downtime in the three weeks still remaining. I don't think I registered.

When he reached Washington, I am convinced, his physical exhaustion caught up with him. It is stressful for anyone to accept the responsibilities of the presidency, but Clinton's reaction seemed extreme. Those who saw him in his first weeks at the White House often found him out of sorts, easily distracted, and impatient. I was watching from afar, and the harried man I saw on television bore little resemblance to the confident, relaxed leader I had known. Coming to the White House early that summer, I concluded that he was almost too tired to think straight. Journalist Joe Klein believes that if Clinton had not been exhausted, he would not have handled the gay issue as ineptly as he did in his first days in office. Not until August of his first year did Clinton get away for a proper rest. Escaping to a low-key vacation in Martha's Vineyard, where he could sleep, play golf, read, and spend time with family, he returned almost restored to full vigor. It is no coincidence that the weeks that followed were among the most productive of his presidency. It may seem odd that so much can turn on a president's sleep. But history and research have repeatedly shown that fitness and stamina are the hidden ingredients of leadership. Especially in high office, a person must exercise judgment that is finely tuned.

All this is not to say that everything done in his transition was wrongheaded. On one major issue facing him, he came down squarely in the right place: he chose a first-rate economic team, established a personal bond with Federal Reserve chairman Alan Greenspan, and began moving in a gutsy direction to bring down budget deficits. But the effects of his early economic decisions would not be felt for many months. In the meantime, Clinton still had to move to Washington and take charge. The transition did not prepare him properly for that immediate challenge. In many ways, it was one of the worst transitions in modern times. The lessons of Reagan, Kennedy, and others who managed it well were forgotten.

Slipping on Banana Peels

262   I have dwelt here on Clinton's transition to the presidency because it is not well understood and had profound consequences. His early weeks in office, by contrast, have been thoroughly described else-

where—most successfully by Elizabeth Drew in her book *On the Edge,* and by Bob Woodward in *The Agenda.* Both had extraordinary access to people around the President. When I came aboard, I was informed that each member of the senior staff was "expected" to sit down regularly with these two authors so they could write accurate books. No other White House had ever agreed to participate in such bizarre arrangements, but there we were. I said okay.

The President himself participated in interviews and I presumed that he had sanctioned the cooperation of everyone else. But he went up in smoke when he read the results, as he should have. Both accounts were devastating indictments. While the two authors describe aspects of the transition, their descriptions of the First Hundred Days are what drove the books forward. To anyone who still doubted, they revealed a White House in disarray, a president leading by the seat of his pants, and an administration apparently in over its head.

Clinton had slipped on one banana peel after another. His first two choices to become attorney general were forced to withdraw. His pledge to end the ban on gays in the military brought howls from the brass, and he partially backed down, upsetting everyone. A Democratic Congress quickly enacted a family and medical leave bill, which the party had long supported, but wisely balked at his economic stimulus bill. It also blocked his efforts to put health care reform on a fast track. From the outside, I and others worried that Clinton was lurching to the left. He seemed to be abandoning the rationale for his presidency and destroying hope for a new era of bipartisan, centrist reform.

Down at the White House, his aides were at sixes and sevens. The staff of the travel office, popular with the press, were summarily fired. A Hollywood friend of the Clintons was then found to have been angling for the contract, which further outraged reporters. The press also slammed Clinton for holding up traffic at Los Angeles International, while Air Force One sat on the ground as he got his hair cut by a Hollywood barber for $200. Later evidence showed other travelers weren't delayed, but the facts never caught up. It was Murphy's Law squared: everything that could go wrong went completely haywire. Clinton's popularity dropped twenty points, down below 40 percent.

Why did this young, promising president stumble and almost come apart in those early days? The proximate cause, as I have argued, was the lack of effective preparation during the transition. "They really weren't ready to govern," observed Senator Daniel

263

Patrick Moynihan. Those mistakes were partly born out of inexperience and hubris. It was a bigger jump from Little Rock to Washington than even Clinton had anticipated. Neither he nor Hillary appreciated what it takes to govern in the most complex political system in the world. Both of them had also blazed successful paths their entire lives, overcoming numerous defeats and setbacks. Not surprisingly, they entertained dreams of becoming the next Franklin and Eleanor. The dreams far outran reality.

It should also be emphasized that his opponents never gave Clinton a decent break. Republicans had controlled the White House so long that they considered him a usurper and many denied him legitimacy from his first day in office. Their attacks on him were often personal and vicious. In contrast to Reagan's first year, when southern Democrats provided the margin of his victories in the House, Republicans stoutly refused to help Clinton in his first months. Senator Bob Dole organized a filibuster that killed off Clinton's economic stimulus plan in his first ninety days. Not a single Republican voted for his budget plan. Simultaneously, the press turned on him. Stories that might have been sympathetic or overlooked his foibles turned unusually harsh. Commentators declared him politically dead just weeks after he took office. No president in recent history has been so denied a honeymoon from the press and Congress.

Joining His Inner Circle

When Bill Clinton is in trouble, he looks for a quick fix. I know. I was one of them.

After leaving the Reagan administration in 1983, I thought it unlikely I would ever return to government service. I had had my turns at bat and was now enjoying journalism. In 1988, the *Washington Post* reported that a newly elected George Bush might select me to run the U.S. Information Agency. I wrote to Bush to say that while flattered, I would appreciate not being considered. I also repeated something I had told him before: that even as I rooted for his success, I thought my first responsibility as a commentator was to provide readers and viewers with as balanced an account as I could. Occasionally, I might have to be critical. Bush, true to character, sent a kind, gracious response.

264   When Bill Clinton won in 1992, it never occurred to me to send a similar note to him. As a Democrat, he would never want any help

from me and presumably he knew I wasn't looking for anything. We never broached the subject.

In a bolt out of nowhere, his chief of staff Mack McLarty called one day in May to say he and the President had been reading my editorials in *U.S. News* urging various courses of action on the administration. Some were critical. Would I join him for lunch to talk? I didn't know McLarty, but agreed and we ate in the White House mess. A short while later, the President himself dropped by to say hello and we talked for a while about his difficulties. McLarty ended the conversation by saying that the White House needed to recruit a Washington veteran to help shore up its operations and wondered if I had any names to suggest. I promised to think about it.

The next Sunday afternoon, Mack called me at home and wanted to know if I had any names for him. I recommended a couple of people from the Carter years—Stu Eizenstat was one. We left it there and he said he might call again. Now I began to wonder what this flirtation was really about.

That Wednesday night I had a speech at Lousiana State University. Starting to drive back to New Orleans afterward, I stopped in a Phillips 66 station to check phone messages and learned that the White House operator wanted me to call. When I checked in, she rang up Mack at home.

"David, we've thought about this a lot and the President wants to talk to you about you personally filling that slot. He's very serious and very eager to talk." I damn near dropped the phone. "Can you come to my house tomorrow night for dinner—just the two of us?"

With the White House in the midst of tense budget talks on Capitol Hill, Mack couldn't get home until after ten the next night, but his wife, Donna, had left us a delicious dinner of lamb. He took me into his confidence about problems that the team was facing, and sometime after midnight, the President called.

"I'm in trouble. I need your help."

Bill Clinton can be highly persuasive one-on-one, and over the next thirty minutes, he made a convincing appeal. How deep a hole he was in. How my experience and judgment could help him out. How I could serve as a bridge to the press, to Republicans, and to people I respected in Washington. How much it mattered to the country. Would I please consider it?

The job they had in mind was two-hatted: to serve as "counselor to the President" and "communications director." They had never appointed a counselor before, so that title was available. As for communications director, George Stephanopoulos had been serving in that capacity. They said he had already agreed to move into a different role as a top political adviser and close liaison with Democrats in Congress.

I said I was willing to consider the counselor post but not communications. If I came, I would be willing to help them find a new communications czar and help oversee that operation, but I didn't want to do that job again. It would also have to be a short stay. Given my Republican ties, it would be difficult enough to assist him with governing, but I emphatically could not remain in the White House during a campaign against the GOP. And I did not want to have my arrival linked to a change in George's status. The President's relationship with Stephanopoulos was on a separate track and should remain there. Should he change positions and I be seen as an instigating force, that would be poisonous for me with the younger White House staff, who adored him. They agreed to take communications off the table and agreed that I would stay out of campaigns, but I could not get a firm answer on delinking me from Stephanopoulos. That would later prove to diminish my effectiveness.

The President said they were extremely eager to move right away with both of us. He would be on a day trip Friday, but the Vice President would call me to follow up. I said this was a major decision and I would like some time to think it over with my family and friends. Anne and I and our kids were going to Bermuda that Saturday morning for a brief vacation, and I would like to reserve a decision until after I got back the following Wednesday. I suggested to Mack that they announce George's future before then.

The next day, Al Gore came crackling through the phone, insisting that I had to make a decision immediately. The chance of a leak is too great, he explained. We think you can do the greatest good here if the announcement catches the world by surprise. He painted a bright picture of how I would join a tight circle of five people: the President, the Vice President, the First Lady, the chief of staff, and me, the counselor. It was important, I said, that if I were to come, I have a direct reporting relationship with the President as well as the chief of staff. Gore seemed to agree.

In the hours that followed, I feverishly sought out the friends and colleagues whose judgment I most trusted and who would protect the confidence of our conversations. Mark Shields, a wonderful partner for five years on *The MacNeil/Lehrer NewsHour,* was one; Ken Duberstein, the last chief of staff for Reagan and a valued friend, was another; so were Mort Zuckerman, Jim Lehrer, and Alan Greenspan.

After recovering from surprise, most had kind words about the contribution I might make but warned that I could be putting my head in a noose. "That's the most partisan White House I've ever seen," Duberstein boomed. "Those kids over there will try to hang you the first chance they get." Mark agreed and had one further piece of advice: stay as far away as possible from Whitewater. He knew some of the players and imagined it reeked with corruption. Sound advice from one and all.

I wanted to talk with a number of other Republicans, including party leaders Bob Dole and Newt Gingrich. I needed to sound them out as to whether it would, in fact, be possible to serve as a bridge from a Democratic president to Republicans on the Hill. I also wanted to get to them in advance of any announcement or leak so I could protect my relations with them. If they thought the idea was preposterous, I doubted I could be effective in the job. In the rush, I was never able to speak to them in advance as I should have.

Meetings were set up for that evening in the White House residence. I was to come in after dinner and see Hillary alone. Her husband would return after eleven from his day trip, and he and I could talk then. The Vice President called several times; Mack was on the road and we talked a bit by phone. Gore made it plain that the President wanted to resolve it that night to get out in front of the press. Late that afternoon, CNN broke the story, saying that the White House was talking with me and that George seemed headed for a demotion. Someone in the White House was intentionally putting out the backstage drama. I was angry and felt very hustled.

Over dinner that night, our son Christopher and daughter Katherine both urged me to go forward. Anne was deeply divided. Three times she had been a "White House widow" and, as pleased as she was that the President was asking for my help (she liked him), she was torn about yet another round. "Why can't we take more time to think about it?" she asked. "This feels like a runaway train." She was right on that point. As I left for my late-night sessions with Hillary and Bill, she said she would go along with whatever was decided, but it was clear she wasn't happy. The ones who pay the heaviest price for government service are always the spouses. Thankfully, she stayed in our marriage in the storms that followed.

Meeting alone with Hillary, I put a series of questions to her. *Do you truly want this to happen?* Yes, absolutely. Bill needs your help, and I am all for it. *From the outside, it appears you are pulling your husband far to the left. Is that what you want?* Not at all. The media misunderstand me. I am actually very traditional in most of my beliefs,

267

especially on social issues. Don't forget I was a Goldwater girl back in the early sixties. It's essential that Bill dominate the center of politics. *Why do you hate the press so much?* I don't really. They've been tough on us from the start, but we need to repair relations. You can help us with that, just as you can help us reach out to Republicans. *What about the Washington establishment? Why haven't you courted some of the most influential people in the city, like Ben Bradlee and Sally Quinn?* We know we should do that. We've been thinking about some dinners this summer at the White House. You can help us there, too. As we went down my list, she had all the right answers.

Well after 11:00 P.M., as I recall, a tired Bill Clinton dragged into the upstairs residence where we were talking. For a while, the three of us chatted and he and I then went into his study, where he poured out his troubles in Washington and asked for a final answer. It was vitally important to his presidency, he said. He needed help. I was the best person for the job. And we had to settle it tonight and announce it first thing in the morning. The news wouldn't hold; our talks were leaking out. Stephanopoulos would have to be part of the same package, because his news was leaking, too. We couldn't wait until after my holiday.

As we went back and forth, he once again pushed all of my buttons. Around 1:00 A.M., I agreed. A few hours later, at 7:30 on a Saturday morning, four of us went into the Rose Garden—President Clinton, Vice President Gore, George Stephanopoulos, and I.

People have frequently asked me since: how could a veteran of three Republican White Houses help a Democratic president? I was at peace with my decision. At the end of the day, I thought it was the right thing to do. The President of the United States was in trouble and was asking for help.

In retrospect, I confess that sometimes I wonder whether I was suffering from a rescue fantasy. Who in the devil was I to think that single-handedly, I might turn things around? Was I so flattered by the request that my ego had spun out of control? Probably more so than I admitted to myself. In truth, the Clinton White House didn't need a Lone Ranger to come riding in; it needed a full posse of veterans from the past with experience and skills—preferably from Democratic ranks—and it needed stronger leadership at the top.

Having worked for three Republicans, I knew that some would also think that I had betrayed the party and was empty of conviction. They would label me the newest member of the world's oldest profession. In fact, I did have to wrestle internally with my beliefs and how they matched up to the president I would serve. It was not the first time. With Nixon and Ford, I had become comfortable ideologically, but my moderate views placed me outside the conservative mainstream of Reagan supporters; now I would be outside the liberal mainstream of Clinton supporters. Because Reagan governed more to the center than he talked, I was okay then. Working for a Democrat would obviously be harder, but if Clinton governed as a New Democrat and pursued a bipartisan reform agenda, I felt I would be okay again. The agenda of the Democratic Leadership Council—home of the New Democrats—was, after all, very close to my own. If Clinton wandered too far from it, I would have to rethink.

But at the time, I was more conscious of other sentiments. As a native of the South, I grew up believing that one answers a call to service. This call was special: it came directly from a president of the United States when he thought his stewardship was in peril. The fact that he was willing to reach out over party lines was to me a good signal, not a bad one. Throughout its history, the country has always performed best when its leadership has woven together broad, bipartisan coalitions. As recently as World War II, FDR tapped two Republicans to serve in key cabinet posts. In 1961, President Kennedy asked—and received—the support of Republicans to serve as secretary of the treasury, secretary of defense, CIA director, and national security adviser! President Nixon recruited Democrat Daniel Patrick Moynihan to serve as his counselor in the White House and later brought in Democrat John Connally as treasury secretary, the man he liked the most. Joining up with President Clinton, I did not pretend to be in the same league, but I was acting in the same tradition. It was troubling to me that the tradition had faded; I hoped that in a small way, I might help to keep it alive because I thought it urgent that Americans seek common ground. From letters and comments that have flowed in, I sense that many others around the country agree.

Many who have been privileged to serve in the White House over the years also feel a personal bond with the Office of the Presidency. We look up to the office itself and believe it the crown jewel of American democracy. We want our presidents to succeed whether they are Republicans or Democrats.

Certainly, those thoughts were uppermost as I stood that morning in the Rose Garden and followed the President to the microphone. "Patriotism must come before partisanship," I said. "It is time to move beyond the scorching partisanship that now pervades 269 Capitol Hill, to move beyond the cynicism that now creeps into so much of our reporting, to move beyond old boxes for our thinking.

Four out of our past five presidents have left office broken by its weight. This presidency must and will have a better outcome. We cannot afford to wait any longer in addressing America's needs."

A few hours later, House Republican leader Newt Gingrich placed the first call to me from the GOP hierarchy. "I want to congratulate you," he said. "You are doing the right thing. This is the way we should practice politics in this country, and I want to help you in any way I can." Over the next eighteen months, he was true to his word, and he has occupied a warm spot with me ever since.

But his voice was rare in those early days. Some Republicans inside the beltway branded me as another Benedict Arnold. This only proved the nasty things they had been saying about me for years, conservatives muttered angrily. The first time he visited the White House, Bob Dole—a man I had long supported—would barely shake hands. More painful was the reaction of former President Bush. He suggested that on television during the 1992 campaign, I had been secretly supporting Clinton all along when I should have been defending him. Remembering how much I wanted him to serve and how I had tried publicly to persuade him to change course as president, I felt wounded.

To this day, some have neither forgiven nor forgotten. But, happily, close friends and most of my former colleagues eventually came to a more benign view. When old hands saw that I wasn't sticking around to campaign for Clinton and continued to speak as a moderate who was respectful of conservatives, that eased the tension.

I did have second thoughts about the process. As much as I saluted Clinton for reaching out across party lines for help, he and Gore wanted to turn my appointment into a public relations coup. The bigger the surprise, the bigger the headline—and the more the ripple effect across the country. Aha, they could say, Clinton is on the comeback trail again! As someone practiced in those arts, I could appreciate their motivations.

Their insistence on a pell-mell decision, however, turned my life upside down. For the sake of their Sunday headline, I wound up on the short end of the stick: my talks with my wife were too short, I never had time to consult Republicans properly, and George and I were shoehorned into the same announcement, hurting us both in the months that followed. I made a mistake in not slowing down that runaway train.

270

Even so, I still think it was right to accept. If anything, a bridging of differences in Washington has grown more important in the years since. Americans are aching for a politics that moves beyond bickering and personal destruction.

As usual, Ronald Reagan had the best and final word. Visiting the capital that summer, his last appearance there, he told a Republican crowd with a smile, "I must say that returning to Washington today really brought back memories. As our plane headed toward the airport, I looked down on the White House, and it was just like the good old days . . . the South Lawn, the Rose Garden . . . *David Gergen.*"

9

Riding the Roller Coaster

THE BILL CLINTON I FOUND in the Oval Office that summer was very different from the fellow who had taken the oath in January. He had wanted to be a transformational president, he had told James MacGregor Burns and Georgia Sorenson shortly before his inauguration. Jefferson, Lincoln, the two Roosevelts, Kennedy—they would be his models. "Not for eighty years—not since Woodrow Wilson had come to office—had a new president offered such a considered strategy of leadership," they wrote.

By summer, Clinton had seen his hopes go smash. As he opened up to me in our early talks, his frustrations flowed to the surface. As he and Hillary had come riding into town, their ideals flying high, they felt they had met resistance at every turn. They were angry with Republicans and the press for denying them a honeymoon. He was also unsparing in self-criticism. Somehow, he felt, he had allowed himself to get way out of position, too far over to the left, and he had to get back to the political center, which he described as his natural home. He recognized that he had presented no core vision and had never come up with the right public message after his inauguration. He took blame as well for what had gone wrong in the White House, right down to the disorganization in his staff.

Worst of all, he had lost his self-confidence. He acted as if the stuffing had been knocked out of him, a far cry from earlier days. As governor, he had always brimmed with optimism. Whatever might befall him on a Monday, he would wake up Tuesday thinking it was a brand-new world, waiting to be conquered. Mistakes were what you learned from, not what you brooded over—or not for long. The first months in Washington had taken a cruel toll, especially because his ambitions had been so lofty.

But if Clinton was down, he wasn't out. He was never a quitter. Instead, he liked to wear out his opposition by hanging in—or, as he put it, "showing up for work every day." He had wanted this office since he was a kid, of course, and he wasn't going to surrender it without a fight. Just as he had rebounded from defeats as a governor and campaigner, he was prepared to do so now as president.

Men who make it to the presidency usually have a reserve of internal strengths they can call upon when in trouble. He certainly did, and in the months that followed, I saw them all emerge: resilience, persuasiveness, a luminous intelligence, courage, a capacity to learn from mistakes, and a deep caring about the public good. They are the best of Bill Clinton—the qualities that carried him to the White House and allowed him to become one of the five presidents of the twentieth century who served two full terms.

Never in my time at the White House did I see him engage in anything unethical or underhanded. There was no corner-cutting or finagling. I knew he still had an eye for women. As men do, we might talk of one or another we had seen during the day. The Vice President liked to join in stories, too. But so far as I could tell, that was all there was—talk. I brought with me an attractive, young, intelligent assistant, Dianna Pierce, who was frequently with him alone, and he never made a pass or an inappropriate remark. Nor did he to any of her female friends. The Clinton I was seeing was a man at his Sunday best.

Not that he was perfect. I've known some public men with tempers, but his was the worst by a magnitude of at least two. Early on, I flew with him to Chicago on a small version of Air Force One, and when he learned that small details of his airport visit with Mayor Richard Daley had been mishandled, he erupted so violently that I wished I had a parachute.

Bill Clinton getting mad is like Mount Vesuvius erupting. At the White House, he would usually blow at least once in the morning and straight into the face of George Stephanopoulos. Perhaps he felt that George was the son he never had and could trust him to take it. Certainly, Stephanopoulos bore up with a stoicism that was commendable. He sensed that if he didn't talk back, Clinton would cool off and, within a few minutes, we could get back to work. A White House photographer once captured the two of them, Clinton exploding and Stephanopoulos passive, their faces inches apart. I

273

imagine that negative went the way of Rose Mary Woods's lost tape. Though brief, those scenes were jarring.

From the beginning, there were also signs of trouble at home. A chipper president would arrive at the office in the morning, almost whistling as he whipped through papers. A phone would ring. It was a call from upstairs at the residence. He would listen, utter a few words, but as we started back to work, his mood would darken, his attention wander, and hot words would spew out. Had we seen the outrageous things his enemies were saying about him now? Why hadn't we attacked? Why was he working so hard and getting so little credit? Why was his staff screwing him again? *What*, I would wonder, had she said to him now?

Perhaps I was overreacting when I also thought that this White House was too paranoid about the outside world. Nothing matched the distrust I had seen in the Nixon White House. But it was that experience—and the price Nixon paid—which made me extrasensitive as I listened to President Clinton, the First Lady, and others in their entourage talk of countless enemies. Sure, I argued, there are folks out there who would like to do you in, but there are plenty of others—in the press, on Capitol Hill, over in Georgetown, up in New York—who will give you a fair shake if you approach them in the right spirit. Make the system work for you, not against you.

My advice did not always go down well. I told myself that this was a White House under siege. It was natural that feelings were raw and jagged. Clinton was smart enough to see that down the road he must address these deeper problems. Otherwise, like Nixon, he could face more serious trouble. But for now, just over four months into his presidency, he had an immediate crisis on his hands: how to pull himself out of a ditch so he could govern. If he didn't do that, all the rest wouldn't matter. If he did, he would take care of the rest later on. Or so I thought. A bumpy ride lay ahead.

The Makings of a Comeback

Over the next seven months, Bill Clinton staged a spectacular comeback. In late May, he stood at 38 percent in the public opinion polls and observers wondered if he were doomed. By late December, he had risen to 58 percent and could take credit for many of the most substantial accomplishments of his presidency—congressional passage of his budget plan, NAFTA, national service, and the Brady Bill; signing of a peace agreement between the Palestinians and Israelis;

and the launch of the Vice President's efforts to "reinvent" government. With the First Lady's plan for health reform also opening to positive reviews, Clinton seemed poised once again to embody great new hopes for social reform.

Some commentators said that since the turnaround started around the time of my arrival, I must have been primarily responsible. Not true. I believe I was one of those who helped, but Bill Clinton was the chief architect of this comeback, just as he has been for others in his life.

Clinton had dug a deep hole for himself and now, rallying, he almost climbed out. He was the one who rediscovered his remarkable strengths and turned them again to his advantage. The rest of us on his team provided a supportive environment. We tightened up operations at the White House, so he wouldn't be burdened with more snafus, but mostly we encouraged him to remember who he was. We were there for him emotionally. We cheered him on when he won and cheered him up when he lost. In psychological terms, we created a "safe space" where he could work things out on his own.

In earlier years, I had learned that men who are elected president usually know a lot more about what works for them than do their staffs. They are also the only ones on the ballot; no one in their employ won a single vote. Conservatives who said "Let Reagan be Reagan" were ultimately right. What better rule now? "Let Clinton be Clinton," I decided. Give him your most honest evaluations but don't try to substitute your judgment for his. Instead, a staff must try to bring out the best in a president.

Both Clintons were eager to shape up the White House operation. Some changes seemed cosmetic to the outside but were dramatic within the microcosm of the White House. Early in the administration, for example, Stephanopoulos had wanted to keep access open to reporters, but Hillary and Susan Thomases had wanted to exile them to the Old Executive Office Building across the street. As a compromise, a door was shut between the press room and the office of the press secretary. Reporters could visit Stephanopoulos and Myers only with permission. That access had never been blocked before, and reporters rightly resented the change. George and Dee Dee weren't happy, either.

In our first conversation, I asked Hillary to have the door reopened, and she immediately agreed. She even wondered why it had not been done before! As tiny as that move was, the press saw it 275 as a symbolic gesture that promised better days were ahead. And for a while, they were. Both Clintons agreed to talk with reporters more and invited them to a round of dinners that summer. As he sensed that they were no longer baying at him, Clinton felt less tense and regained his old ease in talking with them. The war against the press was moving toward a truce.

With encouragement, Clinton also began paying more attention to other centers of power. For too long, he had treated foreign policy as a sideshow—as if he were telling his foreign policy advisers: Keep the world quiet while I fix things at home. In the Cold War, presidents typically spent at least 60 percent of their time on foreign affairs; with Bush, the figure could rise to 75 percent. Clinton early on reversed the tables: domestic affairs probably consumed 75 percent of his time, foreign affairs less than a quarter. Foreign embassies were outraged that their heads of government couldn't get on Clinton's calendar. When a small plane crashed on the White House lawn, people joked that it was CIA director Jim Woolsey trying to get an appointment. No president in more than half a century had been so cavalier toward the larger world.

Now that he was in trouble, Clinton listened more closely to his national security adviser, Tony Lake, and Secretary of State Warren Christopher. They told him that he had the capacity to be a strong foreign policy president but he had to engage. Stop flitting in and out. Each day should begin with a thorough briefing; regularly, he should meet with his whole NSC; once a week, he should sit down privately with his secretary of state. His schedulers had to treat foreign policy as an integral part of White House life. Clinton accepted some of their recommendations. He still waited too long to wrap his mind around a problem; his decisions were still too tactical and improvised, but he was on a better path. On big questions in foreign policy, he usually got it right in the end.

We also tried to slow down the pace within the White House, so there would be less chaos and he would have a chance to breathe and think. Every White House has a degree of internal confusion. Reagan joked that in his White House, the right hand did not know what the far right hand was doing. But the early Clinton White House was beyond the pale. Vice President Gore, who likes tidiness, had the most apt analogy: we could be like ten-year-olds playing soccer. Nobody is ever in position; everyone is swarming around the ball.

And so it was. As the President prepared to enter the Rose Garden for a public ceremony—an occasion that always invited the
276 press to shout out questions—as many as ten to twenty staffers would stream into the Oval Office, mill about, and and pepper him with conflicting advice. One would whisper in his ear; another

would stuff a piece of paper in his hand. It was done with the best of intentions, but to someone accustomed to a buttoned-down Republican style, it was a shock.

In the weeks that followed, Clinton began his recovery by becoming more focused and disciplined. With the rest of us also pushing hard, the White House pulled together and built sturdier relations with the outside world. We were a long way from a well-oiled machine, but we were running more smoothly. More important, his self-confidence was returning. As we say in Washington, he was becoming more presidential. And that strengthened him for what really mattered: getting things done.

Winning Twin Victories

The most significant turning of those seven months came through two critical victories on Capitol Hill. Clinton began struggling during the transition to reconcile his campaign promises with the hard realities of exploding federal deficits. The internal fight was long and messy, spilling over into the first weeks of his presidency. Clinton had promised voters that he would cut taxes for the middle class, and his populist advisers—Carville, Begala, and others—wanted him to keep his pledge. Hillary generally sided with them on economic issues. "We didn't come here to spend all our time cutting deficits created by Republicans," she would say.

But Bob Rubin, Leon Panetta, Lloyd Bentsen, Laura Tyson, and his other economic advisers persuaded him that by first pleasing Wall Street, he would ultimately help Main Street. He had inherited annual budget deficits of over $200 billion a year, and the Congressional Budget Office estimated that on the path it was then taking, the federal government would run up additional deficits of over $300 billion in years to come. Unless he had an ambitious plan for budget reduction that would necessarily include tax hikes, he would spook investors, drive up interest rates, and possibly send the economy into another tailspin. "The budget deficits are a bone in the nation's throat," he told me later. "Until we get rid of them, we can't do anything else. That's why I went after them first."

So, early in his presidency, Clinton made that hard call to present a disciplined budget. Instead of tax cuts, he called for tax increases. To minimize the impact on the middle class, he targeted the rate hikes to the top 5 percent of taxpayers. He also pared back plans for dramatic increases in social spending. Trying to keep his cam- 277 paign pledge of "putting people first," he did call for modest increases in a few programs for "human investment"—among them Head Start, child nutrition, and the Earned Income Tax Credit—but that meant he had to cut deeper in other areas that were politically popular.

There were two pieces of foolishness in his early plan. One was a stimulus package to goose up the economy with $16 billion in short-term spending. With growth already under way, Republicans properly batted it down. Clinton told me his biggest mistake was to entrust passage to Senator Robert Byrd (D-WV), who didn't seem to mind that it died. From now on, Clinton said, he would keep control of his legislative proposals and learn how to get them through himself. The other mistake occurred over his call for a new energy tax that had been pushed by Gore.

Overall, however, Clinton's budget plan was a sound package that in ordinary times would have attracted bipartisan support. It reflected the pragmatism he wanted to bring to Washington. He came in believing that if he did "the right thing," the country would follow and, over time, he would be politically rewarded. He was a "goo-goo" then—what old Washingtonians called a "good government" person.

By the time I arrived in early summer, Clinton had squeaked through preliminary budget victories in both the House and Senate. But they were tougher fights than expected and final passage was still problematic. Republicans had united against him, howling that his tax increases were wrongheaded and would pitch the economy into a recession. Few Democrats liked the plan, either, because it starved some of their favorite causes. If they were going to save his budget, Clinton had to convince them there was something in it for them.

After the horrible accounts I had heard about the White House, I was impressed that in this one area, Clinton was cooking. His economic team was clearly one of the best, and after some early slips his legislative team was also coming together. Two men who deserve more credit than they have received for his early successes as president—chief of staff Mack McLarty and chief legislative assistant Howard Paster—artfully deployed the administration's resources on Capitol Hill. Roger Altman, the number-two man at Treasury, set up a War Room at the White House to focus day-to-day attention on passage. I didn't like the signal that a "War Room" sent to Republicans, but no Republicans were supporting the budget plan anyway, so I didn't say anything. I spent most of my time working with Mack to shore up the White House—along with the President's confidence.

Like many leaders, Clinton is at his peak when his back is to the wall, and he worked the Hill like a man possessed. Day after day, he called, cajoled, begged, pressured, promised—whatever it took. He learned everything he could about each recruit and was masterful in one-on-one conversations. I was reminded of Lyndon Johnson's famous "treatment" of former colleagues on Capitol Hill. Clinton never threatened people the way Johnson did but he could adopt a lot of the same swagger. In Arkansas, Clinton had worked the legislature so hard that they once banned him from the floor. Probably some congressmen wish they could have put a ban on his phone calls after a while. The first call is flattering, the second well received, but a third and fourth?

Clinton had no dams or military bases he could deliver in exchange for votes. Nor was he trusted or even liked by many Democrats. But he could tailor a different argument for each member. More spending for a program down the line. Special consideration on an appointment or a regulatory change. Maybe a presidential fund-raiser. And if those didn't work, he had a clincher in his back pocket: he was the first Democrat in the White House in a dozen years, and the party couldn't afford to let him to fail in his first year. One by one, Democrats reluctantly signed on board.

Clinton won that August by the tiniest of margins. In the House, the tally was 218 to 216, with no Republicans in support. In another party-line vote, the Senate wound up in a 50–50 tie, broken by Vice President Gore. Clinton was holding on by a thread.

Even so, that budget victory was the most important legislative achievement of his presidency. The markets had worried that he would be a free-spending Democrat. When he instead adopted a more prudent plan, Wall Street smiled. When he got Congress to go along, too, it boomed. With the budget under firmer control, Alan Greenspan's Federal Reserve Board felt it safer to lower interest rates. The economy grew more rapidly, inflation fell, unemployment fell, and the stock market rose and rose. Halfway into Clinton's second term, Greenspan announced the economy was in its healthiest shape in half a century. Working families had been left behind during much of the growth in the 1980s and early 1990s, but as labor markets tightened, their incomes finally began to rise in the mid 1990s. The budget went from a deficit of $200 billion to a surplus of

$200 billion. Other factors were at work. But Clinton didn't just preside over the economic boom of the 1990s—he, like Reagan, could claim substantial credit.

IF THE BUDGET VICTORY was the Mount Everest of Clinton's first year, NAFTA was the Annapurna.

The North American Free Trade Agreement was intended to erase trade barriers from the north of Canada to the southern tip of Mexico, allowing some 400 million people to enrich each other economically and culturally. The United States could also assert its global leadership more effectively, pointing the way toward a high-tech, high-growth future. Clinton had examined NAFTA during his campaign and warily supported it—with reservations. It definitely represented "good government." But it was also a political minefield. The core of his political base, Big Labor, was adamantly opposed and many environmentalists were equally repelled. For a Democratic candidate to tell the AFL-CIO that he was pro-NAFTA was almost the equivalent of a Republican candidate telling the Christian Coalition he was pro-choice.

The Bush administration had negotiated the basic framework of NAFTA and left it to the Clinton team to fill in the details, many of which were contentious. Clinton early on directed Mickey Kantor, his trade representative and longtime friend, to seek the best deal he could, but keep a back door open. If Kantor could not win an agreement that most Democrats could support, maybe it was better not to have a deal at all. Clinton wanted an exit if needed. As I joined the White House, NAFTA was percolating along as a secondary issue. But Kantor began closing in on a possible bargain and presented Clinton with a critical choice: Do you want it or not?

That question had touched off a ferocious debate inside. Lined up on one side were the economic advisers who backed NAFTA unanimously. Treasury Secretary Lloyd Bentsen, a Texan, was the strongest advocate. Secretary of State Christopher emphasized the importance of NAFTA to America's world leadership. On the other side were the political advisers, led by Stephanopoulos, Carville, Begala, along with Hillary. They thought NAFTA was a disaster—that he could not win passage, that labor would be angry, and we would once again postpone health care reform, their number-one priority for his first term. Kill it in its crib, they urged.

280

As often happened, I lined up with the economic and foreign policy advisers. NAFTA was not only an excellent agreement but would, I hoped, advance the cause of bipartisanship. Republicans and some moderate Democrats were bound to support it. I was outspoken as an advocate, drawing the ire of many on the other side. Just what we feared, they thought, a Republican mole. Fortunately, I once again found myself in the same foxhole with McLarty.

Clinton was uncertain. David Rockefeller, a constructive force in U.S. relations with Latin America, organized a business delegation to visit the White House to make the argument. They couldn't get an answer. Late one night, the negotiators called Clinton and said, This is it. You have to decide now. He could complete the deal then, which would then commit him to an uphill fight for passage in Congress, or kill it and blame the other side for failure. Critics who claim that Clinton has no backbone, no principles, and no core were proved wrong that night. "Let's go," he said.

Three times overall, then and on two other occasions, I saw Clinton given a clear opportunity to dump NAFTA and walk away without paying a price. The temptations were huge. But each time, he came back with the same answer: this agreement belongs more to George Bush than to us. It isn't ours. But it is something we have to do.

Once committed, Clinton put the White House at "general quarters." Bill Daley, an executive in Chicago and brother of the mayor, signed up to organize the campaign, working with Kantor; Rahm Emanuel dropped other assignments to help Daley; and Bill Frenzel, a former Republican congressman, agreed to serve as an informal link to the GOP. On the outside, business and others rallied grassroots support. Our biggest ally turned out to be Newt Gingrich, who promised that if Clinton delivered a passel of Democrats, he would produce at least 100 Republican votes. Inside the White House, people warned Clinton that Gingrich was lying, that he would screw him in the end.

The unexpected announcement that Yasir Arafat and Yitzak Rabin were coming to the White House to seal their peace agreement gave Clinton an opening on NAFTA. We asked three former presidents—Ford, Carter, and Bush—to come to the White House for the peace signing and then to stick around the next morning for a NAFTA kickoff. Their presence would send the best possible signal that NAFTA served the national interest. As an overflow crowd gathered in the East Room that morning, we were nervous because the cards for Clinton's speech had been mixed up and we feared he might fumble his remarks. Each of the former presidents was effective. Clinton took the microphone, threw out his cards, and spoke

281

with more passion than I had heard from him in months. The new trade agreement, he thundered, was not only good for America, it was good for the world. He would carry this fight to the Congress with every ounce of energy he could. "Now I understand why he's inside looking out and I'm outside looking in," Bush commented.

Over the days that followed, I watched as Clinton simultaneously worked the Hill and reworked tiny details of the agreement with Mexico to bring in undecided votes. A side agreement was added on citrus that helped to swing part of the Florida delegation in favor. Another side agreement was cut on sugar that helped out in Louisiana. Kantor squeezed so many concessions out of the Mexican negotiators that they said, stop calling. So, McLarty picked up the phone and gently pried loose some more. Clinton was working a delicate balance: he needed enough concessions from Mexico to win a majority in Congress but not so many that the agreement would blow up in Mexico City. The chief Mexican negotiator, Jaime Serra, was adept at helping to achieve that end.

When Clinton publicly embraced NAFTA, opinion polls showed that the public opposed it by 60 to 40. Several congressmen told Clinton early on that they would like to help him on NAFTA, but he had to provide cover for them in their districts so they wouldn't be knocked off in the next election. If voters back home were against NAFTA, a Republican in a close district could easily lose his seat; with labor sitting on its hands, a Democrat would be in even worse shape. Reversing public opinion was thus critical to building a successful coalition on the Hill.

Clinton barnstormed the country, and the business community lobbied its constituents with advertisements and public statements. When Americans are asked about trade, their first instinct is protectionist. But it has long been true that if a clear, articulate case is made, opinion will swing over in favor of free trade. It takes presidential leadership to bring the public around, and Clinton provided plenty of it. In truth, we oversold the benefits of NAFTA, just as so many other presidents, such as FDR and Truman, had done on key foreign policy questions. But the polls began moving in our direction.

A huge obstacle still lay in our path: Ross Perot. He was giving us fits. Coming off his nineteen-point showing in the general election a year earlier, he was still a formidable power. Perot deserved credit for alerting the public to the dangers of budget deficits, but his cracker barrel criticisms of NAFTA were scaring people away. "There will be a giant sucking sound" of jobs leaving the country, he kept saying, and his audiences nodded in agreement. If we were going to win, somebody had to take on Perot one-on-one on live television. Our first thought was Lee Iacocca. He visited Clinton in the Oval Office, agreed to help out on the general campaign, but took a pass on Perot.

Who could do it best? A lightbulb went on one morning with Jack Quinn, the Vice President's chief of staff, and he sought me out privately: "I think Gore ought to debate Perot one-on-one with Larry King as moderator. He's excited about it but wants to know what you think." I urged him to move right away. I had watched Gore working with Clinton to persuade congressmen called in for a visit. The Vice President was at least as effective in argument as the President. If he were half as good in a debate, he could beat Perot. Besides, we had to roll the dice to win this one.

Others took a dimmer view. George Stephanopoulos, whose relations with Gore were testy, was flatly against. He had lots of company. Quinn, McLarty, and I were almost alone in favor on staff, but we held the ace card: the Vice President himself. I thought Clinton would have to resolve the conflict, but before the question even went to him that morning, Gore committed himself to CNN. Clinton had no choice but to buy in. Gore had surprised me, not for the last time. I could not remember anything similar since Nixon went his own way in the Checkers speech, not asking Ike.

As we began exploring how the debate would be structured, I wound up as the intermediary with Perot. He had been at his best on NAFTA when he spoke in front of crowds and whipped people up with his wisecracks. He was a terrific showman. I worried that in an open forum, Gore might win on points but Perot would win the crowd—and that would sway the television audience. "Ross," I told him over the phone, "at a minimum, if we have an auditorium or outdoor amphitheater, we will need to split the tickets so that each side is equally represented. But wouldn't it be a lot better for the two of you to have a serious, one-on-one debate in a studio, where you won't be interrupted by an audience? Why not come on together with Larry King right here in the CNN studio in Washington? Isn't that the best way to do it?"

I was certain he would insist on an open audience. He would never give up that advantage. "Let's do it in the Washington studio," he said without hesitation. Something about going *mano a mano* right there on the set appealed to his manhood. "You're on," I answered, trying to hide my delight.

Gore knew that NAFTA would rise or fall on the Perot debate, so he closeted himself to prepare. He also called many of us to his

283

residence for rehearsals. On the final afternoon before the 9:00 P.M. show, he had three of us there: Jack Quinn, television guru Michael Shehan, and me. As he stood at the podium, he was damn near frozen. I had worked with political figures before who had gone tight but this one worried me. Here we were only hours before show time, and one of the most experienced men in politics was barely coherent. I thought for sure that Perot would wipe us out and NAFTA was a goner.

In the next couple of hours, he lightened up a bit but nowhere near enough. "I need to break for dinner and a shower," he said. So he disappeared for a while. Shortly before nine he came downstairs looking fresh, but he was still tight. We were heading toward a disaster.

About twenty minutes before the show, we left his house for the ride across town. I started to pile into the Vice President's limo so we could all keep talking. "Don't get in the limo," Jack instructed me. "You and I and Michael should all ride in the backup. Let Tipper get in there alone with him."

Now, I don't know what happened in those next twenty minutes. But I can say that when Gore got out of that limo on the other end, he was transformed. Clark Kent had turned into Superman. He was ready to crush Perot. I have always wondered: was Tipper his secret weapon, an emotional bulwark for him?

Gore's performance pushed us over the top. Large numbers saw the debate or the clips that followed and resolved their doubts about the agreement. On the eve of the vote, opinion shifted more heavily toward us. Given the protection they needed, clumps of congressmen now began to break in favor. In spite of deep suspicions within the White House, Newt Gingrich also delivered. He and his allies had been quietly rounding up Republican members in favor of NAFTA for weeks. In the end, a majority of Republicans in the House, 132 voted for NAFTA while 43 voted against; among Democrats, only 102 voted for compared to 156 against.

With easy Senate passage, NAFTA marked the high water mark of bipartisanship during Clinton's presidency, even more so than the recent victory on China trade. Passage of welfare reform in 1996 also came close, but in that instance, Republicans maneuvered Clinton into signing a bill that was far more theirs than his. Some of his advisers would resign over it. NAFTA, on the other hand, was a true political marriage. History was also kind to NAFTA. Had Bush completed the agreement, he probably could not have gotten it through a Democratic Congress; had Bush not started the agreement, Clinton

284

probably would not have negotiated it on his own. The agreement succeeded because each man did heavy lifting.

NAFTA was also a textbook case in presidential leadership. At first blush, the United States had signed on to an international undertaking that was unpopular in both the Congress and in public polls. On many occasions in the past, such undertakings have died ignominiously. The Senate Foreign Relations Committee keeps a tally of treaties and agreements signed by the executive branch that have never been approved by the legislative branch and then languish. At last count, there were more than fifty accords on the list. Early on, NAFTA seemed headed for that scrap heap. But Clinton, after fumbling, not only committed himself to a losing cause but also launched a determined and masterful campaign to secure passage.

As Richard Neustadt has pointed out, power can beget power in the presidency. A chief executive who exercises leadership well in a hard fight will see his reputation and strength grow for future struggles. Nothing in American politics is stronger than a president joined in union with Congress. Nothing gives a president more political capital than a strong, bipartisan victory in Congress. That's the magic of leadership. Clinton, after passage of his budget and NAFTA, was at the height of his power as president. Sadly, he couldn't hold.

As IT TURNED OUT, the budget and NAFTA fights were also a foretaste of some nasty things to come for me. After the budget struggle, I had been much agitated by the attitudes of many White House colleagues toward centrist Democrats who had not gone along with the President's plans. Angry epithets were directed toward senators like David Boren of Oklahoma and congressmen like Dave McCurdy. Word went out that they were now pariahs. I thought that was stupid because Clinton professed to be a New Democrat, and men like Boren and McCurdy were a critical part of that coalition. Better to forgive and forget, bringing them back in the fold for future struggles.

In NAFTA, it was the liberals' turn to abandon their president. Congressman David Bonior of Michigan even used his power as majority whip to organize opposition to Clinton. In olden days, that would have been an act of lèse-majesté. LBJ would have run Bonior out of town. So, the day after the NAFTA fight, I was anxious 285 to see if equal justice would prevail. Hillary joined a large staff meeting in the Roosevelt Room—the President wasn't there—where we mapped out next steps. When the right moment arrived, I spoke up to the effect, "I noticed with some interest how the Democratic centrists were punished after they went against the President on the budget vote. I trust that Mr. Bonior will now be treated the same way. After all, he went far beyond what the centrists did to bring down the President."

I had spoken a blasphemy. The room went dead silent. Hillary looked daggers at me. Mr. Bonior, it was agreed, would be invited to the White House for coffee that afternoon in order to be sweet and make up. After all, Bonior was important to the health care fight just ahead. It was instantly apparent that while the President might consider himself a New Democrat, he was in a minority within his own White House. Later, I was told that my comment was an important souring point in my relationship with the First Lady.

There was one other surprise in the aftermath of NAFTA. The President profusely thanked the many members of his own administration and the Democrats who had the courage to stick with him, but he was perfunctory in recognizing Gingrich and the Republicans. A couple of comments here and there, and he moved on. I always regretted that moment. Newt, as one might expect, was angered by how little credit Republicans received for their cooperation. Friends on the Hill told me Newt swore that Clinton would never use Republicans again.

A Fateful Decision

Coming back late one afternoon to my office in December 1993, I was uneasy when I saw the incoming phone message: "Bob Kaiser: Important." Why was the managing editor of the *Washington Post* calling? It was like hearing that your doctor had just phoned after reading your blood tests.

Even so, I hardly appreciated that having finally gained high ground through his legislative victories, Clinton was now heading toward a cliff.

Five minutes later, Kaiser and I were connected. "You know I don't call you very often," Bob said, "and when I do, I hope you'll think it's serious. But we feel we're getting the runaround over there on Whitewater and I want you to know about it." At issue, he explained, was a letter that a *Post* reporter had sent to Bruce Lindsay, one of President Clinton's most trusted advisers and longtime friend from Arkansas. The letter contained questions relating to the fi-

286

nances of the Clintons in the years before they came to Washington. It had arrived two weeks earlier, and so far Lindsay hadn't answered. The *Post*, its nose already twitchy about the Clintons' past, was growing impatient.

"This is the first I've heard about your letter, Bob," I explained. "I'll look into it and get back to you." He knew as well as I did that I was still a relatively fresh face on the Clinton team and that my arrival had been greeted there with minimal enthusiasm by the younger staff. Neither of us was sure how far my influence extended. But Bob and I had also been in the trenches during Watergate—one at the *Post*, the other at the White House—and we remembered how destructive the stonewalling of those days had been. We had also been on the *Yale Daily News* together in the early sixties, when Bob had distinguished himself even then with his investigative reporting. He's fair but tough—and, if misled, very tough.

My first visit that night was with Mack McLarty, whose honesty and friendship I had come to prize. He didn't seem to know about the letter, either. After making further inquiries, I suggested to Mack that Lindsay, Gearan, and I pay a personal visit to the *Post*, sort out what its reporters wanted, and Gearan and I would recommend next steps. Gearan had become the new director of communications. Mack agreed, and a couple of days later, our White House trio set out for an early evening appointment. It may have been a mistake to suggest that we go to them, not the other way around—would we appear too eager?—but I wanted to impress upon the *Post* that in *this* White House, we would be forthcoming.

Waiting for us was a phalanx of editors and reporters who were suspicious about that very point. They laid out a long list of complaints about a lack of cooperation by Clinton aides, dating back to the 1992 campaign, and asked that the White House let them look over a range of documents relating to potential irregularities in Whitewater and a previous gubernatorial campaign. Lindsay argued that the White House documents were incomplete and, if released, would be subject to misinterpretation. More vehemently, he complained that *Post* reporters had been unfair in their Whitewater coverage and that giving over more documents would only trigger new rounds of negative stories. He made a good case, but I thought the *Post* was more persuasive. Gearan and I, comparing notes later, both agreed that the best course was to give the *Post* all the documents it was requesting.

The next day, I made the case for full disclosure to McLarty.

After the *Post* had a chance to look over the documents and begin reporting from them, we should make them available to the entire White House press corps. Of course, as reporters pored over the files, a barrage of negative stories would probably hit us. But if Watergate had taught us anything, surely it was that a president must come clean up front and take his lumps then, rather than hiding the facts, letting them be dragged out piece by piece, and stimulating his opponents to initiate a criminal investigation. The first course could be rough, but the second could be ruinous. McLarty agreed. He promised to set up a meeting with President Clinton at which Gearan and I could present our case.

The meeting was set for seven o'clock that Friday night, December 10, upstairs in the family residence with the President and Mack. Mrs. Clinton, I was informed, would also be joining us. It smelled like a debate was in the works: the Clintons' lawyers would be making the case against disclosure while Gearan and I would argue in favor. Who knew who else might be in attendance to tip the scales? Lindsay? He would be against. Stephanopoulos? Well, maybe he would be for. Best to wait and see.

A couple of minutes before seven, Gearan and I were waiting nervously in the basement of the White House for the elevator to carry us to the family residence on the second floor. It arrived, the doors swung open and, to our surprise, out stepped Mack. He began tugging us back toward the West Wing. "It's already over," he told us. The Clintons had had their lawyers come in early for a private discussion of the documents, had heard their arguments, and had decided not to give over anything. They didn't even want to hear the case for disclosure!

I was furious. Not only was their decision rash and unwise—this was the worst possible way to run a White House—but I felt insulted. They had asked me to join their staff only a few months earlier on the theory that they wanted someone with Washington and press experience to provide personal counsel so they could avoid hitting more rocks. They had also promised full access. Until that moment, they had mostly lived up to their pledges, but here, at a crucial point, they had slammed the door shut.

My flash of anger—rare, I hoped—had an effect. I insisted upon an immediate meeting with the President, and Mack agreed. We would gather the next morning and slip in to see the President after his Saturday radio address. Mack delivered the President to his small study just off the Oval Office so that we could speak quietly over a cup of coffee. George Stephanopoulos joined us, and to my

288

delight, he and I agreed. From the day I was forced upon him, there had been tension between us. On the same side, George and I were a good team.

The President was ready to listen. I made three arguments in favor of full disclosure: first, that the newspaper had a meritorious case and, contrary to others in the White House, I thought it had tried to be fair in its coverage of the Clintons; second, that the Nixon years left no doubt about the need for disclosure in such a case; and, third, that given the nature of the controversy, it was especially risky to take on the *Post*. As the newspaper that vaulted into the top rank of American journalism through its Watergate investigation, the *Post* would never back down on Whitewater. Indeed, it would be bristling for a fight if we poked a stick in its eye.

It wasn't just Bob Kaiser who was tough. *Post* executive editor Leonard Downie had won his spurs in Watergate and was a proud, tenacious successor to Ben Bradlee. They and others at the paper already sensed that the Clinton team had misled them several times in the past. If we didn't try to work out a fair settlement, I told the President, the *Post* would sic a big team of investigative reporters on the White House and that would lead other news organizations into full-throated pursuit. They could drive his presidency over a precipice.

"I agree with you," the President said. "I think we should turn over all of the documents."

But, he added, he didn't feel he could make this decision alone because his wife had been a partner in the Whitewater land transactions. Looking to me, he said, "*You'll* have to speak to Hillary and get her agreement. If she agrees, we'll do it." It wasn't clear why he had left it up to me to make the argument to his wife. I promised to see her.

That Monday morning, I called Mrs. Clinton's office and asked for an appointment. "We'll get back to you," they promised. Checking later that day, I was told that she would like to see me but her calendar was full in the next few days. "Call back." There were times when one could wander into her second-floor office in the West Wing and see Mrs. Clinton rather quickly; she was usually responsive to staff. This time, it was different: over the next several days, I got shrugs and cold shoulders. The stall was on. I couldn't get an audience.

Having promised the *Post* an answer by early in the week, I reluctantly called Downie and told him we needed a little more time. He was sympathetic, up to a point. Frustrated, I went back to McLarty and brought it up with the President; again, I was told, take

289

it up with the First Lady. The days slipped by, then a full week, and I realized that we were in a cul-de-sac. There would be no forward movement without Mrs. Clinton's assent, and she had already made up her mind.

Finally, on a Friday afternoon two weeks after the canceled meeting in the family residence, I was informed that the next day Bruce Lindsay would deliver a one-paragraph letter to the *Post* responding to the request for documents. Its message, in effect: "Screw you."

Early the next week Downie called with an inevitable reply: We feel you're making a terrible mistake. Nothing personal, but we intend to pursue this story relentlessly. And they did.

A growing number of other news organizations joined in the hunt, the *New York Times* and *Newsweek* among the most prominent. Coverage of Whitewater intensified, and within a few weeks, other tantalizing tales were floating out of Arkansas. A drumbeat started up for the appointment of an independent counsel by Attorney General Janet Reno, forcing the Clintons at last to turn over all the papers to the Justice Department and to call for the independent counsel themselves. The Clinton presidency was in free fall. On January 20, 1994—exactly a year from the inauguration—a former federal prosecutor, Edward Fiske, was named independent counsel. "There are no limits on what I can do," Fiske warned and he meant it. By August, when he stepped down, he had opened a broad range of investigations of the Clintons. His successor was a former solicitor general and federal appeals court judge. Within months, Kenneth Starr became a household name.

Perhaps the appointment of an independent counsel was inevitable for the Clintons. I don't think so. I believe that decision against disclosure was the decisive turning point. If they had turned over the Whitewater documents to the *Washington Post* in December 1993, their seven-year-old land deal would have soon disappeared as an issue and the history of the next seven years would have been entirely different. Yes, disclosure would have brought embarrassments. Among other items, Mrs. Clinton's investment in commodity futures apparently would have come to light. But we know today that nothing in those documents constituted a case for criminal prosecution of either one of the Clintons in their Whitewater land dealings. There wasn't anything truly serious there, and disclosure would have shown that.

More to the point, by disclosing the documents, we would have punctured the growing pressure for an independent counsel. Edward Fiske and Kenneth Starr would never have arrived on the scene, we might never have heard of Monica Lewinsky (who had nothing to do with the original Whitewater matter), and there would have been no impeachment. The country would have been spared that travail, and the President himself could have had a highly productive second term.

So much can turn on a single decision in the White House.

It is tempting to blame Mrs. Clinton for the refusal to disclose. She should have said yes from the beginning, accepting short-term embarrassment in exchange for long-term protection of both herself and her husband. She listened too easily to the lawyers and to her own instincts as a litigator, instincts that told her never to give an inch to the other side. Whitewater was always more a political than a legal problem.

But to blame Mrs. Clinton is to accept the false premise that she was supposed to be in charge. She was not. Voters elected her husband to run the government, and he is the one who bears responsibility here. Decisions made within a White House about what to release or withhold from the press belong in the end to him. Should he not have listened to his own inner voice? Why didn't he go to his wife and persuade her that it was in their mutual best interest to take a different path? Why didn't he take charge?

Those questions ran headlong into something fundamental about Clinton and about the style of leadership he brought to Washington.

Three for the Price of One

Bill Clinton is the first baby boomer to reach the White House, bringing with him different attitudes and values than presidents of the past. Like many of his generation shaped by the sixties, he rejects hierarchical structures and has little regard for figures of authority. He prefers loose, freewheeling organizations with a diversity of voices and perspectives. Sitting in the Oval Office, he is as eager to hear from a twenty-five-year-old as a sixty-year-old. That can be thrilling to one, jarring to the other.

One of his strengths is his willingness to share power. He has not tried to micromanage his cabinet officers, and when they have succeeded, he has showered them with praise. They privately complain about the chaos around him and roll their eyes at his personal troubles, but have generally enjoyed working with him. And that's

291

the point: they feel as if they are working *with* him, not *for* him. He puts them on an equal plane. Four of his cabinet officers—Bruce Babbitt, Janet Reno, Richard Riley, and Donna Shalala—have been in their jobs over the course of both terms. Riley at Education, Shalala at Health and Human Services, Carol Browner at the Environmental Protection Agency and James Lee Witt at the Federal Emergency Management Agency have each served longer in their posts than anyone else in history. Clinton's subcabinet has also set a modern record for longevity in office. On average, they have served in place some 3.36 years. The Nixon average was 1.73 years; Carter, 2.47; Reagan, 3.27; Bush, 2.52.

But that same spirit got Clinton into trouble when he tried an even larger experiment within the White House itself—power-sharing on a grand scale. It backfired badly.

In my first hours at the White House, I had asked Mack McLarty if he would sketch out the management chart for me. He drew out a plan that showed a single box on top, one box underneath, and then, just below, a long horizontal line from which dangled many boxes. As best I can remember, our conversation went like this:

"That's me in the second box," Mack said. "The senior staff all report through me up the line, as you would expect."

"Mack, where are the First Lady and the Vice President on this chart?"

He paused for reflection. "Every White House has its own personality, as you know," he said. "In this White House, as you will find, we usually have three people in that top box: the President, the Vice President, and the First Lady. All three of them sign off on big decisions. You'll just have to get used to it."

"Well, I'm not sure I'll ever get used to it, but I'll try." I smiled wanly. Privately, I was reminded of the old nursery rhyme, "Rub-a-dub-dub, three men in a tub, and who do you think they be? The butcher, the baker, the candlestick maker, turn them out, knaves all three."

In fact, it wasn't easy for anyone on staff. The White House is the nerve center of the most complex and powerful government in the world. Every day, thousands of messages arrive requiring an intelligent review; every day, thousands of messages leave telling others how to act and, in some instances, trying to persuade them how to act. Visitors come from Capitol Hill, foreign governments, state and local governments, major corporations, universities, religious groups, and other centers of power. Reporters ask hundreds of questions.

In that whir of activity, it is essential that a White House staff be

292

able to act swiftly and with purpose. The chief of staff, the national security adviser, and others around the president must know which decisions they should make in his name and which must be taken to him for resolution. A steady stream of decision papers moves to the Oval Office hour by hour. The president can take them home overnight to mull, but the next day he will probably need to answer. Sometimes, he can afford to wait, let the issue ripen, seek out more information, but not often. He has to move and keep moving to stay on top. It's okay to make a mistake but not too many. He has to get most of them right the first time, and that's why experience, an inner integrity, a philosophy, and a political sixth sense are so important. The president needs a personal foundation on which to act.

One thing he cannot do is dither. A president must be able to make decisions without hesitation on his own and then, like Harry Truman after he decided to drop the atomic bomb, go home and sleep well at night. He is the only one under our constitutional order who has that awesome responsibility.

To ensure that he has complete and balanced information on which to act, that his decisions are executed swiftly, and that his capacity to govern is protected, the White House staff must devote itself to him with complete attention. Each morning, a member of the staff must wake up asking, "How can I help the President today?" Ultimately, of course, a staff member is answerable to the public and to conscience. But the first instinct must be service to the person elected. All this has always been the case.

Bill Clinton broke the mold. He installed both his wife and his vice president in the West Wing of the White House. No other First Lady had been there before. The chiefs of staff for both the Vice President and First Lady became assistants to the president, also a first. That placed them among the highest aides in the White House and gave them access to important meetings.

It might still have been possible to have a well-managed White House, but Clinton also introduced a three-headed system for decision-making, and that was a rolling disaster as far as I could tell. It caused untold delays, confusions, and divided loyalties. A member of the cabinet or staff might think that the President had decided something on Tuesday only to find that he was in a different place on Wednesday because he had since talked to his wife or the Vice President. An official in the administration who felt the President might not like his idea would first lobby the First Lady or the Veep to line up support, knowing that might turn around the decision in the Oval Office. Or, alternatively, after losing one in the Oval Office, one

293

might appeal to the First Lady to seek a reversal. Almost every fight could be reopened if you were clever enough to game the system.

In most White Houses, it is helpful if a vice president, First Lady, or member of the family occasionally intercedes in delicate matters. Eisenhower used Nixon to tell chief of staff Sherman Adams that he should pack, "and don't forget the vicuña coat"; Nancy Reagan engineered the retirement of chief of staff Don Regan; George W. Bush came to Washington to oversee the departure of chief of staff John Sununu. Some presidents have also found it helpful to introduce a degree of competition and overlapping responsibilities among their aides. Witness the famous clashes within FDR's entourage and the troika under Reagan. But the Clinton operation carried both of these propositions to an extreme.

The messiness of the speechwriting process became the stuff of legend. In February 1993, a group of former White House speechwriters gathered at the home of Bill Safire for the biennial meeting of the Judson Welliver Society, named after the first White House ghost (an assistant to Presidents Harding and Coolidge). After swapping yarns, we watched Clinton make his first Oval Office address to the nation and couldn't get over how young and small he looked in the chair. The stunner came when George Stephanopoulos dropped in late in the evening and revealed that the President's speech had not been put to bed until twenty minutes before airtime. Less than twenty minutes to rehearse! Clinton's reputation in Washington— precious to his capacity to govern—suffered badly as stories like that spread.

Equally damaging were divisions created within the staff. Out the window went the old notion that the "White House staff" is in reality the President's staff, with the First Lady and Vice President maintaining subordinate teams tucked away in the East Wing and Old Executive Office Building. In the new world, the First Lady and the Vice President maintained sizable staffs of their own whose primary loyalty ran to them, not to the President.

Jody Greenstone, a woman of immense talent, had come to the White House as my deputy. Jody and I were tagged as "Bill people" when we arrived and everyone assumed he was our liege, which he was, in effect. But we soon found there were "Hillary people" and "Gore people" who were less interested in the President than in the person they served. Some crossed the barriers. The President, for example, had faith in the political judgment of Maggie Williams, chief of staff to the First Lady, and Maggie managed to serve both principals well. But she was a rarity. His critics had been too tough on

294

McLarty, I concluded. Not only was he denied his own deputy as chief of staff, but he also had to keep these different factions in harness, pulling in the same direction.

Getting One Partnership Right

Fortunately, by the time of my arrival, one of the three principals had seen there were too many chefs in the kitchen and was beginning to step back. With the President's support, the Vice President would take the lead in projects that fit his interest (modernizing government, the environment, overseas commissions), would stay out of projects headed by the First Lady (health care), and would otherwise serve as a close-in adviser and consigliere. Some of the President's aides thought Gore was still crowding Clinton too much—"Does he always have to be standing in the picture?" It was apparent that Gore and Hillary were also competitive, each pursuing power. Even so, the new arrangement that evolved made the best use of a vice president of any White House I have known.

The power and influence of the vice president took a leap forward in the 1970s, when Walter Mondale occupied an office in the West Wing, just down the hall from President Carter. In a city where, it has been said, "nothing propinqs like propinquity," Mondale had immediate access and was a close adviser. Every vice president since has kept a West Wing office. Shortly before Reagan was inaugurated, I called Bob Finch to ask what the key had been to working with the Gipper when Finch had been his lieutenant governor in California. "Weekly lunches," he said. I passed that on to Jim Baker and George Bush, and, sure enough, they set up weekly lunches between President Reagan and Vice President Bush. Those lunches have been a staple at the White House since, providing a valuable forum where the top elected officials of the land can talk privately. In every case, they have also strengthened personal bonds.

In the new Clinton-Gore arrangement, the office reached a higher level altogether. The Vice President became the junior partner to the President. He was more than a man-in-waiting, more than an adviser at the table. Aside from Rubin, he often gave the President some of his shrewdest advice. In their book, *Co-Leaders*, David A. Heenan and Warren Bennis write about the importance of strong number twos who enjoy the confidence of number one. Repeatedly, the co-partner has been essential to the effectiveness of the boss— George Marshall to Harry Truman, Chou En-lai to Mao Tse-tung,

295

Steve Ballmer to Bill Gates, Craig Barrett to Andy Grove. That does not guarantee the junior partner will succeed in his own right if he moves up—other issues arise there—but it does suggest that a president is well served by identifying and then building up the right person to serve in a more powerful vice presidency.

Clinton was self-confident enough that he could bring a potential rival into the center of his campaign and into the center of his presidency. He didn't mind sharing the spotlight. If he had hoped that the Vice President would also be a valuable link to Congress, he may have been disappointed; Gore's ties with some key members were frayed. Gore, however, studied the issues with intensity, often coming to foreign policy meetings having read not only the memos but also the voluminous cable traffic from overseas. Clinton could always find in him an intellectual companion.

I had known Gore for several years and approached him at the White House as a potential ally. Some thought that I was naive—he is trying to manipulate you, they told me. But I found our frequent conversations both productive and enlightening. Every week or two, we would meet alone in his office to talk for up to an hour about how Clinton worked, how the operation was running, and about governance. Ginseng tea would come, and he cut off other interruptions.

Since I left, it has been surprising to see Gore become ensnared by ethical controversies. He came to the the vice presidency as Mr. Clean, and while I was at the White House he was the "go to" guy to keep the administration out of trouble. Someone on staff once came to me with disturbing tales from within the building. I wasn't sure whether to talk directly to the President, so I went in to see the Vice President. Gore immediately went to Clinton and blew the whistle. The trouble ended.

Perils of a Co-Presidency

The President's relationship with the First Lady has been complex and nourishing, yet dangerous. He has leaned on her more than anyone else, and she has been a pillar. Had there been no Hillary in his life, I doubt there would have been a White House, either. But it wasn't easy for him or her when they reached their destination.

Teddy Roosevelt was once asked about his rambunctious daughter Alice and replied that he could spend his time managing her or running the country—but he could not do both. In his first years in office, Clinton had a hard time managing his presidency, his marriage, and himself all at the same time. While he and his wife have a public marriage, no one outside professes to understand it fully. Certainly, I did not, and if it had not become so intertwined with his leadership, I would not write about it here. But one cannot sort out Clinton's presidency without addressing it.

The Bill Clinton I saw needed the emotional approval of his wife on a daily basis. He depended on her, spoke of her, and acted as if she were his Rock of Gibraltar. I saw less of what she received in return but assume she drew heavily from him, too.

When they were in balance, they complemented each other well. Their partnership energized his leadership. She was the anchor, he the sail. He was the dreamer, she the realist. She was the strategist, he the tactician. He was outer-directed, she turned inward. She helped him gain office, he helped her gain power. He leaned to the center politically, she leaned well to the left. She provided an abundance of superego, he came with an extra-large dose of id. He let things bounce off, she internalized them. She was composed, he flew off the handle. He liked to laugh, she was serious. She insisted on a zone of privacy, he told people about his underwear. He thought a lot about the rights of blacks, she focused on the rights of women. She cared most about children, he looked after old folks. Together, they both loved their daughter. Chelsea is their alpha and omega.

But the way they structured their relationship—and the roiling emotions just beneath its surface—posed critical problems in his presidency. Even as Gore stepped back from a place in that top box on the management chart, she stayed there. And it just didn't work. No matter how talented, two people cannot occupy that space, jointly making decisions. On the sawdust trail, a vibrant husband-wife team can lift the spirit and quality of a campaign. In some gubernatorial offices, there may be room for co-equals. There is no place for a co-presidency.

Hillary Clinton ran into a buzzsaw the day she walked into the White House. The first woman with an advanced degree to become First Lady, she has few peers in the candlepower she brought. As a social activist, she naturally thought Eleanor Roosevelt might serve as her role model. But as a student at Duke pointed out to me, Mrs. Clinton did not seem to appreciate that in the popular mind, Mrs. Roosevelt derived her power from the Office of First Lady, while Hillary seemed to draw her power from the Office of the President. That went too far for most Americans. Doris Kearns Goodwin has also noted that Mrs. Roosevelt was so much ahead of her time that she could be seen as eccentric. "There she goes again," a couple might say, chuckling. To older men, Mrs. Clinton seemed more threatening, as if she wanted to knock them off their perch. Early on, Hillary recounted for me comments she had heard from middle-aged men: "I would love my daughter to grow up like you. But I am sure glad my wife isn't."

Over the eighteen months I worked with and nearby Mrs. Clinton, I gained great respect for her as a champion of social causes. While our politics were sharply different, I could see her passions for social justice. Critics say she is interested in power; of course she is. But power for a larger purpose, and that is the mark of a good leader. Yet it wasn't long before I was running afoul of Hillary. Our collision was probably inevitable. The two of us just didn't see eye to eye, starting with policy but extending to this central question of how to run a White House.

Shortly after the President's budget victory in his first summer, the Clintons called together the Vice President, top staff, and political consultants to map out strategy for the fall. We met in the Solarium on the third floor of the residence. Health care, NAFTA, reinventing government—all were on the table. I don't remember what triggered it, but suddenly Mrs. Clinton unleashed a bitter, scathing attack on our efforts in the budget fight. Her words were about the staff, but it was clear the President was her target. We were stupid amateurs, hacks, whatever—the words but not the scene are buried. Her husband was losing his stature, becoming the mechanic in chief. How could we be so dumb? We should just wait and see how much better the health care campaign would be. Her people were organized, knew what they were doing, and would show us a thing or two. How could you guys possibly want to get a Republican trade agreement through Congress now? Are you going to screw up health care, too?

The President defended himself and his staff, and they got into a row—far from the last one in the Solarium. The rest of us sat in embarrassed silence. Many couples have harsh, tense conversations. Most conduct them somewhere else—out of earshot. Apparently, the Clintons had talked that way in front of campaign staffs and even gubernatorial aides for a long time, and their friends ignored it. But the White House is different. One felt party to a massive violation of their privacy. Later on, one of the participants told me that this happened frequently. In the middle of a conversation, she would launch a deadly missile straight at his heart and just before it hit, the missile would explode, the shrapnel hitting the staff. He would respond, and tempers would flare. Get over it, I was told. I never did. Those conversations were demoralizing, deepened the divisions between the Bill and Hillary camps, and made one tiptoe around the principals. Keeping the presidency on track became a heck of a lot harder for everyone.

I do not mean to leave the impression that Mrs. Clinton was a harridan. Clearly, she had internalized her anger over the years, resolving that she should put her energies into working even harder for their joint success. When she saw mistakes made by his team or by him, she couldn't hold back any longer. Her emotions boiled to the surface.

She was also a sensitive, vulnerable woman, as I found. Weeks after our blowup over the *Washington Post* request for Whitewater documents, I agreed to defend the Clintons on NBC's *Today* show. I was trying to show I was a team player. Before going on live that morning, I had a call from Hillary. She and her husband were leaving that morning for his mother's funeral in Arkansas. I expressed sympathy for all she had gone through in recent months. As we talked, she started crying. "You can tell your friends at the *Post*," she said, "that we've learned our lesson. We came here to do good things, and we just didn't understand so many things about this town. It's been so hard."

I murmured a few things and finally said, "I wish I could come over and give you a hug. I would give a lot to cheer you up." I meant it.

Looking back, I wish it had all turned out differently. They did come to Washington to do good things. They were not simply grasping for power. If their relationship had evolved in a different way over the years—or if he had been elected later in life—perhaps it would have been more settled and would not have spilled over into his presidency. They would never have attempted a co-presidency. As it was, they each paid a dreadful price in those days I saw them together. And there was worse still to come.

Debacle in Health Care

Sunday night was an odd time to gather at the White House. But we had reached another critical turning point in Bill Clinton's presidency, and he and Hillary wanted to talk. About a dozen of us gath- 299 ered in the Map Room in the basement of the residence. It was June 1994, and the Clintons' health care plan was on the ropes.

Months earlier, in my first days at the White House, their chief honcho on the project, Ira Magaziner, had come by to talk about the plan he was designing along with the First Lady and President. He wanted to ask about the politics of health and to enlist my support. Though Ira had a penchant for grand schemes, I found him self-effacing and likable. I enjoyed his company.

As he described their plan, then still secret, I could see I was going to play odd man out again. The proposal sounded immensely complex and required far more governmental intrusion into health care than I thought appropriate or politically viable. This initial proposal is not the plan we want at the end of the process, Ira assured me, but it allows us to keep Democratic activists on board while we negotiate our way closer to the center. There we can pick up a majority, including moderate Republicans. You will also like the final plan a lot more than the one you see now.

Never mind my substantive disagreements for the moment, I answered. Let's focus on its legislative prospects. Politics is still the art of the possible, and this plan will be impossible on the Hill, even with Democrats in charge. For thirty years, the only sweeping reforms that have passed have been those with huge bipartisan majorities—Medicare, civil rights, and tax reform, among others. Instead of starting with a bill supported by the left wing of Congress and trying to move toward the center, we should start in the center with moderates from both parties and gradually build a coalition outward. And instead of sending up a detailed plan, give them a skeletal proposal built on three or four core principles and let people on both sides craft a final plan that will attract a bipartisan majority.

"We're beyond that now," Ira responded. While important decisions still had to be made, the Clintons had already set their course. We parted company with his pledge that the plan would become more centrist and less governmental, and my pledge to help so long as that was the case.

Health care, I soon discovered, had already sparked brutal fights within the administration. In a meeting that summer in the cabinet room, Donna Shalala, Secretary of Health and Human Services, pulled me aside to say, "We've got to talk." Over lunch a few days later, she confided her misgivings about the plan taking shape. "I didn't come here to set up a new regulatory bureaucracy in Washington," she said. I snapped to attention. Here was a cabinet officer painted on the outside (unfairly) as an unreconstructed liberal say-

300

ing that the administration should adopt a more market-oriented plan. She was not alone. The entire economic team also had doubts, which they had voiced. The White House was again split into camps: Mrs. Clinton, the political consultants, many other advisers on the populist side; the economics team, Donna, Mack, me on the other. The Vice President stayed out, and Stephanopoulos tried to keep peace. The President, it seemed, was following Hillary's lead.

At health care meetings that summer, the economics group started to muffle their voices. As much as they disliked the plan that was evolving, they saw that only three votes counted: the First Lady, the President, and Ira—and apparently in that order. In one meeting in the cabinet room, only Laura Tyson, head of the Council of Economic Advisers, challenged the First Lady on cost projections. The rest of us men shuffled our feet and held Laura's coat. No need to say who prevailed.

That fall and then again in his State of the Union in 1994, the President sallied forth with his health care plan, the centerpiece of his first term. It was well received at first because Clinton presented it ably and people saw that the administration was gutsy enough to take on one of the country's most difficult challenges. The First Lady also created a sensation when she testified on behalf of the plan in front of both Senate and House committees.

But on close inspection, the plan turned out to be a gift horse to the opposition, especially the insurance industry, small business, and conservative Republicans on Capitol Hill. Rube Goldberg had met his match. Its 1,354 pages, crammed with different commands to the private sector (thou "shall" do this; thou "shall not" do that), provided luscious opportunities for attack. While liberals thought the plan did not go far enough in embracing the Canadian single-payer model, opponents saw it went far enough to kill it. They remembered how the AMA sank Truman's plan by calling it "socialized medicine." The Clintons' plan, they said, was "government-run health care," a slogan that cut deep with the public. "The government shouldn't choose our health care plan. We should choose our own," Harry told Louise in a television ad widely shown and sponsored by the health insurance industry. Swiftly, opponents framed the public debate in a way that ensured our defeat.

Even so, there was still a possibility that significant reform could be rescued if the White House compromised and pushed for a more modest, bipartisan plan. Early in 1994, Senate Majority Leader Bob Dole was genuinely interested in striking a bargain, as was the Democratic chairman of Senate Finance, Daniel Patrick Moynihan.

301

Middle-of-the-roaders on both sides, such as Republican senator John Chafee of Rhode Island, stood ready to help. In May, Dole slipped a note to Moynihan: "Is it time for the Moynihan-Dole bill?" Pat Moynihan still keeps that yellow piece of paper in his Senate desk, a reminder of what might have been.

In the White House, however, sentiment had hardened against compromise. Liberal chairmen of House committees were assuring the Clintons they could get the original plan through the House with only Democratic votes. Forget negotiations with the Republicans, they said, they can never be trusted. They will eventually betray you. The First Lady, burned by mounting criticisms, and by what she saw as double-dealing by some Republicans, was persuaded. "Incrementalism" became a dirty word around the West Wing, and those of us who wanted a bipartisan compromise were marginalized. When staff meetings were called on health strategy, I was increasingly left out.

There was a new man in the White House saddle now, Harold Ickes of New York. Son of a famous adviser to Franklin Roosevelt, he shared his father's fervent belief in government and even his curmudgeonly ways. The Clintons invested great faith in his political skills. With his arrival in January 1994, the balance of power within the White House staff slid firmly over to the liberal side. Moderates were now heavily outnumbered and outgunned. Interest in a bipartisan deal was slipping away from us.

Armed with his note from Dole, Senator Moynihan had signaled to the White House that we now had one last chance for a bill: if we would drop our insistence on universal coverage, he thought he could strike a good bargain with Dole and other Republican senators and hopefully could overcome the continuing opposition of Gingrich. We gathered that Sunday night in the Map Room for a climactic decision.

Early the next morning, the President had a live interview scheduled on NBC's *Today* show, where he would make his final offer. He could now signal a willingness to compromise—which might make it happen—or he could continue going for broke, which would extinguish all hope. As far as I was concerned, the lesson of every president from Roosevelt to Reagan was clear on an issue of this magnitude: take what you can now and come back for the rest later.

I cannot reconstruct the full conversation that Sunday night. There was a chorus of arguments from staff urging the President not to give an inch. The First Lady agreed. I said little. My position was known and, given my growing isolation, I knew I could not sway the conversation. I would only harden up the other side. Our hope was Treasury Secretary Lloyd Bentsen, a former chairman of Senate Finance and still an influential player on Capitol Hill. If we had left health care to Bentsen and Shalala, we would have struck a deal with Congress a long time ago. Lloyd still wanted a compromise now, and finally he cleared his throat to speak. A young staffer immediately challenged him. Then, for reasons never clear, the President exploded. He had already heard more than he wanted. His face was flushed with anger. As long as I am president, he said, I plan to keep fighting for serious reform. I did not get elected to compromise on this issue. We can't trust the Republicans and I am not backing down! We won't compromise!

Looking at my watch, I wrote a note to myself: "At 10:22 P.M. tonight, health care died."

Health care reform never even came to a vote in the House or the Senate. The biggest initiative of Clinton's presidency died in committee. Not since the Vietnam War had there been so large a public policy debacle. And, since then, the number of Americans losing health care insurance has climbed by a million a year and now stands at 44 million. Health care inflation has been rising and Medicare is in serious need of change. As for the President and First Lady, they had crashed to defeat and their bid for greatness went aglimmering.

Lessons from the Health Care Defeat

In their fine book on the health care fight, *The System*, two veterans of the *Washington Post*, Haynes Johnson and David Broder, make the case that even a legislative magician like Lyndon Johnson would have had trouble securing health care reform in the current political environment. Trust in the presidency has declined; the White House commands less authority in pursuing major initiatives; Congress is more fractious; the press is more interested in scandal than substance; and interest groups have acquired greater power. The confluence makes leadership far more difficult, as they say.

Change has been especially difficult in health care. Congress has turned back repeated attempts to overhaul the system, starting with FDR and Truman and running through Nixon and Carter. In Clinton's case, the struggle was complicated because Newt Gingrich and fellow conservatives also saw the health care fight as a vehicle

303

for gaining control of Congress. Why cooperate with Clinton? Why not elect a Republican Congress and apply free market principles to the problem?

In trying to overhaul the $1 trillion health care industry, the Clintons were tackling one of the toughest challenges in public policy; they were walking down a path littered with the skeletons of past reforms stretching back six decades. And they were willing to stake their reputations on the fight. For that alone, they deserve credit for political courage.

In an interview with Johnson and Broder, the President manfully acknowledged, "I set the Congress up for failure." He recognized that the defeat of health care was a case study in how not to lead. Because the mistakes we made at the White House can be an important guide to future presidents trying to undertake bold, difficult initiatives, it is worth pausing to look at them more closely. Several conclusions stand out:

Misjudging the values of the country. A leader must understand the core values of the society of which she or he is a part and seek to govern within those values. Americans have long been the least supportive of the welfare state of any industrialized peoples. We are, as sociologist Seymour Martin Lipset says, an "outlier" among Western nations, and the Republican Party is the most antistatist of any major political party. To propose a health care plan that smacked of government control ran directly counter to our core national beliefs in individualism and laissez-faire.

The plan also ran afoul of the new conservatism. LBJ could pass Medicare in the 1960s because faith in government was at a high point. Three-quarters of the population said they trusted government to do what is right all or most of the time. By 1994, only a quarter expressed similar trust. The Clinton plan flew in the teeth of that change. A leader like FDR would have understood and crafted a plan to match the times.

Misjudging the President's political strength. "Great initiatives cannot be built upon slender majorities," Jefferson observed. Clinton had too slender a base to enact one of the most sweeping legislative reforms of the century. His 43 percent plurality in the 1992 elections and his lack of coattails left him without a sturdy following, and the missteps of his early months in office had weakened him further. Even in the fall of 1993, when he first addressed the country on his

304 health care proposals, he lacked the dominance needed for so large an undertaking. The failure to recognize the limits on his authority was, in the judgment of Johnson and Broder, his "greatest mistake."

There was a tendency within the White House to believe that Clinton could "sell" anything. His formidable powers at the podium would put the opposition to flight. Ira Magaziner even believed that Clinton could "make complexity our ally." But the way the opposition was able to seize the high ground from Clinton shows once again that a White House must first get the substance right before it tries to "sell" anything.

Misjudging the Congress. Clinton himself believes his greatest blunder was in the way he approached Congress, starting with an early decision to bypass traditional committee hearings (and a potential Senate filibuster) by including health reform in a budget reconciliation bill in 1993. Senator Robert Byrd, protecting senatorial traditions, put a prompt halt to that maneuver, but it left a residue of bad feelings on Capitol Hill.

In retrospect, it is clear that leaders in the House could not deliver a majority composed only of Democrats. Those promises from the barons fell apart. Their authority within the Congress had eroded as much as the President's within the country. We needed Republican votes, and contrary to Johnson and Broder, I believe we could have gotten them if we had begun by working with Republican moderates. But there was so much distrust on both sides we never seriously tried that path.

Misjudging interest groups. The AFL-CIO and the American Association of Retired Persons never generated as much support as expected, and the Health Insurance Association of America and the National Federation of Independent Business delivered far more opposition. It was not the campaign contributions but the field operations of the opponents that were devastating. Even Johnson and Broder were surprised. Interest groups, they wrote, "have become crypto-political parties of their own—unelected and unaccountable—employing skilled operatives who at other times run presidential and senatorial campaigns. This is the development that reformers need to address." Talks with health industry representatives persuaded me that if we had been more accommodating early, they might have worked with us. Another missed opportunity.

Mistaking campaigning for governing. Right from the beginning, the emphasis in the White House was not so much in persuading skeptical or uncertain congressmen as in overwhelming them through public pressure. That was especially true of Republicans. The creation of yet another "War Room" sent an unmistakable signal to opponents in the other party that our intention was not a negotiation but unconditional surrender. Newt Gingrich went into the same

305

mode, seeing the health care fight as his best vehicle for capturing the House. He was in no mood for compromise, either. But we should have recognized that War Rooms do not build bipartisan coalitions; they destroy them.

Letting the perfect become the enemy of the good. Until close to the end, I believe that a compromise might have been achieved. Lloyd Bentsen had developed a plan when he was still in the Senate that might have formed the basis of negotiation across party aisles. While incremental, it would have addressed at least parts of the problem. In a campaign for a second term, Clinton could have gained a mandate for further reform and then passed it in 1997–1998, when he was still strong.

In retrospect, it is clear that reform of health care is an issue better suited to the kind of "adaptive work" that Ronald A. Heifetz describes in his book, *Leadership Without Easy Answers*. Heifetz argues that on some public issues a leader should not hand down a solution from on high but should mobilize followers to work through changes in social understanding and behavior. If Lyndon Johnson had simply sent Congress civil rights bills in the mid-1960s, for example, he might have failed. Johnson instead encouraged a process of social ferment, and when the public mood ripened in his favor he then succeeded in passing legislation. We would have done better following that course in health care reform.

A Dangerous Seesaw

One mystery persists: How did we make all these mistakes in health care? How does a future White House avoid them? There is no single answer. All of us in the administration shared in them to one degree or another—the President, the First Lady, Ira, and the rest of us, certainly me. I wish I had fought harder to pull the proposal toward the center. Even though my influence was dimming, I should have invested the last ounce.

Overall, a lack of experience in the White House certainly played a key role. Richard Neustadt has pointed out the cruel irony that presidents undertake their biggest missions early, when they are strong but their teams are still green and prone to mistakes. Even as talented a president as Clinton could not expect to storm the Congress, forcing through a proposal as massive and controversial as his health plan. Adding to the lack of experience was an idealism that was blinding because it was suffused with self-righteousness. It is a

306

common disease in the White House, afflicting Republicans and Democrats alike. Among Clintonites, it was widely thought that the Republicans had engaged in so much malign neglect over the years that the public would rally to Democratic nostrums. People will obviously see we are right and they are wrong. Arrogance, as Neustadt reminds, is as big a danger as ignorance.

But I must record one other observation because it is fundamental to what went wrong in this case. It is not one that I write about happily. President Clinton was not fully himself in this fight. He was not as engaged, politically and intellectually, as I saw him in the budget and NAFTA struggles. True, he gave his utmost in the promotion of the health plan and fought for its passage. But he did not exercise his own, independent judgment in the formulation, presentation, or final resolution of the plan. Even though he had signed off each step of the way, he did not take full ownership of the endeavor nor did he personally marshal the resources of the administration for its success.

The matter goes back to the nature of the partnership he had with Mrs. Clinton and how that partnership was influenced by his own past. To have asked her to lead a national crusade on behalf of health care reform would have been a good idea. She is brilliant and articulate. But to assign her primary responsibility for designing the program and navigating its passage through Congress was to place upon her more of a burden than any First Lady could bear, even Mrs. Clinton.

Primary responsibility for design of the program should have been assigned to the lead cabinet officer in health affairs, Donna Shalala, just as responsibility for design of the budget program is always given to the director of the budget. Ms. Shalala has been a successful president of two universities and a shrewd policy-maker. With marching orders from the President on his goals, she could have drawn upon the expertise of her department, worked with Congress, the cabinet, academics, and outside groups, informed the press, and kept the White House in the loop. The President, First Lady, and Ira could have monitored her closely. What would have emerged is a plan that came as close to achieving the President's goals as possible. The President could have remained out front and taken full charge of passage. The First Lady, too, would have played an indispensable role. That is the way the system is designed to work—and in the past has led to pathbreaking changes in social 307 policy.

As it was, the President, without meaning to, gave the First

Lady "mission impossible." When she was "collecting facts" at public forums around the country, speakers were often chosen who would say what she wanted to hear. When she expressed views, few wanted to contradict her. When she went to Capitol Hill, senators and congressmen were deferential and reluctant to speak candidly. She was like an extremely wealthy person with many suitors who can never be quite sure who is telling the truth.

As experienced as she is in the ways of the world, Mrs. Clinton had never been tested in legislative battle in Washington. She can also have a tin ear politically. To ask that, on her maiden voyage, she take on the most massive social reform in decades, build up a detailed, thousand-page proposal and guide it through a fractious Congress was simply more than she should have been expected to do.

Her critics say, "Well, she wanted it." Perhaps, but we ask presidents to choose what is best for the country. Looking ahead toward the Normandy invasion, the most complex mission in military history, FDR knew that George Marshall, his trusted confidant and a man who had earned it, wanted to head the invasion force. Instead of trying to please Marshall, FDR asked him to remain in Washington because the country needed him there. He sent Dwight Eisenhower in Marshall's place.

The President asked the First Lady in part because he believed in her talents, which was justified. He acted, too, because he wanted to promote women as national leaders, which was welcome. He also liked to share with his wife, which was generous. But does anyone doubt that he also wanted to placate her? Had it not been for his own past, I doubt he would have placed his presidency so fully in her hands.

An incident occurred in December of that year that I now look back upon—perhaps mistakenly—as significant to health care. The *American Spectator* and then the *Los Angeles Times* both broke stories alleging that Arkansas troopers had been used by then-governor Clinton to procure women for him. One of them, the *Spectator* said, was a woman named "Paula" who was brought to the Governor in a hotel room where he exposed himself and asked that she "kiss it." The stories were so salacious that I could not believe them, and I joined in the effort to knock them down. No one foresaw that the *Spectator* piece would encourage Paula Corbin Jones to file suit against Clinton.

308   In the next few days, it became obvious that the stories had privately humiliated Mrs. Clinton and her husband was deep in her doghouse. Like a bouncy golden retriever who has pooped on the

living room rug, he curled up and looked baleful for days. Perhaps I am wrong, but over the next several weeks, I sensed that he was in no mood—and no position—to challenge her on anything. As the New Year opened, we were heading into the most important months of the health care fight with a president who was tiptoeing around the person in charge. I cannot recall him publicly confronting her on any health care issue after that.

That January, Mrs. Clinton's team came up with the idea that in presenting his health care plan in his State of the Union address, the President should hold up a fountain pen and pledge to veto any bill that did not guarantee universal coverage. They were looking for a television "moment" that would be replayed many times. I thought the pen and the threat would only enrage Republicans, possibly dooming an eventual bipartisan agreement. When Democratic leaders came to the cabinet room in advance of the speech, she pushed the idea and the President sat mum. I took a last stab at trying to stop it. As the leaders were leaving, I asked Speaker Tom Foley his reaction. He said he would prefer it not be done. I urged him to express his view to the First Lady, which he did. I asked her if she would reconsider. No, we're going ahead, she replied.

That ended the matter. When the President, during his address, waved his pen in the faces of Republicans, he looked like a matador holding up a red cape. The bulls charged. Later on, I realized that after Mrs. Clinton had given her answer to Tom Foley, it had never occurred to me that I might appeal the decision to the President.

I was learning that the relationship between the President and First Lady had a serious danger I had not understood. It was not just the matter of two heads making decisions. It was becoming clear that their partnership, which works well for them personally when in balance, can also tip out of balance. In fact, it operates like a seesaw. If he goes down in the relationship, she goes up. And vice versa: If she goes down, he goes up. Either way, the person on top is not as tethered to the other. The complementarities are out of whack. For all her idealism, she needs his political genius to succeed. For all his energy, he needs her good head to keep him anchored.

In the health care fight, she was high up on the seesaw. She took charge and he let her go. Apparently, he was in no position to challenge her or to assert himself in a way that would have been better for them both. When the enterprise failed, I was forced to ask: Might he have passed a bipartisan reform plan if the shadow of his past had not hung over his relationship with his wife?

309

A Personal Farewell

By late spring of 1994, I thought I should quietly leave the White House.

When I first arrived, the President and many of the older members of his team—the Vice President, Mack, Bob Rubin, Bill Galston, Warren Christopher, Al From—had been welcoming. So had a few of the younger ones like Mark Gearan and Bruce Reed. And I made new friends like Joel Klein and Vicki Radd. But most of the young members of the staff took umbrage at my plopping down in their midst. I didn't really blame them. After all, they had broken their backs to elect a Democrat. Why wouldn't they be angry when a Republican was slipped through the back door? Why not hire another Democrat? And why should they think well of someone whose arrival was linked to the downgrading of George Stephanopoulos, their hero? Fair questions.

I had pledged to myself that I would try to be a complete team player. "I don't want to displace anybody from a West Wing office," I had told Mack. "I just need a phone and a desk." When they offered the old barbershop in the basement, I accepted. It had no windows and was so tiny that my deputy, Jody Greenstone, and I wound up making phone calls from a couch in the hall. We laughed a lot at the absurdity of it all.

How to talk to reporters was another challenge. I knew many of the veterans and liked talking with them. The President also wanted me to form a link with them. In Reagan days, when I was a link to the press, some had found it easy to blame me for any leaks (I was responsible for some, but not the number supposed). I was determined not to be in that position again and worked hard to protect inside information. By my count, I engaged in only two leaks while there, one inadvertent and the other to help out on a story I can't even remember. Still, I had a press problem: whenever Clinton did something right, stories gave me too much credit. Later on, I started getting more hits than I deserved, so I guess it balanced out. But the positive stories further antagonized my new colleagues.

The hardest part was trying to reconcile my views about policy and governance with my new surroundings. I wore my service under three Republican presidents as a badge of honor. I also believed there was a bridge between Reaganism and what Clinton had espoused in his campaign about personal responsibility, individual initiative, and a healthy economy. The Democratic Leadership

310

Council, a platform for the Clinton candidacy, certainly wanted to weave some of Reagan's ideas into the Democratic fabric. Clinton had told me coming in he wanted to become a bipartisan president. But he had appointed many people to his White House who abhorred everything about Republicans, especially Reagan.

Sometimes at meetings I would think I had made a horrible mistake in joining up. Late at night after the President's budget victory, the younger staff started chanting anti-Reagan slogans. I went home feeling depressed and compromised. I noticed that Lloyd Bentsen went home, too. Had it not been for the countervailing presence of men like Bentsen, Rubin, McLarty, and Christopher, I am uncertain I would have made it through. I came to know what it was like to be a liver transplant.

In the early months, the satisfaction came because my thoughts seemed to count and the President was righting himself. He listened to me with attention and respect, and we got on well. My affection for him grew, even as the mystery about him deepened.

But as he gained ascendancy, my star dimmed. I had a growing sense that partisan members of the staff were saying to each other, "Now that we have gotten out of the ditch, we can do this by ourselves. Why do we need that bastard? Let's get him out of here." It wasn't long before I would read nasty quotes about me in the newspapers, attributed to White House sources. A few of the more senior members of the team rallied to my side, but the knives were out down below. I was cut to shreds and was extremely displeased, but—perhaps dumbly—was too proud to ask the President for help. I just assumed he would put a stop to it and speak up in my defense. He did not.

The telling issue for me was whether I could still make a difference inside. The endgame came with Whitewater and then health care, as I began crossing swords too often with the First Lady. Our disagreements were fundamental and, even though we treated each other respectfully, I guessed she would be happier if I were somewhere else. As the liberal side of the house gained more power, policy was moving in that direction and I was frozen out of meetings. I was also having more trouble persuading the President, who was down on the seesaw and seemed self-absorbed.

There's such a thing as overstaying your welcome at the White House, so I decided to leave by early summer, a year after I had arrived. I would be well away before the off-year election season began. But the President called and asked if I could give him six months of additional service, working with him and Secretary of

State Christopher at the State Department. He said he needed more help there and would appreciate a hand. I accepted because I greatly respected Christopher. Jody Greenstone and Dianna Pierce accompanied me there.

As it turned out, that invitation was a blessing. Christopher and his team were among the finest people I have known in public life. People said that Christopher wasn't a scintillating presence on television, but he had something that counts far more: character and personal integrity. He and Tom Donilon, along with other colleagues there, provided a warm, stimulating haven where I could stay out of the 1994 election fray and also learn more about the practice of American diplomacy. Those were my happiest months in the administration.

That fall, I sent a letter to the President to say that while honored by his invitation to serve, I did want to leave the administration at the end of the year, as we had discussed. I sent the letter early, before the elections, so that it would be clear the results, whatever they were, had not been a factor. I wanted to leave without fanfare. Christopher gave me a gracious farewell from State. Again, I was too proud to ask for anything from the President. A staff-written letter of thanks arrived from the White House. I thought he would say thanks in person. He did not.

Looking back upon my eighteen months, I at first had mixed feelings—proud that for a brief moment, I perhaps helped a president in trouble; angry that I also felt used. The anger has disappeared over time. If you step into turbulent waters, you should expect to get wet. The pride remains.

10

Assessing His Leadership

Few of us can think of Bill Clinton without an emotional bias. One of the best reporters who has ever covered the White House, the late Ann Devroy of the *Washington Post,* told me that whenever she wrote a story evaluating Clinton, her voice mail was full the next morning. If she had been positive, his detractors would shout into her phone; if negative, his supporters would shout. Either way, callers were usually emotional and vulgar.

Not since Nixon has a president been as polarizing. Political scientist George C. Edwards has pointed out that during his first two years in office, approval of Clinton's performance among self-identified Democrats ran roughly 50 points higher than among Republicans. It has remained high throughout his eight years. By contrast, the average difference between the parties for all presidents from Eisenhower through Carter was only 35 percent, and under President Bush was 37 percent. Reagan is the only other outlier: the differences in his approval levels averaged 53 percent, similar to Clinton's early gap. But Reagan never stirred up personal hatred the way Clinton and Nixon have.

I confess that I am conflicted. I admired Clinton early and salute him now for his substantial accomplishments, but I have also experienced many disappointments. Others who have worked for him have also had topsy-turvy reactions. With the passage of six years since leaving his White House, I hope that I can now stand back and write with fairness and respect.

Much has transpired since I departed. Twice he has fallen from grace; once he has come back. After voters turned Democrats out of Congress in the off-year elections of 1994—in effect, a negative referendum on the Clinton presidency—Dick Morris became the next Mr. Fix-It. He was more successful than the rest of us. In fact, the Morris relationship with Clinton rivaled the most famous alliances ever made with a president—Colonel House with Woodrow Wilson, Louis Howe with FDR, Sherman Adams with Ike. Neither Haldeman nor Kissinger, Rumsfeld nor Cheney, Jordan nor Powell, Baker nor Meese, Sununu nor Scowcroft, had such dominion over government. Had it not been for Morris, Clinton might not have recovered and won reelection in 1996.

But in adopting the Morris strategy, Clinton also entered a more cynical phase in his presidency. He stopped pursuing the good in favor of the popular. He went from a "goo-goo" to win-at-any-cost. "I sometimes thought that Bill Clinton had two mind-sets: the Boy Scout and the politician. In the Boy Scout mode, he sees his own goodness and focuses, with lofty dignity, on doing good in the world. . . . When Clinton faces political adversity, he switches into his politician mode . . . he becomes an astute and acute political warrior," Morris writes in his insightful memoir, *Behind the Oval Office*.

As energizing as the Morris period and the reelection were, they also left a deep residue of trouble in Clinton's second term. The decision to launch an early and massive advertising campaign against Republican Bob Dole in the fall of 1995 required the Clinton-Gore team to raise millions of dollars at warp speed. Dropping traditions, they also dropped their ethical standards. After the election, voters were horrified to learn, as opponents put it, that the Lincoln bedroom had been turned into Motel Six and foreign money had poured into the Clinton-Gore coffers. A smell of scandal permeated Clinton's second term. His election tactics and strategy of "triangulation" also infuriated Democrats and Republicans on Capitol Hill. Democrats stood by him during the second term, but Republican mistrust, already deep, turned poisonous. Legislative achievements have been scant since then.

Clinton's "Naked Moment"

314 The Morris period also marked a new phase in the Hillary-Bill relationship. With the defeat of health care and the loss of Congress, the First Lady suffered a psychological blow and went down on the see-

saw. With his comeback under Morris, the President went up. He was now untethered from her. The old cocksureness was returning, along with the cigars. It is not surprising that he then succumbed to the temptation of thong underwear and began a sexual relationship with Monica Lewinsky that continued on and off for eighteen months.

It is difficult for many to sit in moral judgment upon his affairs over the years. Yet he should have appreciated that the rules have changed since Kennedy—that no president and, in fact, no serious presidential candidate can survive in today's climate if he carries on with Kennedy's abandon. My sense is that Clinton did indeed understand the rules had changed and he *tried* to change, too. For reasons that are unclear, he lacked the will and self-discipline to hold himself in check. His relationship with Lewinsky, of course, had even more forbidden aspects—her youth, the fact that she was an intern, the sacrilege of having oral sex in the Oval Office. A man who places a young woman in that position has made a grievous error and must bear that guilt forever.

With his enemies already baying at the gate, it was not just a matter of giving in to an old temptation but acting with extreme stupidity. On *The NewsHour with Jim Lehrer,* historian Stephen Ambrose said in exasperation, "God created man with a penis and a brain and gave him only enough blood to run one at a time."

On January 17, 1998, when Clinton gave a videotape deposition in the Paula Jones case against him for sexual harassment, he was jolted when her lawyers bore in with detailed questions about his relationship with Monica. His immediate instinct was denial. He ducked and dodged through the conversation, leaving a trail of answers that were a focus of his impeachment.

When the story hit the press a few days later, Bill Clinton faced the greatest test of his leadership. This was his "naked moment"—a moment when, as we have seen before, all Americans can pierce the public veil and see the character of the man who lies behind.

Clinton never hesitated. Questioned by press secretary Mike McCurry, he approved a statement that "he's never had an improper relationship with this woman." To his chief of staff Erskine Bowles and his top deputies, he said he did not have a sexual relationship; to his deputy chief of staff, John Podesta, he explicitly denied any oral sex. That afternoon, in a television interview with Jim Lehrer, he assured his audience, "There is not a sexual relationship, an improper sexual relationship, or any other kind of improper relationship." That afternoon, he told journalist Mort Kondracke, "The relation-

315

ship was not sexual." Memorably, he appeared thereafter in the Roosevelt Room and, finger wagging at the cameras, made his famous denial: "I want to say one thing to the American people. I want you to listen to me, I'm going to say this again. I did not have sexual relations with that woman, Miss Lewinsky. I never told anybody to lie, not a single time—never. These allegations are false."

Some savvy observers in Washington believe Clinton was right to evade and lie that January. If he had told the truth, they say, his enemies would have ripped him apart and driven him from office over what was, in the end, a sexual escapade with an eager, consenting woman. It is certainly true that few other presidents have been as maliciously pilloried. While there has never been "a vast right-wing conspiracy" at work, as Mrs. Clinton claimed six days after the story broke, there has been a growing fraternity of Clinton haters. Working in parallel and sometimes in concert, they have poured large sums of money and energy into discrediting him since he entered politics.

Even so, Clinton was wrong. He put his own interests above the national interest, his personal survival above the country's needs. Americans now knew for sure what they had only suspected—their President would lie to save himself. His presidency has never recovered.

Yes, as was said of Nixon, even paranoids have real enemies. But Clinton never came to grips with the lessons of the Nixon experience. Even while enemies are ganging up, a president cannot give in to natural instincts, letting his anger or fear drive his decisions. Nixon could never bear telling the truth about Watergate for fear of what his enemies would do to him and his team. Clinton chose the same course now. One never made it, the other did—but each put the nation through needless hell.

The drama that followed consumed thirteen precious months of Clinton's second term, ending finally in a vote of impeachment by the House on two articles in December 1998 and a vote of acquittal by the Senate on both charges in February 1999. Those months were an ugly chapter as partisan tempers erupted on both sides, political leaders savaged each other, and public discourse reached new lows on television. There were times when the White House had good cause to bare its fangs, just as Republicans had ample reason to be bitter toward Democrats. But even as he survived, Clinton could take little solace. He was the first president in history to testify before a grand jury as a target of a criminal investigation; the first president forced to make a humiliating confession of infidelity; the first while

316

in office to have his sexual life graphically publicized; and the first elected president to be impeached.

The collateral damage was immense. He had compromised his family, friends, cabinet members, and staff. He had cheapened the political process he had worked all his life to improve. His hopes for making his second term one of high accomplishment were lost. And a series of adverse court decisions left the presidency itself weakened as an institution for those who follow him. The presidency is by nature a weak institution within the constitutional arrangement, and it has long been an article of faith among scholars that an incumbent's duty is to leave it as strong as he has found it, perhaps stronger. Others share responsibility for the ordeal the country endured in 1998–1999. His mistakes did not rise to the level of high crimes; he did not deserve to be impeached. But those of us who worked for his success must acknowledge his failures.

Clinton continues to evolve even now as president. Since his acquittal, he has worked aggressively to restore his public standing and to leave behind more achievements. His focus on a place in history has been so intense that his chief of staff has banned the word "legacy" from the lexicon of the staff. But we have enough evidence in hand to begin assessing his leadership, trying to draw lessons for those who follow.

His Core Leadership Qualities

No one can grow up in a relatively poor state, survive a difficult childhood, rise to the White House—and *then* win reelection— unless he has formidable strengths. I was fortunate to be there when Bill Clinton was at his best. What I saw convinced me he wasn't just strong; he had the potential to become one of the best leaders of twentieth-century America. Why he did not is a story we can save for a moment. For now, let me describe the qualities I saw that lifted him to the edges of greatness.

RESILIENCE

"Success is going from failure to failure without loss of enthusiasm," Churchill observed. Clinton has had more than his share of failures as president—the knockdowns early in his presidency, the defeat on health care, Whitewater, the Republican takeover of Congress, his

317

impeachment. But he has never lost his enthusiasm. He is the most resilient president we have had in decades, perhaps as far back as Lincoln. His critics punch him silly, knock him down, and he always gets off the canvas. He may be disoriented for a moment, but he is still fighting.

Presumably that resilience came from a long series of setbacks and recoveries, stretching back to childhood. The stories of his upbringing in Arkansas are already familiar. A more obvious parallel lies in his early days in politics: 1978, the youngest elected governor in the country; 1980, the youngest governor defeated for reelection; 1982, chastened, he is reelected. Then, too, of course were the early setbacks of the 1992 campaign, followed by his capture of the nomination. In both instances, just as in 1993, his wife was a major, steadying force for him.

Some political leaders never survive the first blow they receive after they reach the national stage. The presidential campaign of George Romney imploded in 1968 after he said he had been "brainwashed" in Vietnam. Ed Muskie never recovered from his alleged crying scene in the snows of New Hampshire in 1972. Two good men, two lost campaigns. In politics, the consultants say that such candidates have "glass jaws," crumbling on the first hit. But a candidate who can take a punch and walk back builds up public respect. Voters may not like him very much, but they admire his durability. Over time, Clinton gained political strength because people saw him take so many punches and come back smiling. He was the perpetual "Comeback Kid."

His critics attribute his resiliency to overweening ambition. He's a man who will stop at nothing to get on top and stay there, they say. There's no doubt that Clinton is one of the most ambitious men we have ever had in the modern presidency, at least matching Johnson and Nixon. But I haven't sensed that that is the reason for his buoyancy.

If anything, Clinton combines a natural optimism with a capacity to stand outside himself. He can look on his travails existentially, almost as if he were another person. He might blow up at a small, inconsequential matter, but the big ones seem to roll off him. When a crisis arises, he can just as easily put himself in another person's shoes as in his own. Maybe that is a protective cover he invented for himself to ward off injury as a child. By the time he reached adulthood, the batterings he took never penetrated deeply enough to kill his spirit. His emotional coat of armor became thicker than most men's.

I saw that firsthand the night of Vince Foster's suicide in the summer of 1993. Vernon Jordan and I, who had been at a private dinner party that night, rushed over to find Clinton at the home of the widow, Lisa Foster. I was worried that after so many troubles in Washington, this would be the final straw for the Clintons. If White House life had killed their friend Vince, both of the Clintons might sour forever on their new home and his presidency would come apart. What I found was Clinton consoling everyone else in the room. He was subdued but giving strength to others, not drawing from them. Later, sitting with a small group in his kitchen back at the White House, the President was far more concerned about what this would do to Lisa than to him. He must have known that the suicide—the first by a major administration figure since Defense Secretary James Forrestal jumped out a window at the Bethesda Naval Hospital in 1949—would cause an enormous stir. Yet, if Clinton felt threatened, he didn't show it. His empathy was directed toward Lisa. I went home that night much relieved about the President's mental health. He was tough enough, all right.

Eisenhower liked to say, "What counts is not necessarily the size of the dog in the fight—it's the size of the fight in the dog." Clinton had plenty of fight in him.

BRAINS

Clinton had the firmest, most subtle grasp of public policy of any president I have known, including Nixon. Presidents tend to know a great deal about the politics of issues, not the issues themselves. Clinton insisted upon knowing both, and he knew about issues across the board. One probably needs to go back to Woodrow Wilson or Teddy Roosevelt for parallels.

In economics, for example, nearly all presidents come in knowing only a smattering and don't try to learn more. Instead, they recruit an assortment of macroeconomists, Wall Street veterans, and former CEOs, and then go along with their advice. Clinton had a first-rate team, but was never satisfied until he understood for himself the intricacies behind their thinking. He would happily plunge into a thicket of statistics and jargon, bushwhacking his way to the other side. Only then would he feel comfortable making a decision. Journalists dismiss that as "wonkery," but Clinton put it to good use.

Bob Rubin is properly given credit as the President's economic

319

pillar. Quiet, self-effacing, he held together the economic policy-making and gave wise counsel. Rubin was a primary voice in persuading Clinton to support a serious plan for budget reductions, going forward with the NAFTA treaty, respecting the independence of the Federal Reserve Board, and helping the economics of Mexico and then of Asia during their financial meltdowns of the mid- and late 1990s. Bob Rubin was the MVP of the Clinton years.

As Rubin would be the first to acknowledge, however, Clinton was an apt pupil and soon developed superior judgment on economic issues. What he didn't know when he arrived, he picked up along the way. While the process was messy and he reached results two minutes to midnight, the results were good. In 1993, Clinton frequently exploded in private that Alan Greenspan was keeping interest rates too tight. He wanted to blast him on the public airwaves. But Rubin would stand in front of Clinton's desk in the Oval Office and explain that presidential jawboning would only challenge the chairman's manhood and force up rates more. Clinton would calm down and keep his distaste for the Fed to himself. Over time, Greenspan was vindicated and Clinton twice reappointed him. Together, they helped to make the economic boom the greatest success of the Clinton years.

Through those tutorials and his own probing, Clinton built up his intellectual foundation. When elected, he was barely functional on a computer but learned all about Silicon Valley and how technologies were changing the economy. By the end of his presidency, he was giving the best speeches on science and technology of anyone on the public stage.

Cabinet officers in education, health care, and urban affairs also found that he knew as much about their subject as they did, if not more. When he paid attention in foreign policy—which wasn't as often as he should—he also learned about the subtleties there. More than once Clinton took flight with a soliloquy about the nature of issues that only the experts could follow. Gore could be even more theoretical. Sometimes I wasn't sure if I was in a graduate seminar or the Oval Office.

Not many politicians are original thinkers and Clinton isn't either. His strength is that of the synthesizer—absorbing masses of information, sorting through, and then weaving it together into an artful, new whole. From his college papers through his presidency, as biographer David Maraniss has shown, that has been his pattern. He is also best as a tactician. In politics, where there are many different players in every game, he can analyze the position and the likely

320

next move of each player with canny insight. From that, he can plot the move that will best advance his own interest. That's how he was able to outmaneuver Newt Gingrich during the shutdown of the government in 1995. Gingrich was no match for Clinton as a tactician nor is anyone else in politics today. Clinton, it should be added, has trouble thinking through and adopting a strategy. He is too accustomed to thinking in the short term, always trying to keep his options open. The lack of a long-term strategy has been a serious weakness throughout his presidency.

Clinton is also exceptionally good at listening to multiple perspectives, extracting from each their best points and then integrating these views into a single public policy that can provide progress on a wide front. He has 360-degree vision. And because he understands the connections that exist—how early childhood intervention enhances a child's performance in school, for example—he has been able to fashion sophisticated policies that are a blend of liberal and conservative thinking. Save health care, no other contemporary president has been as adept at domestic policy-making.

Clinton also comes as close as I have seen to a photographic memory, even better than Reagan's. As Maraniss pointed out, Clinton can remember phone numbers he hasn't dialed in years. He can recite chapter and verse from books he has read, whether it's the Bible or political histories. Among my memories is Clinton sitting in the Oval Office in animated conversation. When someone else talked, he would pick up a *New York Times* crossword puzzle and fill in the blanks. He wasn't bored; it was like doodling for him. I might say something about crime, and he wanted to know the name of a character in *Aïda*. I found that daunting.

One Sunday in 1994, a number of us gathered with him for most of the day in the Oval Office to discuss Haiti. He had sent three envoys there—Jimmy Carter, Colin Powell, and Sam Nunn, the former senator—to negotiate with the thugs then in power. Unless they agreed to resign, Clinton was sending in the Eighty-second Airborne. Carter and Clinton talked frequently by phone, comparing notes on the negotiations. Eventually, the Carter team succeeded, and the U.S. troops went in peacefully.

As he was talking with Carter, Clinton would pick up that day's crossword puzzle, the largest of the week. Since it didn't seem to distract him, it amused me to watch, but I wondered what Carter might have been doing on his end of the line. Upon their return, I casually asked one of Carter's aides. Oh, he said, we had a television in our room and sometimes we would watch CNN while the talks

321

were under way. At one point, CNN featured a fashion show and a drop-dead blonde with a slinky dress sashayed down the aisle. Carter, talking to the President, put the phone a little away and exclaimed, Look at that! They still got the job done.

If forced to choose between high intelligence and high integrity in a leader, I would not hesitate to prefer integrity. Obviously, it would have been better if Clinton had achieved more of a balance. Still, the flaws in his character should not blind us to the fact that he is prodigiously bright and his intelligence has served him well. One day, we may be nostalgic for a president who can speak with clarity, wit, and sophistication.

A POLITICAL TOUCH

It is by now common wisdom that Bill Clinton is the most talented politician of his generation. He is not, as it turns out, as good as a president should be at the "inside game" of politics, but he is indeed superb at the "outside game."

I have seen him repeatedly carry out the same pattern of winning people over. Long before he became president, he would enter a group where he was virtually unknown. He would try to meet each and every person there, eliciting their stories, listening carefully, learning their names. Gradually, he would get a sense of who they were and how they thought. He is empathic by nature and, like British prime minister Tony Blair, has the political equivalent of "perfect pitch"—an uncanny ability to read the mood of his audience. People gravitate toward him because he is seductive. Only after he has had time with the group does he begin to put himself forward. By then, he seems their natural leader. That was the Bill Clinton who has become president or first among equals of every group of which he has been a part—from high school to college to Oxford to Yale Law to Arkansas to Renaissance to the National Governors Conference to the Democratic Leadership Council to the White House.

At a public podium, he dances with words, spinning out thoughts and framing issues in ways that leave his friends dazzled and his foes sputtering. He always says too much—not a thought goes unexpressed. And he does not employ memorable phrases— his entries in *Bartlett's* will never be longer than Reagan's. But he is one of the best extemporaneous speakers in public life today. When Bill Safire compiled his updated edition of public oratory, *Lend Me*

322

Your Ears, he chose only one speech by President Clinton—an address he gave after throwing away his notes and speaking from his heart to black ministers in Memphis.

His capacity to understand his audience and to shape arguments to fit has made Clinton a formidable campaigner. In public opinion polls, Clinton has not always been judged well if the focus has been on him alone. But once he is in the arena and has a live opponent, he excels. He is clever at drawing distinctions that make the other fellow's case seem weak, even dangerous, while advancing his own cause. Only once in his presidency has the other side beaten Clinton in a public argument—over the administration's health care proposal—and there, as we have seen, he was not in full control. Time and again, he has put Republicans such as Newt Gingrich in a rhetorical box by framing the debate in terms that made it unwinnable for the other side.

To succeed in the presidency, however, a chief executive must do more than win elections and arguments. He must also persuade other powerful players within the system to go along with him, and on that score, Clinton's political skills have been much less impressive. People inside the system—on Capitol Hill, in foreign capitals, among the interest groups, within the press corps, among the Washington elite—have been wary of him and, increasingly over the course of his presidency, have become distrustful.

That's why one must distinguish between his skills at the outside and inside games.

To be fair, Clinton has been president during an unusually difficult period in public life. Partisanship has been intense on Capitol Hill. Even so, he has made his relations with Congress infinitely worse. The problem has not been the people he has recruited to run his congressional shops. They have been good. The problem has been the way he has run his White House, often treating Congress and other institutions as subservient. Some leaders, like Senator George Mitchell, have gotten on well with him, but others have kept their distance and a few have spoken out caustically. In Clinton's first year in office, Democratic senator Bob Kerrey said publicly what others were saying in private: "Clinton's an unusually good liar." Looking back after Clinton's seven years in office, historians and other presidency watchers surveyed by C-Span in February 2000 concluded that Clinton had the worst congressional relations of any president in the twentieth century.

It is instructive to compare his legislative success record with those of his predecessors in office. In many instances, they, too, had

323

to work with Congresses that were in the control of the opposing party. Eisenhower had a Democratic House in six of his eight years in office; Nixon, Ford, Reagan, and Bush, throughout their terms. The Senate wasn't much friendlier. Both chambers, of course, have been in Republican hands through six of Clinton's years. But save Bush and Ford—who never had a Congress of their own party—earlier presidents racked up significantly better legislative scorecards, as compiled by the *Congressional Quarterly*. Here are the average support scores per year since *CQ* began compiling the statistics in 1953:

Eisenhower	72 percent
Kennedy	84 percent
Johnson	81 percent
Nixon	67 percent
Ford	58 percent
Carter	76 percent
Reagan	63 percent
Bush	52 percent
Clinton	58 percent
Clinton, 1995–99	47 percent

Notably, *Congressional Quarterly* found that in the first year of the Republican takeover, 1995, and in the year of the Lewinsky scandal, 1999, Clinton's scores sank to 36 percent and 38 percent respectively. In no other year ever recorded has a president's success rate in Congress fallen below 40 percent. Even accounting for the rabid opposition that Clinton often faced among Republicans—who, after all, didn't give him a single vote for his first budget and voted en masse to throw him out of office six years later—it seems incontestable that Clinton has been better as an outside than inside leader.

COURAGE

Early on, Clinton had acquired a reputation for caving in at the first sign of political trouble. On his campaign promises to cut taxes for the middle class, reverse policy in Haiti, and stiffen up on China, he seemed to retreat when he entered office. Even on gays in the military, when he whipped up so much hostility from the Right, his allies on the Left accused him of a sellout. "It stinks," Congressman Barney Frank said.

Yet, on many of those same issues, those of us around him in

324

that first year often saw a president exercising a political courage that we admired. Dropping the middle-class tax cut in favor of higher taxes on the wealthy was terrible politics for him. But in light of the worsening deficits, he thought it was the best course for the country and took it. NAFTA was much the same story. When he saw that keeping his campaign pledge on Haiti would encourage boat-loads of Haitians to head for Florida, he thought it better to accept criticism for retreating than to have people die on tiny skiffs at sea. Similarly, on China, he came to appreciate that the Bush policy had been much sounder than he thought. Better for him to eat crow as president, he concluded, than to risk driving China into isolation. He very much wanted gays to serve openly in the military, but after hearing out the Joint Chiefs in person and testing congressional sentiment, he thought that the wisest course was to embrace a less ambitious "don't ask, don't tell" policy. Even gay soldiers would be better served, he decided. Once he understood that, was he wrong to change his mind and follow a different course? To me, that was gutsy.

I was among those who urged a more incremental approach to health care reform. But I had to give him, as well as Hillary, credit for trying. No president in history—not even Harry Truman—has staked as much of his political reputation in order to overhaul the national health care system.

The sadness is that after voters elected a Republican Congress in 1994, he changed. He put down the sword he had raised in behalf of causes he believed in. Only in the beginning of the second term, when he was politically strong, did he become the Boy Scout again— until the Lewinsky scandal broke. Then he lost courage completely, but for a while that was one of his major assets.

CARING

Ronald Reagan tended to care a great deal about people as individuals but not much about group rights. Bill Clinton is the opposite. He can be indifferent to individuals but genuinely cares about the well-being of groups.

Blacks, women, children, the poor, the elderly, the disadvantaged, working mothers, gays, victims of natural disasters, people who play by the rules—all these and more have a living, breathing 325 quality to Clinton and they matter to him. They appeal to him as underdogs, and he has spent a great deal of his presidency working hard on their behalf. Not every group qualifies for his concern. Certainly, the unborn don't. Nor do union members, veterans, and small business owners. He tends to focus on race, gender, and class distinctions, favoring those he thinks are on the short end of the stick.

One might say these are traditional Democratic constituencies, so that of course he "cares." But it goes deeper with him than most public figures. He got into politics with a dual motivation: to become president *and* to "do good" by those left behind. To see him as driven solely by personal ambition is to miss an essential ingredient of his being.

In both the 1984 and 1988 campaigns, the Democratic nominees for president felt they had to kowtow to Jesse Jackson in order to win the black vote. In the 1992 campaign, Clinton consciously snubbed Jackson at a Sister Souljah event in order to show his independence. The difference was that Clinton already had many longtime black friends who would come to his defense and would help him win grassroots support. He had built a network of his own support from years of working with civil rights groups and speaking in black churches. Politically, the snub worked. A forgiving Jackson went on to become one of Clinton's most important sources of emotional and spiritual support during the Monica furor.

As president, Clinton took seriously his pledge to create an administration that "looks more like America." While most of his senior White House staff was made up of white males, Clinton has appointed eleven women to cabinet and cabinet-level positions, in contrast to the eight women similarly appointed over the three terms of Reagan and Bush. He has also named thirteen minorities to such positions, compared to seven under Reagan and Bush combined. At the judicial level, 28 percent of Clinton's appointees have been females (compared to 8 percent for Reagan and 19 percent for Bush). Of all the women who have ever served on the federal bench, 44 percent are Clinton appointees. Some 18 percent of Clinton's appointees to the bench have been black (compared to 2 percent for Reagan and 6 percent for Bush). Of all the African Americans who have ever served on the federal bench, 46 percent are Clinton appointees.

In his policy choices, Clinton also has pushed a series of programs through Congress that favored those in his favored groups. The litany is too long to repeat, but among those passed have been family and medical leave (a bill vetoed by Bush), increases in the earned income tax credit, a higher minimum wage, enlarged programs for child nutrition, and nationwide vaccinations for children.

It has become axiomatic among many black Americans that Clinton has been their best friend in the White House since Johnson, maybe even Roosevelt. To an extent not widely appreciated, Clinton delivered.

Why He Went Wrong

How could a man of such abundant gifts have fallen short? Why did he never fulfill the bright promise he represented? His friends say it was impossible in a town where, as Vince Foster said in his note, "ruining people is considered sport." Washington is a tough town these days, no doubt about it, and his enemies have been unmerciful to Clinton. But students of the future will draw the wrong lessons about his leadership if they stop there. An honest account requires one to look at the rest of the story—the weaknesses that Clinton himself had which held him back. An interest in women and a willingness to lie about it are not the keys. Rather, they are the manifestation of other, more fundamental problems he brought to his presidency. As a friend said to me, sadly, "Bill Clinton would have been a great president if he had not been who he was."

LACK OF AN INNER COMPASS

Biographer David Maraniss reports that in 1981, Clinton gave a lecture at the University of Arkansas, analyzing key figures in politics from Willie Stark to Lincoln, Hitler, and Churchill: "In all political leaders, he told the class, there was a struggle between darkness and light. He mentioned the darkness of insecurity, depression, and family disorder. In great leaders, he said, the light overcame the darkness, but it was always a struggle." Clinton was touching upon his own internal struggle, Maraniss believes, especially with lying and philandering, two traits that had been part of his family life since he was young.

Perhaps we should think of Clinton locked in a titanic struggle between light and dark. But my sense is that description better fits Richard Nixon. Clinton has never shown the darkness of a Nixon. He isn't harboring interior demons the way Nixon was. Clinton is a sunny figure who doesn't want to hurt anybody and feels bad when he does. He can certainly be paranoid and lose his temper, but he 327 isn't a hater. What he hates is other people hating him. He desperately wants other people to like him.

Instead of a struggle between light and dark, my sense is that Clinton's central problem has been the lack of an inner compass. He has 360-degree vision but no true north. He isn't yet fully grounded within. Explaining the success of an earlier president, historian David McCullough once wrote of Harry Truman that "He knew who he was, and liked who he was. He liked being Harry Truman. He enjoyed being Harry Truman." Bill Clinton isn't exactly sure who he is yet and tries to define himself by how well others like him. That leads him into all sorts of contradictions, and the view by others that he seems a constant mixture of strengths and weaknesses.

Whether growing up as the stepchild of an alcoholic and without his real father left Clinton without the kind of disciplining force in his life that he needed, as others have suggested, I am not qualified to say. It is relatively clear that by shaping his entire life since childhood to winning public office and then catapulting into the governorship of Arkansas at age thirty-two, Clinton never had the chance most people have of making their mistakes in private. He was under such intense public scrutiny from early on that when his sexual energy got the best of him, as it did frequently, he learned to lie with gusto in order to cover his tracks. Nor did Clinton ever have time in his early adulthood for quiet reflection and internal growth. He started running grueling, time-consuming political campaigns when he was twenty-seven years old and he has been running nonstop ever since. Like his dad and his idol John Kennedy, he thought he might die young and wanted his cup to runneth over. He never took it from his lips long enough to know the man drinking.

The presidency may be the one job whose pursuit over an entire lifetime makes a person *less* likely to succeed in it. The Nixon and Clinton experiences both suggest that. When he came to the White House, Bill Clinton had an underdeveloped sense of self. Instead of looking within for guidance, he constantly took his cues from the environment outside. Throughout his life, he had relied upon verbal gymnastics to skip past trouble, rather than wrestling trouble to the ground. He had developed an illusion that he was invincible, and that if by chance he couldn't talk his way out of trouble, the women in his life—his mother, Hillary, others—would rescue him.

A politician needs ambition to climb the greasy pole, and that Clinton had in abundance. While he and Hillary wanted to reenact the Roosevelts, he had never endured the hardships of Roosevelt, the seven long years in the wilderness that transformed him from a prince into a man of iron. FDR was ambitious, just like Clinton, but he overcame his narcissism. Clinton has not fully done that. While superb at putting himself into others' shoes, Clinton has viewed too many people as instruments for his own advancement. He and his wife have a self-righteous streak, a sense that they are on a mission that is just and good and that gives them special dispensations in life. If their cause is so pure, how can anyone else question their motive? They can even make members of the staff feel the Clintons are doing them a favor by hiring them.

David Maraniss points out from the late 1980s on, Clinton has linked the two ideas of opportunity and responsibility. The government should ensure that everyone has an equal opportunity, but the individual then has the responsibility to use it well. "Clinton's history, however, shows that taking 'complete responsibility' for all his actions, 'public and private,' was not one of his strong points. The examples come from all parts of his life, large and small."

If he wasn't fully responsible for what went wrong, clearly he could also do it over. In the fall of 1999, Don Van Natta, Jr., in the *New York Times,* suggested "the mulligan" as "a perfect metaphor for his Presidency." The comparison immediately stuck among reporters because it captured a part of him so well. A golfer who takes his shot over is said to be hitting a mulligan. It is considered a benign shot by weekend duffers. Clinton is notorious for taking a second shot if his first slices into the woods. Jerry Ford and Jack Nicklaus played golf with him in Colorado and afterward Clinton claimed to the press that he had scored a respectable 80. An irritated Nicklaus, according to Bob Woodward, whispered to Ford, "Eighty with fifty floating mulligans." It's one thing to take mulligans in golf, however, and another to take them in public life. If nothing ever counts, it becomes easy to compartmentalize, to forget what happened yesterday, to think that only what happens today matters.

Bill Clinton is not a bad man, as his enemies claim. In fact, in most ways, he is a very good and caring man who wants to improve the lives of others. But his career has been so rushed, he has never had time to let roots grow in his interior life. He has spent huge amounts of time helping others but has never taken the time to allow others to help him. In the aftermath of the Lewinsky scandal, he sought help from pastoral counselors. There is growing evidence that he is becoming more integrated and may achieve the redemption he is seeking. Perhaps he shall one day gain the inner grace of Jimmy Carter.

But that will come long after the damage is done to his presi-

329

dency. Henry Adams once wrote that the essence of leadership in the presidency is "a helm to grasp, a course to steer, a port to seek." Clinton had grasped the helm, but because he lacked an inner compass, he had neither a course nor a port that remained firm.

A CAMPAIGN MENTALITY

Lacking a rudder in his own life, Clinton has had a hard time building one in his presidency. In his State of the Union address each year, he has typically listed fifty to sixty initiatives but has never been clear which ones truly matter. Rather than choosing two or three central goals for his presidency, he has continually shifted, depending upon the external political environment.

Fiscal prudence—slashing the deficit, saving the surplus—has been his single constant, and because he has stuck to it with conviction and courage, he has been highly successful. But all else has been in flux. He elevated health care reform into the centerpiece of his first term, but when his bill collapsed, he buried it without a word. In 1997, he announced to fanfare that education reform would be his first priority for the future. It became one among many. He has spoken of Medicare and Social Security reform as his legacy to the next generation. When an opportunity came in 1999 for a bipartisan agreement on Medicare, he spurned it—it didn't fit his political needs at the moment. A president who has a hard time defining himself has found it equally difficult to define his administration. He can frame a debate but not a vision.

Instead of governing with a steady hand, the President has fallen back on what has always worked best for him. After he first lost in Arkansas, Dick Morris convinced him it was not enough to get things done; he also had to pay constant attention to his own reelection. With elections there occurring every two years, he became accustomed to running a permanent campaign.

Naturally, Clinton brought that style with him to Washington, installing his campaign team at the White House. I am unaware of any previous administration in which outside political advisers have exercised as large a role. Stan Greenberg, often with the aid of Mandy Grunwald, wrote the memos that for the first two years were the basis of long-term planning meetings, attended by the President, First Lady, and Vice President. Joining them at the table were James Carville and Paul Begala. When the four consultants fell out of favor after the 1994 election, Dick Morris took their place. In

330

truth, all of these people—along with campaign veterans inside like Stephanopoulos and Emanuel—were among the best political heads in politics. At issue is not their talent. Rather, it is the degree to which the President tried to lead through chronic campaigning.

There were three prongs to his permanent campaign. One was a reliance upon constant polling. All modern presidents have polled heavily—Haldeman put three different pollsters in the field at a time and secretly paid a fourth to keep an eye on the others—but no one before Clinton has taken a poll to determine whether he should tell the truth publicly (the Lewinsky case) or to use American ground troops (Kosovo). The *Wall Street Journal* has reported that President Bush in his first two years spent $216,000 on polls; President Clinton in his first year alone spent $1,986,410, nearly ten times as much. A second prong was a reliance upon War Rooms in legislative battles. That approach had worked spectacularly in the campaign. Why not in the White House? The final prong was his "outside-in" style of governing, as Charles O. Jones has called it. Jones found that during his first year and a half in office, Clinton averaged ten appearances a month on the road to pump his programs, more than twice as many as Reagan did before he was shot. Reagan communicated effectively with both the public and Congress by staying near home. Clinton hit the road, trying to use "bank shots" to score. "We need popular support to keep the pressure on Congress to vote for change," explained Stan Greenberg.

The permanent campaign did work in limited instances in passing legislation; it helped Clinton win reelection; and it was important in staving off congressional investigators. If he had to do it again, Clinton would probably employ the same approach to governing. But he may not see how much damage was done to his leadership, especially on Capitol Hill. It drove away potential allies and made legislative agreements infinitely more difficult. Republicans on Capitol Hill, already combative, became impervious to his outside-in style, nor were Democratic legislators impressed.

A campaign is by definition a zero-sum game: one party wins, the other loses. It naturally introduces the notion of warfare because one path to victory—sometimes the only one—is to annihilate the other side. A warrior must do whatever it takes to win, fair or foul. The other side becomes your enemy and compromise becomes a dirty word.

The idea of governing is wholly different. The parties to a problem can see themselves as partners, not enemies. It can be a game of win-win: each party can win by working out a solution that is mutually beneficial. Richard Neustadt pointed out forty years ago that ours is not a government of separated powers, as is popularly thought, but of "separated institutions *sharing* powers." Approaching public policy disputes in that spirit, the leaders of the executive and legislative branches can bargain in good faith and reach settlements that serve the needs of both. Mutual trust is essential and so is respect. Governing does not end tough, hard fights—nor should it. Still, most of the biggest legislative achievements of the past have come because presidents understood what it means to govern. A permanent campaign is its antithesis.

ETHICAL WEAKNESS

In a survey of fifty-six historians and political observers taken by C-Span earlier this year, Clinton ranked fifth highest among all presidents in economic management and dead last in moral authority—behind Richard Nixon! That contemporary judgment is not likely to change soon.

As a former assistant and longtime friend, I write now with heavy heart. But in evaluating Clinton's leadership, one can no more avoid this subject than leaving Watergate out of the Nixon story. Clinton had, after all, pledged the most ethical administration and knew that, given his past experience, he would face tougher scrutiny and be held to higher standards than his predecessor. Yet, the years that followed brought a cavalcade of scandals, controversies, and mistakes. Some were small, others large, but together they add up to a depressing saga. Run the headlines quickly through your mind: an unprecedented firing of the nation's top prosecutors; the travel office firings; a rifling of Vince Foster's files; criminal referrals over conversations between White House and Treasury aides; the state trooper flap; commodities futures; Webb Hubbell goes to jail; the Paula Jones case; indictments of the governor and others in Arkansas; John Huang; Monica Lewinsky; the reappearance of White House billing records; Filegate; the Paula Jones deposition; Kathleen Willey; Janet Reno's refusal to appoint an independent counsel for campaign finance; an $850,000 settlement with Paula Jones; impeachment; Juanita Broaddrick; a federal judge finds the President in contempt; disbarment proceedings in Arkansas.

332   Nothing here amounts to the assaults upon the constitutional framework of the Nixon years. But there is an unarguable pattern of poor ethics. There are also uncomfortable parallels between the Clin-

ton and Nixon administrations: in each case, the president himself took a lax attitude toward his own ethics. Each allowed an environment to grow up around him that was a breeding ground for others to get into trouble. And then when scandals broke, each allowed his administration to react in ways that made matters worse. For each man, the defects proved self-destructive.

In every organization, ethics start at the top. A president, like a CEO, sets the standards for the whole team. If he fails in his own conduct—as leaders do—he must compensate as best he can by accepting personal responsibility. Nixon should have taken responsibility for Watergate on the day of the break-in, just as Clinton should have immediately taken responsibility for his relationship with an intern. Whether they would have survived is less important than whether they protected the honor of their office. Similarly, a president must demand that others who work for him meet high standards, and if they fail, he must take corrective action. He is just as responsible for the conduct of those around him as he is for his own. That is Leadership 101.

Sadly, Clinton has given the impression for many years that he feels the rules do not apply to him, and if called on infractions, he can bluff his way out. He has a history of walking on the edge and, when he goes over, dodging responsibility. Nor has he insisted that others around him meet high standards. No one can explain why. But those flaws have been at the root of his troubles.

He may not fully appreciate the signals he has sent to people working for him. They have seen that he has trouble disciplining himself and, when cornered, will evade, attack, or lie. At least three times he has lied to his own team on questions that mattered: the draft, Gennifer Flowers, and Monica Lewinsky. Unable to restrain himself, he has been in no position to crack down on others. The signals his people have gotten is that borderline ethics will be tolerated. As night follows day, others associated with Clinton have drifted into trouble. Not many, to be sure. The vast majority who have worked in the Clinton administration are fine, upstanding people. But what spoilers the others were!

A PATTERN OF DENIAL

When accusations have arisen on the outside, the President has con- 333 sistently avoided responsibility and allowed his team to embrace tactics that are self-defeating. Instead of answering charges with facts, the first reaction has typically been to deny all and refuse to divulge the facts. "Deny, deny, deny," he told girlfriends. If stonewalling doesn't work, the second reaction has been to smear the reputation of the accusers. Gennifer Flowers, they said, was seeking "cash for trash." "Drag a hundred dollars through a trailer park and there's no telling what you'll find," they said of Paula Jones. Monica Lewinsky was the "stalker," and Kathleen Willey was "unstable." All else failing, the ultimate defense—see Lewinsky—has been to bury the truth in a tissue of lies. None of this has been pretty.

Once they reached the White House, the Clintons would have sent a clear signal to their appointees that they wanted an open and accountable government had they been forthcoming about Whitewater. After they hunkered down instead, others took their cue and tended to resist elsewhere. White House advisers who pushed for more openness—and there were a good many, including some in the general counsel's office—typically blamed the Clintons' lawyers for that strategy. Lawyers, however, are employees of their clients, not the other way around. Ultimately, the clients are the ones who decide how they wish to be defended.

There is one strong argument in favor of the Clintons' approach: the unfairness of their enemies. From Little Rock to Washington, zealous accusers have been inventing outrageous stories about them and seeking their destruction. Watching how their private lives have been turned upside down and their friends in Arkansas have been badgered, one sympathizes with the Clintons' tendency to draw a self-protective shield around themselves. They know that if they admit the slightest mistake, it will be sensationalized and their accusers will be back for more.

But their experience argues for caution in responding to accusers. It does not suggest stonewalling. With a president who is a lightning rod for attacks, a White House must exercise care, distinguishing between those that are villainous and those that are serious. Demands for information from red-eyed zealots can be ignored, but those from leading news organizations, responsible chairs of congressional committees, and duly appointed federal investigators deserve forthright answers. Unfortunately, the Clinton White House worked itself into such a wrath about its accusers that it tended to give the same answer to everyone: Hell, no! It was the President himself who seemed in denial.

ANGER TOWARD THE PRESS

Clinton's approach toward the press opens another window on his leadership. He has run the most aggressive press operation in modern times, and at times the excesses have become a serious problem for his governance.

To be sure, changes in the press corps forced his hand. In the nine years after I left the Reagan administration, I spent most of my time in journalism, but I was nonetheless surprised upon returning to government to see how much tougher the press challenge has become. Instead of four or five cameras on the lawn in front of the West Wing, I now counted as many as twenty-four. The news cycle has also become continuous, so that the press office must shovel out information and answer calls twenty-four hours a day. CNN has become the fastest way for every government to send its message around the world.

The more disturbing change, I found, is that many journalists today seem more cynical and judgmental than those covering the White House twenty years ago. There are stellar exceptions—Tom Friedman, E. J. Dionne, and Ron Brownstein, to name a few—but I miss members of the older generation, like Lou Cannon, who asked tough questions and still wrote a fair, balanced story. The incentives in the business are tilted now in the wrong direction. Rewards in today's media run toward sensationalism and gossip.

The changes haven't been easy on anyone entering public service of late. When I joined the Nixon administration in 1971, it was widely believed that if you served well and honorably in public life, you could leave government with your reputation enhanced. Today, if you work hard and honorably in government, about the best you can hope for is to leave with your reputation intact.

In my tour with Clinton, I found what it was like to go through the ups and downs. Three or four pieces in the *New York Times* roughed me up a bit; some of their criticisms were justified, others left me puzzled. Then the paper assigned a correspondent to write a fresh profile on me in my new digs at the State Department. A number of colleagues, including Secretary Christopher, told him kind things, for which I was grateful. But when the correspondent filed the piece, it didn't appear. He told me his editors wanted him to report some more, which he did. Still, the story went unpublished. Curious, I talked to a contact at the *Times*. "It was spiked," he said, "too positive." Why would the editors do that? I asked. "Because they

335

feel you haven't earned your redemption yet." Redemption? I asked. "For working for Reagan," he said.

I was thus sympathetic to the frustration and anger that many on the Clinton team, especially the President and First Lady, felt toward the press. They had reason to set up an aggressive operation, and, over time, some of their efforts paid off. Their "rapid response" teams were extremely effective in getting the President's perspective into every story before it hit the streets. In fighting off accusers, his team also perfected the art of the "document dump"—releasing piles of papers to the media before opponents began leaking them out in Congress or in the independent counsel's office. Mike Mc-Curry has earned a spot in the hall of fame for press secretaries.

But I am afraid the Clintons carried too large a chip on their shoulders toward the press and would have had a far more productive relationship if they had been more open and respectful of reporters. Trust is a two-way street. While Clinton in the past year has seemingly moved beyond anger, the earlier atmosphere was decidedly unhealthy. More to the point, as press secretary Joe Lockhart has publicly acknowledged, many on his White House staff fell into a pattern of spinning stories beyond their legitimate bounds. It did not occur so much at the podium in the pressroom. But it happened continuously in phone calls and quiet conversations as one anonymous source or another would tell reporters half-truths or bald-faced lies to put the President, the First Lady, or himself in a flattering light.

As someone who had started a "spin patrol" back in the Reagan years, I was aghast at how it had been corrupted. How could we have taught a younger generation of public officials the wrong lessons about governance? Where had we gone wrong? While officials since the beginning of the republic have been cajoling the press, one of my deepest regrets in public life is a feeling that I have contributed to this deterioration. Spin has spun out of control and we need to put it back in its box. Ben Bradlee, the *Post*'s former editor, has put it well: "This word spinning . . . is a nice uptown way of saying lying."

The excessive spin of the Clinton years is only in part a defense against a changing press corps; it has also grown out of his leadership style. If a White House staff thinks it is engaged in a permanent campaign, it will act as it does in a campaign. And that means telling reporters damn near anything to grab a good headline. A campaign lives from news cycle to news cycle, often fudging or exaggerating. The only thing that matters is to win each day's battle and then the election. After that, people can fold up tents and go home, not worrying about the debris in their wake. The mind-set for governing is entirely different. There people must cock one eye on the next headline but another on the horizon. Governing is a process and to be successful, leaders have to build up a reputation for trust and integrity over time.

Clinton allowed his White House to become too preoccupied with spinning each day's story. Reporters became unclear where the truth stopped and the spin started. After a while, they wondered whether the Clinton team knew themselves. Morality in government begins with officials using words as honestly as possible to describe the truth. Max DePree again: "A leader's first duty is to define reality." In spin—as in war—truth is often the first casualty.

His Loss of Leadership

An invisible thread runs through the Clinton years—from his own internal weaknesses, to the need for a permanent campaign, the continual lapses of ethics, the resort to evasions and spin—and that thread ended in the collapse of his moral authority in 1998. The disclosure of his relationship with Monica Lewinsky and his subsequent lies may have been the precipitating cause, but the explosion that erupted then—in Congress, in the press, and among other major power centers—also reflected a powerful backlash that had been building up for years. Many Americans continued to support Clinton—his approval ratings in his second term have been higher than Reagan's—but people inside the beltway had had enough.

The central point that Neustadt made in 1960 was relevant again: presidential power rests upon the twin pillars of public prestige *and* professional reputation. To govern, a president must build his popularity with the public, but he must also maintain a good reputation in Washington. Clinton now had one and not the other. He lost his capacity to lead.

Living outside Washington, it is easy to be cynical about those who live inside; there is much to be cynical about. But one should not forget that almost everyone who comes to Washington has a streak of idealism and wants to think that whatever the job, she or he is performing something worthwhile. Washington is at heart a village, and the central square is dominated by one institution—the White House. Just as Washington insiders want their children to look upon them with pride, they want the presidency to be a place of honor.

If a newcomer thumbs his nose at the villagers and breaks their

337

rules—even if he is president—he will eventually pay a heavy price. That is what happened to Clinton. In November 1998, Sally Quinn wrote a piece in the *Washington Post* that angered the Clintons but captured the sentiments of the city. Among the one hundred people she interviewed, the dean of the press corps, David Broder, told her, "He came in here and trashed the place, and it's not his place." Bill Galston, a former domestic adviser to Clinton and a noted professor, said, "Most people in Washington . . . are honorable and are trying to do the right thing. The basic thought is that to concede that [Clinton's behavior] is normal and that everybody does it is to undermine a lifetime commitment to honorable public service." Andrea Mitchell of NBC said, "There is a small-town quality to the grief that is being felt . . ." The village has a cardinal rule, I added, "You don't foul the nest."

Reflecting on his presidency, I believe Clinton was elected too early for his own good. That night he declared for the presidency and called me at home, in 1991, he did not sound like a man who expected to win. He talked bravely, but it was apparent that he saw the 1992 race as a warm-up, a chance to run the track and find the money before he went the distance. Apparently, he thought Mario Cuomo would enter, edge him out, win the Democratic crown and then lose to Bush in the finals. That outcome would allow Clinton to argue in 1996 that three straight Democratic nominees—Mondale, Dukakis, Cuomo—had taken the party down to defeat with old-fashioned liberalism. Time for a New Democrat! With voters tired of Republicans in the White House, Clinton could then sweep into power with a rousing victory and a mandate for action.

He would have been a better president had that scenario played out. By 1996, Clinton would have had four more years to mature. He would have become more grounded, more self-disciplined, and lost some of his need to walk on the edge. Perhaps he and Hillary would have also reached a greater equilibrium in their relationship and neither would have felt it necessary to pursue a co-presidency. Their private lives would have had a less disruptive impact upon their public ones. With time, he would have thought more clearly about his priorities as president and how to achieve them.

Can one be certain he would have changed? Of course not. Some elements of personality are deeply ingrained. Perhaps he would have remained self-absorbed and reckless. But history suggests that self-mastery is usually a matter of growth and habit, not genes. Clinton has grown up a great deal during his presidential years. He has grown steadier and steeled himself to the demands of

338

the national spotlight. Toward the end of his presidency, he was demonstrating far more effectiveness than in the beginning.

In his relationship with Lewinsky, according to her notes, he acknowledged to her earlier relationships with women but said he had tried to stop when he was forty years old. He portrayed himself as an addict who had attempted to go straight, fallen off the wagon when she came along and was desperately trying to get on again. Perhaps he was lying (as Lewinsky suspected). But there is a good deal of evidence that when he was around forty, Clinton had become sensitive to how much damage his flings would wreak upon his political ambitions. He saw in 1988 how Gary Hart had been brought down and was scrambling to protect himself. While there were persistent rumors to the contrary, the Clinton I saw up close over eighteen months was clearly working to behave himself. My sense is that he was trying hard to reform and didn't quite make it. If he had given himself four more years to mature before coming to the White House, he might have.

As Historians May See Him

Bill Clinton will almost assuredly go down in history as a man who reached for the heavens and came up with one hand full of stars, the other filled with dust. The ambivalence historians feel toward Johnson and Nixon is likely to attach to him as well.

He was clearly a man of incredible promise—high intelligence, grand dreams, personal resilience, a compelling presence—and, just as clearly, his presidency was marked by significant accomplishment. The economic surge on his watch lifted more boats off the bottom than in any recent presidency. The poverty level dropped to the lowest level in thirty years and the bottom quintile of the population actually enjoyed a higher growth in income levels than did the middle class. While Republicans were the prime movers, Clinton can look with pride in cutting welfare rolls sharply and moving large numbers into the workforce. The 1990s were also a decade that saw an important reversal in key social indicators. Illegitimate births, teenage pregnancies, divorces, crimes, teenage violence, drug usage among young people—rates for all stopped going up and starting dropping while he was president. He cannot claim sole credit, but there would not have been as much progress without his leadership. 339

Even in the area of foreign affairs, Clinton has bragging rights. His critics are harsh, and there have indeed been times when he has been inattentive and dithering. Ad hocism has often reigned. But he has kept the nation out of war, played a constructive role in encouraging the unification of Europe and the expansion of NATO, moved the peace process forward in the Middle East, stopped the genocide in former Yugoslavia, defused the economic crisis in Asia, and helped to keep the world economy on track. He has also reached out to India and is the first president since Carter to pay serious attention to the poorer countries of Africa. One could say of his foreign policy what Twain said of Wagner: "His music is better than it sounds."

Yet, historians will have to weigh the rest of the story. His legislative achievements are important—his 1993 and 1997 budgets, NAFTA, family leave, welfare reform, national service, the Brady Bill, and China's accession to the World Trade Organization. But consider a longer list of major initiatives that have been rejected or have sunk from sight: comprehensive health reform, Social Security reform, Medicare reform, campaign finance reform, tobacco, the Comprehensive Test Ban Treaty, continued fast-track authority in trade, and the Kyoto environmental accords. His record as a legislative leader is definitely mixed.

And then there is the matter of ethics. I have before me a five-volume set entitled *Whitewater,* containing editorials and articles from the *Wall Street Journal* dating back to Clinton's early days. Granted that the *Journal* editorial page is rabidly anti-Clinton. Granted that many charges against him proved baseless and his Republican accusers went too far. But no one can read the record without feeling depressed.

Ironically, what may yet enhance Clinton's stature as a leader is something he has always believed in the most: the future. When Clinton was an undergraduate at Georgetown University, a rather eccentric professor, Carroll Quigley, who taught a mandatory course on Western civilization, heavily influenced him. The highlight of the course was Quigley's lecture on "future preference," in which he argued that progress has depended on people's willingness to sacrifice today in order to secure a better life tomorrow. "Future preference. Don't ever forget that." As biographer David Maraniss points out, Clinton rarely delivered a speech thereafter that did not draw upon Quigley's lecture. He has always believed that if one works hard every day, as he has, the future will be brighter than today.

And so it may be for his reputation. Clinton's star dimmed as he was leaving office, partly because of Gore's close loss in the election, mostly because of his own mistakes. Yet it could wax again if the Democrats recapture control of Congress and the White House in the next few years, especially if the New Democrats are the driving force behind their revival. Before Clinton's victory in 1992, Democrats had lost five of the past six presidential elections; if they win in 2004, they can claim two of the past three, and Clinton could argue that he helped his party defy history. As political scientist Stephen Skowronek has shown, national political movements are usually launched by a dramatic presidential leader but then lose steam over time until presidents who serve at the tail end fizzle out. Clinton was at the tail end of the movement that FDR started and might have been expected to have lasted but a single term, al a Jimmy Carter. Instead, he swept to reelection by refashioning the Democrats, making them more competative and broadly based. As recently as 1980, the Democrats were widely seen as an assortment of minority groups and special interests; today, while continuing to represent minorities, the party has become more representative of the middle class.

Clinton has reason to hope that he has changed the face of international politics as well. The elections of Thatcher in 1979 and Reagan in 1980 triggered a rise in conservative parties in both Europe and North America. By embracing the "Third Way" for their parties, Clinton in the United States and British prime minister Tony Blair have pushed the pendulum in the other direction. Third-way politics became the rage in Europe in the 1990s, so that by the end of the decade, a revitalized left-of-center party ran every major country in Western Europe aside from Spain. Clinton and Blair are both entitled to claim considerable credit.

In future decades, historians may also ask whether Clinton has been more farsighted than he seems today. He has introduced a style of leadership that drives traditionalists to distraction. Rather than having a clear set of goals and principles, as Reagan did, Clinton seems to absorb everyone else's ideas, pick and choose among them, and come up with an ever-changing agenda. There seem to be no ultimate truths in his world and few core beliefs. Those who are more traditional—I am one—prefer that Henry Adams view of a president seeking a helm to grasp, a course to steer, a port to seek.

But we must recognize that there is an alternative view gaining currency today, at least in academic circles. Postmodernism holds that social truths are an artifact of culture and are "socially constructed" by elites, who fashion them to fit their own advantages, as Kenneth J. Gergen has argued. For example, women for centuries were thought prone to hysteria and naturally subordinate. We now recognize that belief was socially manufactured by men and allowed them to maintain their own dominance. By the same token, we live

341

today in a culture with a multiplicity of voices, all espousing their own truths. Clinton's strength, say the postmodernists, is that he is willing to listen and to distill from them policies that are more enlightened than if he were the captive of one ideology. In effect, Clinton is our first postmodern president and should be celebrated as such. That is the argument. We are likely to see these debates play out vigorously in the years ahead.

What is certainly true is that Clinton's policies have advanced the causes of those whose voices have usually been drowned out—from women to blacks to gays and others. As modest as the steps have been at times, those groups now face a brighter future and, for that, he deserves credit.

Indeed, Clinton's greatest contribution may not be what he accomplished in the 1990s but how well he prepared the country for the decades that follow. That "bridge to the twenty-first century" may turn out to be pretty sturdy after all. Economic fundamentals are strong today, social conditions are improving, the world is at relative peace, and the country is poised on the edge of new scientific and technological revolutions. Who would have thought a decade ago the country would be in superb shape? While Bill Clinton will never escape opprobrium for his own past, perhaps one day he will receive generous credit for improving our future.

Conclusion _____

Seven Lessons
of Leadership

SOON AFTER A NEW PRESIDENT takes office, someone usually has a quiet word in his ear: "Did you know that there is still room up there on Mount Rushmore for one more face? At least a small profile." There isn't, in fact; the sixty-foot slabs are taken. But every president tries mightily to win a place equal to the four men remembered there.

In the eyes of historians, none of our recent occupants has come close. Following a tradition started by his father, Arthur Schlesinger, Jr., surveyed thirty-two fellow historians in December 1996, asking them to rate the presidents. Washington, Lincoln, and Franklin Roosevelt once again swept the boards. Jefferson, Jackson, Polk, Teddy Roosevelt, Wilson, and Truman were considered "near great." What was striking was the decline since Truman. His three successors—Eisenhower, Kennedy, and Johnson—barely made it into the top half of the class, scoring "above average." All six presidents thereafter were in the bottom half. Ford, Carter, Reagan, Bush, and Clinton were marked "below average," and Nixon was deemed a "failure."

If that's the case, why should we bother to look for lessons of leadership among recent presidents? For starters, that may not be the case—or at least not for long. As Schlesinger himself has written, presidential reputations wax and wane. Truman and Eisenhower have risen significantly in esteem since leaving office. The same will 343 almost surely happen with Reagan (especially if more conservatives begin writing history), and signs of nostalgia are already popping up around Ford and Bush. Even Clinton may rise in historical estimation.

The larger point is that we need to face reality: it's a lot tougher for anyone to lead the country today than it was in the first half of the twentieth century. Expectations of what a president can accomplish have escalated dramatically, while his capacity for action has diminished even more. A White House today must keep its eye on half a dozen trouble spots around the world and help to steer an international economy, all the while taking responsibility for violence in schools and monitoring research into the human genome. Something is bound to go wrong somewhere, and when it does, a hungry press corps will give relentless chase and partisans in Congress will march cabinet secretaries to Capitol Hill. "It must be realized," Machiavelli wrote, "that there is nothing more difficult to plan, more uncertain of success, or more dangerous to manage than the establishment of a new order of government." And that was long before lobbyists could spend millions on grassroots campaigns to block a president. Not since 1986 has Congress passed bipartisan, blockbuster legislation—the reform of the tax code. No wonder the queue is short for Mount Rushmore.

But that's all the more reason to study the experiences of our recent presidents—to see what worked, what failed, and what can be learned by their successors. Understanding the past is essential to mastering the future. The next twenty years or so will be crucial in shaping the twenty-first century. As the forces of democratic capitalism sweep the world and as technology and science hold out new promise, we may be on the threshold of a new golden age. What could make the difference is the quality of our leadership, starting in the presidency. We need men and women in that job and in the White House who know what it takes to mobilize the energies of the country and can apply themselves with wisdom. There are no off-the-shelf manuals for presidents, but there are rich lessons to be gleaned from past experience.

I do not pretend here to have the final word on any of the four presidents I have served. Their private papers will not be fully opened for some years, and even then will not give us a complete picture. President Kennedy was once sent an inquiry asking him to join a group of historians in assessing past presidents. He exploded in irritation. "How the hell can they know?" he said. "They've never had to sit here, reading all the cables, listening to people all day about these problems." He had a point. The most any of us can offer is our best sense of the picture.

344

My sense is that even if we do not know the details, certain broad conclusions about leadership can be drawn from recent presidents. All the way along in this book, I have offered observations that seemed pertinent. There is no space to review each of them here, but it might be helpful to boil them down to those that are the most essential.

In my judgment, there are seven keys to responsible and effective leadership in the White House. They apply whether the administration is Democratic or Republican, liberal or conservative. In fact, they apply as well to leaders of most other organizations—CEOs, university presidents, military generals, and heads of nonprofit institutions.

1. Leadership Starts from Within

Richard Nixon and Bill Clinton were the two most gifted presidents of the past thirty years. Each was inordinately bright, well read, and politically savvy. Each reveled in power. Nixon was the best strategist in the office since Eisenhower and possibly since Woodrow Wilson; Clinton was the best tactician since Lyndon Johnson and possibly Franklin Roosevelt. Yet each was the author of his own downfall. Nixon let his demons gain ascendance, and Clinton could not manage the fault lines in his character. They were living proof that before mastering the world, a leader must achieve self-mastery. Or, as Heraclitus put it more succinctly, "Character is destiny."

The inner soul of a president flows into every aspect of his leadership far more than is generally recognized. His passions in life usually form the basis for his central mission in office. Nixon's search for a "lasting structure of peace" grew out of his dream of becoming a world statesman, just as the hardscrabble youth of LBJ led to his pursuit of a Great Society. We know, too, that the character of a leader heavily influences his decision-making—both how and what he decides. Ford's pardon of Nixon grew out of his own decency. Reagan showed us the degree to which personality shapes rhetoric as well as the ability of a president to work with Congress and the press. In Nixon and Clinton, we saw that the character of a president also determines the character of his White House—that the men and women around him take their cues from the man in the center. Finally—and most importantly—the character of a president determines the integrity of his public life.

In his small classic, *On Leadership*, John W. Gardner assembles a

345

list of fourteen personal attributes that he believes are important for leaders, public and private. He draws from his own experience as well as from scholars in the field such as Ralph Stogdill, Bernard Bass, and Edwin P. Hollander. A president certainly needs a high measure of all the qualities that Gardner lists: physical vitality; intelligence and judgment-in-action; a willingness to accept responsibilities; task competence; an understanding of followers and their needs; skill in dealing with people; a need to achieve; a capacity to motivate; courage and steadiness; a capacity to win and hold trust; a capacity to manage and set priorities; confidence; assertiveness; and an adaptability of approach.

Of these, integrity is the most important for a president. As former senator Alan Simpson said in introducing Gerald Ford at Harvard a year ago: "If you have integrity, nothing else matters. If you don't have integrity, nothing else matters."

People can reasonably debate how virtuous a public leader must be in private life. Some believe that if a politician has erred in his adult life—by committing adultery, for example—he should be disqualified from high office: "If his wife can't trust him, we can't either." But experience suggests that this standard sets the bar higher than we need or should expect. Consider Franklin Roosevelt. Twenty years after he died, Americans learned for the first time that the Roosevelts did not have a perfect marriage. FDR was a father of five when he had a passionate affair with Lucy Mercer that nearly destroyed his marriage. He broke off the relationship, but it was Lucy, not Eleanor, who was with him on the day of his fatal stroke, and as Doris Kearns Goodwin points out, Eleanor bore the burden of the affair for over forty years. Despite this relationship—and perhaps others—FDR emerged as the greatest president of the twentieth century.

How can one resolve these dilemmas about private virtue? There is no easy or simple answer. The rule that journalists used to apply before the new era of sensationalism has always seemed best to me: when a politician's private life interferes with the way he conducts himself in public, we should draw the line. If he drinks too much, is licentious, uses hard drugs, gambles himself into debt—those go too far. Otherwise, we should show greater tolerance and respect for human foibles. Bill Clinton went over the line not because he had sexual relations but because he engaged a White House intern in the Oval Office and then blatantly lied about it.

While there is room for disagreement about private life, there can be none about the conduct of public life. To govern, a president must have the trust of the public and people within the system. And trust does not come with the job anymore; it must be earned. It is thus vital that a president be truthful and accountable for his actions and insist that his staff meet the same rigorous standards. The government has a right to remain silent on matters of sensitivity, but no right to lie—unless the survival of the nation is at stake—and no right to mislead through excessive spin. Those who preach otherwise do violence to democratic principles.

Beyond personal integrity, it is especially important that the nation's chief executive rank high in what political scientist Everett Carll Ladd called "presidential intelligence"—that ineffable blend of knowledge, judgment, temperament, and faith in the future that leads to wise decisions and responsible leadership. It is dangerous, of course, to have a president who is ignorant of the world and of history. But if brains were the only criterion, Nixon, Carter, and Clinton would have been our best presidents of recent years. Rather, as we saw with Reagan, it is a combination of core competence and emotional intelligence that is a better predictor of effectiveness.

Equally important for presidential leadership is courage. No one can succeed in today's politics unless he or she is prepared to fall on a sword in a good cause. Nixon would never have opened the door to China if he lacked guts, nor would Reagan have survived a bullet and hastened the end of the Cold War, nor would Clinton have ended the deficits and secured the passage of NAFTA. Courage must be tempered by prudence, of course—something that was lacking in the Clinton health care plan—but the sine qua non of leadership is inner strength.

2. A Central, Compelling Purpose

Just as a president must have strong character, he must be of clear purpose. He must tell the country where he is heading so he can rally people behind him. Lincoln's purpose was to save the Union, FDR's to end the Depression and then to win the war. People could say in a single sentence what their presidencies were all about. Among recent executives, only Reagan was clear about his central goals—to reduce taxes, reduce spending, cut regulations, reduce the deficit, and increase the defense budget. By campaigning on those goals, he not only won a mandate but also made substantial progress toward their achievement (with the conspicuous exception of the budget deficit). By contrast, consider Ford, Carter, Bush, and Clinton. They

347

had high hopes, too, but never articulated a central, compelling purpose for their presidencies, and they all suffered as a result.

A president's central purpose must also be rooted in the nation's core values. They can be found in the Declaration of Independence. As G. K. Chesterton famously observed, "America is the only nation in the world that is founded on a creed. That creed is set forth with dogmatic and even theological lucidity in the Declaration of Independence." All of our greatest presidents have gone there for inspirational strength. Lincoln said he never had a political sentiment that did not spring from it. It was not intended to be a statement of who we are but of what we dream of becoming, realizing that the journey never ends. It is our communal vision. That's why a president, unlike a CEO, need not reinvent the national vision upon taking office. He should instead give fresh life to the one we have, applying it to the context of the times, leading the nation forward to its greater fulfillment. The reason Martin Luther King was so powerful when he declared, "I have a dream," was that he was standing at the Lincoln Memorial challenging us to carry out the promises of the Declaration.

Presidents depart from the nation's core values at their peril. The Clintons' health care plan failed in large part because it went against the grain. By contrast, FDR knew his Social Security plan was a sharp departure from past tradition but cleverly structured it so that the government did not pay for it out of general revenues; rather he designed it so that people "saved" for their own future. Making the plan consistent with core values was the secret to its passage.

3. A Capacity to Persuade

For most of the country's history, it didn't matter much whether a president could mobilize the public. From Jefferson until Wilson, the annual State of the Union was a written report to Congress. Even through Truman and Eisenhower, it was more important to be a good broker among interests than a good speaker. Television changed everything. Kennedy and Reagan now stand out in the public mind as the most memorable speakers of the late twentieth century because they were masters of the medium. They both had a capacity to persuade a mass audience through television, and in Reagan's case, he turned it into a powerful weapon to achieve his legislative goals.

If anything, the danger today is that presidents blab on so much that their audiences tune out. George Bush actually gave more public talks per year than Reagan, and Clinton has delivered more than both of them combined. In 1997, Clinton delivered 545 public speeches. He is unusually good at explaining complex public policy issues in simple terms that connect with his audiences, so that in any given forum, he is highly effective. But overexposure has dulled his impact.

4. An Ability to Work within the System

A common mistake among political consultants today is to believe that the only thing that counts in governing anymore is public persuasion. Television has become an indispensable tool for leadership, but as Reagan's success showed, it is still important that a president and his team be effective in working with other elements of our democratic system. Congress remains a coequal branch of government, and the press acts like one.

In effect, a president should see himself as the center of a web. Surrounding him are six different institutional forces with whom he must form successful working relationships, whether by cooperation, charm, or persuasion. The public, Congress, and the press are obviously the most critical. But there are other players who must also be approached with political savvy: foreign powers, domestic interest groups, and domestic elites. All of these outside players expect to have a place at his table and to share in decision-making; most of them will put their own needs first. No one in the twentieth century was better at juggling these many groups than Franklin Roosevelt. He was, as James MacGregor Burns wrote, both the lion and the fox, and that accounted in large measure for his extraordinary success.

Among recent executives, it is surprising how often that lesson has been lost. Nixon, Carter, and Clinton all seemed to thumb their nose at institutions like Congress, the press, and the political elite of Washington. It is difficult enough to govern in today's climate, but they managed to make it almost impossible by doubling the resistance to their agendas. Future presidents ought to go to school on FDR's success in the New Deal, Harry Truman's passage of the Marshall Plan, LBJ's victories in the civil rights bills of 1964 and 1965, and Reagan's passage of his economic program.

349

5. A Sure, Quick Start

If contemporary experience has taught us anything, surely it is the need for a president to "hit the ground running." The difference between Reagan's quick start and Clinton's stumbles put one on the path toward a succession of legislative triumphs and the other on the road to a debacle in health care and a loss of Congress. Had Clinton not been as agile as he was in recovering in late 1993 and then again in 1995–1996, he would have been a one-term president. As it was, he never became the transformational figure he had hoped.

In most institutions, the power of a leader grows over time. A CEO, a university president, the head of a union, acquire stature through the quality of their long-term performance. The presidency is just the opposite: power tends to evaporate quickly. It's not that a president must rival Franklin Roosevelt in his First Hundred Days, but his first months in office—up to the August recess of Congress—are usually the widest window of opportunity he will have, even if he serves two full terms. That's why he has to move fast.

Achieving a smooth, successful start is more arduous than it looks. Those who have been well schooled in national life have a definite advantage. FDR, LBJ, and Reagan knew how to pull the levers of power before they got to the White House; Carter and Clinton had to learn on the job. The campaign itself must also be focused on governing. By giving voters a clear sense of what they wanted to do in office, LBJ in 1964 and Reagan in 1980 both won mandates that greatly strengthened their hands in the months that followed. By contrast, Reagan never sought a mandate in the 1984 campaign, and his second term never matched his first. A well-run transition is a less appreciated but equally important element. Had Clinton settled down in the eleven weeks between his election and inauguration, he would have arrived in Washington with a more experienced White House team, a game plan for his first weeks in office, and a storehouse of personal energy. He lacked all three.

6. Strong, Prudent Advisers

When George Washington was preparing his third annual message to Congress, as biographer Richard Brookhiser has pointed out, he first took suggestions from James Madison and Thomas Jefferson.

He then asked Alexander Hamilton to draw up a first draft, which went back to Madison for a rewrite. Not a bad lot.

The Washington experience underscores a repeated lesson from presidential history. The best presidents are ones who surround themselves with the best advisers. Lincoln wrote down the names of his potential cabinet on the night of his election and from them recruited a team that rivaled Washington's. Teddy Roosevelt, Franklin Roosevelt, Harry Truman—all were noted for the quality of the people around them. Of the presidents I have served, Reagan started with the best White House operation, and Ford wound up with the best cabinet. In each instance, one could see a palpable difference in the dynamics of their leadership.

In the future, we are likely to see the First Lady or the First Man exercise an ever-larger influence upon the political thinking of the president. Hillary Clinton is the first woman in the post with a professional degree, but she will be far from the last. The trend should be a welcome one: a president needs a friend in whom he can confide his private thoughts, and if that person is also an empathic, educated helpmate, all the better. The only caveat is whether the two keep their roles strictly separated. The Clinton experience should be lesson enough.

7. Inspiring Others to Carry On the Mission

One of the most instructive books about the leadership of Franklin Roosevelt starts with his death. Historian William Leuchtenburg shows that the next eight presidents after him all lived in his shadow. Three of them—Truman, Kennedy, and Johnson—were Democrats who consciously set out to complete the New Deal. Two—Eisenhower and Nixon—were Republicans who accepted it and even added on to it. In fact, Nixon was in many ways the last of the New Deal presidents. Even Reagan, who rejected the Great Society, didn't want to disturb the work of his first political hero and adopted much of his leadership style.

The point is that the most effective presidents create a living legacy, inspiring legions of followers to carry on their mission long after they are gone. Among contemporary presidents, only Reagan has come close to doing that. While he never built a coalition to match FDR's, he put a stamp upon his party and upon the nation's political culture that shapes it still. 351

As political scientist Stephen Skowronek has demonstrated, there is a pattern to the way presidents like Jefferson, Jackson, Lincoln, FDR, and Reagan have created a new politics. In each case, they came into power by knocking down an old orthodoxy and in its place built what is now popularly called "a new paradigm." Roosevelt gave the boot to laissez-faire and put government at the helm of the economy. Reagan shifted the balance away from a government-centered system and embraced an entrepreneurial culture. They also built new political movements and created cadres of loyal followers who would pick up their banner when they fell. Inevitably, they also left behind an agenda of unfinished work that subsequent presidents tried to complete.

Today's politics is ripe for a president to come into office and offer "a new paradigm." There may not be an old orthodoxy to knock down; no single regime of ideas is now dominant. But the winds of change are blowing so hard that voters are eager to find a leader who will set forth a clear, steady path into the future. The next president who does that successfully will also be the next to have a living legacy.

THERE ARE, as we have seen over the course of this book, a good many other lessons that recent experience suggests about leadership, but the seven enumerated here seem fundamental. They are the principles upon which to build. They do not guarantee success. Certainly, they offer no guarantee of producing a new candidate for Mount Rushmore. Great crises usually bring forth great leaders, as Abigail Adams once observed, and, for now, neither war nor depression is looming. But these principles do hold out the promise that if they are followed, the nation might once again enjoy a steady stream of presidents who are strong, honest, and effective. Who can ask for more? We might just find that new golden age.

Notes

Preface

11   "with a great shout": James C. Humes, *Instant Eloquence: A Lazy Man's Guide to Public Speaking* (New York: Harper & Row, 1973), p. 223.
11   Just after World War I: Samuel P. Huntington, *The Third Wave: Democratization in the Late Twentieth Century* (Norman, OK: University of Oklahoma Press, 1991), p. 26.
11   John Keegan writes: John Keegan, "Winston Churchill," *Time*, April 13, 1998, p. 114.
12   Arthur Schlesinger, Jr., points out: Arthur Schlesinger, Jr., *The Cycles of American History* (Boston: Houghton Mifflin, 1986), p. 421.
14   Daniel Patrick Moynihan offered a farewell: Ray Price, *With Nixon* (New York: Viking Press, 1977), p. 214.

RICHARD NIXON

1. The Stuff of Shakespeare

19   Arthur Schlesinger, Jr., asked: Arthur M. Schlesinger, Jr., "The Ultimate Approval Rating," *New York Times Magazine*, December 12, 1996, p. 46.
19   "Look," he deadpanned: Stephen E. Ambrose, *Nixon: Ruin and Recovery 1973–1990* (New York: Simon & Schuster, 1991), p. 545.
19   He calls Senator Edward M. Kennedy: John Aloysius Farrell, "Nixon Ranted Against Mass. Democrats, Tapes Show Vietnam Opposition Angered President," *Boston Globe*, October 15, 1999, p. A3.
20   Tip O'Neill: ibid.
20   The Supreme Court is: Ben Macintyre, "Nixon Tapes Testify to Deep Hatred of Jews," *Times* (London), October 7, 1999, p. 21.
20   Nixon rants: ibid.
20   Justice Potter Stewart: George Lardner, Jr., and Michael Dobbs, "New Nixon Tapes Are Released; Depth of President's Antisemitism Detailed," *Washington Post*, October 6, 1999, p. A31.
20   "The Jews": ibid.

20   he instructs Haldeman: Associated Press, October 7, 1999.

20   There are exceptions: George Lardner and Dobbs, "New Nixon Tapes Are Released."

20   Talking about Daniel Ellsberg: Associated Press, October 7, 1999.

20   Ray Price, his principal speechwriter: Ray Price, *With Nixon* (New York: Viking Press, 1977), p. 18.

20   Herbert Stein said: Charles Krauthammer, "Nixon on the Couch," *Washington Post*, op-ed, October 15, 1999, p. A29.

20   Leonard Garment, a former Wall Street lawyer: "Richard Nixon, Unedited," *New York Times*, October 19, 1999, p. 23, col. 2.

21   "seething cauldron of inchoate hatreds": Krauthammer, "Nixon on the Couch."

21   Age of Nixon: Herbert S. Parmet, *Richard Nixon and His America* (Boston: Little, Brown, 1990), p. 620.

21   "I gave them a sword": Interview with David Frost, May 4, 1977.

27   Ike confided his darkest thoughts: Stephen E. Ambrose, "Dwight D. Eisenhower," in Robert A. Wilson, ed., *Character Above All: Ten Presidents from FDR to George Bush* (New York: Simon & Schuster, 1996), p. 80.

28   James Goldman's title: James Goldman, *The Lion in Winter: A Comedy in Two Acts* (New York: Samuel French, 1966).

29   Haldeman recounts: H. R. Haldeman with Joseph DiMona, *The Ends of Power* (New York: Times Books, 1978), p. 73.

30   "each day [is] a chance": Parmet, *Richard Nixon and his America*, p. 565.

31   Bill Safire provided: William Safire, *Before the Fall: An Inside View of the Pre-Watergate White House* (New York: Doubleday, 1975), pp. 96–99.

2. The Bright Side

34   Fred Greenstein's book: Fred I. Greenstein, *The Hidden-Hand Presidency: Eisenhower as Leader* (New York: Basic Books, 1982).

34   Nixon, ever the student: Richard Nixon, *Leaders* (New York: Warner Books, 1982).

37   The book that emerged: Richard Nixon, *Six Crises* (Garden City, NY: Doubleday, 1962).

37   "De Gaulle in his 'wilderness' years": Nixon, *Leaders*, p. 329.

38   "withdrawal and return": Richard Nixon, *In the Arena: A Memoir of Defeat and Renewal* (New York: Simon & Schuster, 1990), p. 26.

38   "the hero's journey": Joseph Campbell, *The Hero with a Thousand Faces* (New York: Pantheon, 1949).

39   Tom Wicker: Tom Wicker, *One of Us: Richard Nixon and the American Dream* (New York: Random House, 1991), pp. 80–110.

41   "a beaten man": Nixon notes, Nixon Presidential Materials, National Archives, August 8, 1974.

41   Robert Blake's biography: Robert Blake, *Disraeli* (New York: St. Martin's Press, 1966).

41   "He commented": H. R. Haldeman, *The Haldeman Diaries: Inside the Nixon White House* (New York: G. P. Putnam's Sons, 1994), p. 271.

42   "inspired people, charged them up": ibid., p. 147.

42   Heifetz: Ronald A. Heifetz, *Leadership Without Easy Answers* (Cambridge, MA: Belknap Press, 1994), p. 252.

42   In his book: Nixon, *In the Arena*, p. 221.

43   one of our best speechwriters: James C. Humes, *Instant Eloquence: A Lazy Man's Guide to Public Speaking* (New York: Harper & Row, 1973).

44   historian Melvin Small: Melvin Small, *The Presidency of Richard Nixon*, American Presidency Series (Lawrence, KS: University Press of Kansas, 1999), p. 185.

44   Invited to the Elysée: Richard Nixon, *RN: The Memoirs of Richard Nixon* (New York: Grosset & Dunlap, 1978), p. 249.

44   "The machine controls our destiny": Nixon, *Leaders*, p. 46.

45   "France cannot be France without greatness": "Living Large," *Wall Street Journal,* November 3, 1993, p. A22.

46   *The Edge of the Sword:* Charles de Gaulle, *The Edge of the Sword* (New York: Criterion Books, 1960).

46   "a manual for leadership": Nixon, *Leaders,* p. 45.

46   "a spirit of confidence": ibid., p. 51.

46   "First and foremost": ibid., pp. 51–52.

47   a memorandum from Haldeman: "Memo of the Month," *Washington Monthly,* November 1973, p. 46.

48   Bob Haldeman records in his memoirs: H. R. Haldeman with Joseph Di-Mona, *The Ends of Power* (New York: Times Books, 1978), p. 83.

49   biographer Joan Hoff: Joan Hoff, *Nixon Reconsidered* (New York: Basic-Books, 1994).

50   "The first act of a leader": Max DePree, *Leadership Is an Art* (Garden City, NY: Doubleday, 1989), p. 11

52   Nixon's principal environmental adviser: "Nixon's Domestic Policy: Both Liberal and Bold in Retrospect," *Presidential Studies Quarterly,* vol. 26, no. 1 (Winter 1996), p. 149.

53   After the library gathering: David Gergen, "The Restless Spirit of Richard Nixon," *U.S. News & World Report,* July 30, 1990, p. 24.

53   Peggy Noonan compared: Peggy Noonan, *What I Saw at the Revolution: A Political Life in the Reagan Era* (New York: Random House, 1990), p. 310.

55   Kissinger laments: Henry Kissinger, *The White House Years* (Boston: Little, Brown, 1982), p. 1095.

55   Haldeman confided to his diaries: Haldeman, *The Haldeman Diaries,* p. 168.

57   he wrote a piece on Asia: Richard Nixon, "Asia After Viet Nam," *Foreign Affairs,* October 1967, pp. 111–25.

58   his first words: author's notes.

61   "The devious and deceitful ways": Small, *The Presidency of Richard Nixon,* p. 309.

61   "his greatest claim to glory": Tad Szulc, *The Illusion of Peace: Foreign Policy in the Nixon Years* (New York: Viking Press, 1978), p. 9.

63   Herbert Stein explained: Erwin C. Hargrove and Samuel A. Morley, eds., *The President and the Council of Economic Advisers: Interviews with CEA Chairmen* (Boulder, CO: Westview Press, 1984), p. 367.

63   the EPA has presided over impressive changes: *Twenty-five Years of Environmental Progress* (Washington, DC: Environmental Protection Agency, 1998).

64   In 1968, some 68 percent of African-American children: Nixon, *RN: The Memoirs of Richard Nixon,* p. 439.

64   Writes Tom Wicker, a southern liberal: Wicker, *One of Us,* p. 506.

3. Why He Fell

65   "but if he has": Merle Miller, *Plain Speaking: An Oral Biography of Harry S. Truman* (New York: G. P. Putnam's Sons, 1973), p. 335.

75   "the man in the arena": Richard Nixon, *Leaders* (New York: Warner Books, 1982), p. 345.

76   Larry Sabato: Larry J. Sabato and Glenn R. Simpson, *Dirty Little Secrets: The Persistence of Corruption in American Politics* (New York: Random House, 1996), pp. 10–18.

76   "there's no doubt": Joel Achenbach, "Rewind to 1972: The Reel Richard Nixon," *Washington Post,* May 4, 1994, p. C1.

77   "I have decided": Herbert S. Parmet, *Richard Nixon and His America* (Boston: Little, Brown, 1990), p. 560.

77   Billy Graham has written: Billy Graham, *Just as I Am: The Autobiography of Billy Graham* (San Francisco: HarperCollins, 1997), p. 456.

77   Herbert Parmet writes: Parmet, *Richard Nixon and His America*, pp. 6–12.

77   eight-page memorandum: Nixon Presidential Materials, National Archives.

78   "You must remember": ibid.

80   "pink right down to her underwear": Stephen E. Ambrose, *Nixon: The Education of a Politician, 1913–1962* (New York: Simon & Schuster, 1987), p. 22.

81   "without great men": Nixon, *Leaders*, pp. 320–21.

82   "has to bring to his work": ibid., p. 321.

82   "Once he has the reins": ibid.

82   "History has had its share": ibid., p. 322.

82   "In evaluating a leader": ibid., p. 324.

82   "Let us be clear": ibid., p. 327.

82   "the average American": Stephen E. Ambrose, *Nixon: Ruin and Recovery, 1973–1990* (New York: Simon & Schuster, 1991), pp. 12–13.

83   "humdrum existence": H. R. Haldeman, *The Haldeman Diaries: Inside the Nixon White House* (New York: G. P. Putnam's Sons, 1994), p. 258.

83   "Because the leader is busy": Nixon, *Leaders*, p. 332.

84   Melvin Small notes: Melvin Small, *The Presidency of Richard Nixon* (Lawrence, KS: University Press of Kansas, 1999), p. 228.

84   in *Politics:* Aristotle, *Politics* (Oxford: Clarendon Press, 1926).

84   Erwin C. Hargrove argues: Erwin C. Hargrove, *The President as Leader: Appealing to the Better Angels of Our Nature* (Lawrence, KS: University Press of Kansas, 1998), p. 4.

84   After struggling for years: Richard Brookhiser, *Founding Father: Rediscovering George Washington* (New York: The Free Press, 1996), p. 133.

85   "the spirit of their constitution": Hargrove, *The President as Leader*, p. 4.

85   "In domestic terms": Raymond K. Price Jr., "The Nixon Presidency: Some Mitigating Circumstances," in Kenneth W. Thompson, ed., *The Nixon Presidency: Twenty-two Intimate Perspectives of Richard M. Nixon* (Lanham, MD: University Press of America, 1987), p. 384.

87   "What a strange man was Richard Nixon": Stephen E. Ambrose, *Nixon: The Triumph of a Politician, 1962–1972* (New York: Simon & Schuster, 1989), p. 330.

87   "They're bastards": Haldeman, *The Haldeman Diaries*, p. 309.

88   "We have yet to fire": ibid.

88   "screw our political enemies": Ambrose, *Nixon: The Triumph of a Politician, 1962–1972*, p. 409.

89   "You won't have Nixon": Parmet, *Richard Nixon and His America*, pp. 429–30.

89   "a free shave": Stephen Hess and Sandy Northrup, *Drawn and Quartered: The History of American Political Cartoons* (Montgomery, AL: Elliot & Clark, 1996), p. 121.

89   "hated and beaten": William Safire, *Before the Fall: An Inside View of the Pre-Watergate White House* (Garden City, NY: Doubleday, 1975), p. 343.

89   "In his indulgence": ibid.

91   Stephen Ambrose points out: Ambrose, *Nixon: The Triumph of a Politician, 1962–1972*, p. 273.

97   "damned good government": Kenneth Franklin Kurz, *Nixon's Enemies* (Los Angeles: Lowell House, 1998), p. 285.

97   July 21, 1969: Haldeman, *The Haldeman Diaries*, p. 74.

98   November 3, 1969: ibid., p. 104.

98   March 4, 1970: ibid., p. 134.

98 March 10, 1970: ibid., p. 136.
98 April 9, 1970: ibid., p. 148.
98 July 25, 1970: ibid., p. 185.
98 September 12, 1970: ibid., p. 193.
98 November 25, 1970: ibid., p. 213.
98 December 5, 1970: ibid., p. 215.
98 May 28, 1971: ibid., p. 293.
98 June 23, 1971: ibid., p. 305.
99 September 13, 1971: ibid., p. 353.
99 according to Stephen Ambrose: Stephen Ambrose, *Nixon: The Triumph of a Politician, 1962–1972* (New York: Simon & Schuster, 1989), p. 447.
99 "It shows you're a weakling": H. R. Haldeman with Joseph DiMona, *The Ends of Power* (New York: Times Books, 1978) p. 110.
99 "I don't care how": Ambrose, *Nixon: The Triumph of a Politician, 1962–1972*, p. 448.
99 "If we can't get anyone": Haldeman with DiMona, *The Ends of Power*, p. 112.
100 "So this is the spine": author interview with Leonard Garment, *The NewsHour with Jim Lehrer*, PBS, June 19, 1997.
101 Victor Lasky: Victor Lasky, *It Didn't Start with Watergate* (New York: The Dial Press, 1977).
102 "the King must be": "Traditional Justice and Demands of the 20th Century," *Times* (London), July 31, 1993.
103 "I get a lot of advice": Haldeman, *The Haldeman Diaries*, p. 311.
104 "Today is a day": William Hamilton and Christine Spolar, "Richard Nixon's Long Journey Ends; Clinton Stresses Totality of His Life," *Washington Post*, April 28, 1994, p. A1.

GERALD FORD

4. A MAN OF CHARACTER

108 "our most underrated": James Cannon, "Gerald Ford: 1974–1977," in Robert A. Wilson, ed., *Character Above All: Ten Presidents from FDR to George Bush* (New York: Simon & Schuster, 1985), p. 171.
108 *New York* magazine: Richard Reeves, "Jerry Ford and His Flying Circus: A Presidential Diary," *New York*, November 25, 1974, pp. 42–46.
108 "Ford is slow": Richard Reeves, *A Ford, Not a Lincoln* (New York: Harcourt Brace Jovanovich, 1975), p. 26.
108 "a safe man": ibid., p. 3.
109 "No journalist did more": John Robert Greene, *The Presidency of Gerald Ford* (Lawrence, KS: University Press of Kansas, 1995), p. 62.
109 "I'm Sorry, Mr. President": Richard Reeves, "I'm Sorry, Mr. President," *American Heritage*, December 1, 1996, p. 62.
109 "couldn't fart and chew gum": Reeves, *A Ford, Not a Lincoln*, p. 25.
110 "Truth is the glue": James M. Cannon, *Time and Chance: Gerald Ford's Appointment with History* (New York: HarperCollins, 1994), p. 235.
111 "more than any other man": ibid., p. xvi.
111 the memoirs of one of Ford's most intimate advisers: Robert T. Hartmann, *Palace Politics: An Inside Account of the Ford Years* (New York: McGraw-Hill, 1980).
115 "Ford to City: Drop Dead": *New York Daily News*, October 30, 1975.
117 "Ladies and gentlemen": Jerald F. terHorst, *Gerald Ford and the Future of the Presidency* (New York: The Third Press, 1974), p. 231.

118   "This one is going to be tough": ibid., pp. 232–33.
118   "I cannot in good conscience": ibid., p. 236.
118   In Pittsburgh: ibid., pp. 237–38.
118   Ford's popularity: ibid.
120   "enough is enough": Greene, *The Presidency of Gerald Ford*, p. 45.
121   "I do not think": Hartmann, *Palace Politics*, p. 254.
121   "asked for prayers for guidance": ibid., pp. 249–52.
121   "Outwardly, nobody was wildly enthusiastic": ibid., p. 261.
123   "I was spending 25 percent": author notes, Ford lecture, Kennedy School of Government, Harvard University, March 16, 1999.
124   "serious allegations and accusations": Hartmann, *Palace Politics*, p. 266.
124   Ford argues specifically: Gerald R. Ford, *A Time to Heal* (New York: Harper & Row, 1979), p. 173.
125   As the *New York Times* noted: ibid., p. 151.
126   "King of the Rock": James MacGregor Burns, *The Power to Lead: The Crisis of the American Presidency* (New York: Simon & Schuster, 1984). See especially chapter 5.
129   "the blooper": "The Blooper Heard Round the World," *Time*, October 18, 1976, p. 12.
130   "a powerful chief of staff": Ford, *A Time to Heal*, p. 147.
130   "It projects the openness you want": ibid., p. 186.
132   "The ayes have it": Hartmann, *Palace Politics*, pp. 183–84.
135   "The principal virtue": Fred I. Greenstein, ed., *Leadership in the Modern Presidency* (Cambridge, MA: Harvard University Press, 1988), p. 210.
137   "The use of history": Richard Neustadt and Ernest May, *Thinking in Time: The Uses of History for Decision Makers* (New York: The Free Press, 1986), p. xv.
138   "based on results": Greenstein, *Leadership in the Modern Presidency*, p. 214.
139   Ford's opening statement: Cannon, *Time and Chance*, p. 235.
139   "head-to-head confrontations" Ford, *A Time to Heal*, p. 87.
139   "We gave Nixon no choice": Cannon, "Gerald Ford," p. 158.
143   "the biggest political mistake": Cannon, "Gerald Ford," p. 170.
143   "a sense of personal openness": Michael P. Riccards, *The Ferocious Engine of Democracy: A History of the American Presidency*, vol. 2 (Lanham, MD: Madison Books, 1998), p. 345.
143   "the passive ways of Congress": ibid., p. 350.
144   correspondent Morley Safer: Betty Ford with Chris Chase, *The Times of My Life* (New York: Harper & Row, 1978), p. 206–7.
144   *Manchester Union-Leader:* ibid., p. 208.
144   "I thought I'd lost 10 million": ibid.
144   "Dear Morley": Sheila Rabb Weidenfeld, *First Lady's Lady: With the Fords in the White House* (New York: G. P. Putnam's Sons, 1979), p. 182.
145   she told Barbara Walters: Ford with Chase, *The Times of My Life*, p. 151.
146   "loneliest moment": Ford, *A Time to Heal*, p. 191.
146   "lying in the hospital": Ford with Chase, *The Times of My Life*, p. 194.
147   Standing there alone: Hartmann, *Palace Politics*, pp. 180–81.
148   "God has been good": Tip O'Neill with William Novak, *Man of the House: The Life and Political Memoirs of Speaker Tip O'Neill* (New York: Random House, 1987), p. 271.

RONALD REAGAN

5. The Natural

153   Bernard Malamud: Bernard Malamud, *The Natural* (New York: Farrar, Straus and Company, 1952).

153   an "amiable dunce": Hugh Sidey, "The Presidency: Learning to Judge Candidates," *Time*, October 24, 1983, p. 29.

153   "Errol Flynn of the B's": Lou Cannon, *President Reagan: The Role of a Lifetime* (New York: Simon & Schuster, 1991), p. 91.

155   living in a cobblestone era: James MacGregor Burns, *Cobblestone Leadership: Majority Rule, Minority Power* (Norman, OK: University of Oklahoma Press, 1990).

155   a collapse of confidence: Seymour Martin Lipset and William Schneider, *The Confidence Gap: Business, Labor, and Government in the Public Mind* (New York: The Free Press, 1983).

155   "Seven fat years": Robert L. Bartley, *The Seven Fat Years: And How to Do It Again* (New York: The Free Press, 1992).

156   Frances Perkins wrote: Frances Perkins, *The Roosevelt I Knew* (New York: Viking Press, 1946), p. 4.

157   Stephen Skowronek writes: Stephen Skowronek, *The Politics Presidents Make: Leadership from John Adams to George Bush* (Cambridge, MA: Belknap Press, 1993).

157   "the era of big government": Ann Devroy, "Clinton Embraces GOP Themes in Setting Agenda; 'Era of Big Government Is Over,' Clinton Tells Nation," *Washington Post*, January 24, 1996, p. A1.

158   "Rule I": Joseph Alsop, *FDR, 1882–1945: A Centenary Remembrance* (New York: Viking Press, 1982), p. 108.

161   "I paid for this microphone": Cannon, *President Reagan*, p. 123.

161   "a simple-minded man": David Herbert Donald, *Lincoln* (New York: Simon & Schuster, 1995), p. 149.

170   "give it all you can": Hedrick Smith, *The Power Game: How Washington Works* (New York: Random House, 1988), p. 333.

171   Steve Hess once wrote: Stephen Hess, *Organizing the Presidency* (Washington: Brookings Institution, 1988), p. 17.

171   "What do we do now?": Lou Cannon, *Reagan* (New York: G. P. Putnam's Sons, 1982), p. 119.

171   "It's just like Georgia": Smith, *The Power Game*, p. 338.

172   "go to the source": Lou Cannon, "Risks of a Scare Campaign," *Washington Post*, March 10, 1986, p. A2.

175   "I hope you're all Republicans": Cannon, *President Reagan*, p. 141.

175   "Honey, I forgot to duck": ibid., p. 123.

175   "All in all": ibid., p.142.

176   "why take a chance?": Lou Cannon, "The Truth in Reagan's Humor," *Washington Post*, April 27, 1987, p. A2.

176   "There is no right to strike": William Allen White, *A Puritan in Babylon: The Story of Calvin Coolidge* (New York: Macmillan Company, 1938), p. 166.

183   "There is no limit": Richard Norton Smith, "Heroic Modesty," *Wall Street Journal*, November 4, 1997, p. A20.

185   "He handles the media": Cannon, *President Reagan*, p. 116.

185   "We have been kinder": Mark Hertsgaard, *On Bended Knee: The Press and the Reagan Presidency* (New York: Farrar Straus Giroux, 1988), p. 3.

185   "I don't know how to explain": ibid., p. 4.

189   "told me after he was elected": Cannon, *President Reagan*, p. 114.

190 Speaker Tip O'Neill thought: David R. Gergen, "After Backstabbing, GOP Backs Gingrich, Sort Of," *Los Angeles Times,* August 27, 1997, p. M2.

191 Adam Clymer writes: Adam Clymer, *Edward M. Kennedy: A Biography* (New York: William Morrow and Company, 1999), p. 326.

192 "We have a leader": Henry Goddard Leach, "We Have a Leader," *Forum,* April 1933, p. 193.

193 "But 40 percent": Cannon, *President Reagan,* p. 496.

193 "[This 1981] show of leadership": ibid., pp. 496–97.

6. A ROOSEVELTIAN STYLE

194 "a near-hopeless hemophilic liberal": William E. Leuchtenburg, *In the Shadow of FDR: From Harry Truman to Bill Clinton* (Ithaca, NY: Cornell University Press, 1983), p. 215.

194 "learned new rhythms": Theodore Harold White, *America in Search of Itself: The Making of the President, 1956–1980* (New York: Harper & Row, 1982), p. 242.

195 "No President ever": Geoffrey C. Ward, *A First-Class Temperament: The Emergence of Franklin Roosevelt* (New York: Harper & Row, 1989), p. xxi.

195 "You know": ibid., p. xii.

196 "Roosevelt without the polio": Garry Wills, *Certain Trumpets: The Call of Leaders* (New York: Simon & Schuster, 1994), p. 37.

197 "On the assumption": Fred I. Greenstein, *The Hidden-Hand Presidency: Eisenhower as Leader* (New York: Basic Books, 1982), p. 354.

198 "The riddle of Reagan's intelligence": Lou Cannon, *President Reagan: The Role of a Lifetime* (New York: Simon & Schuster, 1991), p. 137.

199 "Others who have struggled": ibid., p. 138.

199 "The higher the rank": Daniel Goleman, "What Makes a Leader?," *Harvard Business Review,* November–December 1998, p. 94.

201 "a talent for happiness": Cannon, *President Reagan,* p. 793.

201 "He gave confidence": Leuchtenburg, *In the Shadow of FDR,* p. 214

202 "This guy has a handshake": Cannon, *President Reagan: The Role of a Lifetime,* p. 173.

202 a graying Tarzan: Ronald Reagan, "How to Stay Fit," *Parade,* December 4, 1983, pp. 6–8.

205 "We don't have the technology": Frances Fitzgerald, *Way Out There in the Blue: Reagan, Star Wars, and the End of the Cold War* (New York: Simon & Schuster 2000), p. 205.

205 "We weren't ready": Hedrick Smith, *The Power Game: How Washington Works* (New York: Random House, 1988), p. 613.

205 "a very dangerous spot": "SDI, Chernobyl Helped End Cold War, Conference Told," *Washington Post,* February 27, 1993, p. A17.

206 "I think he saw SDI": "Reagan," *American Experience,* PBS, February 23, 1998.

206 "Reagan's decision to go ahead": Holger Jensen, "Thatcher Says 'Star Wars' Key to Ending Cold War," *Rocky Mountain News,* October 10, 1995, p. 6A.

206 Hedrick Smith: Smith, *The Power Game,* p. 604.

207 "I have no expectation" Sherry Kuczynski, "Leaders and Success: President Franklin D. Roosevelt," *Investor's Business Daily,* February 19, 1998, p. A1.

209 "a war on poverty": David Hoffman, "Prospect of Arms Race Cited; Reagan Sees It as Factor in Soviets' Return to Talks," *Washington Post,* January 24, 1985, p. A14.

7. Secrets of the Great Communicator

210   "Of all the talents": Reid Buckley, *Strictly Speaking: Reid Buckley's Indispensable Handbook on Public Speaking* (New York: McGraw-Hill, 1999), p. xii.

211   "When the slip came through": Lou Cannon, *Reagan* (New York: G. P. Putnam's Sons, 1982), p. 46.

211   "his first screen test": ibid., p. 51.

212   "There have been times": John H. Fund, "The Secret of Reagan's 'Success,' " *Wall Street Journal*, January 23, 1989.

213   "We wouldn't have had a prayer": James Deakin, *Straight Stuff: The Reporters, The White House and the Truth* (New York: Morrow, 1984), p. 165.

213   "The Scaffolding of Rhetoric": Randolph S. Churchill, *Winston S. Churchill, Companion Volume I, Part 2, 1896–1900* (Boston: Houghton Mifflin, 1967), pp. 816–821.

215   "The only time": Warren Bennis, *An Invented Life: Reflections on Leadership and Change* (Reading, MA: Addison-Wesley, 1993), p. 57.

215   The best memoirs: Samuel Irving Rosenman, *Working with Roosevelt* (New York: Harper, 1952).

216   "I won a nickname": " 'Two Great Triumphs': Restoring Economy and Morale," *Washington Post*, January 12, 1989, p. A8.

217   "not the solution": *Public Papers of the Presidents of the United States, Ronald Reagan: January 20 to December 31, 1981* (Washington, DC: United States Government Printing Office, 1982), pp. 1–4.

218   William Kristol and David Brooks: William Kristol and David Brooks, "What Ails Conservatism," *Wall Street Journal*, September 15, 1997, p. A22.

219   "What is most beautiful": Helen Fisher, *The First Sex: The Natural Talents of Women and How They Are Changing the World* (New York: Random House, 1999), p. xxviii.

222   "The crisis we are facing": *Public Papers of the Presidents of the United States, Ronald Reagan: January 20 to December 31, 1981*, pp. 1–4.

222   William Leuchtenburg: William E. Leuchtenburg, *The FDR Years: On Roosevelt and His Legacy* (New York: Columbia University Press, 1995), pp. 35–53. Chapter title is "The New Deal and the Analogue of War."

222   just as effective: James M. McPherson, *Abraham Lincoln and the Second American Revolution* (New York: Oxford University Press, 1990), pp. 93–112. Chapter title is "How Lincoln Won the War with Metaphors."

223   "Leaders achieve their effectiveness": Howard Gardner in collaboration with Emma Laskin, *Leading Minds: An Anatomy of Leadership* (New York: BasicBooks, 1995), pp. 9, 13.

223   stories "about themselves": ibid., p. 14.

223   "The stories of the leader": ibid.

223   Richard Dawkins: Richard Dawkins, *The Selfish Gene* (New York: Oxford University Press, 1976).

224   "In recent world history": Gardner with Laskin, *Leading Minds*, p. 10.

224   "Don't worry, son": Robert Sherrill, "Ronald Reagan: The Man and the Masks," *Washington Post*, January 11, 1987, p. X4

225   James David Barber: James David Barber, "The Oval Office Aesop," *New York Times*, November 7, 1982, section 4, p. 17.

225   "The orator's first test": Garry Wills, *Certain Trumpets: The Call of Leaders*, (New York: Simon & Schuster, 1994), p. 218.

226   "King's oratory urged": Wills, *Certain Trumpets*, p. 218.

226   "It is a stroke of leadership genius": Gardner with Laskin, *Leading Minds*, p. 37.

226   Churchill first developed: ibid., p. 262.

226 "I am not a crook": Kathleen Hall Jamieson, *Eloquence in an Electronic Age: The Transformation of Political Speechmaking* (New York: Oxford University Press, 1988), p. 113.

227 "Adult children of alcoholics": Peggy Noonan, *What I Saw at the Revolution: A Political Life in the Reagan Era* (New York: Random House, 1990), p. 154.

228 more a life story: Ronald Reagan, *An American Life* (New York: Simon & Schuster, 1990).

230 "when life seems hard": Jamieson, *Eloquence in an Electronic Age*, p. 121.

230 "Every 74-year-old president": Sandy Grady, "What a Birthday Party! A Boffo Finish for the Gipper," *Seattle Times*, February 8, 1985, p. A10.

230 "the nation's host": Christopher Matthews, "Politics as Theater," *Washington Post*, May 6, 1984, p. 1k.

230 an element of Reagan's rhetoric: Jamieson, *Eloquence in an Electronic Age*, p. 91.

231 "The moments in which words fail": ibid., p. 129.

231 "I know it's hard": ibid.

231 "The crew of the space shuttle": ibid., pp. 129–32.

232 "The scenes of senseless tragedy": ibid., p. 127.

232 "We will not forget the pictures": ibid., pp. 127–28.

232 "We will not forget the image": ibid., p. 128.

232 "A set of images": ibid.

232 "When visual images": ibid., p. 126.

232 "The entire nation has watched": ibid., p. 133.

232 "You probably don't recognize": ibid.

233 "I think [the situation] was summed up": ibid., pp. 133–34.

234 "showing his age?": Rich Jaroslovsky and James M. Perry, "Fitness Issue—New Question in Race: Is Oldest U.S. President Now Showing His Age? Reagan Debate Performance Invites Open Speculation on His Ability to Serve," *Wall Street Journal*, October 9, 1984.

234 "an issue in this campaign": Lou Cannon, *President Reagan: The Role of a Lifetime* (New York: Simon & Schuster, 1991), p. 550.

234 "when you're faced with two temptations": Remarks at the annual Salute to Congress dinner, February 4, 1981.

235 Paul D. Erickson: Paul D. Erickson, *Reagan Speaks: The Making of an American Myth* (New York: New York University Press, 1985), p. 19.

236 "the only American poet": Noonan, *What I Saw at the Revolution*, p. 227.

239 "What can you say": ibid., p. 255.

239 By his own account: Reagan, *An American Life*, p. 150.

239 "The Eleventh Commandment": Cannon, *Reagan*, p. 108.

241 "I often say": Fred I. Greenstein, ed., *Leadership in the Modern Presidency* (Cambridge, MA: Harvard University Press), p. 277.

242 "A semantic infiltration": ibid., pp. 277–78.

243 historian John Keegan records: John Keegan, *The Mask of Command* (New York: Viking Press, 1987), p. 47.

243 "a calculated stroke": ibid.

243 "But theatricality," Keegan observes: ibid., pp. 47–48.

244 "I have already grown gray": Richard Norton Smith, *Patriarch: George Washington and the New American Nation* (Boston: Houghton Mifflin, 1993), p. 19.

244 "Instantly, rebellion melted": ibid.

244 Hugh Gregory Gallagher: Hugh Gregory Gallagher, *FDR's Splendid Deception* (New York: Dodd, Mead), 1985.

244 "It is not surprising": ibid., p. 190.

244 "The camera seldom lies": Michael K. Deaver, *Behind the Scenes* (New York: Morrow, 1987), p. 42.

245 "My fellow Americans": Celestine Bohlen, "Soviets Formally Denounce Reagan's Joke," *Washington Post*, August 16, 1984, p. A1.

246 "I've never played a governor": Lou Cannon, "Letter from California; Elder Statesman's Mantle Fits, Reagan Finds," *Washington Post*, May 7, 1991, p. A3.

246 "If the voice is a gift": Cannon, *Reagan*, p. 45.

BILL CLINTON

8. DREAMS AND DISAPPOINTMENTS

251 "the most ethical administration": Mary McGrory, "Why Zoe Got Zapped," *Washington Post*, January 24, 1993, p. C1.

256 George C. Edwards has pointed out: George C. Edwards, "Frustration and Folly: Bill Clinton and the Public Presidency," in Colin Campbell and Bert A. Rockman, eds., *The Clinton Presidency: First Appraisals* (New York: Chatham House, 1996), p. 235.

256 Thomas Patterson found: Thomas E. Patterson, *Out of Order: How the Decline of the Political Parties and the Growing Power of the News Media Undermine the American Way of Electing Presidents* (New York: Alfred A. Knopf, 1993), pp. 13–14.

257 James MacGregor Burns and Georgia Sorenson point out: James MacGregor Burns and Georgia J. Sorenson, *Dead Center: Clinton-Gore Leadership and the Perils of Moderation* (New York: Scribner, 1999), p. 71.

258 Thomas Mann and Norman Ornstein have pointed out: Thomas Mann and Norman Ornstein, "After the Campaign, What?," *Brookings Review*, vol. 18, no. 1 (Winter 2000), p. 47.

260 Bob Woodward has detailed: Bob Woodward, *The Agenda: Inside the Clinton White House* (New York: Simon & Schuster, 1994).

261 Machiavelli wrote that a new prince: Niccolò Machiavelli, *The Prince* (New York: Bantam Books, 1966), p. 60.

261 David Maraniss writes in his biography: David Maraniss, *First in His Class: A Biography of Bill Clinton* (New York: Simon & Schuster, 1995), p. 53.

263 Elizabeth Drew in her book: Elizabeth Drew, *On the Edge: The Clinton Presidency* (New York: Simon & Schuster, 1994), p. 24

263 "They really weren't ready": Burns and Sorenson, *Dead Center*, p. 97.

271 "I must say": Roxanne Roberts, "For Reagan, Many Happy Returns: At GOP Fund-Raiser, Ex-President Says Clinton Stole His Ideas," *Washington Post*, February 4, 1994, p. C1.

9. RIDING THE ROLLER COASTER

272 "Not for eighty years": James MacGregor Burns and Georgia J. Sorenson, *Dead Center: Clinton-Gore Leadership and the Perils of Moderation* (New York: Scribner, 1999), p. 77.

282 "giant sucking sound": "Campaign '92: Transcript of the Second Presidential Debate," *Washington Post*, October 16, 1992, p. A34.

290 "There are no limits": Michael Isikoff, "Whitewater Counsel Promises 'Thorough' Probe," *Washington Post*, January 21, 1994, p. A1.

295 David A. Heenan and Warren Bennis write: David A. Heenan and Warren Bennis, *Co-Leaders: The Power of Great Partnerships* (New York: John Wiley, 1999).

302 Dole slipped a note: Haynes Johnson and David Broder, *The System: The*

American Way of Politics at the Breaking Point (Boston: Little, Brown, 1996), p. 372.

303 Haynes Johnson and David Broder: ibid., passim.

304 "I set the Congress up": ibid., p. 609.

304 Seymour Martin Lipset says: Seymour Martin Lipset, *American Exceptionalism: A Double-Edged Sword* (New York: W. W. Norton, 1996).

304 "Great initiatives": Steve Wilson, "The Culprits Who Killed Health Reform," *Arizona Republic,* September 28, 1994, p. A2.

304 "greatest mistake": Johnson and Broder, *The System,* p. 609.

305 "make complexity our ally": ibid., p. 627.

305 "have become crypto-political parties": ibid., p. 630.

306 "adaptive work": Ronald A. Heifetz, *Leadership Without Easy Answers* (Cambridge, MA: Belknap Press, 1994), pp. 129–38.

10. Assessing His Leadership

314 "I sometimes thought": Dick Morris, *Behind the Oval Office: Winning the Presidency in the Nineties* (New York: Random House, 1997), pp. 13–14.

315 "God created man": *The NewsHour with Jim Lehrer,* PBS, April 3, 1998.

315 "There is not a sexual relationship": *The NewsHour with Jim Lehrer,* PBS, January 21, 1998.

315 "The relationship was not sexual": "Clinton: 'There Is No Improper Relationship,'" *Washington Post,* January 22, 1998, p. A13.

316 "I want to say one thing": John F. Harris and Dan Balz, "Clinton More Forcefully Denies Having Had Affair or Urging Lies," *Washington Post,* January 27, 1998, p. A1.

316 "a vast right-wing conspiracy": Brian Duffy and Phil Kuntz, "Clinton's Secretary Testifies Before Grand Jury; First Lady Claims 'Conspiracy' Against Husband," *Wall Street Journal,* January 28, 1998, p. A20.

317 "Success is going": Bruce McCabe, "The Failure Fallacy," *Boston Globe,* May 7, 1987, p. 85.

319 "What counts": "Reporters' Notebook," *Buffalo News,* September 17, 1992, p. B4.

322 When Bill Safire compiled: *Lend Me Your Ears: Great Speeches in History,* selected and introduced by William Safire (New York: W. W. Norton, 1997).

323 "an unusually good liar": Martha Sherrill, "Grave Doubts," *Esquire,* January 1, 1996, p. 86.

324 compiled by the *Congressional Quarterly:* Andrew Taylor, "Clinton Comes Up Short in a Year of Politics Over Substance," *CQ Weekly,* December 11, 1999, p. 2971.

324 "It stinks": Ruth Marcus and Helen Dewar, "Clinton Compromise Delays Showdown Over Ban on Gays," *Washington Post,* January 30, 1993, p. A1.

327 "ruining people is considered sport": Timothy M. Phelps, "Foster's Note: White House Lawyer Cited Misdeeds by FBI, Media, Staff," *Newsday,* August 11, 1993, p. 3.

327 David Maraniss reports: David Maraniss, *The Clinton Enigma: A Four-and-a-Half-Minute Speech Reveals This President's Entire Life* (New York: Simon & Schuster, 1998), p. 17.

328 "He knew who he was": David McCullough, "Harry S. Truman," in Robert A. Wilson, ed., *Character Above All: Ten Presidents from FDR to George Bush* (New York: Simon & Schuster, 1995), p. 40.

329 "Clinton's history": Maraniss, *The Clinton Enigma,* p. 35.

329 "the mulligan": Don Van Natta, Jr., "Taking Second Chances: Par for Clinton's Course," *New York Times,* August 29, 1999, p. 1.

330   "a helm to grasp": Arthur M. Schlesinger, Jr., "Heroes at the Helm," *Newsday*, October 25, 1992, p. 25.

331   The *Wall Street Journal* has reported: James M. Perry, "Clinton Relies Heavily on White House Pollster to Take Words Right Out of the Public's Mouth," *Wall Street Journal*, March 23, 1994, p. A16.

331   Charles O. Jones has called it: Charles O. Jones, "Campaigning to Govern: The Clinton Style," in Colin Campbell and Bert A. Rockman, eds., *The Clinton Presidency: First Appraisals* (Chatham, NJ: Chatham House, 1996), p. 32.

331   "We need popular support": James A. Barnes, "Polls Apart," *National Journal*, July 7, 1993, p. 1750.

332   "separated institutions *sharing* powers": Richard E. Neustadt, *Presidential Power and the Modern Presidents: The Politics of Leadership from Roosevelt to Reagan* (New York: The Free Press, 1990), p. 29.

334   "Deny, deny, deny": Adam Cohen, "The Burden of Proof," *Time*, February 2, 1998, p. 56.

334   "Drag a hundred": R. W. Apple, Jr., "Harassment Case Against Clinton Now at Highest Level," *New York Times*, January 12, 1997, p. A16.

336   "This word spinning": Bill Kovach and Tom Rosenstiel, *Warp Speed: America in the Age of Mixed Media* (New York: Century Foundation Press, 1999), p. 5.

338   Sally Quinn wrote: Sally Quinn, "Not in Their Back Yard," *Washington Post*, November 2, 1998, p. E1.

340   "better than it sounds": William Raspberry, "They Never Learn," *Washington Post*, May 12, 2000, p. A47.

340   "future preference": David Maraniss, *First in His Class: A Biography of Bill Clinton* (New York: Simon & Schuster, 1995), pp. 59–60.

341   Stephen Skowronek has argued: Stephen Skowronek, *The Politics Presidents Make: Leadership from John Adams to George Bush* (Cambridge, MA: Belknap Press, 1993), p. 53.

341   Postmodernism holds: Kenneth J. Gergen (author's brother), *The Saturated Self: Dilemmas of Identity in Contemporary Life* (New York: BasicBooks, 1991).

CONCLUSION

SEVEN LESSONS OF LEADERSHIP

343   Arthur Schlesinger, Jr., surveyed: Arthur Schlesinger, Jr., "The Ultimate Approval Rating," *New York Times Magazine*, December 15, 1996, p. 46.

344   "It must be realized": Niccolò Machiavelli, *The Prince* (New York: Bantam Books, 1981), p. 27.

345   "Character is destiny": Anna Musio, "The Philosopher," *Fast Company*, July 1, 1999, p. 140.

345   John W. Gardner assembles: John W. Gardner, *On Leadership* (New York: The Free Press, 1990).

346   "If you have": author notes, Gerald Ford lecture, Kennedy School of Government, Harvard University, March 16, 1999.

348   "America is the only": Everett Carll Ladd, "The Persistence of the National Idea," *Newsday*, January 3, 1986, p. 71.

349   the lion and the fox: James MacGregor Burns, *Roosevelt: The Lion and the Fox* (New York: Harcourt, Brace, 1956).

350   When George Washington: Richard Brookhiser, *Founding Father: Rediscovering George Washington* (New York: The Free Press, 1996), p. 10.

351 the next eight presidents: William Leuchtenburg, *In the Shadow of FDR: From Harry Truman to Ronald Reagan* (Ithaca, NY: Cornell University Press, 1983).

352 there is a pattern: Stephen Skowronek, *The Politics Presidents Make: Leadership from John Adams to George Bush* (Cambridge, MA: Belknap Press, 1993).

Acknowledgments_____

"Victory has a hundred fathers, and defeat is an orphan," President Kennedy once observed. So it is with a book. There are many I wish to thank for helping to give birth to this one.

Most immediately, I am grateful to a series of my former students at Duke who became my chief research assistants in Washington, assisting in this project before heading to graduate school. They were invaluable and became friends. Laurie Barber spent the past two years with me and Jason Barclay spent one. Earlier, Lisa Halpern spent three years helping me focus on leadership questions. I also want to thank Alex Gordon and Justin Dillon, general research assistants for two years apiece, and Caroline Charles, who managed us all.

Until my agent, Robert Barnett, introduced me to Simon & Schuster, I had not realized what a difference a superb editor can make. Alice Mayhew is now in my hall of heroes. She challenged me at each of the right moments with suggestions and comments that lifted the quality of the work. Without Alice and her colleague Roger Labrie, this book would not have seen the light until Election Day 2008.

I have also gained immeasurably from teaching, first at Duke (1995–1999) and then at the John F. Kennedy School at Harvard (1999–present). The students and faculties have enriched my understanding of both the presidency and of leadership. A year ago, I presented the Terry Sanford Lectures at Duke that are a basis for portions of this work.

Two journalistic organizations have provided a welcome home since the mid-1980s: *U.S. News & World Report* and *The NewsHour* on public television. I am grateful to Mortimer B. Zuckerman, Jim Lehrer, Robin MacNeil, and their staffs—many of them friends—for giving me a chance to report and reflect upon public affairs.

Through teaching and journalism, I have also come to know a num-

367

ber of scholars and authors whose writings and conversations have influenced my thinking. Among the foremost are Richard Neustadt, James MacGregor Burns, Warren Bennis, Howard Gardner, John Gardner, Ronald A. Heifetz, John P. Kotter, Ben Wattenberg, Steve Hess, Kathleen Hall Jamieson, Daniel Goleman, Garry Wills, Fred I. Greenstein, James O'Toole, Barbara Kellerman, and Peter Drucker. Historians Stephen E. Ambrose, Arthur Schlesinger, Jr., David McCullough, Doris Kearns Goodwin, Michael Bechsloss, David Herbert Donald, and Richard Norton Smith have also been rich resources.

Looking back over a longer period, I was blessed that a number of people ahead of me in life were generous in their time and counsel while we served together in government. I count them as life's mentors. Among the ones I especially want to thank are Ray Price, Bryce Harlow, Leonard Garment, Bill Simon, James A. Baker III, and Warren Christopher. Innumerable friends, in and out of government, have been sustaining forces in my life as well. During the ups and downs of the Clinton years, I have been particularly grateful for the support of Mark Shields, Ken Duberstein, Kathy Bushkin, Jody Greenstone, Dianna Pierce, Mack McLarty, Joel Klein, Tom Donilon, Sheryl Handler, Dick Krasno, Jonathan Rose, Joel Fleishman, Craig Biddle, Tom Lovejoy, Mike Ruby, and Christopher Makins.

Ultimately, my greatest sources of inspiration in this endeavor have been the presidents I have served and my family.

As I wrote in the introduction, I believe it a privilege for any citizen to serve in the White House. I thank Richard Nixon, Gerald R. Ford, Ronald Reagan, and Bill Clinton for extending that honor to me. As I have attempted to draw from their presidencies lessons of leadership that might help others, especially the younger generation, I hope that I have demonstrated the respect and affection I feel toward them.

Public service demands its greatest sacrifices not from those in government but from their loved ones. They experience many of the hardships and few of the rewards. I was blessed that my wife, Anne, stood by me, nurtured our children in their early years, endured the long days of isolation, and, in the midst of all that, flowered into the woman she has become. Our children, Christopher and Katherine, are the joys of our life, and they, like Anne, have been an intimate part of my own growth. In thinking about leadership, I have also gained enormously from continuing conversations with my brother Ken and his wife, Mary, both social psychologists and both dear to us. I only wish that my mom and dad could have been here, too.

As for the mistakes and misjudgments in these pages—the defeats, if you will—the paternity is mine alone.

David Gergen

Index

377

*About the Author*_____

DAVID GERGEN has been active in public life for three decades as a senior adviser to presidents, the editor of a national news magazine, a distinguished television commentator, and a teacher. He worked on the White House staffs of four presidents: Nixon (as head of speechwriting); Ford (as a special counsel and chief of the communications team); Reagan (as staff director and director of communications, overseeing the press office and speechwriting staff); and Clinton (as counselor). He has been the editor of *U.S. News & World Report*, a regular commentator on *The MacNeil/Lehrer NewsHour*, a resident fellow of the American Enterprise Institute, and a visiting professor at Duke University. Currently, he is a professor of public service at the John F. Kennedy School of Government at Harvard University and codirector of the school's Center for Public Leadership. He is also editor-at-large for *U.S. News & World Report* and serves as a political analyst for *The NewsHour with Jim Lehrer* and ABC's *Nightline*. He lives in Cambridge, Massachusetts, and McLean, Virginia.

Praise for *Eyewitness to Power*

"Long an astute observer of American presidents, David Gergen in *Eyewitness to Power* provides a trenchant analysis of presidential leadership."
—John Morton Blum, professor emeritus of history, Yale University

"David Gergen [is] one smart fellow. . . . He's a Washington legend and the author of a new book . . . and it's a great book . . . lots of good stories, lots of candy for us political junkies in there."
—Chris Matthews, *Hardball with Chris Matthews*

"*Eyewitness to Power* . . . is filled with warnings about the mistakes and pitfalls that seem to be repeated by every president. Perhaps the biggest mistake for an incoming president would be to ignore what Gergen has seen and learned."
—Michael Kranish, *The Boston Globe*

"The consummate Washington insider . . . Gergen has now written a fascinating book. . . . Terrific."
—Geraldo Rivera, *Rivera Live*

"*Eyewitness to Power* relies on an insider's personal experience to shape larger judgments on 'the essence of leadership.' . . . Gergen provides sympathetic yet weakness-revealing portraits of the presidents he served."
—Robert Schmuhl, *Chicago Tribune*

"After reading this book, it is easy to understand why four U.S. presidents turned to David Gergen for advice and assistance."
—Robert A. Rankin, *The Philadelphia Inquirer*

"One of the smartest guys in Washington . . . Gergen [has written] an excellent memoir."
—Charles E. Cook, Jr., *The San Diego Union-Tribune*

"Intimate without wallowing in tabloid tidbits, Gergen's description of his work at the White House offers valuable sidelight on history, plus pointed thoughts on what qualities citizens truly need from their presidents."
—Mary Carroll, *Booklist*

"Finely etched tales . . . [Gergen's] eye for detail and knack for narrative are to be admired. He brings to life the everyday world of the presidency and provides telling portraits of these fallible yet fascinating leaders."
—*Publishers Weekly*